MICROSOFT OFFICE® 4

FOR WINDOWS™ FOR

DUMMIES®

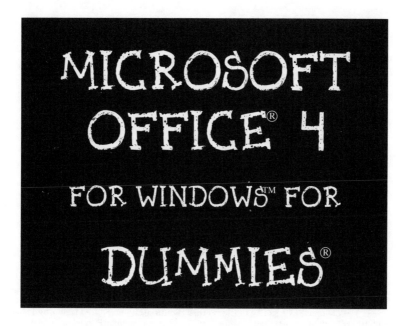

MICROSOFT OFFICE® 4 FOR WINDOWS™ FOR DUMMIES®

by Roger C. Parker

IDG Books Worldwide, Inc.
An International Data Group Company

Foster City, CA ♦ Chicago, IL ♦ Indianapolis, IN ♦ Braintree, MA ♦ Dallas, TX

Microsoft Office® 4 For Windows™ For Dummies®

Published by
IDG Books Worldwide, Inc.
An International Data Group Company
919 E. Hillsdale Blvd.
Suite 400
Foster City, CA 94404

Library of Congress Catalog Card No.: 94-77185

ISBN: 1-56884-183-3

Printed in the United States of America

10 9 8 7 6 5

Distributed in the United States by IDG Books Worldwide, Inc.

Distributed by Macmillan Canada for Canada; by Computer and Technical Books for the Caribbean Basin; by Contemporanea de Ediciones for Venezuela; by Distribuidora Cuspide for Argentina; by CITEC for Brazil; by Ediciones ZETA S.C.R. Ltda. for Peru; by Editorial Limusa SA for Mexico; by Transworld Publishers Limited in the United Kingdom and Europe; by Al-Maiman Publishers & Distributors for Saudi Arabia; by Simron Pty. Ltd. for South Africa; by IDG Communications (HK) Ltd. for Hong Kong; by Toppan Company Ltd. for Japan; by Addison Wesley Publishing Company for Korea; by Longman Singapore Publishers Ltd. for Singapore, Malaysia, Thailand, and Indonesia; by Unalis Corporation for Taiwan; by WS Computer Publishing Company, Inc. for the Philippines; by WoodsLane Pty. Ltd. for Australia; by WoodsLane Enterprises Ltd. for New Zealand.

For general information on IDG Books in the U.S., including information on discounts and premiums, contact IDG Books at 800-434-3422 or 415-655-3000.

For information on where to purchase IDG Books outside the U.S., contact IDG Books International at 415-655-3021 or fax 415-655-3295.

For information on translations, contact Marc Jeffrey Mikulich, Director, Foreign & Subsidiary Rights, at IDG Books Worldwide, 415-655-3018 or fax 415-655-3295.

For sales inquiries and special prices for bulk quantities, write to the address above or call IDG Books Worldwide at 415-655-3000.

For information on using IDG Books in the classroom, or ordering examination copies, contact Jim Kelly at 800-434-2086.

For authorization to photocopy items for corporate, personal, or educational use, please contact Copyright Clearance Center, 222 Rosewood Drive, Danvers, MA 01923, or fax 508-750-4470.

About the Author

Roger C. Parker

More than 600,000 desktop publishers and software users throughout the world rely on books by Roger C. Parker. His list of titles includes *Looking Good in Print: A Guide to Basic Design for Desktop Publishing, The One-Minute Designer, PowerPoint Presentation by Design,* and (with David Holzgang) *WordPerfect 6 SECRETS.* He is also a columnist for publications such as *Techniques Magazine* and *x-height.*

Roger has conducted presentations throughout the world for organizations such as the Consumer Electronics Show, Apple Computer, Creative Seminars, the State Street Bank, Yamaha Audio, and the University of Illinois. He is an activist with the Boston Computer Society.

Roger owns The Write Word, an advertising and consulting firm located in Dover, NH. He can be reached at P.O. Box 697, Dover, NH 03820.

Welcome to the world of IDG Books Worldwide.

IDG Books Worldwide, Inc., is a subsidiary of International Data Group, the world's largest publisher of computer-related information and the leading global provider of information services on information technology. IDG was founded more than 25 years ago and now employs more than 7,200 people worldwide. IDG publishes more than 233 computer publications in 65 countries (see listing below). More than sixty million people read one or more IDG publications each month.

Launched in 1990, IDG Books Worldwide is today the #1 publisher of best-selling computer books in the United States. We are proud to have received 3 awards from the Computer Press Association in recognition of editorial excellence, and our best-selling ...*For Dummies*™ series has more than 12 million copies in print with translations in 25 languages. IDG Books, through a recent joint venture with IDG's Hi-Tech Beijing, became the first U.S. publisher to publish a computer book in the People's Republic of China. In record time, IDG Books has become the first choice for millions of readers around the world who want to learn how to better manage their businesses.

Our mission is simple: Every IDG book is designed to bring extra value and skill-building instructions to the reader. Our books are written by experts who understand and care about our readers. The knowledge base of our editorial staff comes from years of experience in publishing, education, and journalism — experience which we use to produce books for the '90s. In short, we care about books, so we attract the best people. We devote special attention to details such as audience, interior design, use of icons, and illustrations. And because we use an efficient process of authoring, editing, and desktop publishing our books electronically, we can spend more time ensuring superior content and spend less time on the technicalities of making books.

You can count on our commitment to deliver high-quality books at competitive prices on topics consumers want to read about. At IDG, we value quality, and we have been delivering quality for more than 25 years. You'll find no better book on a subject than an IDG book.

John J. Kilcullen

John Kilcullen
President and CEO
IDG Books Worldwide, Inc.

IDG Books Worldwide, Inc., is a subsidiary of International Data Group, the world's largest publisher of computer-related information and the leading global provider of information services on information technology. International Data Group publishes over 220 computer publications in 65 countries. More than fifty million people read one or more International Data Group publications each month. The officers are Patrick J. McGovern, Founder and Board Chairman; Kelly Conlin, President; Jim Casella, Chief Operating Officer. International Data Group's publications include: **ARGENTINA'S** Computerworld Argentina, Infoworld Argentina; **AUSTRALIA'S** Computerworld Australia, Computer Living, Australian PC World, Australian Macworld, Network World, Mobile Business Australia, Publish!, Reseller, IDG Sources; **AUSTRIA'S** Computerwelt Oesterreich, PC Test; **BELGIUM'S** Data News (CW); **BOLIVIA'S** Computerworld; **BRAZIL'S** Computerworld, Connections, Game Power, Mundo Unix, PC World, Publish, Super Game; **BULGARIA'S** Computerworld Bulgaria, PC & Mac World Bulgaria, Network World Bulgaria; **CANADA'S** CIO Canada, Computerworld Canada, InfoCanada, Network World Canada, Reseller; **CHILE'S** Computerworld Chile, Informatica; **COLOMBIA'S** Computerworld Colombia, PC World; **COSTA RICA'S** PC World; **CZECH REPUBLIC'S** Computerworld, Elektronika, PC World; **DENMARK'S** Communications World, Computerworld Danmark, Computerworld Focus, Macintosh Produktkatalog, Macworld Danmark, PC World Danmark, PC Produktguide, Tech World, Windows World; **ECUADOR'S** PC World Ecuador; **EGYPT'S** Computerworld (CW) Middle East, PC World Middle East; **FINLAND'S** MikroPC, Tietoviikko, Tietoverkko; **FRANCE'S** Distributique, GOLDEN MAC, InfoPC, Le Guide du Monde Informatique, Le Monde Informatique, Telecoms & Reseaux; **GERMANY'S** Computerwoche, Computerwoche Focus, Computerwoche Extra, Electronic Entertainment, Gamepro, Information Management, Macwelt, Netzwelt, PC Welt, Publish, Publish; **GREECE'S** Publish & Macworld; **HONG KONG'S** Computerworld Hong Kong, PC World Hong Kong; **HUNGARY'S** Computerworld SZT, PC World; **INDIA'S** Computers & Communications; **INDONESIA'S** Info Komputer; **IRELAND'S** ComputerScope; **ISRAEL'S** Beyond Windows, Computerworld Israel, Multimedia, PC World Israel; **ITALY'S** Computerworld Italia, Lotus Magazine, Macworld Italia, Networking Italia, PC Shopping Italy, PC World Italia; **JAPAN'S** Computerworld Today, Information Systems World, Macworld Japan, Nikkei Personal Computing, SunWorld Japan, Windows World; **KENYA'S** East African Computer News; **KOREA'S** Computerworld Korea, Macworld Korea, PC World Korea; **LATIN AMERICA'S** GamePro; **MALAYSIA'S** Computerworld Malaysia, PC World Malaysia; **MEXICO'S** Compu Edicion, Compu Manufactura, Computacion/Punto de Venta, Computerworld Mexico, MacWorld, Mundo Unix, PC World, Windows; **THE NETHERLANDS'** Computer! Totaal, Computable (CW), LAN Magazine, Lotus Magazine, MacWorld; **NEW ZEALAND'S** Computer Buyer, Computerworld New Zealand, Network World, New Zealand PC World; **NIGERIA'S** PC World Africa; **NORWAY'S** Computerworld Norge, Lotusworld Norge, Macworld Norge, Maxi Data, Networld, PC World Ekspress, PC World Nettverk, PC World Norge, PC World's Produktguide, Publish& Multimedia World, Student Data, Unix World, Windowsworld; **PAKISTAN'S** PC World Pakistan; **PANAMA'S** PC World Panama; **PERU'S** Computerworld Peru, PC World; **PEOPLE'S REPUBLIC OF CHINA'S** China Computerworld, China Infoworld, China PC Info Magazine, Computer Fan, PC World China, Electronics International, Electronics Today/Multimedia World, Electronic Product World, China Network World, Software World Magazine, Telecom Product World; **PHILIPPINES'** Computerworld Philippines, PC Digest (PCW); **POLAND'S** Computerworld Poland, Computerworld Special Report, Networld, PC World/Komputer, Sunworld; **PORTUGAL'S** Cerebro/PC World, Correio Informatico/Computerworld, MacIn; **ROMANIA'S** Computerworld, PC World, Telecom Romania; **RUSSIA'S** Computerworld-Moscow, Mir - PK (PCW), Sety (Networks); **SINGAPORE'S** Computerworld Southeast Asia, PC World Singapore; **SLOVENIA'S** Monitor Magazine; **SOUTH AFRICA'S** Computer Mail (CIO),Computing S.A.,Network World S.A., Software World; **SPAIN'S** Advanced Systems, Amiga World, Computerworld Espana, Communicaciones World, Macworld Espana, NeXTWORLD, Super Juegos Magazine (GamePro), PC World Espana, Publish; **SWEDEN'S** Attack, ComputerSweden, Corporate Computing, Macworld, Mikrodatorn, Natverk & Kommunikation, PC World, CAP & Design, DataIngenjoren, Maxi Data,Windows World; **SWITZERLAND'S** Computerworld Schweiz, Macworld Schweiz, PC Tip; **TAIWAN'S** Computerworld Taiwan, PC World Taiwan; **THAILAND'S** Thai Computerworld; **TURKEY'S** Computerworld Monitor, Macworld Turkiye, PC World Turkiye; **UKRAINE'S** Computerworld, Computers+Software Magazine; **UNITED KINGDOM'S** Computing /Computerworld, Connexion/Network World, Lotus Magazine, Macworld, Open Computing/Sunworld; **UNITED STATES'** Advanced Systems, AmigaWorld, Cable in the Classroom, CD Review, CIO, Computerworld, Computerworld Client/Server Journal, Digital Video, DOS World, Electronic Entertainment Magazine (E2), Federal Computer Week, Game Hits, GamePro, IDG Books, Infoworld, Laser Event, Macworld, Maximize, Multimedia World, Network World, PC Letter, PC World, Publish, SWATPro, Video Event; **URUGUAY'S** PC World Uruguay; **VENEZUELA'S** Computerworld Venezuela, PC World; **VIETNAM'S** PC World Vietnam. 02/28/95

Acknowledgments

Although the author's name appears on the cover, books are team sports. The talents of many others contribute to a book's success.

In this case, from the IDG team, I'd like to acknowledge the contributions of fellow IDG authors John Weingarten and Wallace Wang, plus IDG's strong and supportive editorial team headed by Erik Dafforn and Barbara Potter. I'd also like to acknowledge the support and encouragement of numerous other IDG folk: Publisher David Solomon, Managing Editor Mary Bednarek, Senior Editors Sandy Blackthorn and Tracy Barr, and Acquisitions Editor Janna Custer. Good books result from strong editing, and I feel I've benefited from the best.

On the author's "team" I'd like to acknowledge the enthusiastic support of William Gladstone and Lavander Ginsburg of Waterside Productions and, as always, the patience of my family: Betsy, Christopher, Zachary and — especially — Ryan (who kept me company during several all-night and weekend sessions).

In addition, I'd like to acknowledge the efforts of Marty Taucher, Cheryl Johnson, and Janet Broome at Microsoft's Public Relations office and — most important — the talents of the numerous programmers who conceived and executed the idea of packaging several no-compromise, easy-to-use programs into a single package that is flexible enough to satisfy either first-time or power users.

(The Publisher would like to give special thanks to Patrick J. McGovern, without whom this book would not have been possible.)

Credits

Executive Vice President, Strategic Product Planning and Research
David Solomon

Editorial Director
Diane Graves Steele

Acquisitions Editor
Megg Bonar

Brand Manager
Judith A. Taylor

Editorial Managers
Tracy L. Barr
Sandra Blackthorn
Kristin A. Cocks

Editorial Assistants
Tamara S. Castleman
Stacey Holden Prince
Kevin Spencer

Acquisitions Assistant
Suki Gear

Production Director
Beth Jenkins

Supervisor of Project Coordination
Cindy L. Phipps

Pre-Press Coordinator
Steve Peake

Associate Pre-Press Coordinator
Tony Augsburger

Project Editor
Erik Dafforn

Editors
Diane L. Giangrossi
Barbara L. Potter
Kathy Simpson

Technical Reviewer
Michael J. Partington

Production Staff
J. Tyler Connor
Sherry Gomoll
Drew R. Moore
Mark Owens
Laura Puranen
Dwight Ramsey
Patricia R. Reynolds
Anna Rohrer
Kathie Schnorr
Gina Scott

Proofreader
Charles A. Hutchinson

Indexer
Steve Rath

Book Design
University Graphics

Cover Design
Kavish + Kavish

Contents at a Glance

Cartoons at a Glance
By Rich Tennant

page 13

page 231

page 119

page 159

page 375

page 292

page 64

page 398

page 303

page 418

Table of Contents

· ·

Introduction

● ●

*C*ongratulations on your recent purchase! No, not your purchase of this book — although I'm pleased that you put your trust in me — but on your purchase (or impending purchase) of Microsoft Office 4 for Windows. When you purchased Office 4 for Windows (or Office 4 Professional — we'll be using the terms interchangeably), you purchased the most innovative and exciting computer product to appear within the past few years: a no-compromise collection of software programs that — considered individually or together — can satisfy the most demanding applications.

It can logically be argued that the software programs included in Office 4 are, individually, "best of breed" compared with the available alternatives. But the excellence of Office 4 extends beyond the power of the individual programs included with the suite. Office 4's power comes from a unique combination of information exchange and ease of use. For the first time, power has not become corrupted by complexity.

Who Should Buy This Book

This book is for you, whether you've already purchased Microsoft Office 4 for Windows or are considering purchasing it. It's for you, whether you're a newcomer to computers or an experienced user of Word or Excel who wants to expand on your existing knowledge and master PowerPoint and/or Access.

- If you *haven't yet purchased* Microsoft Office 4 for Windows, this book will help you decide whether Office is worth purchasing. By providing an overview of the Office programs' capabilities and how they operate, this book can help you relate each program's capabilities to your computing needs.

- If you're *about to purchase* Office 4 and are unsure whether to choose Office 4 Professional instead or are considering upgrading Office 4 to Office 4 Professional, the chapters that describe Access 2 will help you decide whether the additional investment is appropriate to your needs.

- If you're new to computers and *have already purchased* Microsoft Office (or your computer includes a preloaded version of Office 4), this book will jump-start your efforts, helping you quickly attain survival-level familiarity with each of the programs.

✔ If you're *familiar with earlier versions of Word or Excel* and are considering updating (or have recently updated) to the latest versions, this book will bring you up to speed on the latest versions. (Whenever possible, I will emphasize new features and show how they compare with those in earlier versions of the programs.)

✔ If you're more familiar with word processing and spreadsheet programs than with presentation, electronic mail, or database programs and want to *expand your horizons*, this book will provide the information you need to get started quickly.

✔ Finally, this book is for you if you want to *work faster* or *produce better-looking documents and presentations*. Whenever possible, I will include design and appearance information that will help you work as quickly as possible, as well as format your pages and presentation visuals so that they command instant respect.

In short, this book provides a foundation that you can put to work immediately and then build on by purchasing specialized volumes (other books in the . . . *For Dummies* series).

Welcome to Information Interchange 101

The programs included with Office 4 take full advantage of the Windows 3.1 environment, permitting you to embed and link data created in one program to projects that you're creating in other programs. This capability not only saves you time but also increases accuracy (by eliminating the need to re-enter data). More important, Office's capability to share data between programs ensures that your print communications and presentations always will contain the same information. *You'll never again include outdated data in a proposal or presentation!*

Following are some of the ways in which Office 4 helps you exchange information between programs:

✔ You can easily insert an Excel chart into a proposal created in Microsoft Word and into a presentation created in PowerPoint. More important, when you make a change in the Excel chart, the Word file containing your proposal and the PowerPoint file containing your presentation are updated automatically.

✔ You can use names and addresses stored in your Microsoft Access mailing list to create mailing labels and personalized letters in Microsoft Word. For the first time, mail merge will be something that you look forward to, rather than leave to expensive consultants (who often are as confused as you are).

> ✓ You can use Word outlines as the basis for PowerPoint presentations and then — after creating your presentation visuals — insert your slides into reports and other publications created in Word.

Although these procedures may sound overly complicated (and a bit unnecessary) now, by the time you reach the end of this book, they'll be second nature to you! By this time next year, you'll wonder how you got by without Office 4.

A new way of looking at your work

Microsoft Office 4 introduces a new way of working with your computer. With Office, your emphasis will subtly switch from a prehistoric (or pre-Windows 3.1) *program-oriented view*, characterized by data files stored with their individual programs (for example, letters and memos stored in a Word subdirectory, charts and spreadsheets stored with Excel, and files containing slides and overheads stored with PowerPoint) to a *project-oriented* view of your work.

Because Office makes it easy to exchange data between programs, Office encourages you to create documents integrating data created with different programs. You'll soon be comfortable creating Word proposals containing Excel spreadsheets and copies of PowerPoint slides and sending drafts to your coworkers for comment using Microsoft Mail.

Your hard disk soon will be organized by projects or by clients. For example, new business memos, meeting notes, budgets and presentation visuals can appear in a NEWBUS subdirectory that also contains your Hot Prospects database. Likewise, correspondence, meeting notes, and time records related to Consolidated Industries can be stored in a Consolidated Industries subdirectory, which itself is divided into subdirectories for storing newsletters, brochures, and billing information.

Office 4 makes it easy to choose the right tool for the job at hand. The Microsoft Office Manager toolbar makes it easy to launch Office applications and switch among them. You'll also appreciate using the Microsoft Office toolbar to launch and locate other frequently used applications (or Windows features such as the File Manager and Print Manager) without having to go through the Program Manager.

Redefining "user friendly"

With the introduction of Office 4, Microsoft has redefined ease of use. ("Hah," you're probably thinking.) But until you work with Office programs and compare them with other programs, the phrase "ease of use" probably has as much credibility as the phrase "reinventing government."

However, you'll become a believer after you've worked with such Office 4 innovations as *AutoCorrect* (which corrects spelling mistakes as you make them), *AutoFormatting* (which takes the work out of creating good-looking documents and presentation visuals), *AutoText* (which enables you to insert frequently used terms as well as formatted tables), *Cue Cards* (which provide step-by-step guidance), and *Wizards* (which take the work out of planning and formatting).

Microsoft's usability studies have paid off in programs that you'll find noticeably easier to use. Microsoft has eliminated unnecessary keystrokes wherever possible, and you don't have to type frequently repeated actions again and again. For example, you can insert day (or month) headings into spreadsheet columns and automatically total the data in rows and columns.

Your mastery of the programs included with Office 4 is eased by the similarities in their menus. Because Office 4 programs have similar menu structures, *after you become comfortable working with one program, you'll find it very easy to transfer your knowledge to the other programs.*

The Word 6 spelling checker offers my favorite example of the way that Microsoft eliminated unnecessary keystrokes. When you launch a competitor's spelling checker, for example, the Spell Check dialog box asks, `Do you want to start spell checking your document?` and then makes you click again to answer in the affirmative. When you launch the Word 6 spelling checker, however, *it goes to work immediately!* A small point, perhaps, but one that represents a philosophy of creating programs around users instead of forcing users to accommodate programs.

Although Microsoft did its homework and created programs that you can use immediately, these programs have virtually unlimited capacity to grow with you as your needs become more sophisticated.

How This Book Is Organized

Before proceeding further, allow me to introduce the various programs that make up Office 4 and to explain some of the things that you can do with each program.

Part I: Working with Words

In the beginning was the Word: Microsoft Word, to be exact. Chapters 1 through 4 describe Microsoft Word 6 for Windows, the latest version of one of the first word processing programs to gain international popularity. Although it is a word processor, Word 6 might better be described as a *document organizer* or *document processor*. Word provides the glue that assembles many of the projects on which you'll be working. You can use Word for everything from simple letters to complex documents such as newsletters, brochures, and books.

With Word 6, you can choose a typeface, type size, and type style for each element of page architecture; import graphics created in other programs; add formatting options such as borders and backgrounds; and prepare a detailed table of contents. Word also allows you to perform about 100 other operations, for which I hope this book provides a basis for exploration at your leisure.

In Part I of this book, you learn how to edit and format text, use the new features of Word 6 (such as AutoCorrect, AutoFormatting, and AutoText) to create effective, attractive correspondence, memos, and multicolumn documents such as newsletters. You also learn how to create and apply styles and templates, as well as how to analyze your document by using Word's Outliner feature and Grammar checker.

Part II: How to Excel at the Numbers Game

Chapters 5, 6, and 7 describe Microsoft Excel 5. If the strong point of Word 6 is that it enables you to format words easily, Excel's strength is in manipulating and displaying numbers. Excel enables you to track budgets, establish cost estimates, and compare the costs and benefits of alternative courses of action. After massaging the numbers to your heart's content, you can display your conclusions in any type of chart or graph by manipulating the data in Excel 5.

In Part II of this book, you learn how to enter data and formulas; work with multilevel spreadsheets; and transform the results of your calculations into attractive, high-impact charts and graphs, which you can then export or link to documents created in other Office applications.

Part III: Suddenly It's Show Time!

Chapters 8 and 9 address the frequently felt (but carefully guarded) secret that most people share: the fear of speaking in public. Not to worry; PowerPoint 4 is here.

If Word helps you look good in print and Excel helps you convert numbers into attractive charts, Microsoft PowerPoint helps you create good-looking 35mm slide presentations, overhead transparencies, and on-screen computer presentations. Indeed, PowerPoint 4 is more than a presentation program; it's a presentation *system* that helps you create all the ingredients you need for an effective presentation: *visuals* (which can be 35mm slides, overhead transparencies, or screen images), *notes* (to help you rehearse your presentation), and *handouts* (which give your audience a tangible reminder of your presentation).

By the time you finish Part III of this book, you'll know how to select the correct presentation format; use the Content Wizard to speed the creation of your next presentation; rehearse your presentation so you'll know how much time to devote to each slide when you deliver your presentation; and prepare support materials, such as notes and handouts. You'll be on the lookout for opportunities to show off your new capabilities instead of hiding whenever the word *presentation* comes up.

Part IV: Working with and Exchanging Information

If you have purchased or upgraded to Office 4 Professional, you also received Access 2. Access is a database program that allows you to store and retrieve information easily. Access permits you to keep track of customers and to analyze what customers bought, how much they paid, and how often they made purchases. Using Access, you can easily store and manipulate even the most sophisticated information.

Chances are that one of your first duties will be creating a name-and-address file of your customers, prospects, and vendors. You also can use Access to track your personal assets and your firm's assets, such as computers, software, VCRs, CDs, books, and other information that could prove invaluable for insurance purposes. Chapters 10 and 11 describe how to create a database and enter information.

Chapter 12 describes how to use Microsoft Mail not only to exchange information with other computer users connected to a network, but also to send drafts of your manuscripts, spreadsheets, and presentations to clients, coworkers, and superiors for their comments.

Part V: Putting It All Together

Chapter 13 describes how to install the Microsoft Office Manager toolbar and how to work as efficiently as possible in the Windows 3.1 environment.

You can set up the Microsoft Office Manager toolbar to load automatically whenever you start Windows. Although you can reduce this toolbar to fit into the right end of the title bar at the top of your screen, you may want to start by making it as large as possible so that the buttons are easy to locate.

Chapter 14 describes how to share information between programs. You learn how to drag Excel charts into a Word proposal; how to base a PowerPoint presentation on a Word document; and how to link data between Word, Excel, and PowerPoint. You learn the differences between (and the relative advantages and disadvantages of) embedding and linking, as well as when to employ each technique.

Chapter 15 focuses on one of the most frequently used examples of information sharing: creating form letters and address labels by merging a letter created in Word 6 with information in an Access database.

Part VI: Part of Tens — 101 Design and Efficiency Tips

You can never divorce appearance from content. Regardless of the tool you use — a proposal created in Word, a spreadsheet created in Excel, or 35mm slides created in PowerPoint — the people you're trying to persuade always unconsciously judge the importance of your words by their appearance. Thus, Chapters 16 through 23 discuss ways of creating attractive documents and presentation visuals.

In addition, content can never be divorced from efficiency. If you're working inefficiently, you simply don't have the time you need to refine your ideas and present them as effectively as possible. Several of the chapters in this section describe shortcuts that may save only a couple of seconds individually but that save significant time cumulatively, giving you the time and mental alertness required to refine your ideas and present them as succinctly as possible.

Appendix and Glossary

If you haven't installed Microsoft Office, you'll appreciate the information contained in the appendix. This information reviews computer hardware requirements and helps you decide how much of each program module you have to install (and how much to leave off, in case hard disk space is limited).

Microsoft Office 4 For Windows For Dummies concludes with a glossary that defines over one hundred of the most important terms associated with Office programs. (I love glossaries; they introduce new ideas quickly and make it easy to review important terms.) Often, the best way to master a new software program is to master the language that it uses.

How to Use This Book

Although I may have started with Chapter 1 and plodded through to the glossary, there's no reason why you have to be so linear.

Each part of this book was planned and written as though it were a separate book on the topic, even though space was (obviously) limited. Yet within itself, each part attempts to be as complete as possible, providing an introduction to the program for newcomers as well as information that helps experienced users make the most of the program.

Accordingly, feel free to turn directly to the part of this book that contains the information you need. (You may find yourself starting with the appendix, if you haven't yet installed Office 4.) I constructed each section as a self-contained minibook with an internal sequence designed to help a novice attain comfort status quickly. Each part begins with the basics (for readers who are encountering the program for the first time) and advances to increasingly specialized and advanced topics.

How much do you need to know?

This book assumes that you have minimal working knowledge of Windows 3.1 (or Windows 3.1 for Workgroups). It assumes that you know how to turn on your computer, install programs, navigate through the Program Manager, and launch programs by clicking their icons. If you're not comfortable with these procedures, you may want to purchase Andy Rathbone's incomparable *Windows For Dummies* as well as this volume. (Notice that I didn't say *instead of*; after all, fair is fair!)

The following sections summarize the other important information that you need to know.

Conventions

To avoid confusion later on, it's important that we all speak the same language from the start. This book uses these conventions:

- ✔ When looking at the screen, notice the blinking *cursor* and the *I-beam pointer*. Move the mouse. Notice that the I-beam pointer moves to follow the mouse's movement.

- ✔ *Clicking* refers to pressing the left mouse button one time. Clicking is how you activate buttons in the toolbar, for example.

- ✔ *Double-clicking* refers to pressing the left mouse button twice in rapid succession. Double-clicking typically activates a different command.

- ✔ *Dragging* (a fraternity prank popular at Halloween) is used to select text to be moved, deleted, or formatted. To drag, place the insertion point to the left of the text that you want to select, hold down the left mouse button, and move the mouse in the desired direction. When you release the mouse button, the text remains selected. You can tell when text is highlighted because it appears in white against a black background.

- ✔ *Clicking the right mouse button.* In Word 6, the right mouse button finally becomes useful. Clicking a text or graphic object with the right mouse button displays Word's shortcut menus, which permit faster access to cut, copy, paste, and format commands.

Icons used in this book

This icon points to things that may be easy to forget but are helpful if remembered.

These sections reveal tricky, high-performance techniques that you may not have thought of.

Look out! This icon tells you how to avoid trouble before it starts.

Skip this if you want; it's nerdy stuff that just might impress your trivia buddies.

This icon gives you tips about how to create the most aesthetically pleasing documentation or presentation.

Finally, this stopwatch gives you the shortcut to completion — miles ahead of the competitor.

Keyboard shortcuts

You can access many commands through keyboard shortcuts. These shortcuts typically involve holding down the Ctrl or Alt key (typically located to the left and right of the spacebar on your keyboard) in combination with one of the function keys (the keys with F1, F2, F3 along the top of the keyboard), although any key can be used as a keyboard shortcut.

In most cases, you can customize Office 4 applications so that you can access virtually every command and feature through a keyboard shortcut, eliminating the need to take your hands off the keyboard and reach for the mouse to open a menu or click a toolbar button.

Why (and How) I Wrote This Book

I wrote this book for several reasons. One reason was that I'm genuinely impressed by what Microsoft has accomplished. I've been a PowerPoint fan since version 1, way back when, and I've worked extensively with the programs that make up Office 4. I wanted to share my experiences with these programs as well as some of my enthusiasm for the way in which Office 4 integrates the programs.

I had two additional goals in mind when I set out to distill thousands of pages of program documentation into a book limited to approximately 400 pages. My goals can be summarized as *survival* combined with *long-term efficiency*.

On the survival level, I want to help you put Office to work immediately, increasing your productivity and helping you expand your repertoire of things you can do with your computer. (There's more to life than memos and spread-sheet calculations.) I want to help you do things that only "power users" could do before, such as print envelopes, use styles for efficiency and consistency, and use such features as Word's Outliner to analyze and reorganize your print communications.

I also want to help you create attractive 35mm slides and overhead transparencies, which will help you speak more confidently in public. These days, it's not enough just to be able to put your ideas on paper; you have to be able to stand up and present them in person, too. (Gulp!)

On the other hand, I want to help you get into the habit of *doing things the right way from the start*. Anybody can be "productive" if he or she is willing to sacrifice efficiency. You've probably heard the story about an infinite number of monkeys banging on an infinite number of typewriters and rewriting the complete works of Shakespeare. You can always be "productive" if you're willing to work two, three, or ten times as hard as necessary, but that's not the right way to go through life. I want to help you work as efficiently and attractively as possible.

How much is covered in this book?

As I write this paragraph, I'm staring at a 1,000-page book on Word that another publisher prepared. Below it is another 1,000-page book on Excel. Below *that* book (deservedly so) is a three-inch-thick book on macros. So how can I presume to write "just" a 400-page book covering *all* Office programs?

The answer lies in selectivity and subjectivity. Rather than try to describe every command and every *nuance* of every command (for example, on rainy days, use the Shift key instead of the Ctrl key), I tried to limit myself to two tasks: providing an informed introduction to what you can reasonably expect to accomplish with each program, and describing the most efficient ways of achieving survival status with each program and instantly putting the program to work.

Therefore, each section of this book describes the sequence of commands that I feel you're going to immediately need to accomplish relatively simple, everyday projects. Rather than introduce the nuances of data interchange at the beginning of the book, for example, I start with the basis of creating, saving, and printing documents in Word. Creative exchange of information between programs doesn't show up until Part V, by which time you should be comfortable with the programs included in Office 4 (or Office 4 Professional).

Efficiency and growth

My other goal is to help you learn to do things right from the start. Many heavy users of word processing programs still don't use styles as efficiently as they can because the importance of styles wasn't fully explained until those users graduated to "self-trained power user" status. I'll also provide design advice because, from day one, the appearance of your documents and presentation visuals influences their effectiveness.

Sometimes I may err on the side of conservatism, especially with regard to toolbar shortcuts. Often, shortcuts (such as simply clicking a toolbar button) can lead to problems. Accordingly, I frequently stress the importance of opening menus and selecting commands rather than blindly clicking toolbar buttons. Although toolbars, wizards, and AutoFormatting can help you move forward quickly, it's important that you *recognize the limitations of these features* and be able to create and modify your own templates, rather than becoming overdependent on the ones provided with the programs.

Remember also that it's possible to type fairly quickly by looking at the keyboard, but there's a glass ceiling in terms of the speed that you can ultimately attain. *Although learning to "touch-type" may be harder in the beginning, you'll soon be able to type faster than those who must watch the keyboard while typing.*

By helping you build on a firm foundation from the start, this book will enable you to proceed much further than users who depend too much on Office 4's automation features. You'll have fewer bad (or at least inefficient) habits to break down the road.

Getting Started

Enough talk, already — let's get started! Turn to Chapter 1, or (if you're already familiar with Word 6) turn to the part that describes the program that you need to master first. (The nice thing about a book is that you can always go back and read the sections you skipped.)

I hope that you enjoy reading this book as much as I enjoyed writing it.

Roger C. Parker
Dover, New Hampshire

Part I
Working with Words

In this part...

Word 6 for Windows is the cornerstone of the powerful Microsoft Office building. Consistently heralded as
the greatest word processing program on earth, Word 6 can
turn you from an assistant pencil sharpener to a publishing
whiz in no time. With Word 6, you can create newsletters,
pamphlets, and even a letter to Mom.

Notice I said Mom, not MOM. There's a difference. One
corrects your errors and shows you better ways to do
things. The other gave birth to you.

If you're really confused, don't worry. Just turn the page and
jump right in.

Chapter 1

Getting Ready to Write the Great American Novel

• •

In This Chapter

▶ Loading Word 6 for Windows

▶ Creating your first document with the help of one of Word's wizards

▶ Choosing between Normal, Outline, and Page view

▶ Changing screen magnification and using the Full Screen feature

▶ Hiding and revealing the ruler

▶ Revealing, hiding, and editing Word's toolbars

▶ Showing or hiding scroll bars and the status bar and using the "Go to" shortcut

▶ Showing and hiding codes, and the importance of the last paragraph mark

▶ Saving, previewing, and printing your first document

▶ Activating Word's Automatic Save feature

▶ Closing documents and exiting Word

• •

*E*nough talk. The best way to master a software program — or even take over control of your office — is to get right down to work. By working with Word, you'll not only get a better idea of just how easy it is to work with Word 6 for Windows, but you'll also learn how to customize your working environment — rearrange the office, as it were — to suit your personal working style.

To start Word, double-click the Microsoft 6 program icon in the Windows 3.1 Manager. Or, if you're clairvoyant (or started reading this book from the appendix, like a lot of people seem to do these days — trendy, I guess) and have already installed MOM — the Microsoft Office Manager — click the Word icon in the Microsoft Office Manager toolbar located at the top of your screen (see the appendix for details on this wonderful timesaving feature). Strangely enough, as shown in Figure 1-1, the Microsoft Word icon resembles a slanted *W* with a piece of paper emerging from the bottom. (Clever, those people working in the rain forests of Redmond, Washington!)

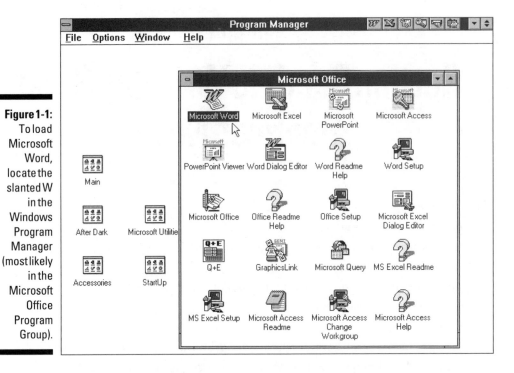

Figure 1-1:
To load
Microsoft
Word,
locate the
slanted W
in the
Windows
Program
Manager
(most likely
in the
Microsoft
Office
Program
Group).

The first thing you see, after you hear the usual whirring and grinding sounds from your computer, is the Word screen (see Figure 1-2). You can begin working at this point by simply typing, or you can enlist the aid of one of Word 6's wizards to help you format your document. You'll be returning to this opening screen in a few minutes for a guided tour — please line up with your partner and keep together with others in your group — but you'll start by examining wizards, one of Office 4's features that make Word and the other Office programs so easy to use.

Working with a Wizard

If you're in a hurry and want to write a letter showing off your spiffy new computer, using a wizard may be helpful. To work with a wizard, open the File menu by positioning your mouse arrow on the word File and clicking once with the left mouse button. When the menu opens, move the arrow down until New is highlighted (or appears against a blue background). Release the mouse button.

Figure 1-2:
Word's
opening
screen — a
face you'll
learn to
love.

You should now be at the New dialog box, which presents you with a list containing *templates* — previously formatted documents with borders, margins, typeface, and type size choices already made for you — as well as a list of wizards, which help you choose between them.

Position the arrow over the down arrow in the Template list box and — holding down the left mouse button — scroll through the list. When you come to Letter Wizard, click it with the mouse button and click OK (or press the Enter key with your right pinky). This action introduces you to the first friend you're going to make in your new office, the Letter Wizard (see Figure 1-3).

Whenever you're presented with a list of options, get in the habit of double-clicking on the desired option rather than simply highlighting the option and clicking the OK button in the dialog box (or pressing Enter). In most cases, this simple technique can save you a lot of time and unnecessary wrist movement (and will impress your friends and lead to so many raises that you will be able to retire early).

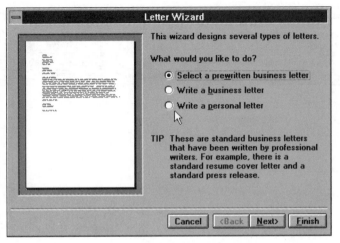

Like all Microsoft's wizards, the Letter Wizard asks you questions and does things in the background on the basis of your answers. Also like the other members of the wizard family — Mama, Papa, and Little Bear Wizard — the Letter Wizard thoroughly explains each of your alternatives and gives you an opportunity to change your mind before proceeding further.

You can begin exploring Letter Wizard by clicking on the circles — or *radio buttons* — next to each of the three alternatives. Notice that an explanation of the option appears immediately next to the word *TIP*. Also notice that there are two types of wizards: *content wizards* that, in this case, help you choose the words, and *appearance wizards* that help you determine format — or appearance.

Just for fun, click the Select a prewritten business letter button and click the Next button, which advances you to the Letter Wizard's list of frequently used types of letters (see Figure 1-4).

Whenever you see an underlined letter in a menu or dialog box, you can choose the command or option associated with it by pressing the underlined letter on your keyboard. When you want to choose the Next button, press the N on your keyboard rather than taking your hands off the keyboard and then using the mouse to click it.

Scroll down to Letter to Mom (we have to maintain a certain decorum, plus one's probably long overdue) and click Next. This Letter Wizard screen then asks you whether you're printing the letter on Letterhead stationery or Plain paper. Select Letterhead stationery followed by another click on the Next button.

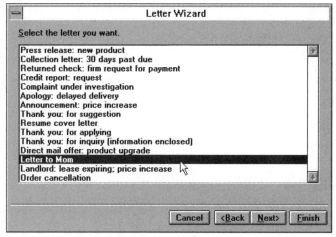

Figure 1-4:
The Letter
Wizard
offers you a
portfolio of
prewritten
letters,
which
provides a
basis for
customization.

At this point, I'd like to introduce you to another nice wizard feature. Click the Back button with your mouse. Notice that the wizard merely sighs — instead of impolitely expressing impatience over your frustrating, indecisive nature — and returns you to the previous screen where you can change your mind. At any point, Microsoft's wizards allow you to back up and change your mind. You won't change your mind now, so click the Next button to get back to the Wizard screen. This makes it easy for you to explore alternative wizard scenarios (some of which may be adapted for pay-per-view TV). The next three screens show you just how well thought-out Word's wizards really are:

✔ The top part of the screen contains three radio buttons that allow you to specify the location of your firm's letterhead (at the top, left, or right of the page) and asks you how much space the letterhead design requires (picky, picky — they should have said "logo" instead of "letterhead design" — maybe they'll ask my opinion next time; I'm easy, for a price, of course). When you are finished making changes, click Next.

✔ The next wizard screen asks you to enter the recipient, in this case Mom's name and address, as well as make any desired changes in your address (which you entered when you installed Word). Make any desired changes and click Next.

✔ This wizard screen asks you "Which style would you like?" and offers you your choice of Classic, Contemporary, and Typewriter. Click the radio button next to your desired choice and click Next.

The final Letter Wizard screen asks you whether you want to Create an envelope or mailing label, Display Help as you work, or Just display the letter. Choose the last option and click the Finish button. Your letter to Mom appears on the screen of your computer (see Figure 1-5).

When Word first loads, you can immediately begin a new document by starting to type when Word's blank opening screen appears. Later, to begin a new document without the assistance of a wizard, choose the File menu followed by the New command in the drop-down menu. You can accept the default Normal template by just clicking on OK or pressing Enter when the New dialog box appears.

Exploring the Word 6 for Windows Screen

Now that you have some words on the screen to play with, you can explore some of the features of the Word 6 for Windows screen. One of the reasons for Word's popularity is the way that you can customize it to suit your specific working habits. Even if you don't immediately use these customization features, it's worth knowing about them from the beginning so you'll know how to access them as your word processing needs become more sophisticated. (*The more you get, the more you want!*) Word 6 for Windows is a program you'll probably never outgrow.

Using, hiding, and revealing the horizontal and vertical scroll bars

One of the first things you'll likely want to do is see how the letter to Mom ends. Unless you sold your Mercedes to buy a 21-inch computer screen, you probably can see only a portion of the letter. Notice the vertical bar — sort of like a side view of an elevator shaft — running up the right side of the screen. This bar, called the *vertical scroll bar*, contains (from top to bottom) an upward-pointing arrow, a square box, and a single arrow pointing down.

Click the down arrow. Notice how each time you click the downward-pointing arrow, another line of your letter appears. To move faster, click the scroll box and — holding down the left mouse button — drag the scroll box down the scroll bar. Notice how you can quickly see more of the top or bottom of your letter by dragging the box up or down. Click in the space below the scroll box. Instead of advancing down a single line at a time, you're presented with the new window-full of your letter.

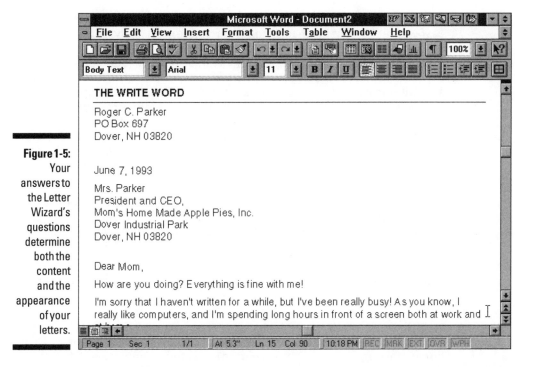

Figure 1-5:
Your
answers to
the Letter
Wizard's
questions
determine
both the
content
and the
appearance
of your
letters.

The horizontal bar along the bottom of the document window works the same way, only instead of moving the image of the letter up or down, it moves it from left to right.

If you are working in Page Layout view (Word's various views are described below), there will be two pairs of double-headed arrows visible at the bottom of the vertical scroll bar: a pair pointing up and a pair pointing down. These pairs of double-headed arrows help you quickly move around a multipage document. If you click the upward-pointing pair of arrows, you're taken to the top of the preceding page. If you click the downward-pointing arrows, Word takes you to the bottom of the next page.

Choosing a different view of the document

Word allows you to view your document from a variety of perspectives. These perspectives alter the appearance and amount of text and graphics that appear on the screen. One of the nice things about working with Word is that you can customize the screen to your working habits as well as the particular task at hand. One of the most important customization options is your ability to work in different views.

Word offers you several ways to view your document: *Normal, Outline,* and *Page Layout* view. I'll examine them in the order you're most likely to use them:

- ✔ **Normal** view is the most efficient way to do most of your typing and editing because it lets you concentrate on the content of your document without being distracted by its appearance. Normal view suppresses *headers* (information like document titles and sections repeated at the top of every page), *footers* (information repeated at the bottom of every page), and *page numbers* (which tell what time it is — sorry!). Normal view also helps you and your computer work faster by suppressing column formatting — the text extends the width of the page. To access Normal view, open the <u>V</u>iew menu and select <u>N</u>ormal.

- ✔ **Page Layout** view provides you with an accurate look at how your document will look when printed. Page Layout view shows headers, footers, and text in side-by-side columns. You get a page view of your document. To access the Page Layout view, open the <u>V</u>iew menu and select <u>P</u>age Layout view.

- ✔ **Outline** view will interest you more later, when you use different level headings to organize long documents.

Instead of opening the View menu each time you want to change views, get in the habit of clicking on the three View buttons located at the extreme left of the horizontal scroll bar. The Normal button is located at the extreme left of the three buttons. The Page View button is in the middle of the three and resembles lines on a piece of paper. The Outline View button, on the right of the other two view buttons, resembles lines that are indented.

The button displaying the currently active view appears pressed in and lighter than the others. To change views, simply click one of the other buttons.

Customizing Normal view

One of the best tips I can give you for working more efficiently in Word is to show the formatted text with a draft font when working in Normal view. Word's *draft* font is a large, easy to read sans serif typeface that always looks the same, regardless of the actual type used in your document. In addition, all text set in Word's draft font appears the same, regardless of the size and style it is actually being set in. The only formatting options shown are bold and italics, indicated by underlining. You'll probably find that the draft font in Normal view is easier on the eyes than serif fonts, especially if you frequently work with fonts like 11- and 12-point Times New Roman.

To replace formatted text with a draft font in Word's Normal view:

1. **Open the Uiew menu and select Normal (unless you're already in Normal view).**

2. **Open the Tools menu and select Options.**

3. **When the Options dialog box appears, select the View tab (see Figure 1-6).**

4. **Click the check boxes next to the Draft Font and Wrap to Window options. Click OK or press Enter on your keyboard.**

Remember, you don't need to reach for the mouse to click the OK button when you want to close a dialog box; simply press Enter.

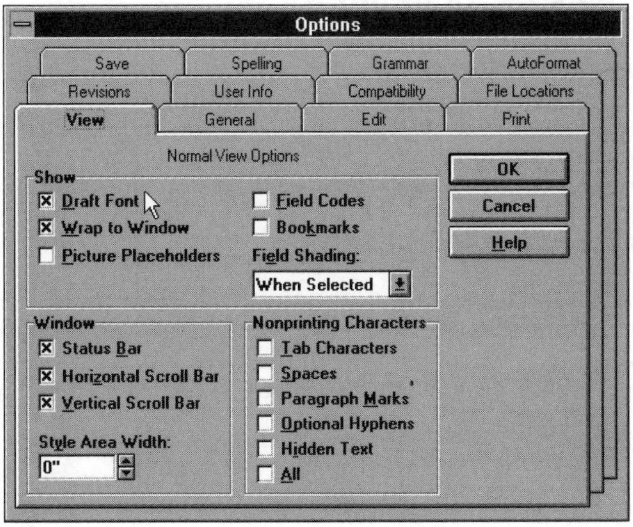

Figure 1-6:
The Options dialog box displays tabs reflecting different categories of Word features that you can customize. Choose the View tab when you want to select Draft font for easier editing.

Options

Save	Spelling	Grammar	AutoFormat
Revisions	User Info	Compatibility	File Locations
View	General	Edit	Print

Normal View Options

Show
- ☒ Draft Font
- ☒ Wrap to Window
- ☐ Picture Placeholders
- ☐ Field Codes
- ☐ Bookmarks
- Field Shading: When Selected ▼

OK
Cancel
Help

Window
- ☒ Status Bar
- ☒ Horizontal Scroll Bar
- ☒ Vertical Scroll Bar

Style Area Width: 0"

Nonprinting Characters
- ☐ Tab Characters
- ☐ Spaces
- ☐ Paragraph Marks
- ☐ Optional Hyphens
- ☐ Hidden Text
- ☐ All

Hiding the scroll bars

You may want to hide the horizontal or vertical scroll bar — or both — in order to gain some additional working area on your computer screen. To do this, choose the Tools menu followed by the Options command. When the Options dialog box appears (refer to Figure 1-6), click the View tab, which brings it to the front. In the Window area of the View tab, click the check box next to Horizontal Scroll Bar and/or Vertical Scroll Bar. Click OK or press Enter. When you return to Normal view, the scroll bars will be gone.

Note, however, that when you remove the horizontal scroll bar from the screen, you also lose the Normal, Outline, and Page Layout view buttons. This means you'll have to open the View menu every time you want to change views.

Note that when you click a check box with an *X* in it, the *X* is removed. Click once again, and the *X* reappears. This process is called *toggling* an option. You'll frequently encounter the same feature in menus. When there's a check mark by a command in a menu or dialog box, the command or option is active. Clicking on it removes the check mark (and deactivates the command).

Using the status bar and hiding it when you want a change of scene

Also at the bottom of the screen is the status bar. And even though there may be times when you want to hide it in order to gain some more document-editing space, the status bar is one of Word's most useful features. The leftmost section of the status bar displays the number of the page you're currently working on, the section number, and the total number of pages in the section. Whenever you select a command, however, this information is replaced by a description of what the selected command does.

There's an important keyboard shortcut associated with the left portion of the status bar. Double-click the left side of the status bar — clicking twice in rapid succession — and Word takes you to the Go To dialog box where you can go directly to a desired page number or advance to a Bookmark, Footnote, or Endnote (see Figure 1-7).

Double-clicking on the left side of the status bar is a shortcut to the Go To dialog box. You can get to the desired page by simply entering the name of the page you want to go to and pressing Enter. Or, if you want to move forwards (or backwards) four pages for example, enter **+4** or **-4** in the Enter Page Number text box of the Go To dialog box.

The remaining section of the status bar displays the current position of the insertion point on the page, followed by a clock. The next few boxes display other Word features and, in some cases, permit you to reach these Word features by double-clicking on the appropriate features box.

Figure 1-7:
The Go To
dialog box,
accessible
by double-
clicking on
the left
section of
the status
bar, permits
you to jump
directly to
any desired
page.

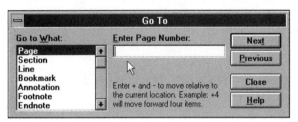

✔ The text in the box with the grayed-out REC turns black when you're recording a macro. This box is also a shortcut: by double-clicking on it, you can begin recording a macro.

✔ When the grayed-out MRK text turns black, revision marking is active, permitting you to track, display, and print changes in your document. There also is a shortcut: double-clicking on the MRK box takes you to the Revisions dialog box, which will allow Group Think, or a committee mentality, to interfere with your pristine words.

✔ When EXT is black instead of grayed out, the keyboard is extending a selection — marking text for editing, deletion, or movement. Double-clicking on this box has the same effect as pressing the F8 function key. (The function keys are usually located along the top of your keyboard, but may also be located on the left side of the keyboard.) You can then highlight text using the up-, down-, left-, and right-arrow keys.

✔ Have you ever noticed that sometimes when you're typing in the middle of a sentence, the words you're entering are replacing existing text instead of pushing the text to the right? That's probably because you've accidentally pressed the Ins — or Insert — key on the right side of your keyboard. If the Insert option (which is the default) is on, OVR is grayed out in this box; if the overstrike option is on, OVR is black.

✔ Finally, when the letters WPH turn from gray to black, it means that Word's Intrusion and Loyalty Detector is on and it senses that there's an ex-WordPerfect user at the keyboard and WordPerfect Help is active. (In case Word's Intrusion and Loyalty Detector doesn't work, you can activate Help for WordPerfect users switching over to Word by double-clicking on this box.)

Because so many useful features are displayed in the status bar, you're likely to want to leave it on all the time. If you decide to hide it, however, open the Tools menu and select Options. When the Options dialog box appears, click the View tab and click the box next to Status Bar. This action causes the status bar to disappear — or, if it is not visible, to appear when you close the dialog box. (Another *toggle*, right?)

Changing screen magnification

Suppose that you are tired of seeing just a portion of your letter and want to see how the whole letter looks.

One option is to open the View menu and select Full Screen. Doing so hides all menus, scroll bars, and the status bar (everything except the Microsoft Office Manager toolbar if you have it visible — see the appendix). You can move through your letter by using the up-, down-, left-, and right-arrow keys. And you can still open menus by clicking along the top of the screen in their approximate location.

To escape from Full Screen view, press Esc (this key is usually at the upper left of your keyboard). You're immediately returned to Normal or Page Layout view.

You can also use Word's Zoom feature to change screen magnification. Open the View menu and choose Zoom. When the Zoom dialog box appears, you can select the placement of the document on your screen (see Figure 1-8). You can show it at actual size (100%), twice actual size (200%), 75%, or you can scale it to the width of your screen (Page Width). If you have a 21-inch monitor, you can show the Whole Page. And you can display up to six pages at a time by clicking on Many Pages. (Clicking on the little screen below Many Pages allows you to specify how many pages by *dragging* — or holding down the left mouse button as you highlight the number and position of the pages you want to display.)

This list could go on and on, but nine times out of ten, you'll probably find working in Page Width most comfortable. Click the OK button to exit the Zoom dialog box.

Before returning to the letter, you should explore two more features of the Word screen that Microsoft Word has in common with other Microsoft Office programs: toolbars and the ruler (my teacher in parochial school always used to hit me with one).

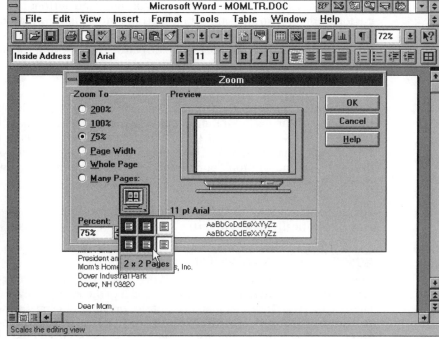

Figure 1-8:
The Zoom
dialog box
allows you
to fine-tune
how Word
will display
your
document
on your
computer's
screen, or
monitor.

Let's go bar hopping!

Word's toolbars offer an alternative way to choose commands. Instead of
opening menus or trying to remember keyboard shortcuts, you can use
toolbars for quick and visible access to important commands by simply clicking
buttons. To see which toolbars are available, open the View menu and select
Toolbars. The Toolbars dialog box (Figure 1-9) shows which toolbars are
currently displayed and which can be displayed.

Figure 1-9:
The
Toolbars
dialog box
shows you
which
toolbars are
currently
visible and
which ones
can be
added.

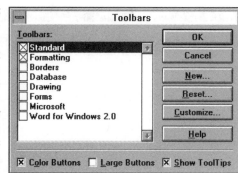

Each toolbar displays a different category of command buttons and can be customized. The two most important are the Standard and Formatting toolbars. These automatically appear when you first install and start Word — you may not be aware that you can hide them. You can also create your own toolbars, reflecting your choice of the commands you most often want to use — or have the most trouble locating.

Note that in the bottom of the toolbox, you have the option of adding color to the toolbars, by using Color Buttons, as well as enlarge the toolbars, by using Large Buttons — although with Large Buttons fewer toolbars can be displayed. Note the mark in the Show ToolTips check box. When this option is active, a description of each button's purpose appears when the mouse arrow passes over each button.

For now, take a look at the Standard and Formatting toolbars. Some of them may automatically appear when the function associated with them is chosen.

Exploring the Standard toolbar

The Standard toolbar offers access to Word's most frequently used commands, arranged from left to right in roughly the order of their frequency of use (see Figure 1-10). You'll find commands visible for opening, closing, saving, and printing files; using the spell checker; cutting, copying, and pasting text; copying formats: and changing your mind (Undo and Redo). The Standard toolbar also makes it easy to insert tables or load Excel — so you can insert a spreadsheet in your Word document — as well as set up multicolumn documents.

Take a few minutes now to slowly move the arrow over each button to familiarize yourself with its function. (If nothing appears when you place the arrow over a button, open View, choose Toolbars, and make sure that the check box next to Show ToolTips is checked.)

Figure 1-10:
Word's Standard toolbar offers you fast and easy access to your most frequently needed commands.

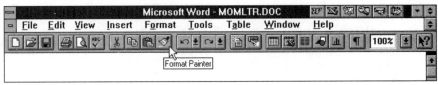

Note the contents at the extreme right of the Standard toolbar. The box with the number displays the current zoom magnification. Click the box with the downward-pointing arrow, and you'll be able to choose a different magnification level.

The button to the left of the box displaying current screen magnification is the Paragraph button. Observe what happens to Mom's letter when you click it (see Figure 1-11). Suddenly, it looks like a bunch of flies have walked across your screen after being doused in India ink.

Notice that a dot indicates each space between words, and a paragraph mark (insert mark) appears each time the Enter key was pressed. There are three reasons the Paragraph button is so valuable.

✔ If your document ever exhibits strange word or paragraph spacing, the Paragraph button will help you discover whether you've inadvertently entered two spaces between words (or none at all) or pressed the Enter key twice after paragraphs.

Paragraph button

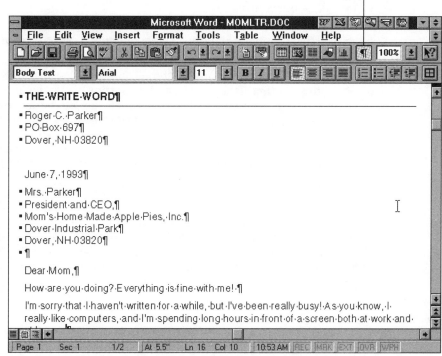

Figure 1-11:
Click the Paragraph button in the Standard toolbar when you want to display spaces between words and paragraph marks.

✔ Word stores character and paragraph formatting in the paragraph mark at the end of each paragraph. If, while editing your document, you inadvertently erase a paragraph mark along with text, the paragraph will join the next paragraph and — equally important — *adopt the formatting of the next paragraph*. This can lead to some strange surprises!

✔ If you insert nonprinting, or *hidden,* text into your document — words for your lover only, perhaps — these hidden words will be revealed when you click the Paragraph button.

The Paragraph button is another example of a *toggle*. The first time you click it, the feature becomes active. Click it again, and the word and paragraph spacing marks disappear from your screen.

If you want to be more selective in what you reveal when you click the Paragraph button, open the Tools menu and select Options. When the Options dialog box appears, select the View tab. In the Nonprinting Characters portion of the View tab located at the lower right, you can specify which nonprinting characters you want to display. You can choose to display from among the following options: Tab Characters, Spaces, Paragraph Marks, Optional Hyphens, Hidden text, or All. Click OK or press Enter to return to your document after you've made your choices.

Exploring the Formatting toolbar (where people go to look good)

The Formatting toolbar is equally useful — and its functions a bit more intuitive (see Figure 1-12). The three boxes on the left side of the Formatting toolbar display the formatting of the text where the insertion point is located. Visible are style, typeface, and type size. In each case, clicking on the downward-pointing arrow to the right of the box permits you to make another choice by scrolling through a list of alternatives. Moving to the right — by clicking B, I, or U — you can choose to make type bold, italic, or underlined. Clicking more than one option is possible (if you want text to be bold italic, for example).

The four buttons with lines in them on the right side of the Formatting toolbar permit you to specify the alignment of text columns. You can align text left, centered, right, or full justified. The button with the numbers permits you to create a numbered list; use the button with the dots to create a bulleted list. The buttons with the left and right arrows are for indenting text or eliminating text indents. The last button — with the square — is for playing tic-tac-toe. No, actually it's the Borders button.

Figure 1-12:
The
Formatting
toolbar.

Press the Borders button to display the Borders toolbar, which permits you to specify the width and placement of lines around an imported graphic or a table. Click the downward-pointing arrow next to the first box, the Lines box, and you can choose lines of different thicknesses or choose double, dashed, or dotted lines. Click the downward-pointing arrow next to the Shading box, the last box in the Borders toolbar, and you can select backgrounds in various shades of gray, a solid (in other words, black) background, or a crosshatch pattern.

After making any desired choices, click once again on the Borders button, the last button in the Formatting toolbar, and the Borders toolbar will disappear (see Figure 1-13).

Editing toolbars (places where editors go after work)

Don't feel that just because a toolbar exists, you have to go there. Like just about every other aspect of Word, you can customize Word's toolbars — with the exception of the Standard toolbar. You can do the following things:

- ✔ Add command buttons to the toolbars.
- ✔ Remove unwanted command buttons.
- ✔ Rearrange the order of the buttons of the toolbars.

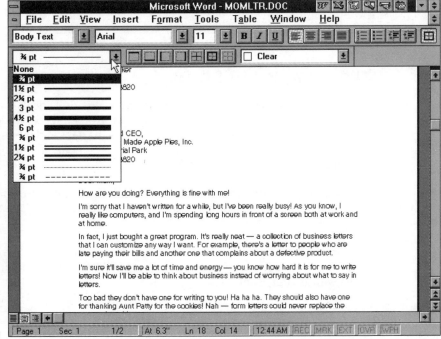

Figure 1-13: The Borders toolbar appears when you click the Borders button in the Formatting toolbar. Click again, and it disappears.

To customize Word's toolbars (see Figure 1-14), open the Tools menu and choose Customize. When the Customize dialog box appears, click the Toolbars tab. Select the Categories you want to modify by clicking the appropriate name. This action displays other buttons which you can add to the toolbar. Notice that a description of the buttons appears as you click each button. To add a button to the toolbar, drag it to the toolbar. To remove an existing button, click it and drag it off the toolbar. To rearrange the toolbar, drag the button to a new location on a toolbar. When you are finished, click Close or press Enter.

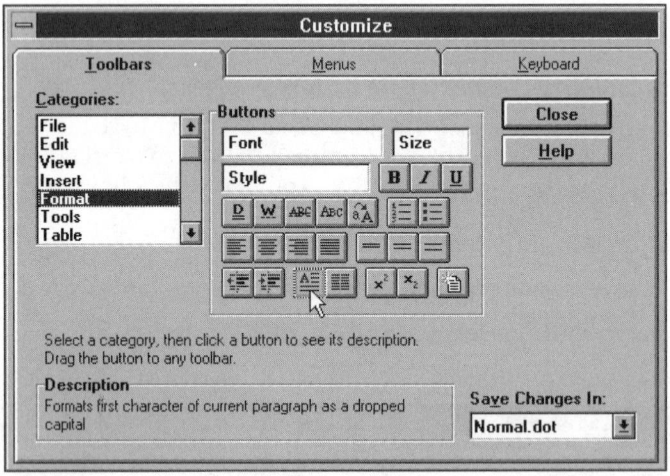

Figure 1-14:
You can customize Word's toolbars by adding, removing, and rearranging buttons.

Exploring Word's ruler

Open the View menu and select Ruler (unless it's already a checked item in the menu). A horizontal ruler will appear along the top of the screen under any toolbars that may be visible. The ruler shows the margins and tabs of your document and, if you're creating a multicolumn document, the column placement and the distance between the columns.

You can easily reformat your document by dragging on the appropriate ruler markers; in other words, you can change margins, add tabs, or adjust column spacing.

Most importantly, by double-clicking on the ruler, you can go directly to Word's Page Setup dialog box, where you can adjust the details of your document layout with greater accuracy.

Resist the temptation to display every toolbar and screen option available. Of the options discussed so far, you'll probably find the scroll bars, the status bar, and the Standard and Formatting toolbars to be most useful. You may find that the ruler takes up space that can be better used to display more of your document.

Saving Mom's Letter

You should now save Mom's letter so you can take a break and return to work on it later. (Next year, perhaps?)

To save Mom's letter, open the File menu and select Save. This action causes a problem because Word doesn't know what you want to call the document. Word accordingly takes you to the Save As dialog box where you can specify a filename and a location for the file (see Figure 1-15). Because you haven't given the document a name yet, Word suggests you save it with the default based on the document number. But this can make it difficult for you to locate the letter at a later date, so I don't recommend following Word's suggestion.

Figure 1-15:
Word's
Save As
dialog box
prompts you
to name
your
document
the first time
you save it.

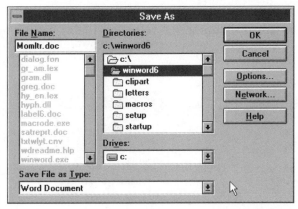

Accordingly, replace the DOC1.DOC default by replacing it with a more meaningful filename, perhaps MOMLTR, and clicking on OK or pressing Enter. (You could just as easily call it MOMBEG. But remember that you're limited to eight letters — no hyphens or spaces allowed — and that Word will automatically insert the *.doc* suffix.) Happier, Word now saves the letter. (Later on I discuss locations other than the Word 6 subdirectory where you can save files.)

After you've named and saved the document the first time, you can work much faster if you use Word's keyboard shortcut for Save: Hold down the Ctrl key while pressing the letter *S*. Get in the habit of saving frequently. It's cheap insurance. (You can also click the Save button — the third from the left on the Standard toolbar — the one that looks like a diskette (if you're working with the Standard toolbar visible).

Activating AutoSave

You've covered a lot of ground so far, but there's something else you should do before you print Mom's letter. This is a final bit of customization that can, quite literally, save you hours of work. Bear with me. Do it, and at some point in the next few years, you'll send me a letter of thanks.

Open the Tools menu and select Options. When the Options dialog box appears, click the Save tab and click in the check box next to Automatic Save Every (box) Minutes. Either accept the default figure of 10 minutes or use the up/down arrows to change the default to a longer or shorter interval. (I prefer 5 minutes because I value my time and hate trying to remember what I've just written.) Click OK or press Enter.

After you've done this simple procedure (see Figure 1-16), Word automatically saves your work at the interval you've specified. Why is periodically saving your work so important?

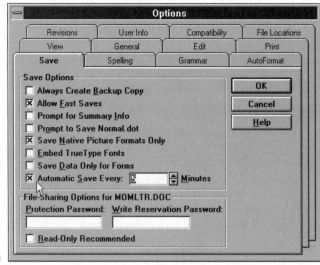

Figure 1-16:
Selecting
Automatic
Save in the
Options
dialog box.

Consider how computers work. Until you save your work, all of your creativity, editing, and formatting don't exist in the computer's memory. That means all of your work will be lost if your dog chases your cat across the room and unplugs your computer, you cross your legs and unplug your computer, or a thunderstorm 200 miles away momentarily interrupts the power going to your computer. Poof!

Ever try to re-create greatness? It can't be done!

So save yourself a lot of hassle and utilize Word's Automatic Save feature. The few seconds for which it interrupts your work — and the fact that Word will prompt you to name a new, previously untitled file five minutes into your work — will be more than repaid by the hours it saves when you try to go back and describe the emotions John felt when leaving Mary after she decided to undertake a new life in Tibet with June (who had recently left Swarthmore and joined the Red Army because she was ashamed of Bill's baby).

Previewing and Printing Mom's Letter

So what's Mom's letter going to look like when it's printed? There are two ways to find out: using Word's Print Preview feature or actually printing the letter.

Putting Print Preview to work

To preview your letter to Mom, open the File menu and select Print Preview. (Or, if you're working with the Standard toolbar visible, click the fifth button from the left — the one that looks like a magnifying glass in front of a piece of paper with a folded-over upper-right corner.) Either alternative takes you to Word's Print Preview, which comes complete with its own toolbar (see Figure 1-17).

When you move the mouse onto the screen, notice how the icon resembles a magnifying glass with a plus sign. This icon is called the Magnifier. Position the Magnifier over the date and click (with the left mouse button — you knew that!). Notice what happens: the Magnifier zooms and magnifies the part of the page over which it is located. Doing so allows you to work at greater accuracy on just a part of your document. You'll appreciate this feature when you start working with frames and imported graphics.

When you magnify just a portion of a page, notice how the plus sign inside the Magnifier icon turns into a minus sign. Click once again, and you're returned to a view of the full page.

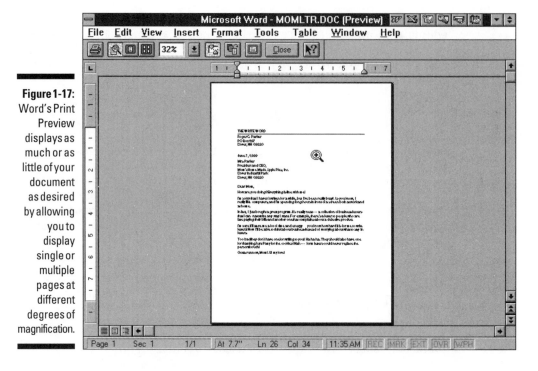

Figure 1-17:
Word's Print Preview displays as much or as little of your document as desired by allowing you to display single or multiple pages at different degrees of magnification.

Take a few minutes to examine the Page Preview toolbar. You can do a lot with it. Here's a description of each button on the Print Preview toolbar, from left to right:

- ✔ The Print button allows you to go directly from Print Preview to Print without closing Print Preview and then opening the File menu and selecting Print — a great time-saver.

- ✔ The Magnifier button turns the insertion point into the Magnifier icon again if you've lost it to the insertion pointer while editing. (Yes, you can edit in Word's Print Preview mode.)

- ✔ The One Page button allows you to display a single page.

- ✔ The Multiple Pages button allows you to display more than one page at a time. Click the Multiple Pages button — the fourth one from the left — and drag downward towards the lower right of your screen. You can display either two or three pages side by side, or stack up to six pages on the screen. (Of course, the more pages you display, the smaller they'll be. But that's what the Magnifier icon is there for! Plus, haven't you always wanted a *really big* computer screen? Here's your excuse to get one!)

✔ Word refers to the next items — a box and a pull-down menu — as the Zoom Control (sort of like "Houston Control, this is Alpha One, over!" without astronauts). By clicking on the downward-pointing arrow, you can change the degree of Print Preview magnification, permitting you to quickly switch between Page Width and Whole Page views.

✔ The next icon — the one that looks like the scale in a doctor's office (which is always set ten pounds heavier than your bathroom scale at home) — hides or reveals the Print Preview ruler.

✔ The Shrink to Fit button is really nifty and especially useful when working with long documents. If you, like me, always end up with letters that have "Sincerely" and your name isolated on the last page, try pressing the Shrink to Fit button. Often, it will be able to locate "wasted" space on the previous page and bring "Sincerely" and your name to the bottom of that page (helping save your temper and the forests of the world). If it doesn't work, Word will apologize and tell you that "After several attempts, Word was unable to shrink the document by one page."

✔ You should be able to tell *me* about the Close and Help buttons by this point.

Click Close to return to your document, or — here's a nice feature — if you're working with the horizontal scroll bar revealed, you can return to your document by clicking on the Normal or Page Layout view button.

Get in the habit of changing views by clicking on the Normal and Page Layout buttons just left of the horizontal scroll bar. Doing this can save you from performing a lot of unnecessary steps and, thus, save you a lot of time.

Printing your work

To print Mom's letter, open the File menu and select — what else? — Print! This action brings you to the Print dialog box where you'll probably be spending a lot of time in the coming months and years (eternity?). The Print dialog box is where you can choose from alternate printers, if you have more than one connected to your computer, as well as — if your document contains more than one page — choose which pages you want to print (see Figure 1-18). Depending on the type of printer you have installed, you can also choose quality options and, if your printer has more than one tray, choose which tray the first and following pages will use.

Figure 1-18:
The Print dialog box allows you to choose a printer and, if your document contains more than one page, choose which pages you want to print and in what order.

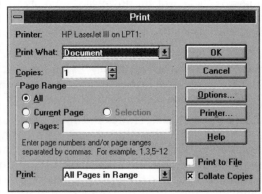

You should now be prepared to print. Turn on your printer, give it time to warm up, and when it indicates it's ready, often by a reassuring green light next to the word *Ready*, click OK or press Enter. A few minutes later, Mom's letter appears in all its splendor and glory.

Print button limitations

Instead of opening the File menu and clicking on Print, you could have started printing by clicking on the Print button in the Standard toolbar. There are both advantages and disadvantages to using the Print button, however.

The advantage, of course, is that it's faster. The *disadvantage*, however, is that Word immediately starts printing your document, bypassing the Print dialog box. As a result, even if you only want to print the current page or a range of pages (for example, pages six through eight), Word prints your entire document. By bypassing the Print dialog box, the Print button prevents you from specifying multiple copies of a document and Word from automatically collating your copies.

The lesson is a good one: choose your features carefully. "Shortcuts" often have unintended side effects!

Closing Mom's Letter and Exiting Word

Well, it's way past midnight and time to stop. You can either close Mom's letter and leave Word loaded (or running) or close Mom's letter and Exit—or turn off—Word 6 for Windows.

If you want to close the letter file and keep Word running, open the File menu and select Close. If you've made any changes since the last save, Word will ask you if you want to save the changes and offer you the following options: Yes, No, Cancel, or Help (see Figure 1-19).

✔ Click Yes, or press Y, if you want to save the document and return to a blank Word screen.

✔ Click No, or press N, if you don't want to save recent changes.

✔ Click Cancel (or press the Esc key on your keyboard) if you're suddenly struck with an anxiety attack and don't want to make up your mind just yet.

✔ Click Help, or press H, if you're really worried!

Figure 1-19:
You're always given a chance to save changes made since the last time you saved before closing a file or exiting Word.

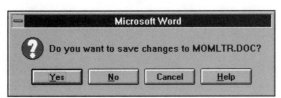

After selecting Yes, you'll be presented with a blank Word screen, ready to begin a new file (perhaps a letter to Dad based on a different wizard).

If, however, you want to not only close the letter but also exit Word (perhaps because you're going to turn off your computer and visit the gang at the Formatting bar), open the File menu and select Exit. You'll find Exit at the bottom of the File menu, below the names of any files you may have already saved.

Once again — if you've made any changes since the last save — Word will ask you if you want to save the changes and present you with the same four alternatives. If you click Yes, and if no other Word documents were open, Mom's letter will disappear and Word 6 for Windows will close, returning you to the Windows Program Manager. Select File⇨Exit Windows, and click OK when asked to confirm leaving Windows. It's now time to turn off your computer and to congratulate yourself on covering so much ground.

Chapter 2
Choosing the Right Words

● ●

In This Chapter

▶ Opening an existing Word document

▶ Moving through a Word document

▶ Selecting text for replacement, deletion, or movement

▶ Using Word's shortcut menus

▶ Restoring deleted text (and changing your mind again)

▶ Using drag-and-drop editing

▶ Using AutoCorrect and AutoText to save time and increase accuracy

▶ Using the Spell Check and Thesaurus features

▶ Adding words to your personal spell-check dictionary

▶ Checking your Grammar (and your Grampar)

● ●

*T*his chapter focuses on choosing the right words for your message, because no matter how smart dem folks at Microsoft are, they couldn't possibly have prepared a wizard for every type of letter that you're likely to need — and if they had, those wizards would be "optional at extra cost." (If Microsoft would cooperate, we could all sit back and just exchange wizard codes with one another.) Until that happens, your ability to communicate effectively in print depends on your ability to edit previously typed words: changing the order in which you introduced ideas and deleting extra, unnecessary, redundant, repetitious, and superfluous words. You can boost your productivity by making the most of Word's editing tools and its keyboard and mouse shortcuts.

Opening a Previously Saved File

You can open a previously saved file in two ways. The first way is to use the File menu, at the bottom of which Word automatically displays the last four files that you saved. Just scroll down the File menu, past the commands, and release the mouse button when you come to the file you want.

You can increase the number of files displayed at the bottom of the File menu by opening the Tools menu, choosing Options, and clicking the General tab. At the bottom of the list of check boxes, you'll find Recently Used File List next to a box that displays the four files you saved last. Click the up and down to increase or decrease the number displayed in this list, or enter a new figure in the box. You may want to enter a larger number if you have a large-screen monitor and typically work on several projects at the same time. (I have my file list set at eight, just in case you're interested.)

The other way to open a previously saved file is to open the File menu and choose Open. This command takes you to the Open dialog box, where you can wander through the various drives and subdirectories located on your computer (or your network, if your computer is connected to one) in search of your file.

When you locate the desired file, you can open it in either of two ways:

- Clicking the filename and then clicking OK (or pressing Enter)
- Double-clicking the filename (double-clicking a listed item in a menu saves time and effort)

Moving through a Word Document

You can navigate through Word documents by using either mouse or keyboard shortcuts. The mouse shortcuts are easy to master. But although keyboard shortcuts initially take more time to learn, *in the long run* you'll find the time savings to be significant enough to warrant mastering them. (And you won't have to go for mouse-arm therapy so often!) Equally important, you'll find that other software programs (Aldus PageMaker, for example) use the same keyboard shortcuts for moving around a document, so you'll be doubly rewarded for your efforts.

Using the mouse to navigate from word to word, screen to screen, and page to page

Word automatically opens documents at the top of the first page. Notice the blinking insertion point. Type **TYPE**. Notice that the word *TYPE* appears in the upper-left corner of the screen, right before the first word in your document. (Before you go any further, press the Backspace key — the gray key with the left-pointing arrow located at the right edge of the top row of your keyboard — four times to eliminate *TYPE*. It's important to start with a relatively clean slate.)

If you're working with the vertical scroll bar displayed, you can view the rest of your current document in the following ways:

- To advance down one line at a time, click the down arrow.

- To move to an approximate location in your document, drag the scroll box in the vertical scroll bar in the desired direction.

- To advance down one window at a time, click the scroll bar *below* the scroll box.

- To return one window at a time to previous locations in your document, click the scroll bar *above* the scroll box.

- To advance to the top of the next page, click the twin down arrows at the bottom of the scroll bar.

- To return to the top of the preceding page, click the twin up arrows in the scroll bar. (Notice that these double arrows disappear if you select Normal or Outline view.)

Using keyboard shortcuts to jump from word to word and page to page

You also use the arrow keys to advance through your document, as follows:

- Each time you press the down-arrow key, you move one line down in your document.

- Each time you press the up-arrow key, you return to the preceding line.

- To move up and down through your document faster, hold down the Ctrl key while pressing the up- and down-arrow keys. This action advances you up or down one paragraph at a time.

- Pressing the PgDn key (or Page Down, on some keyboards) moves you down through the document one window at a time.

✔ Pressing the PgUp key (or Page Up, on some keyboards) moves you up through the document one window at a time.

✔ Holding down the Ctrl key while pressing the Home key takes you to the beginning of your document.

✔ Holding down the Ctrl key while pressing the End key takes you to the end of your document.

Using Word's ingenious Go To command

The Go To command makes it easy to use either mouse or keyboard shortcuts to navigate your documents. If you're working with the status bar displayed at the bottom of the screen, Word offers a simple way to go to the top of the following or preceding page by using your mouse. Follow these steps:

1. **Double-click the page-number area of the status bar.**

   The Go To dialog box appears (see Figure 2-1).

2. **Click the Next or Previous button to go to the top of the page of your choice.**

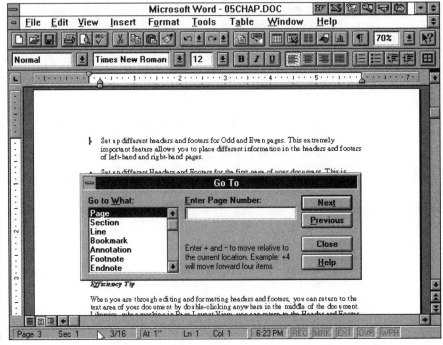

Figure 2-1:
The Go To
dialog box
makes it
easy to
advance to
the top
of the
following or
preceding
page.

If you're not working with the status bar displayed, you can use the Go To command without taking your hands off the keyboard. Follow these steps:

1. **Press Ctrl+G.**

   The Go To dialog box appears.

2. **Press Alt+T to advance to the top of the Next page.**

   Each time that you press Alt+T, you advance another page.

3. **Press Alt+P to return to the top of the Previous page.**

   Again, each time you press Alt+P, you move one page closer to the beginning of your document.

When you're in the Go To dialog box, if you know the number of the page that you want to go to, you can type it in the Enter Page Number box. The Next button immediately turns into a Go To button; clicking that button advances you to the desired page. You also can enter a plus or minus sign, followed by a desired number of pages. Enter **+2**, for example, if you want to advance two pages; enter **–5** if you want to move five pages.

Selecting Text

Selecting text is the cornerstone of word processing. You must select text before you can delete it, move it, replace it with different text, or change its appearance (with character or paragraph formatting, described in the next chapter).

Word offers you four ways to select type:

- ✔ Drag the mouse.
- ✔ Click and double-click the mouse.
- ✔ Press the Shift key in conjunction with an arrow key.
- ✔ Press the F8 function key, followed by an arrow key (and, if desired, the Shift key).

Using the mouse to select text

Dragging is the easiest and most intuitive way to select type with the mouse. Simply position the mouse pointer in front of the first letter of the first word that you want to select; hold down the left mouse button; and drag through the text that you want to delete, format, move, or replace. Release the mouse button when you reach the end of the last word that you want to eliminate or modify. You'll know that text is selected when it appears in *reverse video* — white text against a black background.

But Word offers you even *better* ways to select text with the mouse, as follows:

✔ Double-clicking a word selects the word as well as the space that follows it. (This is a nice Word feature that eliminates an unwanted space before the next word or a punctuation mark.)

✔ Holding down the Ctrl key while clicking inside a sentence selects the entire sentence.

✔ Triple-clicking inside a paragraph selects the entire paragraph.

✔ Clicking the *selection bar* (the margin) to the left of the first word in a line selects the entire line.

✔ Double-clicking the selection bar to the left of a paragraph selects the paragraph.

✔ Vertically dragging the mouse in the selection bar to the left of the text selects multiple lines, whether those lines are contained in the same paragraph or different paragraphs (see Figure 2-2).

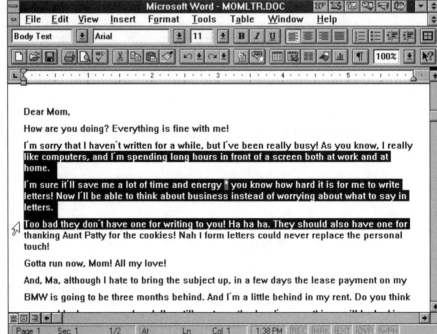

Figure 2-2:
Selecting
multiple
lines and
paragraphs
by vertically
dragging
in the
selection
bar to the
left of the
text.

Using the keyboard to select text

Rather than always removing your right hand from the keyboard and reaching for the mouse, you should try to get in the habit of selecting type by using keyboard shortcuts. The easiest way to select text with keyboard shortcuts is to hold down both the Ctrl and Shift keys while pressing the left- and right-arrow keys, as follows:

- Ctrl+Shift+right arrow selects text to the right of the insertion point. You can select as much text as you want, as long as you don't release the Ctrl and Shift keys.
- Ctrl+Shift+left arrow selects text to the left of the insertion point.
- Ctrl+Shift+up arrow selects the text before the insertion point in the current paragraph. Each subsequent time that you use this shortcut, it selects the entire preceding paragraph.
- Ctrl+Shift+down arrow selects the text after the insertion point in the current paragraph. Each subsequent time that you use this shortcut, it selects the entire following paragraph.

Using special keys

Hold it, there's even more! The following additional keyboard shortcuts are available to speed you on your way toward the perfect deletion or edit:

- Press Ctrl+A to select an entire document — highlighting all text, including footnotes (but excluding headers and footers). This shortcut makes it easy to change the typeface or type size throughout an informal letter or manuscript set in a single typeface and type size.
- Press the F8 function key to activate the selection process. After that, any movement with the mouse or arrow keys selects text from the current insertion point. If you're working with the status bar displayed, you'll know that you're in Select mode when the EXT(end) button turns black. To deactivate the Selection key, press the Esc key or, if the status bar is present, click the EXT(end) button.

If you regularly work with the status bar visible, you can select text with the mouse or the keyboard arrow keys by clicking the grayed-out EXT(end) indicator instead of pressing the F8 function key. When the EXT(end) indicator is highlighted, you don't need to hold down the left mouse button when you select text with the mouse; each time you press the mouse button, text will be highlighted from the preceding selection point to the end of the current sentence.

Editing Text

Editing involves deleting words, replacing old words with new words, and moving words to new locations. You can edit text in several ways:

- ✔ Replacing text
- ✔ Using Cut, Copy, and Paste
- ✔ Using drag-and-drop editing
- ✔ Spiking

Deleting and replacing text

You can press either of two keys to eliminate individual characters and selected text: the Backspace key (typically gray, with an arrow pointing to the left), at the top of your keyboard; and the Delete key, which often is located in more than one place, such as below the Insert key above the arrow keys and below the 3 key in the numeric keypad. (Experts predict that keyboards will be standardized by 2026 — six months before voice-recognition standards become universally accepted.)

Although the Backspace and Delete keys can be used to throw away unwanted characters and text, they differ in three important ways:

- ✔ The Backspace key eliminates characters to the left of the insertion point.
- ✔ If text (or a graphic) is selected, the Delete key eliminates it.
- ✔ If no text has been selected, the Delete key eliminates characters to the right of the insertion point.

Nothing is permanent; you can always change your mind. If you want to restore text after you delete it, choose Edit⇨Undo Clear (or press Ctrl+Z). To restore it, choose Edit⇨Repeat Clear. If you used the Backspace key to delete text or selected text and then entered new text, the menu command changes to Edit⇨Undo Typing (the keyboard shortcut still is Ctrl+Z) or Edit⇨Redo Typing. Word offers you multiple levels of Undo capability during each work session, but you can't undo work that you did before you saved your work and exited Word.

You do not have to delete text before you type replacement text. Simply select the text and type the replacement text over the old text. If you type more words than can fit in the space occupied by the deleted text, Word pushes the additional words and paragraphs to the right. If you replaced a long word with a short word, Word pulls the following words to the left and eliminates the excess space.

Avoid accidentally pressing the Insert key (or Ins, on some keyboards). Word's default mode is Insert — that is, if the insertion point is between two words and you start typing, the words that you type will push the existing words apart. If you accidentally press the Insert key, however, you enter Overtype mode. You can tell when you're in Overtype mode because the OVR button in the status bar becomes darker. When you're in Overtype mode, new text doesn't push existing text out of the way; it appears over the existing words, letter by letter. This situation can cause a great deal of grief and lost work.

Using Cut, Copy, and Paste (also known as Jump, Holler, and Shout)

It's important to note the distinction among the Cut, Clear, Copy, and Paste commands as well as to get into the habit of using keyboard shortcuts rather than opening the Edit menu and choosing the commands.

The following commands are located in the Edit menu:

- ✔ Cut removes text from your document and places it in the Windows Clipboard (a procedure that's sort of like an air-traffic-control holding pattern over Atlanta), from which you can relocate the text to a different location in the same document or in a different document. The keyboard shortcut for Cut is Ctrl+X (think of extracting a tooth — sorry!).

- ✔ Copy leaves the text in its original location and places a copy in the Windows Clipboard, allowing you to place the copy in a different location in the same document or in a different document. The keyboard shortcut for Copy is Ctrl+C.

- ✔ Paste refers to putting whatever is in the Windows Clipboard in your document. After you pick something up from the Clipboard, you must put it back down in a new location. The keyboard shortcut for Paste is Ctrl+V, chosen not for some arcane reason (V is Eastern European for Vlocation) but because it's right next to the X and C keys, where your left hand can locate it easily.

- ✔ Clear is not the same as Cut. When you cut text, it goes to the Clipboard, from which you can move the text to another location. But when you clear text, it disappears. Cleared items do not dislodge existing items in the Clipboard, whereas when you cut or copy an item to the Clipboard, that item replaces anything that was already there. (For a new alternative, see the section on the Spike later in this chapter.) The keyboard shortcut for Clear is the Delete key.

Quick, Get the Menu!

Word offers an even easier way to access the Cut, Copy, and Paste commands than opening the Edit menu or memorizing keyboard shortcuts. To copy or move selected text, you can use Word's shortcut menu. Follow these steps:

1. **Position the mouse pointer on the selected text (if it's not already there), and click the *right* mouse button.**

   Word's shortcut menu appears.

2. **Choose Cut or Copy (see Figure 2-3).**

   Either of these commands places the text in the Clipboard, ready for you to paste it in a different location. (The Paste command is highlighted if you previously cut or copied text to the Clipboard.)

3. **Position the mouse pointer where you want to paste the text.**

4. **Click the right mouse button.**

   The shortcut menu reappears. Notice that Cut and Copy are dimmed but Paste is highlighted.

5. **Choose Paste.**

   The text appears in the desired location.

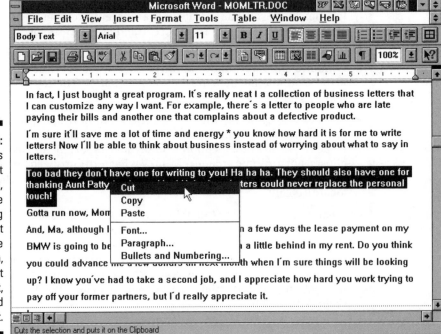

Figure 2-3: Word's shortcut menu, accessible by clicking the right mouse button, makes it easy to cut, copy, and paste text.

Drag and drop (till you drop!)

Drag-and-drop editing is an important shortcut that eliminates the need to cut and paste. Instead of removing text from the screen, placing that text in the Windows Clipboard, and retrieving the text from the Clipboard, you simply hold down the left mouse button and *drag* the text to a new location. You *drop* the text by releasing the mouse button.

Drag-and-drop editing works within a document as well as between documents. If, for example, you have two documents open, you can simply drag and drop text between the two documents. (As you will learn in a later chapter, drag-and-drop editing now works between documents created in different programs, allowing you to drag an Excel chart into a Word document, for example.)

To drag and drop a paragraph in a new location, follow these steps:

1. **Select the paragraph by using the mouse or one of the keyboard shortcuts.**

2. **Place the mouse pointer on the selected paragraph and hold down the left mouse button.**

3. **Drag the paragraph to the new location.**

4. **Release the mouse button.**

Notice that while you drag, the selected text remains in its original location, although a rectangle below the mouse pointer indicates that the pointer contains text. As you move through the document, a vertical line indicates where the text will be dropped if you release the mouse button (see Figure 2-4).

Drag-and-drop editing is not limited to cutting and pasting. To copy text rather than cut it, hold down the Ctrl key as you drag the text. This procedure leaves the original text intact and places a copy of it in a new location.

Drag-and-drop editing works best when both the original and the destination location are inside a single window — that is, when you can see both locations without scrolling. If you are cutting and pasting text from page to page in a document, you may find that drag-and-drop editing is less satisfactory. Positioning the text precisely is difficult because the screen often scrolls in larger increments than you want.

Spike (the new kid on the block)

Traditionally, the Clipboard could accommodate only one item at a time. If you wanted to move several items, you had to cut and paste them one at a time. The Spike, just in from Jersey, permits you to cut and paste multiple items.

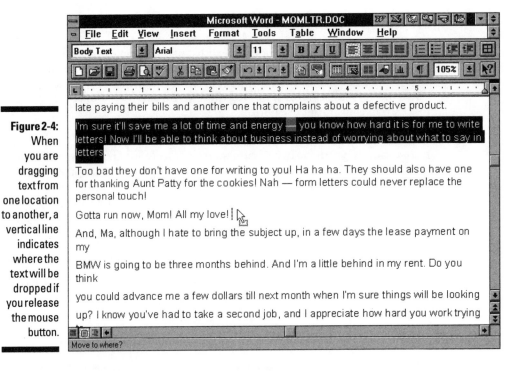

Figure 2-4:
When
you are
dragging
text from
one location
to another, a
vertical line
indicates
where the
text will be
dropped if
you release
the mouse
button.

Think of the Spike as being a sort of a super Clipboard that allows you to add multiple items without replacing items that already are in the Clipboard. To move items to the Spike, follow these steps:

1. **Select the text that you want to move.**

2. **Press Ctrl+F3.**

Repeat these steps as many times as desired.

To insert items from the Spike into a document, follow these steps:

1. **Position the insertion point in your document where you want the Spike's contents to appear.**

2. **Press Ctrl+Shift+F3.**

   All the items appear in the document, in the order in which they were placed in the Spike — just like pieces of paper speared by a spike on your desk. (Quiz: How did Microsoft come up with "Spike" as the name of this feature?)

Saving Time and Ensuring Accuracy with AutoCorrect, Spell Check, and AutoText

One of the reasons that Word is such a pleasure to use is the fact that Microsoft included several features that can save you hours in the years ahead.

Big Brother (not to be confused with Big Bird) is watching!

Spelling checkers have been around for a long time, but the spelling checker in Word 6 is the first to use AutoCorrect. AutoCorrect is Microsoft's version of Big Brother (without the holding company). AutoCorrect checks your spelling *as you type*, correcting mistakes as you make them. (The procedure is like driving with a spouse with whom you've lived too long or like lying to people who know you too well: they know you're lying, you know they know you're lying, and they know you know they know you're lying . . . it's all very complicated.)

AutoCorrect is an extremely valuable asset for three reasons:

 ✔ AutoCorrect comes with a selection of common typographical errors and corrections.

 ✔ You can add your own mistakes to the AutoCorrect dictionary (for example, I almost always have trouble with *tommorrow* and *inadvertantly*).

 ✔ Most important, you can use AutoCorrect to quickly insert correctly spelled phrases, such as the name of your firm (if you happen to work for a firm owned by five brothers from the Balkans).

Type the sentence **John adn I went to teh market.** Notice what happened when you pressed the spacebar after typing *adn*. The instant you pressed the spacebar, Word automatically transposed the *d* and the *n*, resulting in a correctly spelled *and*. When you pressed the spacebar after *teh*, Word spelled *the* correctly.

To get a better idea of how AutoCorrect works, choose Tools⇨AutoCorrect. The AutoCorrect dialog box appears, displaying some of the words that Microsoft added to AutoCorrect (see Figure 2-5). In addition, check boxes permit you to tell Word to be on the lookout for certain common types of spelling errors.

The AutoCorrect dialog box also permits you to add your own typical misspellings. To inform AutoCorrect to be on the lookout for the words that you misspell, type your favorite misspelled word in the Replace box, type the

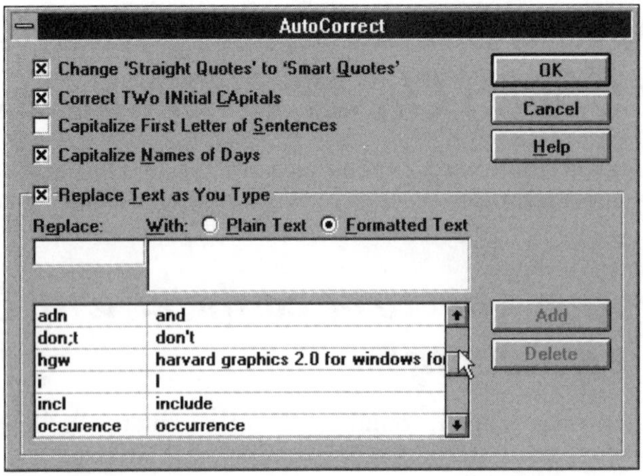

AutoCorrect

- [X] Change 'Straight Quotes' to 'Smart Quotes'
- [X] Correct TWo INitial CApitals
- [ ] Capitalize First Letter of Sentences
- [X] Capitalize Names of Days

OK
Cancel
Help

[X] Replace Text as You Type

Replace: With: ○ Plain Text ● Formatted Text

adn	and
don;t	don't
hgw	harvard graphics 2.0 for windows fo
i	I
incl	include
occurence	occurrence

Add
Delete

Figure 2-5:
Word's
AutoCorrect
dictionary
comes with
common
misspelled
words.

correctly spelled version in the With box, and then click the Add button. Now, whenever Word encounters the misspelling that you entered, it will replace that word with the correctly spelled word.

The only thing you have to watch out for is entering a misspelled word in the With box. If you do, the word will be misspelled consistently.

If you make a mistake in entering a word in the AutoCorrect dialog box, select the misspelled word; click the Delete button; and repeat the process, trying to type a little more carefully this time.

You also can use Word's AutoCorrect feature as a shorthand way to correct hard-to-spell, frequently used names or technical terms. Suppose that you work for a law firm called Orowitz, Kennelwitz, Minnetonka, O'Frien, and Plamer. Chances are that you misspell the firm's name every time it comes up. Instead of running the risk of offending your boss or clients, you can enter **okm** in the AutoCorrect Replace box and enter the complete name of the firm in the With box. That probably will be the last time you'll ever have to type the firm's name; from then on, every time you type **okm**, the letters will be replaced by the correctly spelled-out words.

Spell checking your work

Typographical errors never do anyone any good. Spelling errors destroy the credibility of your words. Fortunately, Word makes it easy to check the spelling of your documents. To activate Word's spelling checker, choose Tools⇨Spelling (or use the F7 function key shortcut). You also can start the spelling checker by clicking the Spelling button in the Standard toolbar (the one with the check mark and the letters *ABC*).

You can spell check your entire document or a single word. To spell check a single word, place the insertion point anywhere inside the word and then activate the spelling checker.

When Word encounters a misspelled word, it stops and offers several alternative spellings (see Figure 2-6). In most cases, the first option is the correct one; you can accept it by clicking the Change button. If you don't like the first option, scroll through the list of options until you find a more appropriate alternative. Then highlight the word you want and click Change.

Figure 2-6:
Word's
Spelling
dialog box
offers
alternative
spellings
and also
permits you
to add
proper
nouns and
technical
terms.

Rather than highlighting an alternative and clicking Change, you can accept a spelling checker alternative by double-clicking the word.

Word's Spelling dialog box offers several other important options:

- ✔ Click the Ignore button if the highlighted word in the document is correctly spelled — if the word is a proper noun or a technical term, for example.

- ✔ Click Ignore All if you use the word in the document more than once. Thereafter, Word ignores that word throughout the current document.

- ✔ Click Change All if you think that you misspelled the word in the document more than once.

✔ Click <u>A</u>dd if you're going to encounter the word in other documents. Word adds the word to a custom dictionary. (You can create additional dictionaries for specialized documents.)

✔ The AutoCo<u>r</u>rect button is new in Word 6. After you select the correct spelling for a word, click this button to add the word to the AutoCorrect dictionary. Thereafter, the word will be corrected automatically as you type it. This procedure can save you a lot of time if you continually misspell the same words and haven't taken the time to enter them in the AutoCorrect dictionary.

✔ Clicking the <u>O</u>ptions button allows you to tell Word to ignore words in uppercase type and words that contain numbers. If you typically work with acronyms or formulas, these options will save you a lot of time. The <u>O</u>ptions button also allows you to add, edit, or remove specialized words in dictionaries.

✔ The <u>U</u>ndo Last button is one of my favorites. Often, when working with the spelling checker, I react too quickly, accepting the first suggestion when another suggestion would be more appropriate. I usually don't realize this, however, until after I click the <u>C</u>hange button. <u>U</u>ndo Last permits me to go back and rectify my spelling error, if not the error of my ways. (Don't you wish that life had an <u>U</u>ndo Last button?)

If you want to quit the spelling checker temporarily and return to work on your document, simply click the document. The Spelling dialog box remains visible. When you want to resume the spell check, click the <u>S</u>tart button.

When Word finishes spell checking your document, it displays the message `The spelling check is complete.` Click the OK button to return to your document.

Working with AutoText

AutoText is a feature that allows you to store and retrieve formatted text and graphics. Think of AutoText as being a permanent hard-disk-based Clipboard. You can save all sorts of items with AutoText, including formatted tables.

AutoText differs from AutoCorrect in two ways: you can use it to save graphics as well as text; and you must select AutoText and scroll through the list of available choices before you can insert the text or graphic.

Use AutoCorrect to insert frequently used abbreviations that you want Word to spell out automatically. Use AutoText to insert infrequently used text and graphics.

To begin your exploration of Word's AutoText feature, create a typical boilerplate paragraph, which you will include in all the proposals submitted to potential clients. You could, for example, type the following text:

All proposed fees are non-negotiable. Terms include a 40 percent deposit and signed purchase order by a company officer at the start of the project and a 30 percent progress fee upon the approval of first drafts. The remaining 30 percent is due within 10 days of project completion. A 1 ¹/₂ percent service charge will be applied for all accounts more than 15 days overdue. Client agrees to assume any and all collection and legal fees caused by late payment.

This paragraph certainly isn't something that you're going to want to type more than once! Therefore, it's an ideal AutoText candidate. To add this paragraph to Word's AutoText options, follow these steps:

1. **Select the text.**

2. **Choose Edit⇨AutoText.**

    The AutoText dialog box appears (see Figure 2-7). The selected text automatically appears in the Selection window. Notice that the Name box contains a portion of the selected text. (You can substitute a different name, if you prefer — in this case, for example, *Terms*.)

3. **Click the Add button.**

    The AutoText dialog box closes, and you return to your document.

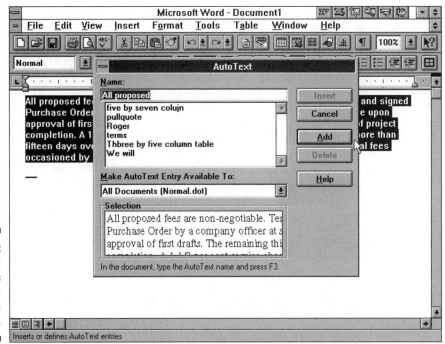

Figure 2-7:
Selected text appears in the Selection window.

Get into the habit of using meaningful names to identify AutoText selections — for example, Logo, Closing, Terms, and Payment Due. This practice permits you to insert the desired text without opening the AutoText dialog box.

You can insert AutoText text into a document in two ways: the easy way and the hard way.

The hard way is to choose Edit⇨AutoText, which displays the AutoText dialog box; select the desired text; and click the Insert button. If numerous AutoText objects appear in the dialog box, you may have to scroll through the list.

You can save time by double-clicking the name of the desired AutoText selection rather than selecting it and clicking the Insert button.

The easy way is to type the name of the selection that you want to use and then press the F3 key. If you named a selection Terms, for example, you would type **Terms** in your document and then press F3; instantly, the paragraph would appear.

Notice the two radio buttons in the AutoText box in the Insert As portion of the text. If you accept the default setting, Formatted Text, the selection appears in the typeface and type size in which it originally was formatted. If you click the radio button next to Plain Text, however, the text is formatted the same as adjacent text.

If you find that you aren't using some of the AutoText selections, choose Edit⇨AutoText to display the AutoText dialog box, highlight the unwanted selection, and click the Delete button.

Using Find and Replace

There are both obvious and not-so-obvious reasons to make extensive use of Word's Find and Replace feature. One obvious reason is to move to a desired location quickly. Suppose, for example, that when you opened a file to your mom, you wanted to go directly to the part that asks for money to help pay for your BMW. You can go directly to the BMW section of the letter by choosing Edit⇨Find. When the Find dialog box appears, type **BMW** and click OK. Word takes you directly to *BMW*.

Using the Find feature

A not-so-obvious application for Find is locating all occurrences of a word or phrase that you think you overused. If the word or phrase shows up frequently, you've overused it.

A final application for the Replace function is reusing a document simply by changing the client's name. For example, Find and Replace permits you to change a proposal for Acme Widgets to one that you can send to Beta Software.

To access Word's Find feature, follow these steps:

1. **Choose Edit⇨Find (or press Ctrl+F).**

   The Find dialog box appears.

2. **In the Find What box, enter the word or phrase that you want to locate.**

   If you're repeating a previous search, click the down arrow next to the Find What box to display a list of your last four searches.

3. **Accept the default, which is to check the entire document, or make a selection in the Search drop-down list to search forward or backward from the insertion point.**

4. **To limit your search to specific criteria, click the appropriate check boxes.**

   You can search for words that use the same combination of uppercase and lowercase letters as your Find What entry; you can search for entire words, instead of partial words; and you can search for words that contain the same letters or sound similar to your selection criteria.

5. **Click the Format button if you want to search for words in a specified Font, Paragraph, Language, or Style.**

6. **Click the Special button if you want to search for particular punctuation marks or section breaks.**

7. **Start the search by clicking the Find Next button.**

8. **After reaching the first selection, click the Cancel button if you want to close the Find dialog box and work on your document.**

   Click the Find Next button again if you want to search for the next occurrence.

If you click the Replace button in the Find dialog box, you go to the Replace dialog box (see Figure 2-8). You also can display the Replace dialog box at any time by choosing Edit⇨Replace (or pressing Ctrl+H).

The Replace dialog box offers more options than the Find dialog box does, but you use it in a similar way. In the Find What box, enter what you're searching for, or click the down arrow and select one of the last four words or text strings that you searched for. Enter replacement text in the Replace With box or click the down arrow and select one of the words or text strings that you used previously. To start the search, click the Find Next button.

Figure 2-8:
The Replace
dialog box
allows you
to substitute
words
automatically
or on a
case-by-
case basis.

When Word locates the desired selection, you can do any of the following things:

- ✔ If you want to do nothing and continue searching, click the Find Next button.

- ✔ If you want to quit the search, click the Cancel button.

- ✔ Click Replace if you want to use replacement text in place of the text that Word just located.

- ✔ Click Replace All if you want to replace every occurrence of the selected text with the replacement text. (This is known as trust.)

As before, you can narrow the search to words that contain a specific combination of uppercase and lowercase characters, to entire words, or to words that contain a specific combination of letters or that sound similar to a certain word.

Using the Thesaurus

One of the pleasures of working with Word 6 is its expanded Thesaurus feature, which makes it easy to locate the right word and find alternatives to overused words.

To use the Thesaurus, start by selecting the word that's giving you trouble. Then choose Tools➪Thesaurus (or press Shift+F7). The Thesaurus dialog box appears (see Figure 2-9).

You do not have to select a word to use the Thesaurus. Simply placing the insertion point anywhere inside the word will suffice.

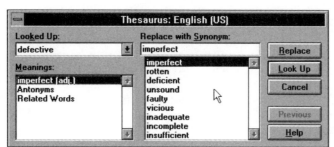

Figure 2-9:
The
Thesaurus
dialog box.

When the Thesaurus dialog box appears, you can replace the word with one of the displayed suggestions or look up other words. You can do any of the following things:

✔ To replace the selected word with one of the suggestions in the Thesaurus dialog box, highlight the replacement word and click the Replace button (or double-click the replacement word).

✔ To continue searching for a word with precisely the right nuance, select the closest synonym in the dialog box and click the Look Up button. A new set of words appears. One of the words in this list might be the one you want.

✔ If you're still not satisfied, click one of the words in the Meanings list. In many cases, you can choose nouns, adjectives, or verbs that have definitions similar to the selected word. Alternatively, click Antonyms to see words that mean the opposite of the word for which you're searching.

✔ If you want to view the last word that you looked up and the synonyms for that word appeared in the dialog box, click the Previous button.

✔ Click Cancel if you despair of writing and want to become a firefighter instead.

When the right word appears, highlight it and then click the Replace button. (Or rewrite the sentence!)

In many cases, the Thesaurus serves mainly to spark your creativity. You don't have to use one of the suggested words; instead, you may come up with another way to express your thought or argument. Often, the best way to use the Thesaurus is to look for antonyms, which frequently help you approach the sentence that you're writing or editing from a new perspective.

Checking Your Grammar

Even the best writers fall into traps. These traps can be caused by a lack of coordination between thinking and typing — you may be so involved with what you're writing that your brain gets ahead of your fingers — or by such problems as the use of overly long sentences, misplaced or missing punctuation marks, or the use of *it's* when *its* is more appropriate. The grammar checker is useful for correcting some of these problems, locating sentence fragments left over from editing, and identifying passive verbs, overused contractions (for example, *you'll* instead of *you will*), and misused words.

By checking your errors before they leave your office, the Word 6 grammar checker helps you improve your writing and prevents potentially embarrassing errors.

To check your grammar, choose Tools⇨Grammar. Each time the grammar checker encounters a questionable word, sentence, or punctuation mark, the Grammar dialog box appears (see Figure 2-10). The questioned text is highlighted in the document and also displayed in the Sentence box of the Grammar dialog box. In the Suggestions box, an alternative word or phrase appears, as well as an explanation of any punctuation problems or grammatical rules involved.

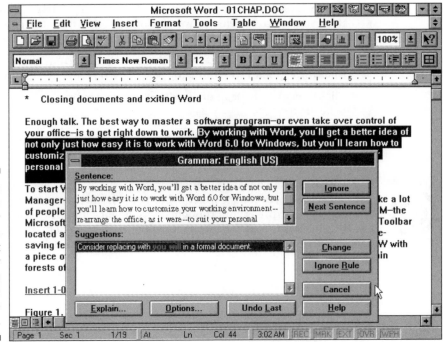

Figure 2-10: Word's grammar checker can help prevent potentially embarrassing errors and improve your writing.

Each time the grammar checker stops, you have several options:

✔ If you disagree with the grammar checker, click the Ignore button. The grammar checker moves forward, stopping again when it encounters another potential problem.

✔ Click the Next Sentence button if you like the sentence the way it is (or you despair of ever making it right and want to make a fresh start with another sentence).

✔ Click the Change button if you want to accept the grammar checker's suggestion.

✔ Click the Ignore Rule button to skip further occurrences of the same type of error.

✔ Click the Explain button to see more information about your infraction (and ways to avoid it in the future).

✔ Click the Options button to choose between formal or informal writing styles and to turn off the spelling checker, which by default operates while you check your grammar.

✔ Clicking the Undo Last button makes it easy to change your mind.

✔ Clicking Cancel allows you to return to your document without making further changes.

After you finish checking your document, the grammar checker displays a Readability Statistics window for your document (see Figure 2-11). You may want to pay particular attention to the number of sentences per paragraph, the number of words per sentence, and the number of characters per word in your document. You'll also want to pay attention to the number of passive sentences.

Figure 2-11:
Oh, no!
After
checking
your
grammar,
you'll
receive a
report card.

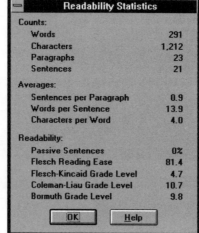

Readability Statistics	
Counts:	
Words	291
Characters	1,212
Paragraphs	23
Sentences	21
Averages:	
Sentences per Paragraph	0.9
Words per Sentence	13.9
Characters per Word	4.0
Readability:	
Passive Sentences	0%
Flesch Reading Ease	81.4
Flesch-Kincaid Grade Level	4.7
Coleman-Liau Grade Level	10.7
Bormuth Grade Level	9.8

OK   Help

The 5th Wave   By Rich Tennant

"NOPE - I'D BETTER WAIT 'TIL ALL MY FONTS ARE WORKING. A HATE LETTER JUST DOESN'T WORK IN *Filigree Flowerbox Extended*."

Chapter 3

Expanding Your Horizons with Advanced Tools

*O*utlining makes it easy for you to step back and get an overall view of your document. By hiding text temporarily, leaving just the headings visible, you can easily observe the overall development of your ideas.

Equally important, Word 6's AutoFormatting feature is based on applying styles to your headings. When you apply styles to Level 1, Level 2, and Level 3 headings and also use a Normal style for body copy, you're setting the stage for allowing Word's AutoFormatting to generate professional results quickly. You also can use this feature to try different appearances for your document.

Working with Word's AutoFormatting, Style Gallery, and Outline Features

The best way to become familiar with Word's AutoFormatting and Outline features is to create a short test document that contains several short paragraphs of Normal text separated by subheads styled Level 1, Level 2, and Level 3.

Enter nonsense text, and then apply Word's default Level 1, Level 2, Level 3, and Normal styles to the various headings and short paragraphs. Keep your paragraphs short so that you'll have space to see several heading levels in one screen. (If your computer tends to crash, you may want to save the document as CHP3TEST.) Your sample document may resemble the one shown in Figure 3-1.

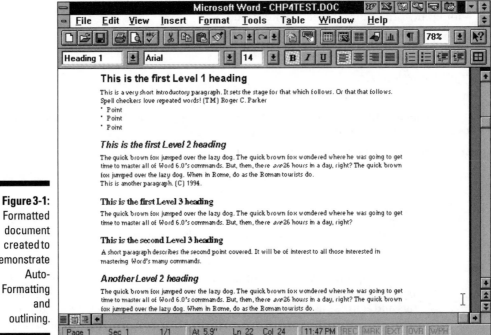

Figure 3-1:
Formatted
document
created to
demonstrate
Auto-
Formatting
and
outlining.

Applying AutoFormatting (all by yourself)

To apply AutoFormatting to your test document, choose Format⇨AutoFormat, or click the AutoFormat button in the Standard toolbar (the button that looks like a page with a star shining in its upper-left corner). If you choose Format⇨AutoFormat rather than the button, the process takes a bit longer and Word notifies you that it is about to format your document automatically.

If you click the Options button in the AutoFormat dialog box that appears, Word displays the AutoFormat tab of the Options dialog box. This tab explains the types of changes that Word is about to make in your document, including applying styles to headings and lists, eliminating extra paragraph marks and spaces, and replacing symbol characters and bullet characters with typographically correct characters and symbols.

At this point, you can instruct Word to be less comprehensive in its changes by clicking the check box next to each formatting option that you want to leave undisturbed. Click OK to continue. Word then automatically reformats your documents and, once again, displays the AutoFormat dialog box.

At this point, as shown in Figure 3-2, you can

✔ Accept or reject all changes

✔ Review and reject individual changes

✔ Choose a custom appearance with the Style Gallery

Figure 3-2:
You can accept Word's changes or choose different formatting options from the Style Gallery.

Click the Style Gallery button if you want to go to the "fitting room" and try on different "looks" for the document. When you click the Style Gallery button, Word takes you to the Style Gallery dialog box, where you can choose among a variety of existing styles, as shown in Figure 3-3.

As you scroll through the list of available templates, notice that the typography of the different heading levels changes. Notice also that the position and spacing of the bulleted list change. Compare Memo 1 and Memo 2, for example, as well as Letters 1, 2, and 3. Notice that the second option of each category typically adds a paragraph rule below Level 1 headings.

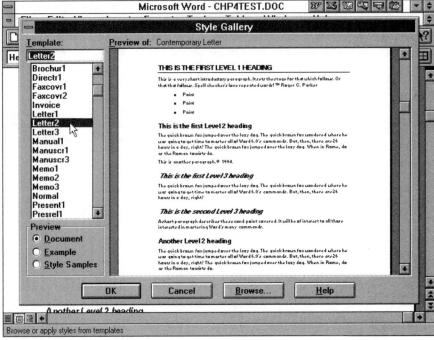

Figure 3-3:
The Preview window of the Style Gallery dialog box permits you to apply different templates to your document temporarily.

To preview a Style Gallery template, click on the desired Style Gallery option — for example, Letter1, Report 2, and so on.

1. **Unless you choose a different option by clicking on a different radio button, Word will apply Style Gallery templates to your current document, as indicated by the click mark in the radio button next to** **Document.**

2. **Click the radio button next to** **Example** **if you want to see an example of a sample document formatted with the highlighted template. Click the scroll bar below the scroll box to see more pages of the document.**

   Often, only the first page of a manuscript or report appears, and you have to advance through the document to see how the following pages are formatted with the styles included with the document. Check out the differences between Letters 1, 2, and 3 as well as the difference between Memo 1 and Memo 2.

3. **Click the radio button next to** **Style Samples** **if you want to see examples of the additional styles included with the highlighted template.**

4. **Click OK or press Enter when you are satisfied with the appearance of your document.**

Click Accept when Word returns you to the AutoFormat dialog box or click Review Changes if you want to see exactly what was done to improve the appearance of your document.

Be aware that if instead of choosing Format⇨AutoFormat you click the AutoFormatting button in the Standard toolbar, your options are entirely different:

- ✔ Word applies formatting automatically, without giving you a chance to decide which formatting options you want to change and which you want to preserve.

- ✔ You do not get a chance to review (and reject, if desired) each formatting change.

- ✔ You do not get a chance to choose a different style from the Style Gallery.

Once again, you see that toolbar buttons often limit your options. Just as the Print button does not permit you to select a different printer or to print only the current page (or a selected range of pages), the AutoFormatting button speeds the process by limiting your control.

Using the Style Gallery at a later date

Nothing is forever with Word 6. What if, at a later date, you decide that you want to apply a different template to your document? Simply choose Format⇨Style Gallery and, once again, review the different templates available. You can press the arrow keys on your keyboard to scroll through the list of available templates. When you see the one you like, double-click its name (or click OK when the name of the template is highlighted).

Click the Browse button if your computer is connected to a network and you want to try templates stored on hard disks on other computers.

Do not save your document after you apply AutoFormatting or apply a new template from the Style Gallery because you will be reusing it to demonstrate other Word features.

Allow Me to Show You to Your Table

Word 6 enables you to use tables to organize and present information in row-and-column format. Tables help you present information to readers in a way that facilitates comparisons. Details that otherwise would be lost in paragraphs become transparently obvious when displayed in a table. When you present information in row-and-column format, you can eliminate unnecessary words, allowing the information to appear by itself, free from other distracting words like nouns and adjectives.

Consider the following example:

> The LX series comes complete with plastic steering wheel, AM radio, two-way adjustable seats, and front-wheel hydraulic braking. The LX-2 package includes the Semi-Luxury Module, which includes a wood-spoked steering wheel; AM/FM radio; precision eight-day, spring-wound analog clock; four-way adjustable seats; and hydraulic braking. The LX-3 includes eight-way, heated power seats; a hand-tooled-leather steering wheel; CD-ready AM/FM cassette stereo; digital clock; and computer-controlled Anchor-Lok braking.

Pretty complicated, eh? Text set in paragraphs makes it hard for readers to visualize and compare information. Present the same information in a table, as in Figure 3-4, however, and the differences between models become obvious.

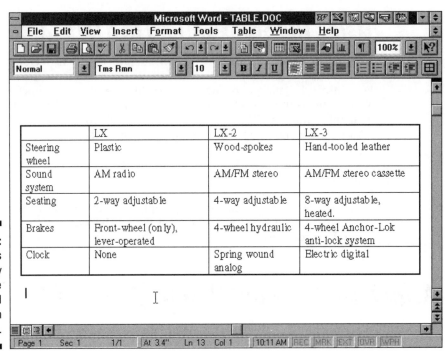

Figure 3-4:
Tables make it easy to compare detailed information at a glance.

In addition to their obvious function in displaying information in row-and-column format, tables play less obvious roles. Often, when information is presented neatly on a page, the underlying structure is a table, even if you can't immediately identify it as a table because of a lack of horizontal and vertical rules.

For example, the structure used to create To, From, Date, and Regarding fields in a fax sheet is based on a table. Likewise, you can use a "borderless table" — a table without a grid created by horizontal and vertical lines — to create a good-looking letterhead with clearly organized locations for name, address, and phone/fax information. Notice that the text in the left column of Figure 3-5 is left-aligned, text in the center column is centered, and text in the right column is right-aligned. Positioning text is often easier using tables than it is using left, right, and centered tabs.

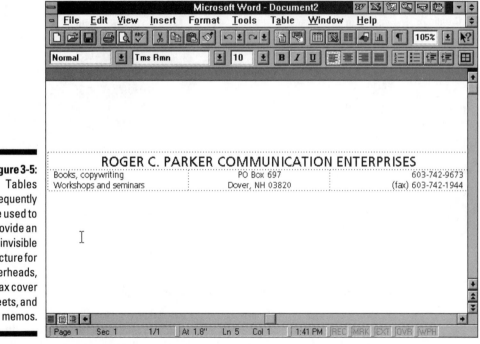

Figure 3-5:
Tables frequently are used to provide an invisible structure for letterheads, fax cover sheets, and memos.

Adding, deleting, and formatting tables

You can add a table to a document in two ways:

- Click the Insert Table button in the Standard toolbar, (the one to the left of the Insert Microsoft Excel Worksheet button with the big X), and when the table sample appears, drag to the lower right and include as many rows and columns as you want. Notice that as your table expands, the status bar tells you how many rows and columns you're creating, as shown in Figure 3-6.

- Choose Table⇨Insert Table.

Figure 3-6:
Creating a table by clicking the Table button in the Standard toolbar and dragging to the desired size.

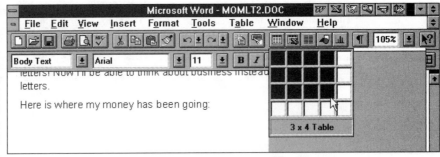

Before you proceed, it may be useful to review a few important terms associated with tables:

- A *Row* refers to information displayed horizontally. A *column* refers to information displayed vertically.

- *Cell* refers to the intersection of a row and column.

- *Headings* appear at the top of columns and rows. Headings are repeated on the following pages automatically if the table can't be printed on a single page. Headings can be *joined* or *split*. In the letterhead example shown in Figure 3-5 earlier in this chapter, the top row was joined to create a large cell that extended over the three columns below.

Deleting and modifying tables

To delete a table, select the entire table *and the insertion point before it*; then choose Edit⇨Clear or press the Delete key. If you hold down the left mouse button and drag through the entire table, or choose Table⇨Select Table (or press Alt+F5) and press Delete, you delete only the *contents* of the table, not the table itself.

Short-term versus long-term efficiency

Word's two ways of adding tables provide another argument for learning to do things the right way instead of instinctively using the first obvious toolbar button. If you use the Standard toolbar's Table button in the preceding example, you'll have to go back and format the table. Because so many variables are involved, including row and column headings (headings are repeated automatically on each page, if the table occupies more than one page) and border and shading options, you may end up spending more time than you would have if you'd used the "old-fashioned," menu-oriented method of adding a table.

If you insert a table by choosing Table⇨Insert Table, Word displays the Insert Table dialog box. This dialog box not only forces you to specify the number of rows and columns for your table but also permits you to use Word's Table Wizard and Table AutoFormatting features to save time (and, perhaps, create a better-looking table).

Here's how to choose between Word's Table Wizard and AutoFormatting options.

✔ If you click the Wizard button after defining the number of rows and columns for your table, Word takes you through a seven-step interrogation — or, more politely, a series of prompts that result in a table formatted to your specifications. You can not only define the layout you desired, but also the align-

ment of column headings. In addition, Word can save you time by eliminating the need to type frequently used headings, such as months, quarters, days of the month, or a series of months. You also can define text and number alignment within the cells of the table.

✔ If you click the AutoFormatting button, Word displays the Table AutoFormat dialog box, in which you can specify the appearance of your table now instead of later, saving you more time. Word offers 33 AutoFormatting options.

By scrolling through the Formats list and previewing the formats in the Preview window, you can choose the best format for your document. (If you have access to a color printer, be sure to click the check box next to Color so that you can preview your work in color.) Click the OK button when you find a format that you like.

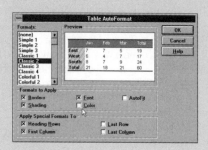

You will probably find it easier to use Word's shortcut menu to delete a table as well as to access many of the formatting options described in the following paragraphs (see Figure 3-7). After selecting the entire table, click the right mouse button. The Table shortcut menu appears. Now, if you choose the Cut command from this menu, the entire table disappears. Don't worry — if you change your mind, you can replace the table by choosing Edit⇨Undo Cut (or pressing Ctrl+Z).

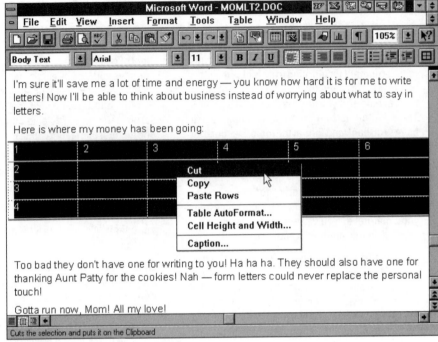

You rarely will guess the right size for a table the first time. In most cases, you'll find it necessary to add or delete rows and/or columns.

- ✔ To *add a row* to a table, place the insertion point in the row above where you want the new row to appear and choose Table⇨Insert Rows. A new empty row appears, and the information in the existing row moves to the next row down.

- ✔ To *add a column* to a table, place the insertion point in the column to the left of where you want the new column to appear and choose Table⇨Select Column. When the column is highlighted, choose Table⇨Insert Columns. A new column appears, and the information in the existing column moves to the next column to the right.

- ✔ To *delete a row or a column*, choose Table⇨Delete Cells. When the Delete Cells dialog box appears, click the radio button next to Delete Entire Row or Delete Entire Column. The remaining rows or columns move up (or to the left) to fill the gap. Do not choose the first two options — Shift Cells Left or Shift Cells Up — unless you are positive that you want to delete an individual cell, not the entire row or column. (These options make it very easy to mess up your table.)

Formatting tables

Word's shortcut menus enable you to format tables quickly. Notice that a different set of menus appears when only a single cell (or the contents of a single cell) is selected.

If text in a single cell is selected, for example, a different set of formatting options becomes available, including the following:

- ✓ Merging or splitting cells
- ✓ Adjusting cell height and width
- ✓ Adding borders and shading to the entire table
- ✓ Using borders and shading to emphasize individual cells
- ✓ Specifying typeface, type size, type style, and alignment options for row and column text

The typical reason for merging cells is to create a header that extends over two columns. To merge cells, select the cells that you want to merge and choose Table⇨Merge Cells. Instantly, the dotted border between the cells disappears, creating a single cell.

Split cells when you want to divide a single cell into two or more horizontal cells. Splitting may be necessary, for example, if you want to highlight separate components of a single month's revenue or expenses. To split a cell, place the insertion point in the cell that you want to divide and choose Table⇨Split Cells.

The easiest way to add borders and shading to an entire table is to position the insertion point anywhere in the table and then choose Table⇨Table AutoFormat or click the right mouse button and choose Table AutoFormat from the shortcut menus. Scroll through the list of formatting choices in the Table AutoFormat dialog box, previewing alternatives in the Preview window. Double-click your desired choice or highlight your choice and click OK.

Alternatively, to add borders and backgrounds to an entire table, select the entire table by dragging (or choose Table⇨Select Table, or press Alt+F5), and then choose Format⇨Borders and Shading. When the Borders and Shading dialog box appears, choose Preset Grid. This option places a thick border around the entire table and uses thin lines to separate individual cells.

To format only a row or column, place the insertion point in the desired row or column and then choose Table⇨Select Row or Table⇨Select Column. When the row or column is highlighted, choose Format⇨Borders and Shading.

To format the contents of a single cell, place the insertion point in the cell and double-click; then choose Format⇨Borders and Shading. When the Borders and Shading dialog box appears, click the Borders tab or the Shading tab and choose the formatting options you want to use.

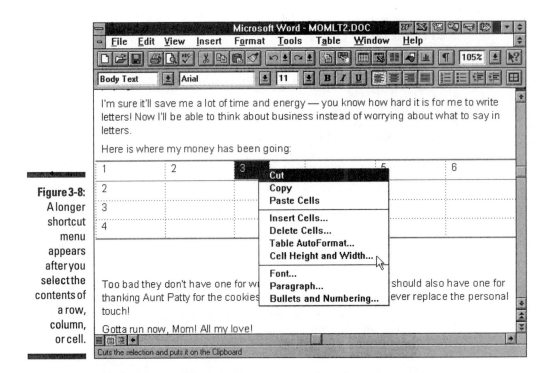

Figure 3-8:
A longer
shortcut
menu
appears
after you
select the
contents of
a row,
column,
or cell.

To adjust cell height and spacing, choose Table⇨Cell Height and Width, or (if you have highlighted the text in the cell) click the right mouse button and choose Cell Height and Width from the shortcut menu (See Figure 3-8). When the Cell Height and Width dialog box appears, click the Row tab if you want to increase the height of a cell or adjust the amount of space between text and the left border of each cell. You can also align text left, centered, or right.

Click the Column tab if you want to specify the width of individual columns precisely or choose AutoFit (from the Cell Height and Width dialog box) if you want Word to do this for you. You also can increase the Space Between Columns increment by entering a precise measurement. The larger the number you enter, the more space appears between text in the column and the margins of the column.

If you want to format text in a row or column, select the row or column by dragging or choose Table⇨Select Row or Table⇨Select Column. Then click the right mouse button to display the shortcut menu and choose Font. Word displays the Font dialog box. Click the Font or Character Spacing tab and make the desired changes (or choose Format⇨Font). Choose Format⇨Paragraph and then click the Indents and Spacing tab if you want to adjust the right and left indents, line spacing, and tabs or to add or modify tabs. Click the Text Flow tab if you want to keep text from splitting across pages if the table will be printed ·on more than one page. Click the Bullets and Numbering tab if you want to further refine the appearance of the text in a row or column.

If you want to format the text in a single cell, place the insertion point in the cell; click the right mouse button to display the shortcut menus; and choose Font, Character, or Bullets and Numbering.

Entering and editing table data

You can enter and edit table data in two ways:

- Click the desired cell and start typing.
- Place the insertion point in the leftmost cell and press the Tab key each time you want to advance to the next cell to the right in the same row. Press Shift+Tab to move backward (to the left) in the row.

To move to the same cell in the preceding or following row, press the up- or down-arrow key on your keyboard.

Saving tables as AutoText entries

After you format the perfect table, you may want to copy it to the AutoText dialog box so that you can reuse your formatting.

To make a formatted table available as an AutoText entry, follow these steps:

1. **Place the insertion point anywhere in the table and choose Table⇨Select Table (or press Alt+the number 5 on your keyboard's numeric keypad).**

2. **Access the Table shortcut menus by clicking the right mouse button.**

3. **Choose Copy.**

4. **Choose Edit⇨AutoText.**

   The AutoText dialog box appears.

5. **Enter a different name in the Name box, or accept the default name (the text that appears in the upper-left cell).**

6. **Click the Add button.**

Saving Time by Working Efficiently

Efficiency leads to quality. Unless you're working at peak efficiency, taking advantage of all the time-savers built into Word 6, you won't have time to fine-tune your thoughts and the way they appear on the page. Accordingly, readers will discount your message every time that they encounter a clumsy grammatical construction or an unstyled paragraph that sticks out like a sore thumb.

This section covers several convenient Word features that can help you work as efficiently as possible.

Using bookmarks to find specific locations

If you're in the middle of a long document and suddenly have to return to page 1 for a second, you can easily forget where you were and waste valuable time searching for the last insertion-point position. Just as you can insert taxicab receipts and bar tabs into books to help you locate your place, you can add invisible electronic bookmarks to Word documents to help you move to a desired location quickly.

To add a bookmark to your document, position the insertion point in the desired location, and choose Edit⇨Bookmark. When the Bookmark dialog box appears (see Figure 3-9), a list of already created (if any) bookmarks appears. Name the new location in shorthand (for example, CURLOC, my favorite, which stands for "current cursor location"). You are limited to a single word — no spaces and just 40 characters. Click the Add button when you finish.

Press Ctrl+Home and review the beginning of your document, or go anywhere in the document. To return to where you were when you got distracted, follow these steps:

1. **Choose Edit⇨Bookmark.**

   The Bookmark dialog box appears.

2. **Select the bookmark name that corresponds to your desired location.**

3. **Click the Go To button to advance directly to the location of the bookmark.**

4. **Click the Close button to return to your work.**

To reposition a bookmark, follow these steps:

1. **Choose Edit⇨Bookmark.**

   The Bookmark dialog box appears. Notice that the name of the last bookmark you used is highlighted.

Figure 3-9:
Bookmarks
help you go
directly
to any
document
location.

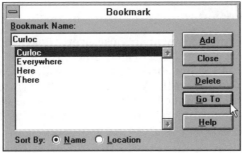

2. **This feature makes it easy to reposition the bookmark that you've been using to keep track of your current location because all you have to do is click the Add button to relocate it.**

You also can use the Edit⇨Go To command to locate bookmarks. If you have added several bookmarks to your document (for example, Beginning, Middle, and End), the Go To command can speed your work. To use the Go To command, follow these steps:

1. **Choose Edit⇨Go To or double-click the page-number location in the status line at the bottom of the screen.**

   The Go To dialog box appears (see Figure 3-10), with Bookmark highlighted.

2. **Click the down arrow next to the Enter Bookmark Name box and scroll through the list of available bookmarks.**

3. **When the name of the desired bookmark is highlighted, click the Go To button and then the Close button.**

   Word takes you directly to the desired location.

Figure 3-10:
The Go To
dialog box
helps you
advance to
a desired
bookmark
quickly.

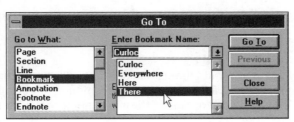

Numbering pages

To add page numbers to your documents, choose Insert⇨Page Numbers to display the Page Numbers dialog box (see Figure 3-11). In the Position list, indicate whether you want page numbers to appear at the Bottom of Page (Footer) or Top of Page (Header). In the Alignment list, indicate whether you want the numbers to appear at the Left, Center, or Right of single-page documents or at the Inside or Outside margins of two-page documents. You receive immediate feedback on your choices in the Preview window.

Figure 3-11:
Choosing a
location
for page
numbers in
the Page
Numbers
dialog box.

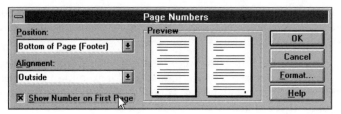

If you don't want to number the first page of your document, which is the convention for letters and documents with cover pages (such as reports and proposals), click the check box next to Show Number on First Page to deselect that option and to remove the number from the first page.

Click the Format button if you want to fine-tune the appearance of page numbers, perhaps replacing numbers with letters or with Roman numerals if you want to use a different numbering style for the introduction of a document than for the body of the document.

Dating your documents (instead of your therapist)

There are two ways you can add the current date and, if desired, time to your documents (three, actually, if you count the old-fashioned way of typing in the information). One is to have Word insert the information as *text*, the other as a *field*.

✔ If you instruct Word to add date and time information as text, the date and time will remain the same, even if you open or print the document months later.

> ✔ If, however, you instruct Word to insert the time and/or date as a *field*, Word will *automatically update* time and date information whenever you open the file or print the document.

To have Word insert date and time information, place the insertion point where you want the information to appear in your document. Select Insert⇨Date and Time. When the Date and Time dialog box appears, select the desired format from the options presented.

> ✔ If you want to insert the information as *text*, just press OK or Enter. This is the best choice for a one-of-a-kind document (such as a letter) that you are likely to save on your computer and refer back to at a later date and you want to be able to verify the date it was sent.

> ✔ Click in the check box next to Insert as Field if you want Word to automatically update the date and time every time you open the file or print the document. This is the right choice if you're creating a document template (such as a form letter you frequently send — perhaps an acknowledgment of an order or a politely worded "no thanks" letter to someone who has sent you a résumé) and want to *automatically add the current date* every time you use the template.

Creating and sorting lists

One of the major improvements that Word 6 represents over Word 2 is its capability to format, number, and sort individual lists. (In certain other word processing programs, if you have two or three separate lists and use the automatic numbering feature, the second list's numbering starts where the first list's numbering ended, even if the lists are separated by several pages!)

To experiment with Word's powerful sorting and numbering feature, begin by entering the following text:

> **The Merry wives of Windsor. Charles Windsor, of New Dover, New Hampshire, of course. Elaine, Carrie, Xaveria, Frieda, Paula, Sandy, Sandi.**

To sort the list, select the text and then choose Table⇨Sort Text. When the Sort Text dialog box appears, accept the default settings and click the OK button. When you return to your document, the list is sorted properly. Notice what happened with *Sandy* and *Sandi*; Word sorted by searching all the letters in the word, using the last, and only different, letter to decide whether *Sandy* or *Sandi* appears first.

Next, with the list still selected, choose Format⇨Bullets and Numbering. When the Bullets and Numbering dialog box appears, click the Bulleted tab if all the entries in your list are of equal importance. Select the bullet type that is most appropriate for your document. You can choose large or small bullets, empty or filled diamonds, and arrows or asterisks.

Click the Numbered tab if you want to indicate levels of importance. Choose Multilevel if your list contains several levels. Click the Modify button if you want to change the color of the bullets, choose a different bullet symbol, or adjust the distance of the indent.

Click OK when you are satisfied with your choices. When you return to your document, your list is reformatted to your specifications (see Figure 3-12).

If you want to format a list quickly without sorting it first, select the list and then click the Numbering or Bullets button at the right end of the Formatting toolbar.

If the listed items extend over two lines, notice that the second and later lines of each item are aligned with the first line instead of with the bullet because the bullets (or numbers) hang to the left of the text. If you want the second and later lines to align with the bullets instead of with the indented text, click the check box next to Hanging Indent to deselect the default in the Bulleted and Numbered tabs.

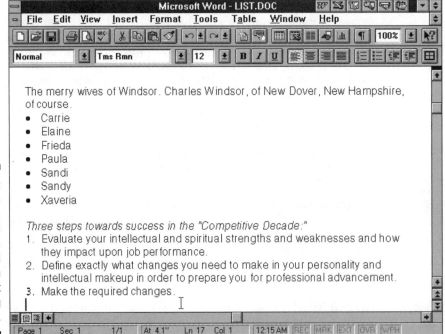

Figure 3-12:
Comparison of a sorted and bulleted list and a numbered list with default hanging indents.

Protecting your words from accidents and prying eyes

Privacy is becoming increasingly important as more and more computers are connected on networks. Although *you* may never be tempted to read a coworker's mail or look at his credit card statement (unless, perhaps, he went to lunch and left his desk unlocked), there's something a bit more tempting about peeking at a résumé, employee evaluation, or personal letter that you encounter while browsing through the hard disks connected to a network.

Word makes it easy to protect your documents. You can save an important document with a 15-letter, *case-sensitive* (that is, the uppercase and lowercase letters have to be in the correct locations) password (or combination of letters, numbers, symbols, and spaces) that must be re-entered to open the file.

To protect a document that you're working on, follow these steps:

1. **Choose File⇨Save.**

   Choose File⇨Save As if you're protecting a previously saved document.

   The Save As dialog box appears.

2. **Click the Options button.**

   The Save tab of the Options dialog box automatically appears.

3. **When the Save tab appears, enter your password in the Protection Password box at the bottom of the tab.**

   Notice that asterisks — not the actual characters that you type — appear on-screen.

4. **When you finish, click OK.**

   The Confirm Password dialog box appears.

5. **Type the password exactly as you did before and then click OK (see Figure 3-13).**

6. **When your retyped password is accepted, click OK.**

To open a protected document, choose File⇨Open. Select the name of the file you want and click OK. When the Password dialog box appears, enter your password *exactly as you typed it before* and then click OK. If you typed your password correctly, the file opens.

You also can *write-protect* a document. Write protection allows other users to read the document but not modify it. This procedure makes it easy to *post* (make available) Word documents on a computer network. When you post a document on a network for other users to read, but not modify, do not enter

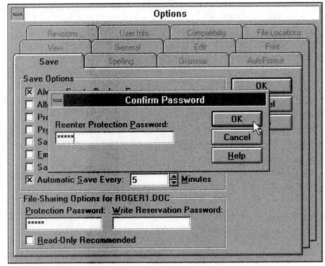

Figure 3-13:
Word forces
you to enter
your
password
twice, to
make sure
that you
remember it.

your password in the Protection Password box; instead, enter your password in the Write Reservation Password box. Other users who do not have the password can access the file by clicking the Read Only button when the Password dialog box appears.

Opening and saving documents in other word processing formats (you traitor, you!)

At times, you may need to open a document that originally was saved in a different word processing program. This situation may occur frequently if you have upgraded from another version of Word for Windows or if you used Word for the Macintosh or a competing word processing program.

To open a document created in another word processing program, choose File⇨Open, and click the down arrow next to List Files of Types. Select All Files. You then can navigate through the subdirectories on your hard disk to locate the subdirectory that contains the desired file. Click the Network button if you want to search the hard drives of other computers connected to the network. Click the down arrow next to the Drives box if you want to read a file on a different hard drive on your computer or on a 5¹/₄- or 3¹/₂-inch floppy disk.

In the list of available files, select the desired file and click OK (or double-click its name). Word informs you that a conversion is in progress.

To save a file in a different format — perhaps so that it can be read by a user of an earlier version of Word for Windows or a user of Word for the Macintosh or (horrors!) a user of a competing product — choose File⇨Save As. Click the down arrow next to the Save File as Type box, and select the desired file type.

If you experience difficulties opening and saving files in other formats, experiment with various formats, including Text Only and Rich Text Format.

Automating your work with macros

Books approaching a thousand pages have been written about creating macros with Word. Needless to say, the subject can become as complicated as you want it to be.

But the basic principle behind macros can be stated very simply: *Macros permit you to execute complicated keyboard sequences quickly and accurately by executing an easy-to-access file.* Any time you find yourself repeating the same operation frequently (for example, entering the same keystrokes or opening the same dialog box time after time), you should consider whether a macro can save you time and increase your accuracy.

Working with macros involves two primary steps: recording the macro and running the macro. If necessary, you may need to edit the macro; in certain cases, you have to delete it and start all over.

So that you have an example to work with, create a simple document with two common problems that require attention: the near-universal habit of pressing the spacebar twice after each period, and the habit of pressing the Enter key twice after each paragraph. (Old habits are hard to break!) These extra spaces can be very noticeable, especially in justified text.

To create your demonstration document, follow these steps:

1. **Type several short sentences and paragraphs, pressing the spacebar twice after each period and pressing the Enter key twice after each paragraph.**

2. **When you finish, click the Paragraph button (the third from the right, with the two vertical bars with the bulge pointing to the left) in the Standard toolbar.**

   This button reveals the spaces and paragraph marks that you entered in your document. The two dots following each period indicate that two spaces were entered.

3. **Format your paragraph by using a large type size.**

4. **Go to Page Layout view (by opening the <u>V</u>iew menu and choosing <u>P</u>age Layout or by clicking the Page Layout button located in the horizontal scroll bar).**

Your finished sample should look like the example shown in Figure 3-14. Notice the two dots indicating two spaces after each period and the two paragraph marks after the paragraph.

Creating a macro

To create a macro, follow these steps:

1. **Choose <u>T</u>ools⇨<u>M</u>acro.**

   The Macro dialog box appears.

2. **Enter a name in the <u>M</u>acro Name box (see Figure 3-15).**

   The name must begin with a letter and consist of a single word. For this example, enter **Nospace**.

3. **For later reference, enter the purpose of the macro in the Descri<u>p</u>tion box.**

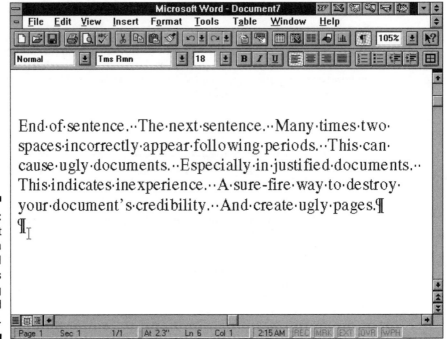

Figure 3-14: Sample text with unwanted spaces following periods and paragraphs.

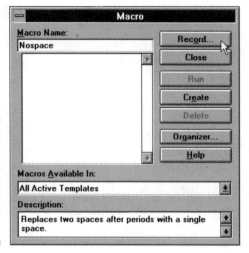

Figure 3-15:
Naming and
describing a
new macro
in the
Macro
dialog box.

4. **Click the Record button.**

   The Record dialog box appears.

5. **Indicate where you want the macro to appear.**

   Click the Menus icon in the Record dialog box if you want the macro to appear in the Macro dialog box. Click Keyboard if you want to assign a keyboard shortcut to the macro. Click Toolbar if you want to assign the macro to the toolbar.

6. **When you finish, click Close.**

   The two-button Macro Record toolbar appears (see Figure 3-16), indicating that all keyboard sequences and actions taken in dialog boxes now are being recorded.

7. **Choose Edit⇨Replace.**

   The Replace dialog box appears.

8. **Enter two spaces in the Find What box and enter one space in the Replace With box.**

9. **Click the down arrow next to Search and then select All.**

10. **Click the Replace All button.**

11. **When Word prompts you that it has finished searching, click the OK button.**

12. **Click the Close button.**

13. **Click the Stop button (marked with a black box) in the Macro Recorder toolbar.**

Congratulations! You've just created your first macro!

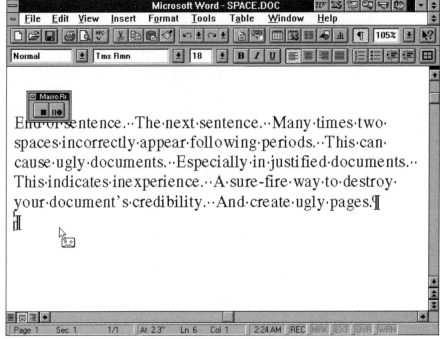

Figure 3-16:
The Macro
Recorder
toolbar and
the cassette
icon
attached to
the mouse
pointer
show that
you are
recording a
macro.

Before proceeding further, choose Edit⇨Undo Replace All. This command returns your sample document to its original condition so that you can demonstrate the performance of your new macro.

Running a macro

To demonstrate your new macro, choose Tools⇨Macro. When the Macro dialog box appears, select the name of your recently created macro; the name appears in the Macro Name box. Then click the Run button. Instantly, the screen reflects the operation of the macro: the two spaces following periods are replaced by single spaces.

Editing and deleting macros

If your macro didn't perform as desired, you can fix it in several ways by selecting Tools followed by Macro, which displays the Macro dialog box:

✔ You can delete the macro and start again by clicking the Delete button.

✔ You can record over the macro by selecting its name and clicking the Create button. Click OK when Word informs you that you are about to replace an existing macro.

✔ If you're especially adventurous, you can edit the macro by clicking the Edit button. Clicking this button displays a screen that contains the text of your macro. Good luck!

The preceding sections barely scratch the surface of what you can accomplish with macros. With a little imagination, you'll undoubtedly come up with your own macros for performing repetitive functions such as resizing windows; formatting text; inserting and relocating bookmarks; and opening, saving, and backing up files. Let your imagination be your guide and be on the lookout for repetitive tasks and ways to work more efficiently.

Your macros can be as sophisticated as you desire. As you become more comfortable with Word, you can insert conditional statements and prompts that ask the user to insert text, just as the Content Wizards did in Chapter 1.

Chapter 4

You, Too, Can Be a Media Baron!

● ●

In This Chapter

▶ Adding headers and footers

▶ Setting up multicolumn documents

▶ Adjusting column spacing and adding lines between columns

▶ Adding, resizing, anchoring, and formatting frames

▶ Creating headlines that span more than one column

▶ Reusing frames

▶ Importing, resizing, and cropping graphics

▶ Adding captions

▶ Using drop caps to attract attention to new stories

▶ Combining multiple text files into a single Word document

● ●

So far, we have concentrated on single-column documents: pages containing type that extends across the page in a single unbroken line. In this chapter, we'll make the jump from correspondence to publications by looking at the four major differences between letters and newsletters. Publications, as contrasted to correspondence, are characterized by headers and footers, the use of multicolumn formats, imported graphics (which can be illustrations or scanned photographs), and whiz-bang techniques such as oversize drop caps.

Basically, this chapter introduces Word's extensive desktop-publishing capabilities.

By the time you finish this chapter, you should be ready to challenge Rupert Murdoch's press empire by publishing your own newsletter and ultimately to take over the *Daily Mail*! (Or at least the *Daily News*.)

Keep Your Footers off My Headers!

Headers and footers can improve both the appearance and readability of your documents. Headers and footers improve the appearance of your documents by adding white space to the top and bottom of your pages. This white space provides a pleasing contrast to the grayness of your text and focuses your reader's attention on your words and accompanying graphics.

You can adjust the distance between headers and footers and page edges, as well as the distance between text columns and headers and footers. You also can use Word's Header and Footer feature to add top and bottom borders to your pages — horizontal rules (lines) that frame your text, define the top and bottom margins of your pages, and add visual weight to your pages.

In addition, headers and footers improve the readability of your documents by helping your readers locate information quickly. You can repeat certain information on each page, such as the publication title, the section or chapter title, and the author's name. You also can add the page number to headers or footers. The advantage of adding page numbers to headers and footers, instead of using Word's Insert⇨Page Numbers command, is that you can include the word *Page* before the number in a header or footer, as well as enjoy more formatting and placement flexibility.

Headers and footers can be used to add temporary information that will help you — the creator of the document — manage your manuscript more effectively. You can add the date and time of printing, for example. By temporarily adding the date and time of printing to document headers or footers (and removing them when it's time to print your final copy), you can keep the various drafts of your manuscript straight, avoiding the embarrassment of inadvertently submitting an early draft.

Adding headers and footers

To add with headers and footers, choose View⇨Header and Footer, regardless of your current document view. This command places you in Page Layout view and reveals the header area of the page as well as the Header and Footer toolbar (see Figure 4-1).

If you have ToolTips enabled, Word displays the purpose of each button as you move the mouse pointer over the various buttons in the Header and Footer toolbar. Most buttons are self-explanatory. For example, clicking the calendar or clock button adds (respectively) the date and time when the document is printed. The first button at the left end of the toolbar switches between each page's header and footer. The next two buttons, Show Next and Show Previous, permit you to switch quickly between headers and footers on odd- and even-numbered pages.

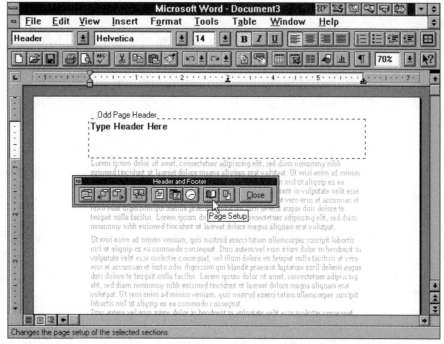

You can enter text in the Header area and format it using the drop-down typeface and type size menus and the bold, italic, and justification buttons in the Formatting toolbar or choose Format⇨Font, Format⇨Paragraph, or Format⇨Style.

Perhaps the most important button in the Header and Footer toolbar is the Page Setup button. Clicking this button takes you to the Layout tab of the Page Setup dialog box. In the Headers and Footers section of this tab, you can do the following things:

- ✔ Set up different headers and footers for the first page of your document. This is especially important for single-sided documents (such as letters, proposals, and reports), which typically don't include page numbers or section information on the first page.

- ✔ Set up different headers and footers for odd and even pages (see Figure 4-2).

After you click the Different Odd and Even check box, you can switch between the headers and footers for odd and even pages by clicking the Show Next and Show Previous buttons in the Header and Footer toolbar.

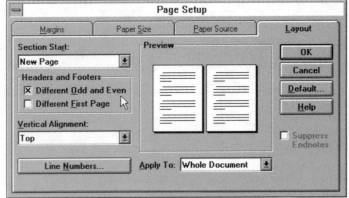

Figure 4-2:
Specifying
different
headers and
footers for
odd and
even pages
in the Page
Setup dialog
box.

When you finish editing and formatting headers and footers, you can return to the text area of your document by double-clicking anywhere in body of the document. Likewise, when you are working in Page Layout view, you can return to the header or footer editing area by double-clicking the grayed-out header or footer area of the page.

Adding white space above and below headers and footers

You can use headers and footers as design elements by controlling the amount of white space between the top of the header and the top of the page. Likewise, you can control the distance between the bottom of a footer and the bottom of the page.

To adjust the distance between the top and bottom edges of a page and the headers and footers, follow these steps:

1. **Choose View⇨Header and Footer, if necessary, to display the Header and Footer toolbar.**

2. **Click the Page Setup button.**

   The Page Setup dialog box appears.

3. **Click the Margins tab.**

4. **Type the desired measurement in the From Edge boxes next to Header and Footer, or click the up or down arrow to adjust the distance.**

5. **Click OK to close the Page Setup dialog box.**

You have to adjust the white space only one time; Word will adjust the header or footer distance for both odd and even pages.

To adjust the distance between headers and footers and adjacent text while working in Page Layout view, click the bottom edge of the bottom-margin boundary (a white rectangle) in the vertical ruler. When the mouse pointer becomes a double-headed arrow, drag it up to reduce the space between the text and header, or drag it down to add space between the header and the top of the text that follows. The horizontal line indicates the new text boundary (see Figure 4-3).

Again, you have to make this adjustment only one time; Word changes the distance for headers or footers on both odd and even pages.

You also can adjust the distance between text and adjacent headers and footers in Page Layout view. Follow these steps:

1. **Choose <u>V</u>iew⇨<u>Z</u>oom⇨<u>W</u>hole Page.**

2. **If the rulers aren't displayed, choose <u>V</u>iew⇨<u>R</u>ulers.**

   The white area of the ruler indicates the top and bottom text margins.

3. **Drag the top- or bottom-margin boundary to extend or reduce the text area without changing the location of headers and footers.**

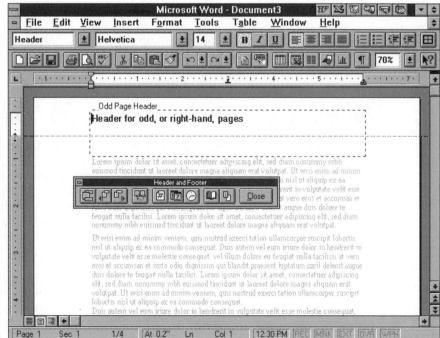

Figure 4-3: Adjusting white space between headers and text by dragging the bottom-margin boundary in the vertical ruler.

Adding border rules to headers and footers

In addition to building white space into your documents and providing space for the publication name, section and chapter titles, author name, and page numbers, you can use headers and footers to add top and bottom borders to your pages.

To add a top or bottom border rule to your pages, follow these steps:

1. **Choose** <u>V</u>**iew**⇨**Header and Footer (or double-click the header or footer area of your document in Page Layout view).**

2. **Choose** <u>V</u>**iew**⇨<u>T</u>**oolbars and then click the Borders check box to display the Borders toolbar.**

   This toolbar includes a drop-down menu that contains lines of different thicknesses, as well as buttons that represent different placement alternatives. The Borders toolbar also includes a second drop-down menu that contains a variety of background fills.

3. **Select a line of the desired thickness from the line drop-down menu.**

4. **To add a border below the header text, click anywhere in the header text and then click the Bottom Border button (see Figure 4-4).**

   The line appears below the text.

5. **To eliminate unnecessary clutter, choose** <u>V</u>**iew**⇨<u>T</u>**oolbars, and click the Borders check box to hide that toolbar.**

Text does not have to be present before you can add header and footer rules. Using this technique, you can add borders to headers and footers that do not contain text.

Inserting WordArt into headers and footers

The disadvantage of the approach in the preceding section, of course, is that you have little or no control of the length or position of the lines that create the top and bottom page borders. The borders extend across the width of the header or footer, and you cannot nudge them away from adjacent text. Borders that appear below text can be especially troublesome. Refer to Figure 4-4; notice that the descenders of the *p* and *g* in the above example bump into the border, making the word *pages* hard to read. This effect communicates a devil-may-care attitude rather than a professional one.

If you want total control of header and footer rules, click the Drawing button (the one that contains a circle, square, and triangle) in the Standard toolbar. When the Drawing toolbar appears, you can draw rules of a precise width and place them exactly where you want them.

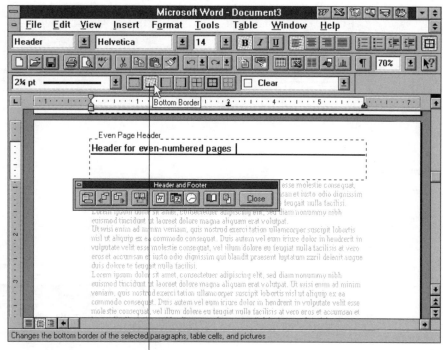

Figure 4-4:
Adding a header rule by using the Borders toolbar.

Bottom border button

You can, for example, use a combination of thick and thin lines to emphasize the text area of multicolumn documents. You also can use a thick line to draw attention to the footer text and a thin line below the thick line to define the width of the page and add weight to the page (see Figure 4-5).

In addition, you can use WordArt to create borders that surround a page. To create a border around each page, follow these steps:

1. **Choose View➪Header and Footer.**

2. **Click the WordArt button in the Standard toolbar.**

   The Drawing toolbar appears.

3. **Click the Line style button, and choose a line of the desired thickness.**

4. **Click the Rectangle drawing tool (see Figure 4-6).**

5. **Starting in the upper-left corner of the header area, drag the handles until the box is the desired distance from the text.**

When you leave Header and Footer view, the border appears on all pages.

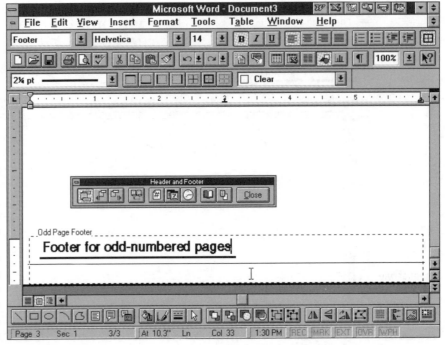

Figure 4-5:
Using
WordArt to
place
header and
footer
borders
exactly
where you
want them.

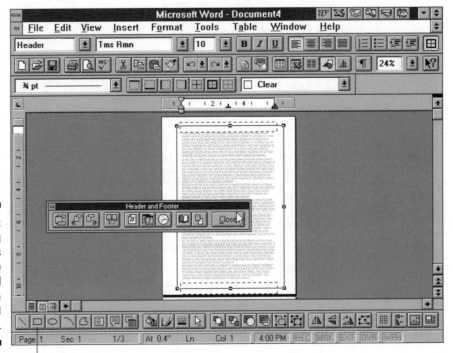

Figure 4-6:
Using
WordArt's
Rectangle
drawing tool
to create a
box around
every page.

Rectangle tool

You easily can check the appearance of multiple headers and footers. Choose View⇨Zoom⇨Many Pages to display three side-by-side pages. These reduced-size pages on your screen permit you to see how headers and footers function when they are applied to a series of pages.

Setting Up Multicolumn Documents

Most serious documents contain more than one column. Using multicolumn documents has numerous advantages. Following are some of the most important reasons to use these documents:

- ✔ Because type size and line spacing determine the line length, multicolumn documents permit you to use a smaller type size, which means that you can fit more words on a page. Long lines of text that extend across a page require a relatively large type size or extra line spacing to keep readers from rereading the line that they just finished reading.

- ✔ Multicolumn documents make it easy to build white space into each page, permitting you to include columns of white space that form a pleasing contrast with the text.

- ✔ Multicolumn documents offer more opportunities for creative placement of photographs and other graphics. Small illustrations, scanned images, and charts can be placed in the narrow columns of white space. Larger graphics can begin in a text column and extend into the adjacent column of white space. Likewise, large horizontal graphics can extend across multiple columns; a large photo, for example, can extend over two columns of a three-column grid.

 When you work with multicolumn documents, always begin by choosing File⇨Page Setup and reviewing the left and right margins in the Page Setup dialog box. Although Word's default margins are appropriate for correspondence and single-page documents, when you work with multicolumn documents, you should reduce the size of the margins to make better use of the space on the page.

Word 6 offers you two ways to set up multicolumn documents. The first method is to click the Column button in the Standard toolbar and then highlight the number of columns that you want to create (see Figure 4-7). This method instantly transforms a single-column document into a multicolumn document.

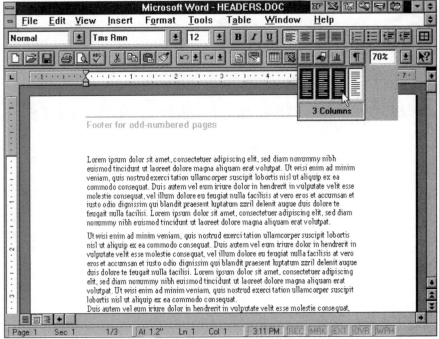

Figure 4-7:
Create
columns
with default
measure-
ments by
clicking the
Column
button in the
Standard
toolbar.

As you have seen several times, however, several compromises are built into the use of the buttons in toolbars. The disadvantage of using the Column button is the fact that the columns are of equal size, which may not be what you want. In addition, the distance between columns is fixed at a half-inch. For most layouts, a half-inch gutter between columns is far too generous, creating awkward gaps between columns and resulting in a page that lacks cohesiveness.

You also can adjust column width by dragging the column markers in the ruler. Although it appears to be an easy procedure, this option can lead to irregular column spacing.

A better, more precise method is to use Word's Columns dialog box (see Figure 4-8). To access the Columns dialog box, choose Format⇨Columns.

Notice that the Presets section of the Columns dialog box offers several placement options, including combinations of wide and narrow columns (with your choice of the narrow column appearing on the left or right side of the page). The wide column is twice the width of the narrow column, making this arrangement especially suitable for newsletters and documentation.

Figure 4-8:
The Columns dialog box allows you to specify columns of different widths, add vertical lines between columns, and fine-tune column spacing.

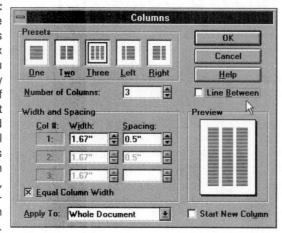

The Number of Columns box allows you to create columns of *equal width* by entering the desired number of columns or clicking the up or down arrow.

Alternately, you can click the Equal Column Width check box to deselect that option and then create columns of different widths and define the spacing between them in the Width and Spacing portion of the dialog box.

To add a vertical line between columns, click the Line Between box.

Get into the habit of reducing Word's default half-inch column spacing by entering a new Spacing measurement in the Width and Spacing area (or by clicking the up or down arrow). Factors that influence correct column spacing include the type size that you're using, the text alignment that you're using, and the presence or absence of vertical rules between columns.

Too much space between columns creates a spread-out page, which makes it difficult for readers to make the transition from the bottom of one column to the top of the next column. Too little space between columns encourages readers to jump the columns, reading across the column gap instead of returning to the beginning of the next line in the same column.

I'm Innocent! This Is a Frame-Up!

Much of Word 6's desktop-publishing capabilities are based on frames. Think of frames as being containers into which you can insert text, illustrations, scanned photographs, charts, or tables. The advantage of frames is that they offer a combination of flexibility and accuracy that otherwise is unavailable. Unlike text, a frame can be dragged anywhere on the page — even beyond the text area.

Frames can be locked to specific locations on a page so that text flows around them as it is edited, or they can be locked to paragraphs so that they float in your document, depending on how the text to which the frames are anchored changes as additions and deletions are made in adjacent paragraphs. Frames make it easy to lock captions to images, as well as to enhance the appearance of your document by adding borders and background fills to text and graphic elements. Equally important, you can use frames as containers for headlines that span more than one column.

Creating, moving, and resizing frames

To insert a frame into a document, follow these steps:

1. **Choose Insert⇨Frame.**

   The mouse pointer turns into a cross.

2. **Click the spot in your document where you want to insert the frame (keeping the left mouse button held down) and create a rectangle of the desired size by dragging (the mouse) diagonally down from left to right.**

3. **Release the mouse button when you finish drawing the frame.**

   The frame appears in your document as a border of diagonal lines (see Figure 4-9).

Notice the blinking insertion point. If you want, you can begin typing immediately, if you are creating a headline that spans two columns or a pulled quote.

Also notice the diagonal lines that create the border of the frame. When you click the border, the mouse pointer changes to a four-headed arrow, and you then can drag the frame anywhere in the document or (if more than one page is visible on-screen) to a different page.

Clicking the border again displays eight resizing handles around the frame. By dragging one of the side handles, you can make the frame wider. You can drag the frame beyond the boundaries of a column so that the frame extends over two or more columns.

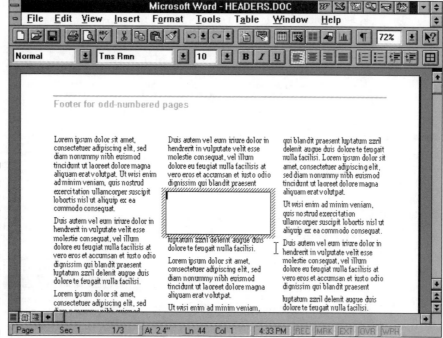

Figure 4-9:
A new
frame ready
to be
formatted,
moved, or
resized, or
to be filled
with text or
graphics.

Formatting and positioning frames

To format a frame, select it, and then click the right mouse button to display the Frame shortcut menu (see Figure 4-10).

The Frame shortcut menu allows you to Cut, Copy, and Paste. More important, the menu offers immediate access to the Frame Borders and Shading dialog box and to the Frame dialog box.

Start by selecting Borders and Shading. This command displays the Frame Borders and Shading dialog box, which contains two tabs.

The Borders tab allows you to determine the style, thickness, and color of the line that surrounds the frame. The From Text option allows you to define the distance between the text inside the frame and the border. This option is useful if you are creating pulled quotes or sidebars and don't want the text to bump into the frame border.

Word constantly keeps you informed by previewing changes in the Border area of the dialog box as you make them. For example, in Figure 4-11, the text in the Border window has been indented 6 points from the border, providing more white space than Word's default 1-point indent.

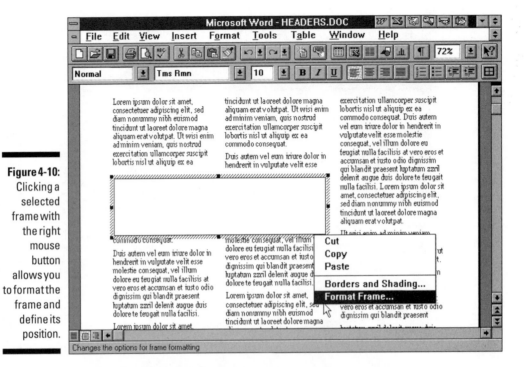

Figure 4-10:
Clicking a
selected
frame with
the right
mouse
button
allows you
to format the
frame and
define its
position.

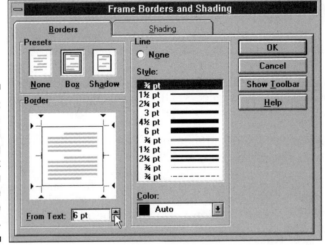

Figure 4-11:
The Frame
Borders and
Shading
dialog box
allows you
to format the
appearance
of the frame.

If you click the Shading tab, you can apply solid or tinted backgrounds (shades of gray) behind the contents of the frame. For example, you can choose Solid (100%) if you want to create reversed text.

After you format the appearance of the frame, it's time to format the position of the frame and its relationship to the page on which it appears, as well as to adjacent text. The Frame dialog box (see Figure 4-12) is one of Word's most important dialog boxes because of its numerous options and the role that those options play in allowing you to use frames for tables, text, and graphics. To show the Frame dialog box, select the frame and choose Format⇨Frame.

Figure 4-12:
The Frame dialog box permits you to position frames carefully and to define their relationship to the page and the adjacent text.

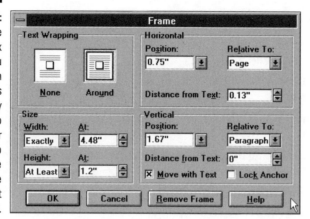

The Text Wrapping portion of the dialog box defines the horizontal relationship of adjacent text to frames. If you choose None, text will not wrap around the frame. Thus, a narrow frame will be surrounded by white space if that frame is not as thick as the column in which it appears. If you accept the default setting, Around, text appears along the left and right sides of narrow frames.

The drop-down menus in the Horizontal section allow you to specify the frame's distance from the text and to align the frame. You also can determine how much white space will separate the frame from adjacent text.

The drop-down menus in the Vertical section allow you to position the frame and define its distance from adjacent text. More important, you can allow the frame to move when adjacent text is edited. If you want the frame to follow adjacent text, click the Move with Text check box. If you click the Lock Anchor check box, the frame and its contents remain stationary even if adjacent text moves during editing.

Use the Width options in the Size portion of the Frame dialog box to allow the frame to expand or contract to accommodate its contents, or to specify minimum (At Least) or exact sizes. Likewise, the Height options allow you to specify exact, minimum, or automatic sizing.

Placing text in a frame

To see how all these commands work together, follow these steps:

1. **Select the frame by clicking it and drag it into the first column.**

   Notice the blinking insertion point.

2. **Type** Major announcement due today.

3. **Format the text in 28-point Helvetica Bold.**

4. **Click the frame border and then click the right mouse button to display the shortcut menu.**

5. **Choose Borders and Shading to display the Frame Borders and Shading dialog box.**

6. **When the Borders tab appears, choose the None option (in the Preset area) to remove the border.**

7. **Click the frame again and then click the right mouse button to display the Frame shortcut menu.**

8. **Choose Format Frame to display the Frame dialog box.**

9. **Set the following Horizontal options:**

   - Position: Left
   - Relative To: Column
   - Distance from Text: 0"

10. **Set the following Vertical options:**

    - Position: Top
    - Relative To: Margin
    - Distance from Text: 0"

11. **Click OK to close the Frame dialog box.**

12. **Click the middle handle at the bottom of the frame, drag it into the frame until it just about touches the descending _y_ in _today_, and then release the mouse button.**

When you finish, your headline should look extremely professional (see Figure 4-13)!

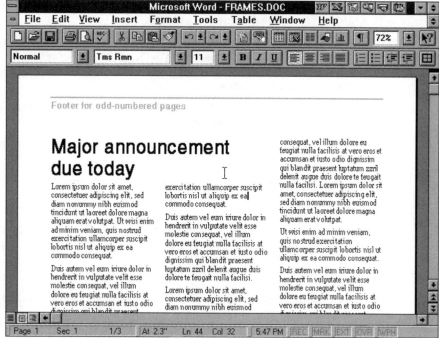

Figure 4-13:
Headline in frame spanning two columns.

Didn't your mother ever tell you to never throw anything away?

Time is money. Anything that you can do to save time pays off in increased income or increased leisure time. In addition, adaptive reuse contributes to increased consistency. Frames, combined with Word's AutoText feature, offer you many opportunities for creative recycling. After you create a distinctive frame style, for example, you can save it and retrieve it at a later date.

In this section, you'll create a frame style for pulled quotes and sidebars. *Pulled quotes* are short sentences — often quotations — that summarize ideas contained in the adjacent text. *Sidebars* are mini articles that elaborate on an idea or topic that is discussed briefly in the adjacent article.

To create a frame style, follow these steps:

1. **Choose Insert⇨Frame and drag the mouse to create a frame that spans two columns.**

   Don't worry about the exact placement of the frame; you can fine-tune its placement later.

2. **Enter the desired text, and format it so that it will form a strong typographic contrast with adjacent text.**

   For example, if you are using a serif typeface (such as Times Roman) for body copy, choose a sans-serif typeface (such as Helvetica Bold Italic) for the pulled quote. Choose a type size that's larger than body copy but smaller than headlines.

3. **Click the border of the frame and then click the right mouse button to display the Frame shortcut menu.**

4. **Choose Borders and Shading to display the Frame Borders and Shading dialog box.**

5. **When the Borders tab appears, set the following options:**

   - Choose None in the Presets area.
   - Click the top of the Border box.
   - In the Style list, click the $4\,{}^1\!/_2$ pt line.
   - In the From Text list, choose 6 points.

6. **Click the Shading tab, choose 25% Custom Shading, and click OK.**

7. **Click the border and then click the right mouse button to display the Frame shortcut menu.**

8. **Choose Format Frame to display the Frame dialog box.**

9. **In the Size area, set the Width at 2.2 inches and the Height at Auto.**

   (Setting the Auto option is extremely important because it allows the pulled quote to shrink or expand to accommodate the text that it contains.)

10. **Click OK to close the dialog box.**

11. **Click the border of the frame and position the pulled quote as desired by dragging the mouse, perhaps between the two text columns.**

    Make sure that you don't create awkward text wraps — lines that are too short for comfortable reading. Also, avoid placing pulled quotes in columns of justified text, as this placement typically results in ugly word spacing and excessive hyphenation in the short lines to the left and right of the pulled quote.

12. **Add an extra carriage return after the last line of the pulled quote, to ensure that the screened background will extend far enough below the quote to frame it properly.**

When you finish, your pulled quote could look like the example shown in Figure 4-14 (although I hope that you'll experiment and develop your own pulled-quote frame).

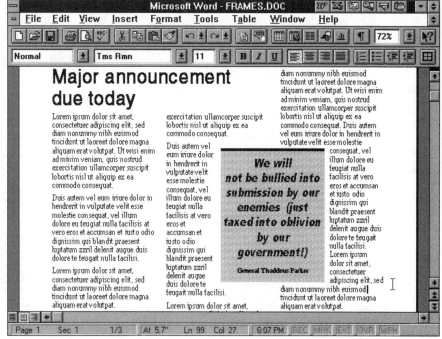

Figure 4-14:
A pulled
quote
formatted
with a top
border and
shaded
background.

Select the frame again, and click the right mouse button to display the Frame shortcut menu. Choose Copy from the shortcut menu. Then choose Edit⇨AutoText to display the AutoText dialog box. Notice that the Name box contains the first line of text in your pulled quote and that the Selection box displays the pulled quote. When you click the Add button, the formatted frame, containing formatted text, is saved and will be available for future use.

To reuse the frame, place the insertion point in a document where you want to insert the frame, and choose Edit⇨AutoText. When the AutoText dialog box appears, click the name of the frame you want to use, and click Insert. Select the existing text in the frame, and replace it with other text. Notice that the height of the pulled quote increases or decreases automatically, depending on the amount of text in the new pulled quote (see Figure 4-15).

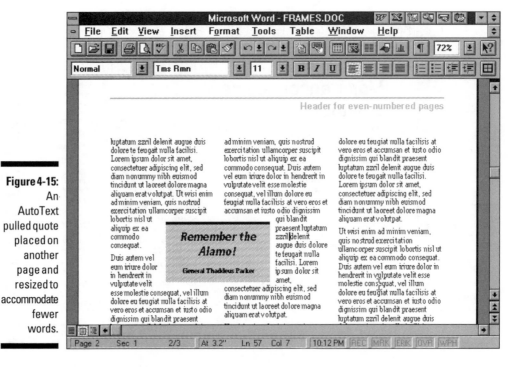

Figure 4-15: An AutoText pulled quote placed on another page and resized to accommodate fewer words.

Become an Importer of Fine Art!

Important as frames can be as containers for text, they are even more important when used as containers for graphics. Although you can insert pictures into your Word documents directly, there are significant advantages to placing them in frames, which give you more flexibility in positioning them on the page.

Don't define *graphics* too narrowly. Graphics can be any of the following things:

- The extensive clip art collection included with Word 6
- Custom illustrations created with drawing programs such as Adobe Illustrator, Aldus Freehand, CorelDRAW!, Visio, and ABC Flow Charter
- Scanned photographs

Inserting, resizing, and cropping graphics

Start by inserting a picture by itself. Place the insertion point in the text where you want to insert the picture, and choose Insert⇨Picture to display the Insert Picture dialog box (see Figure 4-16).

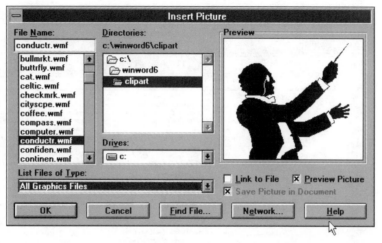

Figure 4-16:
The Insert
Picture
dialog box
makes it
easy to
locate and
preview
images.

Scroll through the list of available pictures (change Directories and Drives, if necessary, to locate the desired image). If you want to limit your search to certain types of images, specify the image type in the List Files of Type drop-down menu.

To evaluate each image before you place the file in your document, choose the Preview Picture option.

When you find an appropriate image — a scanned photograph, an illustration, or off-the-shelf clip art — click OK or double-click the filename. Word displays your document in Page Layout view, and the illustration appears at the inser-tion-point location (see Figure 4-17).

To resize the photo, first click it to display the eight resizing handles, and then drag the handles as desired.

✔ To stretch the image horizontally or vertically, drag one of the middle handles. Drag into the image to make it smaller; drag away from the image to make it larger. The distortion is likely to become very noticeable.

✔ To increase or decrease image size proportionately, drag one of the corner handles. This method maintains the illustration's original *aspect ratio* (height-to-width relationship). Dragging toward the illustration makes it smaller; dragging away from the illustration makes it larger.

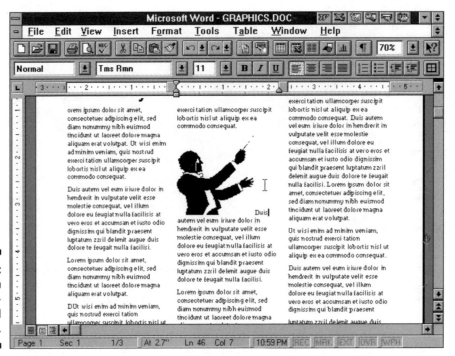

Figure 4-17:
Illustration
before fine-
tuning and
resizing.

Figure 4-18 shows the illustration from Figure 4-18 after being proportionately enlarged. Notice that the text in the column hides the illustration. You'll learn how to correct this problem in the following section.

Cropping involves removing parts of the graphic at the top, bottom, or sides to focus attention on the important parts of the illustration. To crop a graphic, hold down the Shift key while dragging one of the middle handles into the illustration. Notice that the two-headed arrow immediately turns into the cropping tool when you press the Shift key (see Figure 4-19).

When you release the mouse button, the image is resized, and adjacent text shifts to replace the discarded parts of the graphic.

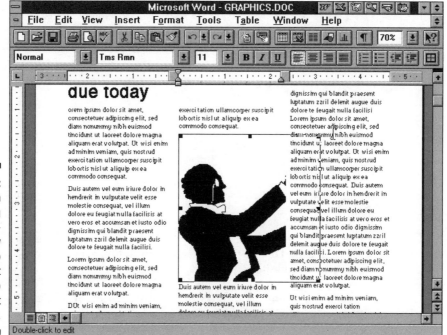

Figure 4-18: Illustration after being proportionately enlarged so much that it extends into an adjacent column.

Figure 4-19: Cropping unnecessary areas from an image.

Reformatting imported images

Click the image with the right mouse button to display a shortcut menu that offers the following options:

Cut
Copy
Paste
Edit Picture
Borders and Shading
Caption
Frame Picture

Choose Cut, Copy, or Paste if you want to perform one of these familiar functions.

Choose Edit Picture if you want to edit the illustration. Also choose Edit Picture if you want to add text to the illustration, to combine illustrations, or to recolor an image or change its fill patterns.

Choose Borders and Shading if you want to add a line around the graphic to separate it from adjacent text.

Choose Caption if you want to add an automatically numbered caption to identify the graphic. Clicking the Caption option displays the Caption dialog box, in which you can enter the caption text and indicate where you want the caption to appear (see Figure 4-20). Word automatically updates caption numbers as you add or delete graphics.

The final shortcut menu option, Frame Picture, offers an easy way to place the imported graphic in a frame. After you frame a picture, the last command in the shortcut menu is Format Frame. Choosing this option displays the Frame dialog box, in which you can resize the frame and accurately position it on the page.

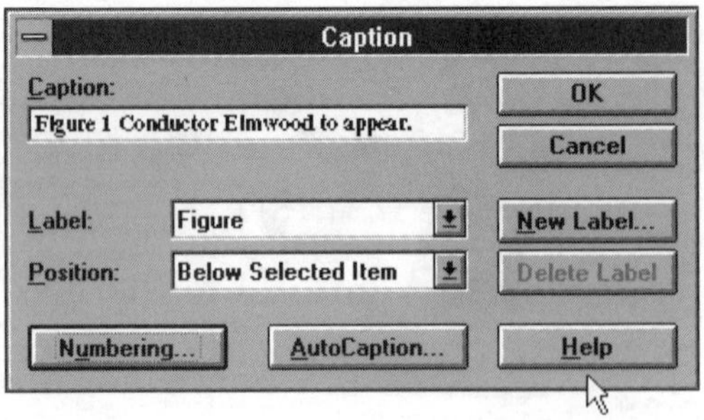

Figure 4-20:
Word makes it easy to add and correctly number captions.

One advantage of the Frame Picture option becomes obvious immediately: the portion of the illustration that was obscured by text in Figure 4-18 now is visible. The graphic now extends into the adjacent column, and the text in the column now wraps around it (see Figure 4-21).

Because you are working in the Frame dialog box, you can lock the graphic to adjacent text, allowing the graphic to move up if the preceding text is deleted or to move down if text is added before it. You also can anchor the graphic to a specific spot on a specific page.

Adding Drop Caps to Attract Attention to New Stories

Drop caps are another new feature in Word 6. *Drop caps* are oversize letters that typically are found at the beginning of an article, helping to create a transition between the headline and the body text.

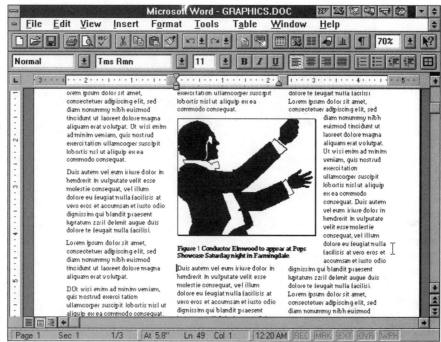

Figure 4-21: Choose the Frame Picture option if you want to anchor the graphic to adjacent text or to a specific page position.

Drop caps used to be difficult to create, but no longer — Word 6 can create good-looking drop caps automatically.

Have no illusions, however: drop caps remain surprisingly complicated, even in the best, most expensive page-layout programs. Whether the quality of the drop caps that Word produces is up to your standards is something that you'll have to decide for yourself.

To add a drop cap, follow these steps:

1. **Highlight the first letter of the paragraph in which you want the drop cap to appear.**

2. **Choose Format⇨Drop Cap.**

   The Drop Cap dialog box appears (see Figure 4-22).

3. **Start by specifying the desired position.**

   In most cases, the appropriate choice is Dropped. If you are working on a single-column document with a deep left-hand margin, however, and if sufficient space is available, you can choose In Margin instead.

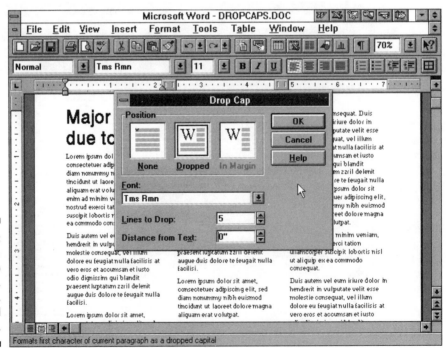

Figure 4-22:
Choosing a drop-cap size, location, and typeface.

4. **Select the desired typeface for the drop cap by clicking the down arrow by the font box.**

   In most cases, you will choose the same typeface used for the adjacent text, although you may want to also experiment with different typefaces.

5. **Specify the size of the drop cap by entering a figure in the <u>L</u>ines to Drop box or by clicking the up or down arrow.**

6. **Click OK and behold your new drop cap (see Figure 4-23)!**

Figure 4-23: The completed drop cap draws the reader into the paragraph.

In many cases, you may need to select the drop cap and reposition it so that it aligns properly with the adjacent paragraph.

You often can improve the appearance of paragraphs that contain initial caps by setting the first line of text in uppercase text. Uppercase text provides a smooth transition between the drop cap and the rest of the paragraph.

I'm Waiting for Your Article!

Another characteristic that separates publishing activities from conventional word processing is the group orientation of many activities. When you're writing a letter, article, or résumé, you're likely to do so by yourself, in a linear front-to-back fashion. As a result, your document might consist of a single file.

But as you begin to use Word to prepare more complex documents (such as newsletters, proposals, and reports), several people are likely to write different sections of the documents. You also may prepare a proposal or report as a series of Word files written at different times.

To combine several files into a single Word document, place the insertion point in the document where you want to insert the new text, and choose Insert⇨File. In the File dialog box, scroll through the various directories and subdirectories on your computer or network until you find the appropriate file (see Figure 4-24). Then double-click the filename. Instantly, Word adds the text of that file to your document.

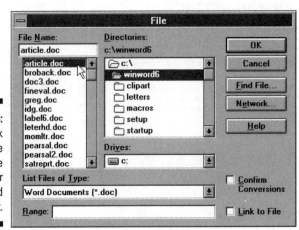

Figure 4-24:
Double-click a filename to insert the file into your Word document.

Part II
How to Excel at the Numbers Game

"A CONSULTANT TOLD US THAT POLYESTER CAN CAUSE SHORTS IN THE SYSTEM, SO WE'RE TRYING AN ALL LEATHER AND LATEX DATA ENTRY DEPARTMENT."

In this part...

*I*t's time to put away your abacus and begin your Excel-lent adventure. Whether you're scared or excited by the prospect of diving into the numbers-oriented world of spreadsheets, this section should allay your fears and heighten your excitement. Get ready to find out what all the spreadsheet fuss is about. You'll learn what spreadsheets are good for and how they can make your life easier — or at least less dependent on your pocket calculator. And, thank goodness, you don't even need an MBA to put Excel to work. In fact, if you understand fourth-grade math (or know some patient fourth-graders who can help you), you're all set.

Chapter 5

Look, Ma! I'm an Accountant!

• •

In This Chapter

▶ Learning spreadsheet lingo (and finding out what the heck spreadsheets are good for)

▶ Putting stuff in: creating a worksheet

▶ Making it calculate: using formulas and functions

▶ Making it pretty: no-sweat formatting

▶ Sending it to the printer

• •

*M*ost folks who've been around computers for a few years credit (or blame) the first spreadsheet program for getting the computer revolution off the ground. Who cares? You just want to get your work done faster and with fewer errors. Excel allows us non-rocket scientists to work with numbers as though we were NASA engineers. (Well…almost.)

What Is a Spreadsheet, Anyway?

If you use, or have seen your accountant using, those green sheets of ledger paper with lines that make it easy to enter information in neat rows and columns, you know what a spreadsheet is. A computer spreadsheet is just the electronic equivalent of green ledger paper.

So what's so wonderful about electronic spreadsheets? Why not just use the paper variety?

Are you kidding? With that icky old paper-and-pencil method, you have to perform calculations by hand. Blech! The worst part is that when you change numbers that affect your calculations, you have to perform the calculations — by hand — all over again.

Wait, it gets worse. Often, the numbers that you change require you to perform not just one calculation, but many calculations. Excel does it all automatically. Change a number, and zap! — all the calculations are updated faster than you can say $E=mc^2$.

Laziness is the mother of invention

Back in 1979, two lazy business students (nothing personal, guys), Dan Briklin and Bob Frankston, decided to devise a way to spend less time with their homework so that they'd have more time for more important activities, such as drinking and parties.

What to do? Perhaps they could put their new computers to work recalculating their business homework. So they did what any lazy business student would do: they wrote the first spreadsheet program. (Hey, I said they were lazy, not stupid.) They called the program VisiCalc, as in Visible Calculator. Pretty clever, huh?

Every spreadsheet program since then, including Excel, owes its existence to Dan and Bob. Thanks, Dan and Bob!

Forecasting and budgeting are two of the primary uses for spreadsheets. The big advantage of using an electronic spreadsheet for this purpose is the ability to look at a variety of "what-if" scenarios. After entering all the budget figures, for example, you may want to see what would happen if the cost of goods goes up ten percent or if you give yourself a million-dollar raise.

Spreadsheets also are handy places to store lists. Because creating a name and address list in Excel is so easy, you may decide that it's the tool of choice for simple data management. Excel provides most of the tools you'll need for manipulating simple databases, such as sorting and searching.

The menu structure and toolbars bear a striking resemblance to Word's (and PowerPoint's, for that matter), so you should feel pretty much at home as soon as you start Excel. (See Figure 5-1.) Speaking of starting Excel ...

- ✔ You start Excel the same way that you start the other Office programs. Click the Microsoft Excel button in the Microsoft Office Manager toolbar, or double-click the Microsoft Excel icon in the Windows Program Manager.

- ✔ If you're not sure which toolbar button does what, you can just move the mouse pointer over the button to display a ToolTip that shows the name of the button. The left side of the status bar displays a longer description of the button's function.

- ✔ Excel spreadsheet files are called *workbooks*, each of which may include up to 256 individual *worksheets*. Each worksheet contains up to 256 vertical columns and 16,384 horizontal rows.

- ✔ Worksheets are identified by their sheet tabs; you can use the shortcut menu to rename them. To rename a sheet, right-click the sheet tab, and then click Rename. Enter a new, more descriptive name in the Rename Sheet dialog box, and then click the OK button.

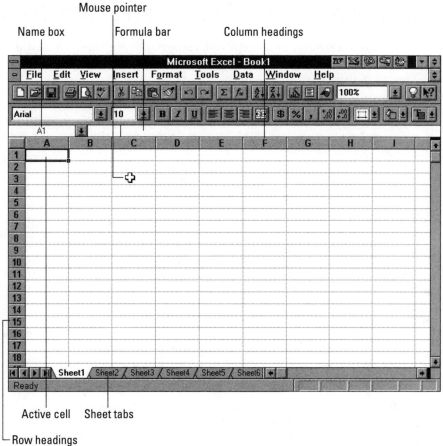

Figure 5-1:
The initial
Excel
screen, with
a blank
worksheet
awaiting
your input.

Name box

Mouse pointer

Formula bar

Column headings

Active cell   Sheet tabs

Row headings

✔ Columns are designated with letters (A, B, C, and so on), and rows are
numbered (1, 2, 3, and so on).

✔ The intersection of a row and a column is called a *cell*. Any data that you
enter into a worksheet — whether that data is numbers or text — is
entered into cells.

✔ Cells are designated by their column letter, followed by their row numbers. For example, the cell at the intersection of column G and row 12 is
cell G:12.

✔ Because your computer screen can display only a small portion of a
worksheet, you'll use the scroll bars and other navigation techniques to
get to the far reaches of larger worksheets.

Putting Stuff In: Creating a Worksheet

To enter data into a worksheet, just move to the cell in which you want to place the data and start typing. It's just that simple. As you type, the data appears both in the cell and in the formula bar.

Three little buttons appear in the formula bar as soon as you start typing. The button marked with the red *X* is the Cancel button; the one with the green check mark is the Enter button; and the one with the *fx* symbol is the Function Wizard button.

Excel's no dummy. Whether you enter text, numbers, or even dates, it knows what you want and responds appropriately (usually).

- ✔ Text is automatically aligned at the left side of the cell, and numbers (including dates, such as Feb. 10, 1995) are aligned at the right side.

- ✔ Complete a cell entry by clicking the Enter button, pressing an arrow key to move to another cell, or pressing Enter on your keyboard.

- ✔ When you press the Enter key to complete a cell entry, the cell pointer moves down one row. This method is best for entering a column of data.

- ✔ You can cancel a cell entry before completing it by pressing the Esc key or clicking the Cancel button in the formula bar.

- ✔ Press the Backspace key to erase cell data one character at a time before completing the cell entry.

- ✔ You can correct data that has already been entered by typing a new entry or by pressing the F2 key, which puts you in Edit mode. In Edit mode, you can correct the data just as you would before completing a cell entry. When you are in Edit mode, you must complete the cell entry by clicking the Enter button or pressing Enter; you can't complete the edit by pressing an arrow key, as you can when you first enter data in the cell.

- ✔ Press the Delete key to erase the contents of a cell.

Names, ranges, and addresses

If the cell to which you want to go is visible on-screen, the easiest way to get to it is to click it. That cell then becomes the active cell, and its *address* (column letter and row number) appears in the name box to the left of the formula bar.

The name box isn't called the name box for nothing. You can assign descriptive names to cells and *ranges* (a group of two or more cells). You can use the name box to assign names and also to move to named cells and ranges.

Excel is an easy date

If you've worked with older spreadsheet programs, which require you to enter dates in a very rigid format (such as @DATE(95,2,10) for February 10, 1995), you can thank your lucky stars (or Bill Gates) that you have Excel.

In Excel, you can enter dates just about any way that you'd normally write them. For example, you can enter **2/2/95, Feb 2, 1995,** or **February 2, 1995.** You may still want to format the dates so that they appear the way you want, but at least it's easy to get the dates into your worksheets. (Formatting is covered later in this chapter.)

Assigning names can make finding portions of a worksheet much easier. For example, it's a lot easier to figure out where your budget's 1995 income area is if it's called 1995 income instead of F22 through J43.

To assign a range name, follow these steps:

1. **Select the range of cells you want to name by dragging (holding down the left mouse button while dragging the mouse).**

   The range is highlighted, and the first cell in the range becomes the active cell. The active cell's address appears in the name box.

2. **Move the mouse pointer into the name box (the left box in the formula bar).**

   The mouse pointer assumes the shape of an I-beam.

3. **Click the name box.**

   The cell address is highlighted and moves to the left side of the selected range.

4. **Type the name that you want to assign to the range.**

5. **Press Enter.**

   The name that you assigned appears in the name box.

To move to a named range, follow these steps:

1. **Click the name box.**

2. **Type the name of the range to which you want to move.**

3. **Press Enter.**

   The range name that you entered is highlighted, and the cell in the upper-left corner of the range is the active cell.

> ✔ Use the name box to jump to any cell address or range. Just click the name box and then enter the address or range. To move to range W5 through X15, for example, click the name box, type **W5:X15**, and press Enter.
>
> ✔ Range addresses are always separated by a colon (:), as in B3:C8.

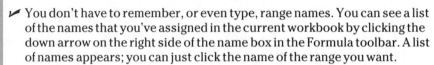

> ✔ You don't have to remember, or even type, range names. You can see a list of the names that you've assigned in the current workbook by clicking the down arrow on the right side of the name box in the Formula toolbar. A list of names appears; you can just click the name of the range you want.
>
> ✔ You'll find that a lot of the time you spend working with spreadsheets involves selecting ranges before formatting and performing other types of worksheet manipulation.

Copying text and numbers

All the Office programs use the same methods to copy data. Select the cell or range that you want to copy, click the Copy button in the Standard toolbar, move to where you want to deposit the copied data, and then click the Paste button. Easy.

There's an even easier way to copy data if you're copying to adjacent cells. Position the mouse pointer on the *fill handle* (the little thingy in the lower-right corner of the cell pointer) and drag in the direction in which you want to copy.

> ✔ Excel is so smart, it usually knows when a cell entry should be incremented. For example, if you enter **January** or **Monday** (or **Jan** or **Mon**) and use the fill handle to drag to the right or down, Excel creates an incremented series — for example, January, February, March or Mon, Tues, Wed.
>
> ✔ If you drag the fill handle up or to the left, Excel creates a decremented series — for example, January, December, November.
>
> ✔ Hold down the Ctrl key as you drag the fill handle to increment a cell entry that Excel isn't smart enough to figure out on its own. If you enter **1** in a cell and use the fill handle without Ctrl, you'll get 1, 1, 1. With Ctrl, you'll get 1, 2, 3.

> ✔ The Ctrl key has the opposite effect when you use it to copy a cell that Excel normally would increment. If January is entered in a cell, Ctrl causes Excel to copy the cell without incrementing.

Help, Mr. TipWizard!

Excel's help facility works just like the help facilities in the other Office programs. Excel, however, has one unique help feature that you may find more helpful than anything else (aside from this book, of course). The TipWizard is like a coach who watches what you do and suggests more efficient ways of doing it. This feature is watching all the time, so you don't need to do anything to activate it.

You do, however, need to do something to see the advice that the TipWizard has to offer. When the TipWizard has a suggestion, the light bulb on the TipWizard button in the Standard toolbar "lights up," turning yellow. Click the TipWizard button, and the suggestion appears in its own TipWizard toolbar below the Formatting toolbar.

Suppose that you didn't know about Excel's incrementing capability, and you typed **Jan**, **Feb**, and **Mar**. The TipWizard would tell you that there is a better way to create a series, as you see in Figure 5-2.

ıØ If you want more detailed instructions about the TipWizard's suggestion, click the Tip Help button on the right side of the TipWizard toolbar.

ıØ To remove the TipWizard toolbar and reclaim some screen real estate, click the TipWizard button in the Standard toolbar.

ıØ It's not a bad idea to leave the TipWizard toolbar on the screen all the time so that you can see new tips as they arise. If you leave the TipWizard on-screen when you exit Excel, it will be there waiting for you with a random Tip of the Day the next time you start Excel.

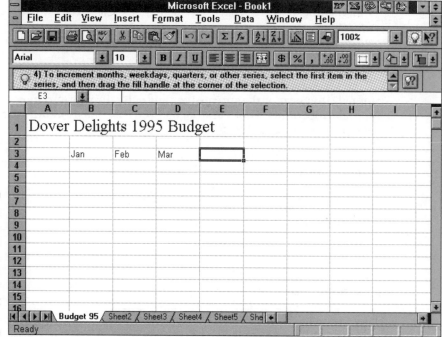

Figure 5-2:
The
TipWizard
toolbar,
showing a
better way
to increment
a series.

Save, save, save

In case you missed it in the Word section, I'll tell you here: you'd better save your documents on a regular basis, or you'll be sorry.

To save a workbook, including all its worksheets, click the Save button (the one marked with a picture of a disk) in the Standard toolbar.

The first time you save, you'll need to enter a name for the file and then click OK. If a Summary Info dialog box appears, enter any additional descriptive details you want to use and then click the OK button.

After you name and save the workbook, you can click the Save button to safeguard your work at regular intervals — say, every 10 or 20 minutes.

✔ Excel automatically assigns an XLS extension to your filename.

✔ Click the File menu and choose Save As to assign a new name to a workbook.

Making It Calculate: Using Formulas and Functions

Without the capability to perform calculations, Excel wouldn't have much of an advantage over the paper-and-pencil alternative. To get Excel to do your mathematical bidding, you create formulas or use one of its zillions of pre-defined formulas called *functions*.

To create simple formulas, move to the cell where you want the result of the formula to appear on the spreadsheet and enter the appropriate cell references and math operators. The operators that you'll use most often are + (addition), – (subtraction), * (multiplication), and / (division).

To create a formula in B5 to multiply the contents of B4 by the contents of B3, follow these steps:

1. **Click cell B5, and type = (the equal sign).**

   All formulas start with an equal sign. Don't ask me why.

2. **Type B3 or click cell B3.**

   It's often easier to click (or *point to*) cell references than it is to type them.

3. **Press * (asterisk).**

   The asterisk is the multiplication symbol.

4. **Type B4 or click cell B4.**

5. Press Enter.

The result of the formula instantly appears in B5. The formula in the formula bar should look like this: =B3*B4.

✔ The way that Excel normally displays data on-screen, you can't see which cells contain formulas and which contain only numbers. The formula bar is the giveaway. You can tell whether a cell contains a formula by looking at the formula bar.

✔ Be very careful not to delete or edit cells that contain formulas; that can really ruin your day.

✔ If you do accidentally wipe out a formula, click the Undo button in the Standard toolbar before you do anything else.

✔ It's easy to enter formulas incorrectly (for me, at least), so it's important to proofread your worksheets to see whether the numbers make sense. If you have a formula that should be multiplying 5 by 100 and the answer you get is 48,673, something is wrong!

Copying formulas

The procedure for copying formulas generally is the same as for copying any other kind of data. When you copy formulas, however, Excel understands that you normally want the copies to be relative to their new location.

Suppose that the numbers in row 3 are the number of hours your employees worked last month and that the numbers in row 4 are their wages, in dollars per hour. If you copy the formula in B5 (B3*B4) to cell C5, you'd want the copy to change to =C3*C4. And that's exactly what happens.

Excel uses relative addressing, so when you copy a formula, Excel copies the logic of the formula rather than the formula itself. The logic that Excel uses when you copy =B3*B4 from B5 to C5 is "Multiply the contents of the cell two rows up by the contents of the cell one row up."

It's especially important to look at the formulas that Excel creates as you copy. Excel makes assumptions when you copy formulas. And you know what can happen when *you* assume.

Having SUM fun

The most frequently used Excel function is the SUM function for adding a range of cells. Functions have a slightly different syntax from that of the formulas that you create; they begin with the equal sign, but that's where the similarity ends.

After the equal sign comes the name of the function, followed by parentheses that contain the function's arguments. *Arguments* are the data or cell references that the function needs to perform its calculations. In the case of the SUM function, the only argument is the range of cells to be summed.

To sum a range of cells, follow these steps:

1. **Click the cell where you want the result of the function to appear and type** =SUM(.

2. **Type the range of cells to be summed (for example,** F12:F24) **or drag the mouse over the range.**

3. **Type**) **and press Enter to complete the entry.**

   The sum of the range appears instantly.

   ✔ You can include more than one range in the SUM argument by separating the ranges with a comma. =SUM(F12:F24,G18:G33), for example, returns the sum of both ranges.

   ✔ The easiest way to sum a range is to have Excel do all the work for you. Just move to the result cell, and click the AutoSum button (it looks like a sideways *M*) in the Standard toolbar. Excel creates a formula with the SUM function and includes the adjacent contiguous range. The program doesn't always guess the correct range, but it's worth a try.

   ✔ Lots of other Excel functions are worth exploring. To see a list of functions and their descriptions, click on Help⇨Contents. Then click Reference Information⇨Worksheet Functions⇨Alphabetical List of Worksheet Functions. As you scroll through the list, you can get more detailed information about the function by clicking its name.

   ✔ As you start using functions, you'll find that you don't have to remember their syntax if you use the Function Wizard button in the Standard toolbar.

Making It Pretty: No-Sweat Formatting

Although entering a bunch of numbers, text, and formulas can provide you needed feedback, you may not end up with anything very attractive. Changing various formatting attributes can turn a dull, lifeless worksheet into a powerful persuader. And persuasion, after all, often is what worksheets are designed for. You want your boss to approve your budget proposals, and a beautiful worksheet will give the boss the impression that you gave it more thought.

Excel offers an almost unlimited variety of formatting options. Fonts, borders, number styles, and alignment are just some of the tools that you can use to prettify your worksheet.

As a general rule, formatting follows this sequence: select the cell or range of cells to be formatted, and then choose the formatting that you want to apply. For example, if you want to make the entries in a range of cells bold, drag the mouse over the range, and then click the Bold button in the Formatting toolbar.

- Most formatting affects cells or ranges of cells. Choose Format⇨Cells to display the Format Cells dialog box, which contains all the cell-formatting options. Notice the tabs for the formatting categories at the top of the dialog box. Click a tab to move to the portion of the dialog box that contains that category's options.

- The Formatting toolbar contains buttons for many of the most common formatting tasks, including fonts and sizes; bold, underline, and italic; alignment options; and common number styles. With most of these buttons, you're just a click away from formatting happiness.

- If you apply any formatting by mistake, immediately click the Undo button to remove the formatting.

- After applying a variety of formatting attributes to a range, you may wonder how you'll remember exactly what you did so that you can format another range the same way. No problem — just click one of the formatted cells, click the Format Painter button in the Standard toolbar, and then drag across the range that you want to format like the original range. Voilà!

- With all the formatting options at your disposal, it's easy to get carried away. You may be tempted to use too many options in a worksheet — 15 fonts, 10 border styles, all the colors in the rainbow. You can create a real mess. If you're not a professional designer, keep your worksheets simple.

Using AutoFormat

If you're not a designer, but you long for fancier formatting than you can pull off on your own, Excel provides some professional help in the form of AutoFormat.

To use AutoFormat, select the data that you want to format, and then choose Format⇨AutoFormat. The AutoFormat dialog box appears, offering a variety of standard formatting options. Click one of the names in the Table Format portion of the dialog box. The Sample portion shows an example of the formatting that will be applied.

When you find the Table Format that tickles your fancy, click the OK button. Poof! All formatted.

- After using AutoFormat, you still may need to apply some specific formatting to portions of the worksheet. If you want to call attention to a particular cell or range, for example, you could increase the size or change the color of the data in those cells.

✔ If you want to restrict the types of formatting that AutoFormat will apply, click the Options button in the AutoFormat dialog box; then deselect the Formats to Apply options that you don't want AutoFormat to use. If you carefully selected the fonts that you want to use, for example, remove the check from the Font check box by clicking it.

Adjusting column widths

It won't be too long before you find that a lot of your data is truncated, scrunched, weird, or otherwise not displayed the way you intended. This problem often is the result of too-narrow columns.

You can adjust columns by positioning the mouse pointer on the right border of the column heading (column headings are the letters) and dragging left to decrease the column width or right to increase it.

✔ You can let Excel figure out the optimal width for the column by double-clicking the border line in the column heading. You'll end up with a column that's just a bit wider than its longest entry.

✔ You may not want a particular column to be adjusted for its longest entry if, for example, one of its entries is a long title. If you use the automatic-column-width feature, you could end up with a column that is way too wide. To get around this little problem, click the column heading to select all the cells in the column; then hold down the Ctrl key and click the cell that you want to exclude from the automatic adjustment. Finally, from the menu bar, click Format⇨Column⇨AutoFit Selection.

Sending It to the Printer

After you finish putting together your masterpiece worksheets, the next step is getting them on paper. That's a lot better than having people crowd around your computer to view the worksheet on-screen, don't you think?

For quick and dirty printing, just click the Print button in the Standard toolbar. For more control of the printing process, click File⇨Print, or press Ctrl+P on your keyboard. The Print dialog box appears. In this dialog box, you can choose whether to print only the range that you've selected, the selected worksheets, or the entire workbook. You also can specify how many copies and which pages to print.

After making your choices, click the OK button to begin the printing process.

✔ Be sure that your printer is turned on, has paper loaded, and that the on-line light is on.

✔ Click the Page Setup button in the Print dialog box to change additional print options, such as orientation, margins, and grid lines.

✔ The Header/Footer tab of the Page Setup dialog box also allows you to add headers and footers: text that appears at the top (*headers*) or bottom (*footers*) of every page.

✔ After you change specifications in the Print and Page Setup dialog boxes, click the Print toolbar button to use the new settings the next time you print, therefore bypassing any dialog box interruptions.

✔ Before sending the document to the printer, check it out with Print Preview. You can get to Print Preview by clicking the Print Preview button in the Print dialog box or the one in the Standard toolbar. Using Print Preview can save you a lot of paper.

Chapter 6

And This Chart Proves Conclusively...

*I*t's easier to explain things and to persuade others that you're headed in the right direction if you chart your course. And because, as we all know, a picture is worth a thousand words, using charts can make you seem more convincing (or at least more verbose). Of course, it's a given that people with a lot to say *must* know what they're talking about...right?

Turning Numbers into Charts

Excel enables you to create gorgeous (or ugly — it's your choice) charts to graphically represent the numbers in your worksheets. As with every other aspect of Excel, the vast number of charting options can be overwhelming. But take heart — after you have your data entered in a worksheet, creating a chart is just a matter of letting Excel know which information you want to use, what type of chart you want, and where to put it.

You don't even need to know much charting lingo to create charts, but familiarity with a few terms will help keep you on the right track.

Even the most basic charts contain at least one data series. A *data series* is just a set of values for a particular category. Sales figures for January, February, and March, for example, are one data series. The cost-of-goods figures for the same period are another data series.

Most charts have an x-axis and a y-axis. Don't get freaked out by the terminology — the *x-axis* is the horizontal plane, and the *y-axis* is the vertical plane. (I hope that's plain enough.)

The way that most data is set up in a worksheet, the x-axis (sometimes called the *category axis*) is used to plot the values in the data series over time. The y-axis (sometimes called the *value axis*) is used to plot the amount of the numbers.

> ✒ You'll find that it's easiest to create Excel charts if your data is set up in normal table format, using contiguous rows and columns. Don't insert any blank rows or columns into the table.

> ✒ You can create a chart in the same sheet that contains the worksheet data or in a different sheet. There is no particular advantage to placing the chart in its own sheet, unless you are creating an on-screen presentation.

> ✒ Adding a new data series to a chart is as easy as dragging and dropping. Select the data in the new series, position the mouse pointer on the bottom border of the selection so that the pointer becomes an arrow, drag the series into the chart, and release the mouse button.

> ✒ Don't go nuts and chart everything in sight. Chart only the data that can really benefit from graphical representation.

Using the ChartWizard

Wouldn't it be great if Excel could simply create the chart for you, if it *knew* what you wanted and where you wanted it?

Get real! Excel's good but not *that* good; you've got to give it a little help. Fortunately, when you use the ChartWizard, you need to provide surprisingly little help.

Follow these steps to create a chart with the ChartWizard:

1. **Select all the cells of the table that include the column and row headings and the data to be charted.**

   The column headings will be used as x-axis labels, and the row headings will be used in the chart legend.

2. **Click the ChartWizard button in the Standard toolbar.**

   The mouse pointer becomes a crosshair with a tiny chart attached, as shown in Figure 6-1.

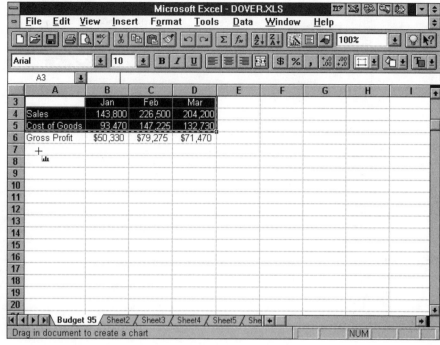

Figure 6-1:
The
selected
chart data
and the
ChartWizard
mouse
pointer.

(If you want to create the chart in its own worksheet, instead of clicking the ChartWizard button, click Insert⇨Chart⇨As New Sheet. The remaining steps are the same.)

3. **Drag the mouse down and to the right to select the portion of the worksheet that you want the chart to occupy.**

Figure 6-2 shows the area where the chart will appear.

4. **Release the mouse button to display the first ChartWizard dialog box, shown in Figure 6-3.**

(The dollar signs in the range just mean that Excel is using absolute cell addressing; no need to give them a second thought.)

5. **Click the Next button or press the Enter key to display the second ChartWizard dialog box.**

This dialog box, shown in Figure 6-4, allows you to choose the chart type. The default, which I'll stick with for the example, is a column chart. Don't spend too much time worrying about the chart type now; you can change the chart type at any time, as you'll learn in the following section of this chapter.

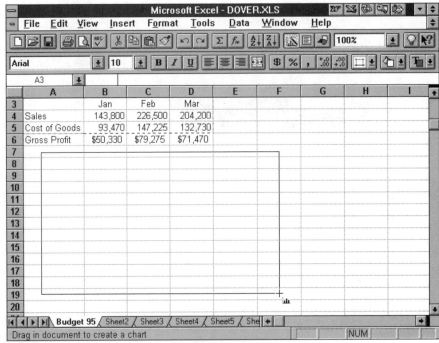

Figure 6-2:
Where the
chart will
appear.

Figure 6-3:
The range of
cells to be
included in
the chart.

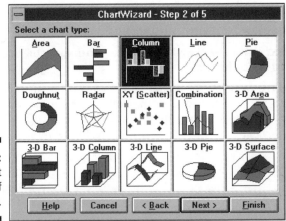

Figure 6-4:
The vast
array of
chart types.

6. **Click the picture of the chart type that you want to use and then click the Next button or press Enter to display the next ChartWizard dialog box (see Figure 6-5).**

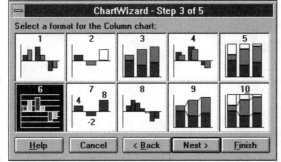

Figure 6-5:
The formats for the chart type.

7. **Click the picture of the chart format that you want to use and then click the Next button or press Enter to display the fourth ChartWizard dialog box (see Figure 6-6).**

The left side of this dialog box shows a preview of the chart and allows you to specify whether to use rows or columns for the data series (they're in rows in the example). The right side of the dialog box asks which rows (from the data you placed in your spreadsheet) to use for the x-axis labels (first 1 row is correct here because you want only *Jan, Feb,* and *Mar* as x-axis labels) and which columns (again, from the data on your spread-sheet) to use for the legend text (first 1 is correct here, too).

As you make option changes in this dialog box and the next one, your changes are reflected in the preview of the chart.

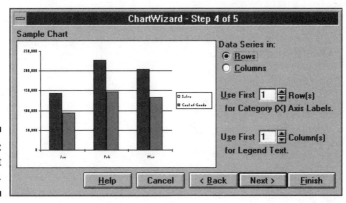

Figure 6-6:
Some chart options.

8. **Make any necessary changes and then click the Next button or press Enter to display the final ChartWizard dialog box (see Figure 6-7).**

   This dialog box allows you to specify whether you want to add a legend, as well as chart and axis titles.

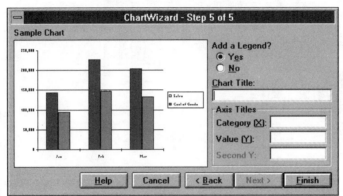

Figure 6-7: Options for legends and titles.

9. **After entering the titles you want, click the Finish button or press Enter to insert the finished chart into the worksheet, as shown in Figure 6-8.**

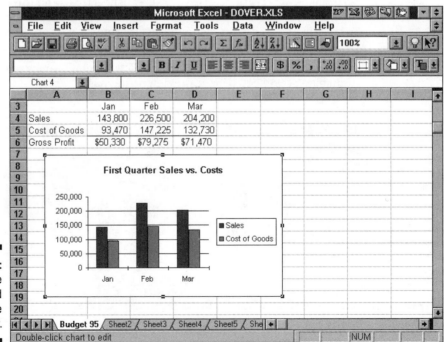

Figure 6-8: The completed chart in the worksheet.

- The little doohickies on the corners and the sides of the chart's border, called *handles*, indicate that the chart is selected.

- To resize the chart, position the mouse pointer on one of the handles and click and drag.

- You can reposition the chart by placing the mouse pointer inside the chart and clicking and dragging.

- As the status bar says, you can double-click the chart to edit individual objects within the chart. To change the formatting of the chart title, for example, double-click the chart, click the chart title, right-click to display the shortcut menu, and choose Format Chart Title to display the Format Chart Title dialog box.

- After editing the portions of the chart that you want to change, get out of Edit mode by clicking outside the chart. You must exit Edit mode to work with the worksheet data and make the view scroll bars reappear.

- Any changes that you make to the numbers in the worksheet are reflected immediately in the chart.

Changing chart types

If, after expending all that brainpower to create a chart with all the elements just the way you want them, you realize — horror of horrors — that you've selected the wrong chart type, don't sweat it. Changing chart types couldn't be easier.

To change the chart type, follow these steps:

1. **Make sure that the chart is in Edit mode.**

   You can tell that you're in Edit mode by the hashed border that surrounds the chart. If the chart isn't in Edit mode, double-click the chart.

2. **Click the Format menu and then click Chart Type.**

   The Chart Type dialog box appears. It should look pretty familiar because it's almost the same as the second ChartWizard dialog box, in which you originally chose the chart type.

3. **Click either the 2-D or 3-D option button in the Chart dimension portion of the dialog box and then click the picture of the chart type you want to use.**

4. **Click the OK button (or press Enter) and — poof! — the chart type changes, as shown in Figure 6-9.**

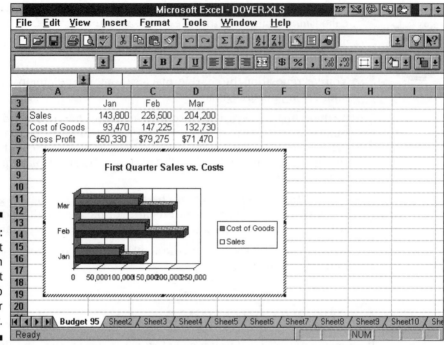

Figure 6-9:
The default
column
chart
changed to
a 3-D bar
chart.

✔ Changing the chart type can produce unexpected and disastrous results. If the chart looks really messed up after you change its type, click the Undo button in the Standard toolbar right away. It's also not a bad idea to save your workbook before making any major change such as this.

✔ You may need to reposition or resize the chart after changing its type.

Picking the best chart type for the job

Excel doesn't give you a mind-boggling variety of charts just for the fun of it. OK, they're a bunch of fun-loving guys and gals out there in Microsoft land, but sometimes they do things for a reason.

In this case, the reason is that some chart types are better than others for presenting some types of data. This book isn't big enough to describe all the nuances of all the various chart types, but here are some basic rules of thumb.

Column charts, Excel's default chart type, often are used for comparing two or more related data series at a specific point in time or a small amount of data over time. The column chart works for the example because it involves two data series (sales versus cost of goods) over time (a three-month period).

Bar charts are column charts turned on their sides; the columns are horizontal instead of vertical.

Pie charts are great for displaying proportional relationships among data items, such as the share that each month's sales contribute to sales for the quarter. The pie chart's primary limitation is that it can display only one data series, so it wouldn't work for the example.

Doughnut charts are similar to pie charts and are used for the same purpose. They have one major advantage over pie charts, however: they can be used to plot more than one data series. A doughnut chart that contains more than one data series uses a separate ring for each series.

Line charts are used to emphasize the continuity of data over time. These charts are also a good choice for showing trends. They are especially useful for showing large sets of data, such as sales of a product over a five-year period. Several of the line-chart formatting options are particularly useful for charting highs and lows, such as snowfall or stocks, and sometimes are referred to as high-low and high-low-close charts.

Area charts are essentially line charts with the spaces between the lines filled in.

Radar charts are similar to line charts but are often used to compare the whole value of several data series.

XY charts use both axes for values. This arrangement allows you to plot relationships between two data series, such as the effect of temperature on an electronic component's failure rate.

Combination charts allow you to combine two chart types to contrast multiple data series. For example, you might use the column-chart portion of a combination chart to plot store sales and a line chart to show the store's projected sales.

✔ Many of the chart types are available in 3-D, which just gives you a different look for the chart. Use this option if you like it.

✔ There are no hard and fast rules about which chart type must be used in each situation. What I've provided are just general guidelines. Experiment with different types and the many other options for making your charts get your points across as effectively as possible.

Printing Charts

If you have charts on separate sheets, printing them is no different from printing worksheets. Printing a chart that is in the same sheet as your worksheet data is also the same as printing a worksheet, as long as you include the range that the chart occupies in the print range.

To print only the chart in a worksheet, follow these steps:

1. **Double-click the chart to put it in Edit mode.**

   The chart will have a hashed border when it's in Edit mode.

2. **Click the File menu and then click Print (or press Ctrl+P).**

   The Print dialog box appears. The only option in the Print What portion is Selected Chart.

3. **Click the OK button.**

✔ Before clicking the OK button, it's a good idea to click the Print Preview button so that you'll know whether you're about to print the right stuff. If the preview looks good, click the Print button in the Preview window.

✔ Make sure that your printer is turned on, paper is loaded, and the on-line light is on.

✔ If you have a page-type printer, such as a laser printer, and your chart doesn't print properly, your printer may not have enough memory. You have two options. The first option is to add more memory to your printer. The guru who installed Office for you can help you with this process. (You'll probably have to come up with some money, though.) Your other option is to try printing the chart at a lower quality setting that won't require as much printer memory.

To print at lower quality, click the File menu in the menu bar and then click Page Setup. Click the Page tab of the Page Setup dialog box. Click the down arrow next to the Print Quality section and then click on Medium. Click OK to clear the dialog box and try printing again. If you still have no luck, you can repeat the process; this time, in the Page tab of the Page Setup dialog box, choose Low quality in the Print Quality box.

Chapter 7

Excel Features That Make Economists of Us All

*I*f I took a poll to find out how many readers of this book already know about the features covered in this chapter, I suspect the results would show that there are only six ... and three of them work for Microsoft.

If you really want to get the most out of Excel, you need to go beyond the obvious and expected features. For a glimpse into some useful and unexpected features, read on.

Finding Answers with Goal Seek

The typical worksheet works something like this: enter data, create formulas, get answers. Bor-ring! Wouldn't it be great if you could just tell Excel what answer you want and have it adjust the data so that you get that answer? Your wish is Excel's command.

The feature that performs this magical feat is called Goal Seek. Just tell Goal Seek what result you want and which cell value to change to get that result.

To find the answer that you've been seeking, follow these steps:

1. **Click the cell in which you want the new answer to appear. (This cell must be a formula.)**

2. **Click Tools⇨Goal Seek.**

   The Goal Seek dialog box appears, with the address of the selected cell in the Set cell text box (see Figure 7-1). Remember: those dollar signs indicate that the cell reference is absolute instead of relative.

3. **Click the To value text box and enter the answer that you want.**

   For example, you may want to find out what sales figure would be required to generate a gross-profit figure of $100,000, so you would enter **100000** in the To value text box.

4. **Click the By changing cell text box.**

   This box is where you tell Excel which value to change to reach your goal.

5. **Click the cell containing the value that you want Excel to change to get to your answer.**

   The cell to be changed must contain a value (a number), not a formula.

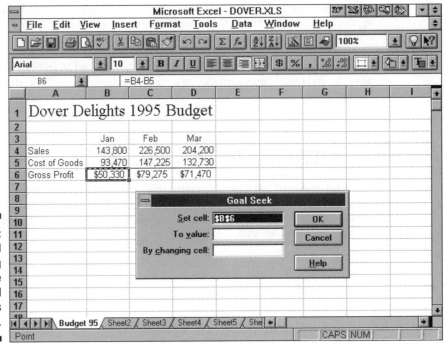

Figure 7-1:
The Goal Seek dialog box with the Set cell address entered.

6. Click the OK button.

As you can see in Figure 7-2, the changes have been made to provide the result that you requested, and the Goal Seek Status dialog box shows the target value and the current value, which should be the same.

7. Click the OK button to accept the changes or click Cancel to have the numbers revert to their original state.

✔ In some cases, the goal you are trying to reach is so complex that it may take your computer a while to find it. Be patient.

✔ In rare instances, Goal Seek may not be able to find the value that will give you exactly the answer you want, but it will get as close as possible.

✔ If you click the OK button in the Goal Seek Status dialog box by mistake and want the numbers back the way they were, click the Undo button in the Standard toolbar before doing anything else.

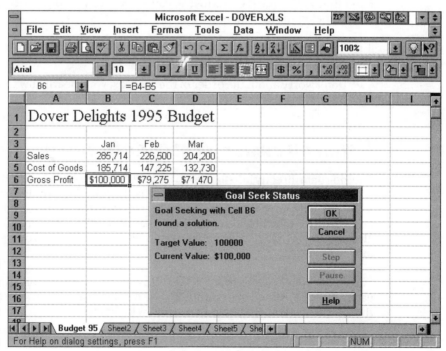

Figure 7-2:
Goal Seek
successfully
completed.

Sorting Tables and Other Cool Database Stuff

Excel isn't just for breakfast — I mean, spreadsheets — anymore. It can be the most efficient program for working with simple (and even not-so-simple) databases. As far as Excel is concerned, a database is just a bunch of information in table format that you want to store and manipulate.

To create an Excel database table, start by entering column headings to label the items of information that you want to include. For a customer list, for example, you might have items such as FIRST NAME, LAST NAME, and AD-DRESS. Each of these items is called a *field*. All the items in a single row of the table are called a *record*. So the database consists of a bunch of records that consist of a bunch of fields.

Enter the data for the records just as you enter data in a normal worksheet, directly below the field-name labels.

- ✔ Enter the field names (column headings) in UPPERCASE so that Excel automatically detects them as field names.

- ✔ Don't worry about the order of the records; you'll learn how to sort them a bit later in this chapter.

Using an easier form of data entry

Entering data directly into the database table is easy enough, but it does have some drawbacks. First, if you have lots of fields, you'll be scrolling back and forth, and you won't be able to see the first fields in the record as you enter the last. Second, each time you enter a new record, you'll have to find the next row after the end of the table. As your table grows, finding the last row can become more difficult.

Excel allows you to enter new records into a data form and automatically places each record at the end of the table. To use the data form, make sure that one of the cells in the table is selected, then follow these steps:

1. **From the menu bar, click Data⇨Form.**

   The data-form dialog box — with the name of the current sheet in the title bar — appears, displaying the first record (see Figure 7-3).

2. **Click the New button.**

   All the fields in the dialog box are cleared so that you can start entering a new record.

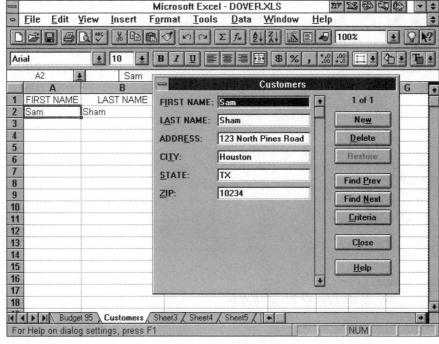

Figure 7-3:
The first
record
displayed in
the data
form.

3. **Enter the data for the first field and then press the Tab key to move to the next field.**

4. **Continue entering data until all the fields for the record are entered and then click the New button again (or just press Enter).**

   Each time that you click the New button, the new record is placed at the bottom of the table, the text boxes are cleared, and you can start entering the next record.

5. **After entering all the records for this session using the data form, click the Close button.**

✔ Don't forget to save your work every 10 to 20 minutes by clicking the Save button in the Standard toolbar.

✔ Format the fields in the existing records before using the data form. Each new record will use the formatting that you applied. If you format the Name fields with bold, for example, all new names will be bold.

✔ You can get into trouble if you enter ZIP codes as numbers. Before you enter new records with the data form, enter the ZIP code field in the first record as text so that Excel won't drop leading zeros. To do this, enter an apostrophe (') in front of the ZIP code.

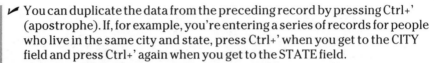
✔ You can duplicate the data from the preceding record by pressing Ctrl+' (apostrophe). If, for example, you're entering a series of records for people who live in the same city and state, press Ctrl+' when you get to the CITY field and press Ctrl+' again when you get to the STATE field.

✔ If you mess up a record, you can click the <u>R</u>estore button if you catch your error before adding the record to the table. If you've already added the record, you can edit it in the table after closing the data-form dialog box. Alternatively, you can click the Find <u>P</u>rev or Find <u>N</u>ext button until the offending record is displayed in the form and then click the <u>D</u>elete button.

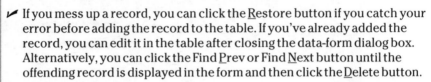
✔ Be consistent in the way that you enter records. You may want to merge some of the data with a Word document or another program. Use the same mixed-case format and don't use any spaces or punctuation in the fields.

✔ You can edit records in the data form. Display the record that you want to use by clicking the Find <u>P</u>rev or Find <u>N</u>ext button or click the <u>C</u>riteria button so that you can enter search criteria. If you mess up some of the data as you're editing, click the <u>R</u>estore button.

Sorting it all out

Sorting databases is something that you'll do frequently. You may want to sort the list by last name to make it easier to find a particular person in the list; perhaps you'll want to sort the list by ZIP code if you're creating mailing labels.

Doing a simple table sort is just a click away. (Well, two clicks, really, but why quibble?) To sort the table, follow these steps:

1. **Click any cell in the column by which you want to sort the table.**

   If you want the table sorted by last name, for example, click any cell in the column that contains the last names. That's one click, if you're counting.

   Figure 7-4 shows an unsorted table with a cell in the LAST NAME field selected.

2. **In the Standard toolbar, click the Sort Ascending button (to sort from A through Z) or the Sort Descending button (to sort from Z through A).**

   See? Just two clicks.

   Figure 7-5 shows the table sorted by last name.

✔ You can undo a sort by clicking the Undo button in the Standard toolbar immediately after sorting.

✔ If you want to sort by more than one field at a time, you'll need to use the Sort dialog box, which you open by clicking <u>D</u>ata⇨<u>S</u>ort from the menu bar. Then click <u>S</u>ort by last names and <u>T</u>hen by first names so that all the Smiths, for example, would be listed together, alphabetized by first names.

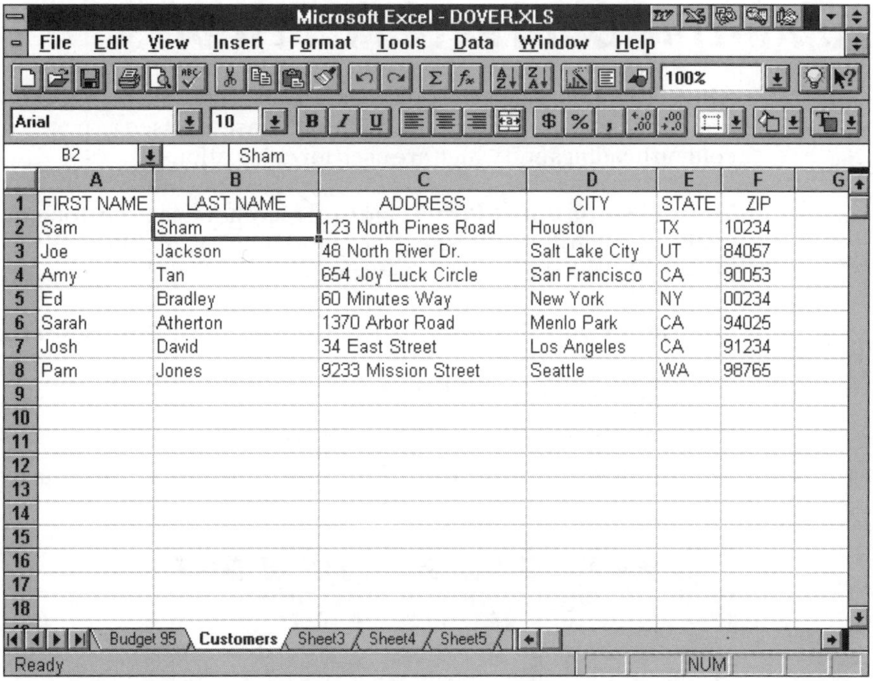

Figure 7-4:
Ready to
sort on the
LAST NAME
field.

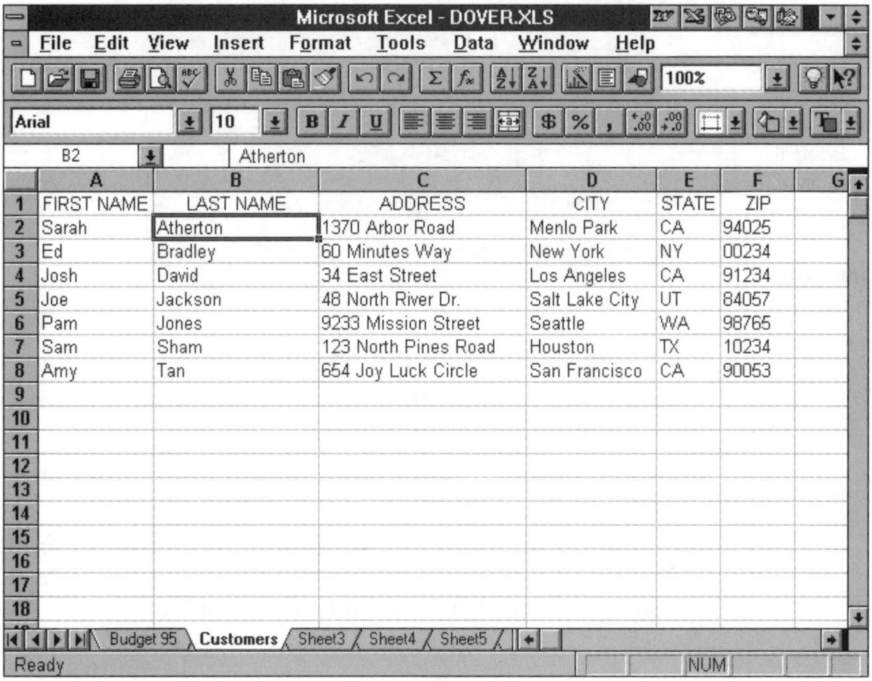

Figure 7-5:
No longer
out of sorts.

Analyzing Data with PivotTables

A PivotTable allows you to look at data in an Excel database in different ways. You can specify which fields from the database are used as page, row, and column headings and which are used for calculations.

You could use a simple PivotTable to display how many customers live in each state. Although PivotTables can be quite complex, creating this sort of PivotTable with the PivotTable Wizard is a snap.

To create a PivotTable with the PivotTable Wizard, follow these steps:

1. **Click any cell in the database.**

2. **From the menu bar, click Data⇨PivotTable.**

   The first PivotTable Wizard dialog box appears, as shown in Figure 7-6.

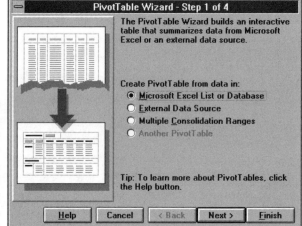

Figure 7-6: The first of four PivotTable Wizard dialog boxes.

3. **Click the Next button or press Enter.**

   The second PivotTable Wizard dialog box appears with the range of your table entered, as shown in Figure 7-7.

4. **Verify that the range is correct and then click the Next button or press Enter.**

   The third PivotTable Wizard dialog box appears (see Figure 7-8). This dialog box is where you specify which fields to use in the PivotTable. The field names appear as buttons on the right side of the dialog box.

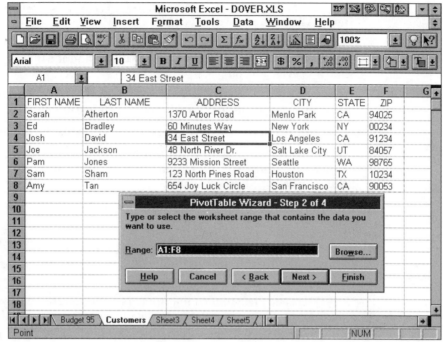

Figure 7-7:
The entire
table is
selected
automatically.

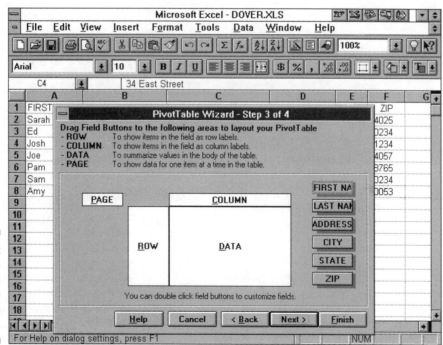

Figure 7-8:
Ready to
create the
structure
of the
PivotTable.

5. **Drag the appropriate field-name buttons into the PAGE, ROW, COLUMN, and DATA portions of the dialog box.**

   To create a simple PivotTable to count the number of customers in each state, drag the STATE button into the ROW portion and then drag STATE into the DATA portion.

   Notice that the STATE button becomes Count of STATE when it's dropped into the DATA portion of the dialog box, as shown in Figure 7-9.

6. **Click the Next button to display the final PivotTable Wizard dialog box.**

7. **In the PivotTable Starting Cell text box, enter a cell reference for the upper-left corner of the new PivotTable, as shown in Figure 7-10, or just click in a cell on your worksheet.**

8. **Click the Finish button to finish creating the PivotTable shown in Figure 7-11.**

✔ If you don't enter a reference for the PivotTable Starting Cell in the final PivotTable Wizard dialog box, the PivotTable will replace your database. Ouch!

✔ The Query and Pivot toolbar that appears when you create a PivotTable gives you tools for manipulating the PivotTable. You can clear this toolbar by clicking its close box.

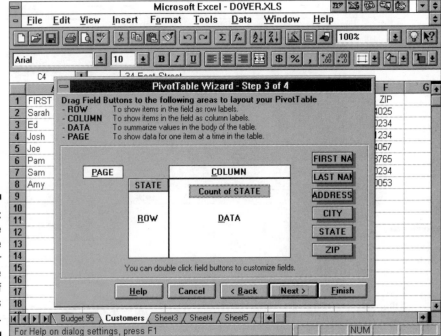

Figure 7-9: The PivotTable set up for a simple count of customers per state.

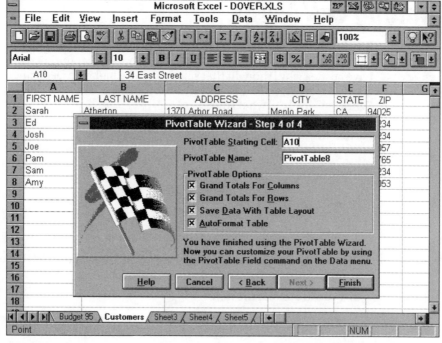

Figure 7-10:
The final
PivotTable
Wizard
dialog box
with a
starting cell
entered.

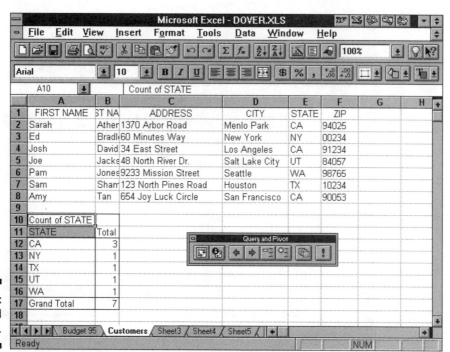

Figure 7-11:
The finished
PivotTable.

Adding Cell Notes

It's hard enough for me to remember why I made certain assumptions when I entered the data for my worksheets. Ten minutes after the entries are made, I have no idea why I thought that sales would be higher in December than June. It's even worse for other people who are looking at the worksheet, trying to figure out why I did what I did.

Fortunately, Excel makes it easy to add hidden notes that can explain a cell entry—assuming, of course, that you have an explanation. Perhaps you want to explain that the numbers in the Cost of Goods cells are a particular percentage of the Sales values.

To add a cell note, follow these steps:

1. **Click the cell to which you want to add a note.**

2. **From the menu bar, click Insert⇨Note to display the Cell Note dialog box, shown in Figure 7-12.**

3. **Type the text of the note.**

   You can add as much text as you want, but keep in mind that you want people to read the note. If it's too long, they may not bother.

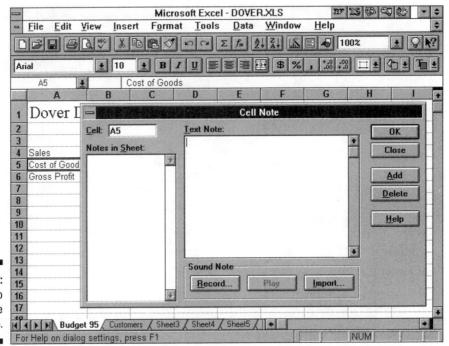

Figure 7-12: Ready to add a note for cell A5.

4. Click the OK button.

A small red rectangle appears in the upper-right corner of each cell with a note attached, as shown in Figure 7-13.

5. To see a note for a particular cell, click the cell; then click Insert⇨Note.

The Cell Note dialog box appears, with the note for the current cell displayed in the Text Note box.

✔ You can edit notes by clicking Insert⇨Note and then clicking the note you want to edit in the Notes in Sheet portion of the dialog box.

✔ If your computer has sound-recording capabilities, you can record spoken notes to attach to your cells. You can play a recorded note by double-clicking the cell that contains the recorded note. (It just might make your day to hear your boss shouting, "What the h*** were you thinking here? Are you on some kind of new medication?")

✔ Normally, notes don't print when you print your worksheets. If you want to print the notes with the worksheets, click File⇨Page Setup. In the Page Setup dialog box, click the Sheet tab, and then click the Notes check box in the Print area of the dialog box.

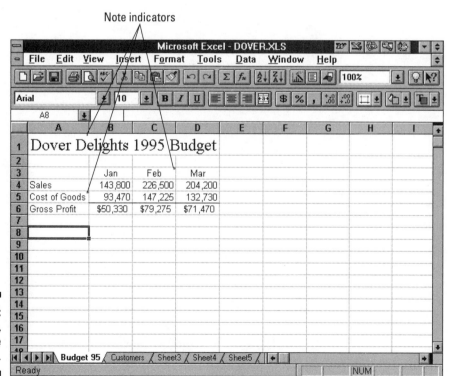

Figure 7-13:
Cells A1, A5, and C3 have notes.

Part III

Suddenly It's Show Time!

The 5th Wave   By Rich Tennant

"These two-color handouts are really going to give our presentation style!"

In this part...

*T*he third leg of Microsoft Office is PowerPoint, a special-ized presentation application. With PowerPoint at your side, you can sell ice in Alaska by using unique slides, overhead projections, and even (gulp) computers.

So after you've written the killer report and crunched all the numbers, coordinate your information into one slick presentation with PowerPoint.

Chapter 8

What Do You Mean *I* Have to Make the Presentation?

*P*resentations are as different from speeches as night is from day (although both are characterized by reduced lighting levels — sorry!). Contrary to what you may expect, however, presentations are a lot easier to prepare and deliver than speeches. This is true because when you deliver a speech, you're all alone: You're doing a (supposedly) serious version of stand-up humor with nothing but your voice to capture and maintain your audience's interest and enthusiasm.

Presentations are easier because you have an important crutch — visuals. These visuals can take the form of 35mm slides, black-and-white or color overhead transparencies, or computer images displayed on a monitor or projected on a screen. These visuals provide a framework for your presentation. Presentation visuals free you from the tyranny of following a "word-for-word" speech and allow you to do what you already do best: communicate on a one-to-one basis. With this comfort zone, you can now make your presentation an opportunity to look forward to rather than an opportunity to change your mind and move to Boise.

The purpose of this chapter is to help you make the transition from "speeches" to "presentations." You'll take a closer look at the elements that go into a successful presentation and show how PowerPoint 4 can help you make not only a successful, but an *enthusiastic*, transition from the back of the room to the front of the room. (If I could do it, you can, too. No one was ever more shy in front of a group than I used to be. Now my friends tell me I'm insufferable!)

The Four Essential Elements of Presentations

Presentations differ from speeches because presentations are more tangible. Speeches, for the most part, exist only on paper, which is read and then discarded (or stored in the bottom drawer of your desk for posterity). In contrast, presentations involve the following four printed elements:

Slides. Slides are the primary speaker-support materials. The term *slide* can be misleading sometimes because it refers to four types of visuals: 35mm slides, black-and-white transparencies, color transparencies, and images displayed on a computer screen or placed on a screen by a projector driven by a computer.

Outline. PowerPoint allows you to print your presentation in Outline view. A printout of your presentation's outline contains slide titles and the text of bulleted lists. The outline is valuable because you easily can review your presentation at a glance to make sure that you have covered all the points and that your arguments appear in a logical sequence.

Notes. Notes refer to printed pages containing *thumbnails*, or reduced-sized copies of each of your visuals, plus the points you want to discuss while the presentation is being projected. Notes permit you to review and rehearse your presentation without referring to the actual slides or overheads. Notes reduce the chance of getting finger marks on the slides or getting them out of order. Notes also permit you to review your presentation on an airplane or in a hotel room.

Handouts. Handouts permit you to provide your audience with a tangible reminder of your presentation and the points that you covered. Handouts allow your audience to review your presentation and share it with others who were unable to attend. Handouts add posterity to your presentation.

A presentation is more than the sum of its parts. Your ability to inform, motivate, or persuade will be weakened if just one of the above elements is missing. For example, without notes, you'll find it difficult to rehearse your presentation, and you may inadvertently omit important points. Without handouts, your audience will have nothing (other than their scribbled notes) to remind them of your sterling words. And organization is certain to suffer if you don't have a printed outline to refer to.

But, never fear, PowerPoint makes it easy to prepare all four parts. Let's get started.

Getting Started with PowerPoint

Microsoft PowerPoint 4 is both the most advanced and the simplest route between the concept of an idea and its presentation that has ever been developed. One of the reasons for this point, of course, is Microsoft's long experience with PowerPoint; PowerPoint was the first presentation program to appear. PowerPoint takes the work — and the worry — out of standing up in front of a group and opening your mouth.

There are two ways to run PowerPoint. The easiest way is to click on the PowerPoint icon in the Microsoft Office Manager toolbar at the top of your screen (see the appendix for installation instructions). The PowerPoint icon is the third from the left. If you haven't installed the Microsoft Office Manager toolbar, you can run PowerPoint by opening the Program Manager and clicking on the PowerPoint icon located in either the PowerPoint group or the Microsoft Office group, depending on how you've organized your Program Manager (see Figure 8-1).

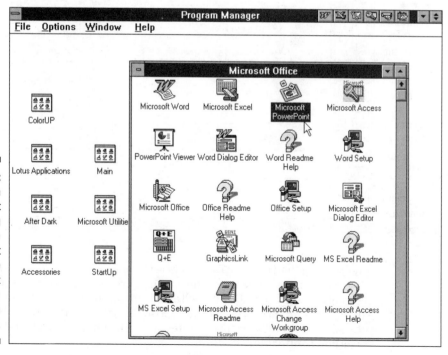

Figure 8-1:
You can run PowerPoint by clicking on the PowerPoint icon in the Microsoft Office program group.

Microsoft's commitment to continuing education is reflected by the first screen to appear, the Tip of the Day. A different tip appears every time you load the program, as shown in Figure 8-2. You can disable these tips by removing the check mark (by clicking it) from the Show Tips at Startup check box, but then you'd be missing out on some great ideas. The tips provide an easy way to improve your ability to prepare and deliver more effective presentations by covering topics from design issues to a review of the commands and keyboard shortcuts that can help you work more efficiently.

If your morning coffee hasn't yet taken hold but you want to look busy, click on the Next Tip button in the Tip of the Day dialog box. Or if you feel that you can never learn enough and you want a mini-seminar on PowerPoint, click on the More Tips button, which presents a list of Tip of the Day contents, subdivided into categories. To close this window, double-click in the control box at the upper-left corner of the window.

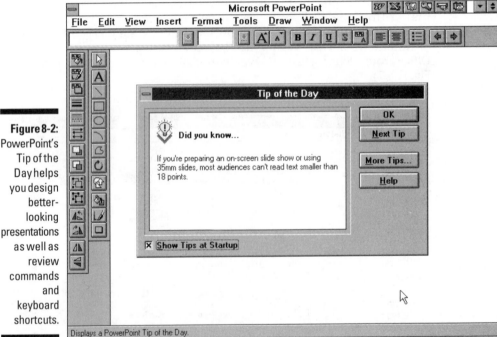

Figure 8-2:
PowerPoint's Tip of the Day helps you design better-looking presentations as well as review commands and keyboard shortcuts.

After reading the Tip of the Day, click on OK or press Enter, which takes you to PowerPoint's opening screen. The opening screen offers you four ways to begin creating a new presentation as well as a fifth option that permits you to open an existing presentation (see Figure 8-3). You choose the fifth option when you're a veteran PowerPoint user (in a chapter or two, just hold your horses!). The PowerPoint options include the following:

✔ The AutoContent Wizard option takes you by the hand and gives you a powerful jump-start in choosing the words for your presentation. This option helps you avoid the stress and procrastination of facing a blank screen. The AutoContent Wizard works by asking you questions about the purpose of your presentation and formats your presentation on the basis of your responses.

✔ The Pick a Look Wizard option concentrates on the appearance of your presentation visuals and support materials (notes that you'll refer to while delivering your presentation as well as audience handouts). You'll choose this option often after you get the hang of presentation planning and pacing.

✔ The Template option permits you to scroll through a list of available presentation templates and preview each option.

✔ Choose the Blank Presentation option if you have a good idea of the content of your presentation and you want to get it into workable form as quickly as possible, without being distracted by the appearance of your visuals. After you have all of your ideas in place, you can apply a template or reformat your presentation from scratch.

✔ The Open an Existing Presentation option duplicates the File⇨Open command and presents you with a list of previously created presentation files.

Figure 8-3:
PowerPoint's opening screen allows you to work as independently as you want on new presentations or to continue working on an existing presentation.

You can also choose from among these options in the New Presentation dialog box, which appears every time you select File⇨New.

Working with the AutoContent Wizard

PowerPoint's AutoContent Wizard presents the shortest distance between your ideas and a finished presentation. Jump right in with the AutoContent Wizard to immediately get your feet wet so that you can become familiar with presentation planning in general and PowerPoint in particular.

In the PowerPoint dialog box, double-click on AutoContent Wizard or click on its radio button and then click on OK or press Enter. The first AutoContent Wizard dialog box welcomes you to PowerPoint Land. Just click on the Next button after you read the introductory paragraphs.

Things get more interesting in the second AutoContent Wizard dialog box, as shown in Figure 8-4. The Wizard comes out and bluntly asks, "What are you going to talk about?" If you can't answer this question at this point, perhaps you should turn off your computer and do some serious thinking about the goals of your presentation. If you *can* provide the answer, your response becomes the title for your presentation. The second AutoContent Wizard dialog box also confirms your name and your firm's name. You can also enter a different company name, if you're preparing a presentation for someone else, and other information, such as the date of your presentation or the name of the event where the presentation is going to take place — the 1994 Consumer Electronics Show, for example. This information is repeated on your presentation visuals and handouts. When you're finished entering the information in this dialog box, click on the Next button.

Each AutoContent Wizard dialog box contains a Back button as well as a Next button. These buttons enable you to change your mind at any point, back up, and choose a different title or type of presentation.

The third AutoContent Wizard dialog box, shown in Figure 8-5, encourages you to be even more focused in your thinking. It offers a selection of presentation categories. Each time you choose a category, a different agenda (or list of topics) appears. These topics help you begin thinking about the contents and pacing of each type of presentation by providing a framework for your thinking. Your options include the following:

- ✔ Recommending a Strategy
- ✔ Selling a Product, Service, or Idea
- ✔ Training
- ✔ Reporting Progress
- ✔ Communicating Bad News
- ✔ General

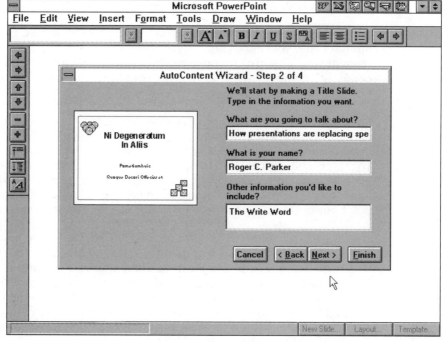

Figure 8-4:
The second
AutoContent
Wizard
dialog box
invites you
to provide a
title for your
presentation.

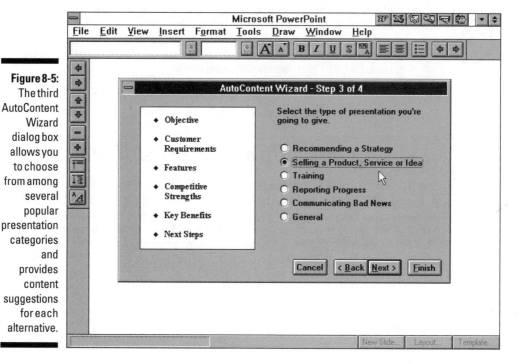

Figure 8-5:
The third
AutoContent
Wizard
dialog box
allows you
to choose
from among
several
popular
presentation
categories
and
provides
content
suggestions
for each
alternative.

Click on the Recommending a Strategy option and click on the Next button.

The final AutoContent Wizard dialog box exists primarily so that you can back up and change your mind about any previous responses. This dialog box also reminds you that you can choose a different look for your presentation by choosing Format⊏>Pick a Look Wizard. Click on the Finish button after you finish reading this information.

Clicking on the Finish button takes you to the Outline view of your presentation and also displays PowerPoint's Cue Cards (see Figure 8-6). The headings visible in the Outline view guide you through the task of developing the content of your presentation. The Outline view also offers suggested titles for each of your slides and prompts you to develop bullet points to support each title. The Cue Cards show you how to use PowerPoint more quickly and efficiently. At this point, you can make several decisions, which include the following:

✔ You can temporarily hide the Cue Cards so that you gain some valuable working space on-screen by double-clicking on the control bar at the upper-left side of the Cue Cards title bar. After you hide the Cue Cards, you may notice that the Outline view of your presentation doesn't extend completely to the right side of your monitor. To fill your monitor with your outline, click on the upward-pointing arrow at the upper-right side of the Presentation title bar to make the Outline view as large as possible. To restore the Cue Cards, select Help⊏>Cue Cards.

✔ Rather than hiding the Cue Cards, you can minimize them to an icon — resembling a hand with two cards in a V formation — at the bottom of the screen by clicking on the downward-pointing arrow at the upper-right side of the Cue Card title bar. Simply double-click on the Cue Cards icon to reveal the Cue Cards when you need them.

✔ You can select the view of your presentation by choosing to work in Slide view rather than Outline view.

Entering and editing text in Outline view

Notice that the first line of the outline contains the title that you entered in the second AutoContent Wizard dialog box (refer to Figure 8-4). The topics that follow in the Outline view are appropriate for the type of presentation you instructed the AutoContent Wizard to choose. The text that appears in each topic is *boilerplate* or idea-generating text intended to get your creative juices flowing when you follow the instructions in the Outline view, answer questions, or provide the information requested.

Figure 8-6:
Your
AutoContent
Wizard
journey
ends with an
outline that
helps you
develop the
content of
your
presentation
and Cue
Cards that
help you
choose
the most
comfortable
view for
working
on your
presentation.

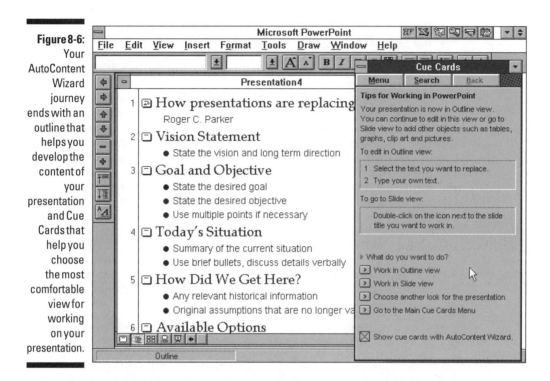

Working with PowerPoint's Cue Cards

PowerPoint's Cue Cards offer an easy way to figure out how to do the tasks you most frequently need to produce or deliver a presentation. The introductory Cue Card lists tips for working in PowerPoint. Click on the bottom option that tells you to go to the main Cue Cards menu. The first Cue Card screen presents the ten tasks that users most frequently need help in accomplishing. Each task is introduced by a small button with an arrow pointing to the right.

Because the AutoContent Wizard opens in Outline view, the first Cue Card visible deals with editing in Outline view or switching to other views. For more information about any topic, click on the button adjacent to the task. The appropriate Cue Card immediately appears, describing the steps necessary to accomplish the task. If the topic is too long for a single Cue Card, a Next button appears at the lower-right side of the Cue Card.

After you have finished reading the Cue Card (or Cards), click on the Back button, which eventually returns you to the introductory Cue Card.

If the task for which you need assistance isn't listed on the Cue Card, click on the Search button, which opens the Help program's Search dialog box. You can then either type a word describing the appropriate task or scroll through the alphabetical list of topics until you encounter the desired topic. After you locate the topic, select it (click on it with the left mouse button) and click on the Show Topics button. This step reveals a list of other topics in the bottom text box. Select one of the listed topics and click on the Go to button. Or, even better, simply double-click on the topic. Either approach takes you directly to the Help screen describing the task.

Information you enter into each outline topic automatically appears on the appropriate slide when you switch to the Slide view of your presentation. (You can, of course, replace boilerplate text with your text in PowerPoint's Slide view, in which case your changes will appear in the outline when you return to Outline view.)

Notice the icon — or rounded-corner box — next to each topic. Each icon indicates that the adjacent text appears on a different slide. Notice also that the icon next to the first slide is a bit different than the icons introducing the slides that follow (refer to Figure 8-6). The triangle and circle in the first icon indicate that this is a title slide. Unlike the slides that follow, title slides do not contain arguments or information. They are intended to appear on-screen while you introduce yourself and discuss your goals for the presentation.

To see more of the presentation — the remaining slides — you can do any of the following actions:

✔ Click on the downward-pointing arrow at the bottom of the vertical scroll bar located along the right edge of the screen. This action scrolls the screen one line at a time, revealing more of the Outline.

✔ Click on the elevator box in the vertical scroll bar and drag in a downward direction. This action permits you to quickly advance through your presentation.

✔ Click just below the elevator box. This action advances you through your presentation one window at a time.

Notice how the suggested slide titles in the Outline provide you with a framework for your presentation. The slide titles and bulleted points may not be exactly what you need, but they provide a starting point that you can massage into shape. To replace the *boilerplate*, or *placeholder*, text in the outline with the actual words that will develop and support your argument, do the following:

1. **Position the mouse pointer to the left of the title or bulleted item that you want to replace and select the words by dragging to the right.**

   The words now appear in reverse: white type against a black background.

2. **Type the desired text and press Enter.**

3. **Select the text in the next item that you want to replace, type the new text, and press Enter.**

   Do this step for each item that you want to replace.

4. **To add another bulleted item under a heading, simply press Enter and type the text that you want to add.**

   Notice that a new bullet appears each time you press Enter.

Previewing your work

To preview a completed slide, simply double-click on the slide icon next to the slide you want to view. This action takes you to Slide view and shows how your words will appear when formatted with the typeface, type size, type styles, and colors of the default PowerPoint presentation template. (Later in this chapter, I'll describe how to choose a different presentation format and create your own default PowerPoint template — but that's a story in itself! I digress....)

If you want to enlarge the view of the slide so that it fills the whole screen — without the distraction of PowerPoint's menus, toolbar, and scroll bars — place the mouse pointer over the Slide Show button (the fifth button from the left, that looks like a screen) located at the lower-left side of the horizontal scroll bar. The words `Slide Show` appear above the button, and a description of the Slide Show feature appears in the status bar at the bottom of the screen. Click on the button and notice how the slide is enlarged to fill your entire screen, providing an even better view of the slide. To return to normal view, press the Escape key — the gray key to the left of the function keys at the top of the keyboard.

To return to Outline view, place the mouse pointer over the second button from the left on the horizontal scroll bar. The words `Outline view` appear above the button, and a description of this view appears in the status bar at the bottom of the screen. After you click on this button, you return to the Outline view from which you started.

Rearranging slides in Outline view

Rearranging the order of your presentation is easy when you are in Outline view. Simply follow these steps:

1. **Click and hold down the mouse button on the slide icon whose position you want to change and move the mouse pointer to the right.**

   The slide icon turns black and all the text, both title and body, appears in reverse. More important, the four-headed "movement" arrow appears.

2. **While you hold down the left mouse button, drag the icon to the position where you want the highlighted text to appear.**

   Notice that a horizontal line appears that indicates where the highlighted text will be located after you release the mouse button.

3. **Release the mouse button.**

   The renumbered slide appears in the new location.

Changing the level of outline points

You can promote or demote outline levels, making some points subordinate to others, by following these steps:

1. **Position the insertion point in front of the first word in the outline level of the slide you want to change, type the new text for the new level, and press Enter.**

   Notice that the insertion point appears in the next outline level.

2. **Click on the Demote button (the right-pointing arrow on the toolbar to the left of your screen) to make the new text appear at a lower level than the original text or click on the Promote button (the left-pointing arrow) to make the new text appear at a higher level.**

   The demoted text is introduced by a >> (indent more) symbol and appears to the right in a smaller type size. The promoted text is introduced by a << (indent less) symbol and appears to the left in a larger type size.

3. **To demote or promote text that already exists in a slide, simply position the insertion point anywhere in the appropriate text and click on the Demote or Promote button.**

   The line will be pushed to the right or the left and will be introduced by the appropriate symbols, depending on which button you choose.

Once again, you can review your work by double-clicking on the slide number. Notice how the text has been reformatted.

To move from Outline view to Slide view, you can also click on the Slide view button, located to the extreme left of the horizontal scroll bar at the bottom of your screen. The Slide view is your normal "working" view and contains the slide you're working on plus PowerPoint's menus, toolbars, and scroll bars.

Adding and deleting slides in Outline view

Suppose that you think of a new topic that you want covered by its own slide. You can easily insert a new slide in the outline. First, position the insertion point at the end of the last line of the slide before the location where you want to add the new slide. Then you can do one of the following actions:

- ✔ Choose the Insert⇨New Slide command.
- ✔ Press the Ctrl+M keyboard shortcut (makes sense to me; how about you?).
- ✔ Click on the New Slide button at the bottom of the screen (the third button from the right).

When a new slide icon appears, start typing. The first line you type is the title. After you type the title, press Enter. The next line you type is the first outline level. Be sure to press Enter after each outline level you type.

To delete a slide, click to the left of the slide number. The slide icon and all text appears in reverse. Then you can do one of the following actions to delete the slide:

✔ Select Edit⇨Cut if you want to place the deleted slide in the Clipboard and insert it into another outline.

✔ Select Edit⇨Clear if you're done with the slide forever.

✔ Press the Backspace key.

✔ Press the Delete key.

Instantly, the selected slide disappears and the remaining slides are renumbered.

Hiding and revealing outline levels

Organization is one of the most important keys to success. To get a better idea of the sequence of your presentation visuals, you can choose to show just the slide titles in Outline view. This kind of outline eliminates the distraction created in viewing not only slide titles but also the supporting details contained on each slide. Because more titles can fit on-screen or on each printed page, you can get a better overview of your presentation sequence. You can hide the topics for individual slides or for your entire presentation.

To hide everything but the titles throughout your entire outline, click on the Show Titles button, the third button from the bottom of the toolbar to the left of your screen (see Figure 8-7). Instantly, you can see your entire presentation at a glance by viewing just the titles.

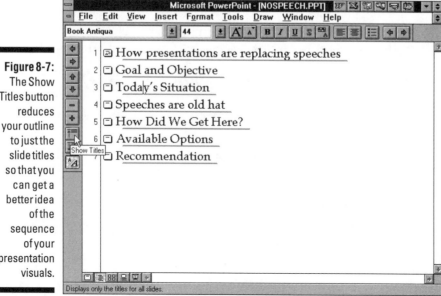

Figure 8-7:
The Show Titles button reduces your outline to just the slide titles so that you can get a better idea of the sequence of your presentation visuals.

To once again reveal your complete outline, click on the Show All button, the second button from the bottom of the toolbar to the left of your screen (the one with the downward-pointing arrow and more horizontal lines). Clicking on this button restores all the outline levels.

To hide the text in an individual slide so that just the title appears, position the mouse pointer in the title of the slide and click on the Collapse Selection button in the toolbar to the left (the one with the minus sign). To reveal the collapsed text, click on the Expand Selection button (the one with the plus sign).

Printing an outline

Printing the outline of your presentation allows you to share your presentation with your clients, coworkers, and supervisors so that you can get their comments and suggestions as early as possible — instead of later, at deadline time, when it's too late to incorporate their suggestions.

To print the Outline view of your presentation, follow these steps:

1. **Choose the File⇨Print command (or use the Ctrl+P keyboard shortcut).**

   The Print dialog box appears.

2. **Click on the downward-pointing arrow next to the Print What pull-down menu.**

3. **Click on Outline view to select it.**

4. **Be sure that the appropriate printer — if you have more than one attached to your computer — appears at the top, next to the word Printer.**

   If the appropriate printer doesn't appear in the dialog box, click on the Printer button, highlight the desired printer, and choose OK.

5. **After you're satisfied with the settings, click the OK button or press Enter.**

Saving your work as a PowerPoint file

After you get your outline in the shape you want it in, you should save the file. To save your work, do the following:

1. **Choose File⇨Save (or use the Ctrl+S keyboard shortcut).**

   The Save As dialog box appears.

2. **Enter a filename in the File Name box.**

   PowerPoint automatically applies the .PPT extension, which identifies this as a PowerPoint 4 presentation.

3. **After you have verified that the file will be saved in the correct directory, click on OK or press Enter.**

Working with the Pick a Look Wizard

Using the Pick a Look Wizard offers a totally different way to work with
PowerPoint. Select File⟳New to return to the New Presentation screen shown
earlier in this chapter (see Figure 8-3). This time, instead of clicking on the
AutoContent Wizard radio button, click on the Pick a Look Wizard radio button
and then click OK.

You're presented with a nine-slide sequence of dialog boxes that will help you
format, or determine, the appearance of your presentation by offering choices
for appropriate layout, colors, and typography *before* you develop the ideas.

After the first Pick a Look Wizard screen appears, read it and click on the Next
button. The second Pick a Look Wizard screen is more important. It asks you
which presentation format you're going to use to deliver your presentation.
Click on the radio button next to a desired format and click on the Next button.
Your alternatives include

- Black-and-white overheads
- Color overheads
- On-screen presentation
- 35mm slides

This decision is vital because color choices should be determined by the
presentation format. Color overhead transparencies, for example, require light
backgrounds and dark type; however, color slides work best with dark backgrounds and light type.

The third Pick a Look Wizard dialog box presents you with a choice of
PowerPoint's four most popular and distinctly different presentation formats
and allows you to preview them (see Figure 8-8). The dialog box also provides
access to other presentation templates installed when you loaded PowerPoint
onto your hard disk.

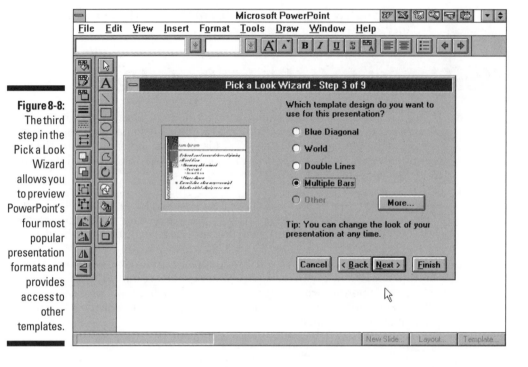

Figure 8-8:
The third
step in the
Pick a Look
Wizard
allows you
to preview
PowerPoint's
four most
popular
presentation
formats and
provides
access to
other
templates.

Feel free to experiment by clicking on the radio buttons next to the Blue Diagonal, World, Double Lines, and Multiple Bars options. As you click on the options, a different thumbnail preview of your choice appears in the Preview window.

To see how your choice of presentation format influences the color decisions that Pick a Look Wizard chooses, click on the Back button, which returns you to the second Pick a Look Wizard dialog box. Choose another presentation format (such as 35mm slides), click on the Next button (which returns you to Step 3), and notice that the thumbnail preview appears in a different color. These new colors are more suitable for 35mm slide presentations.

After you are satisfied with your choice in the third dialog box, click on the Next button.

Previewing additional options

If—picky, picky you—you didn't find exactly the look you were after in the third Pick a Look Wizard dialog box, don't despair. Instead, click on the More button, which advances you to the Presentation Template dialog box where you can preview every layout available for the presentation format you have chosen (see the accompanying figure).

You can drag the elevator box to scroll through the list of available templates, or you can use the up- and down-arrow keys. To preview a template, simply click on its title, and a preview appears in the preview window, appropriately colored for the presentation format you have chosen.

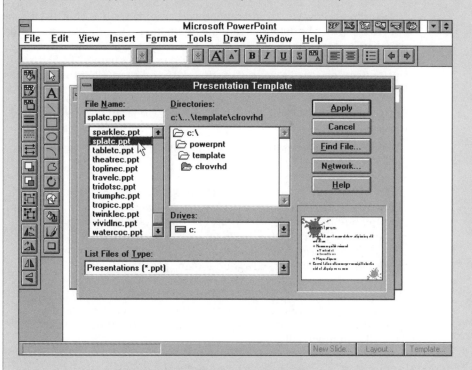

After you have selected the filename of a desired template, click on the Apply button, which returns you to the Pick a Look Wizard dialog box. (You can also select the name of the template without clicking on the Apply button by doubling-clicking on the template's filename.)

Step 4 in the Pick a Look Wizard allows you to determine how you want to print your presentation. Click on the check boxes next to the options you want to print. These options include Full Page Slides, Speaker's Notes, Audience Handout Pages, and Outline Pages. When you have selected all the desired options, click on the Next button.

The next series of four Pick a Look Wizard dialog boxes is extremely important and represents an important advance over previous versions of PowerPoint (as well as most other presentation programs). These dialog boxes include the following options that allow you to add repeating information to your pages:

- ✔ Slide options allow you to add repeating text to each slide. This text can be your firm's title (the default, available by clicking in the check box next to your firm's name), or you can enter the title of your presentation (so it appears in small print on every slide) or your client's name. The Slide Options screen also allows you to add a date and/or number to your slides by simply clicking in the check box next to the desired option.
- ✔ Notes options permit you to add repeating text, page numbers, and dates to your notes.
- ✔ Handout options and outline options also allow you to add repeating text, page numbers, and dates to these pages.

Click on Finish when you are through formatting the outline options. The ninth Pick a Look Wizard congratulates you on your work and gives you the option of changing your mind by pressing the Back button or completing your presentation by clicking the Finish button. Suddenly, you advance to the Slide view for the first slide in your presentation. At this point, your presentation has been formatted, and you're guaranteed a good-looking presentation!

Note the repeating text and the symbols for the slide number and date along the bottom of the slide in Figure 8-9. The two slashes indicate where the printing date of the presentation will appear. The two pound signs indicate where the slide number will appear.

At this point, you can work directly on each slide by responding to PowerPoint's prompts to add titles, subtitles, and other text to each slide. By working in Slide view, you get the immediate feedback and pleasure of seeing your words as they will appear in the typeface, type size, and color determined by the Pick a Look Wizard. The advantage of working in Slide view is that you aren't tempted to add more text than there is room for. You can insert line breaks to avoid long lines followed by short lines. The disadvantage, of course, is that you can become distracted by the beauty of your slides, instead of concentrating on the words.

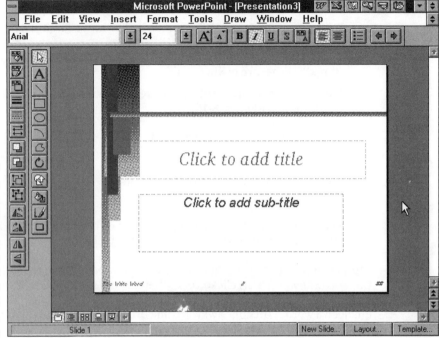

Figure 8-9:
The Pick a
Look Wizard
concludes
by bringing
you to the
Slide view
of the
formatted
slide.

Working in Slide View

Most people spend most of their time working in Slide view, fixing up their slides by editing and deleting text; adding new slides; and adding illustrations, regular charts, organization charts, or tables. When necessary, you can also choose a different presentation template (or combination of layout, colors, and typography).

Entering, editing, and deleting text

In Slide view, the first thing you want to do is replace the title and subtitle in the first slide with something more appropriate to your presentation (unless, of course, you want your title to be "Click to add title"). To replace the title and subtitle placeholders, follow these steps:

1. **Click anywhere inside the Click to add title box (see Figure 8-9).**

   A border of diagonal lines appears, and the insertion point begins blinking in the center of the rectangle.

2. **Enter the desired title.**

   For my example, I typed "Steam Railroading In the Twenty-First Century."

3. **Click inside the Click to add sub-title box and enter the desired subtitle.**

   I typed "The return of King Coal."

4. **Click anywhere on the title and observe the results of your artistic excellence (see Figure 8-10)!**

If you didn't get the titles quite right the first time, you can easily select the text for editing it in any one of three ways:

- ✔ Double-click on a single word to select it.

- ✔ Triple-click to select a sentence.

- ✔ Highlight text for deletion or replacement by holding down the left mouse button and dragging through the text to select it.

In my example, I double-clicked on the word *Railroading* and replaced it with the word *Engines*. Then I clicked elsewhere on the slide to see the result of the change (see Figure 8-11). Notice how the line breaks were adjusted after I changed a word. To fix this awkward line break, press the Enter key after the word *the* in the first line. This action balances the line lengths and avoids awkward word splits.

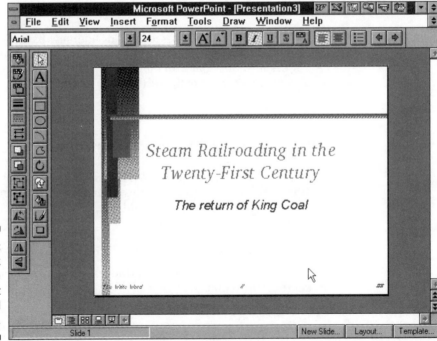

Figure 8-10:
Step back
and admire
your first
formatted
slide.

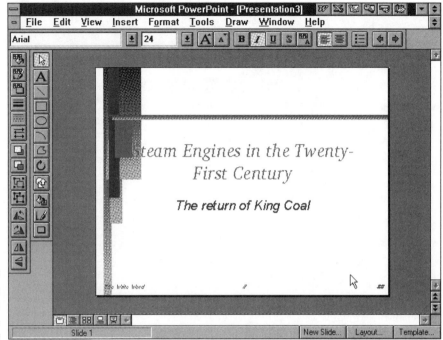

Figure 8-11:
Editing the
slide's title.

I included the example in Figure 8-11 to emphasize the importance of paying attention to details when working with PowerPoint (or any other software program). Because so much happens in the background, it is easy to be lazy and to get lulled into a false sense of security. Your audiences will prejudge your words on the basis of the way you handle details. Always remember that small mistakes — even those as small as an awkward line break — appear really huge when projected!

Adding slides

There are two steps involved in adding slides while you're working in Slide view. First, you must inform PowerPoint that you want to add a slide. Second, you must choose the type of slide you want to add: a single bulleted list, a two-column bulleted list, a chart, a table, and so on.

There are several ways you can add a slide to your presentation. You can select Insert⇨New Slide (Ctrl+M), or you can click on the New Slide button along the lower-right side of your screen. Either alternative takes you to PowerPoint's New Slide dialog box, shown in Figure 8-12, where you can choose the type of slide you want to add. Each choice represents a slide layout consistent with the format of the starting template you chose in the Pick a Look Wizard. You can choose from 20 different types of slide layouts. To see them all, use the vertical scroll bar.

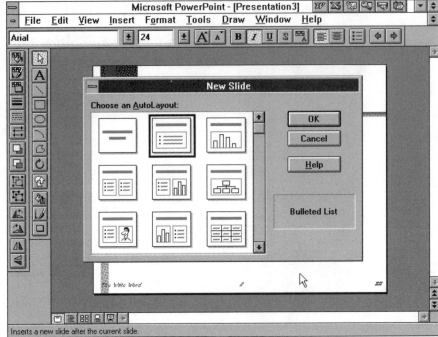

Figure 8-12:
The New
Slide dialog
box
presents
you with 20
different
types of
slide layouts
to choose
from by
using the
vertical
scroll bar.

Each time you click on one of the thumbnail layouts in the New Slide dialog box, a brief description of the layout appears at the lower right. Each layout contains a title plus a bulleted list, an organization chart, and a table; or a combination of a bulleted list and an illustration, graph, table, or organization chart.

Adding a bulleted list to slides

To add a single bulleted list to the slide, click on the middle AutoLayout thumbnail on the first row and click on OK or press Enter. (Double-clicking directly on the sample also selects it.)

Get in the habit of double-clicking on options to select them rather than clicking once and then clicking on the OK button or pressing Enter. Double-clicking saves time as well as wear and tear on Righty, your wrist, and Mickey, your mouse. (With apologies to the Lefties in the audience, of course. Political correctness, and all . . .)

Once again, click on the Click to add title box and enter a desired title. To add an additional supporting point, click on the Click to add text box, enter the text for the supporting point, and press Enter. If you want to add more supporting points, continue to type the text and press Enter for each point you want to

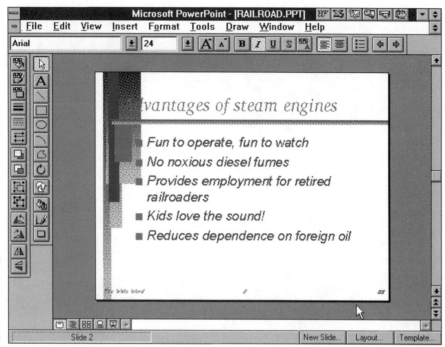

Figure 8-13:
A formatted
slide with a
bulleted list.

make. If you accidentally added an extra Enter, don't worry: Simply backspace over it, and it disappears. After you have finished, click elsewhere on the slide. To get a feel for what the slide should look like, examine Figure 8-13.

Adding a two-column bulleted list

To add a two-column bulleted list slide, click on the New Slide button or select Insert➪New Slide or use the Ctrl+M keyboard shortcut to add another slide. In the New Slide dialog box, PowerPoint provides the last AutoLayout thumbnail selected as the default selection. To choose your new selection, select the AutoLayout thumbnail in the middle of the left-hand column. The words 2 Column Text appear in the description box to the right. Click on OK or press Enter.

After the new slide appears on-screen, click in the title area and type the title. Then click on the Click to add text box on the left and type the text for each point you want to include in this column. Be sure to press Enter after each point. Then click in the second column's Click to add text box and type in the text for each point you want to include in this column. Again, be sure to press Enter after each point. Your slide should look something like the one in Figure 8-14.

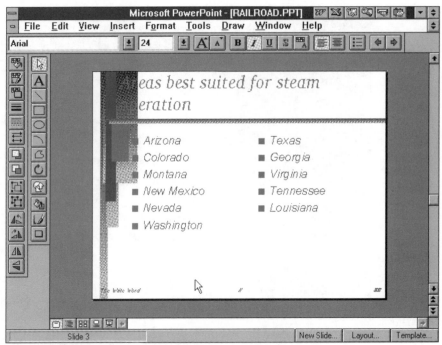

Figure 8-14:
A completed
two-column
bulleted list.

Notice, once again, that the first line of the title is noticeably longer than the second line. Get in the habit of reviewing your work as you create it. Use the Enter key to break slide titles at logical pauses so that the lines are approximately the same length.

Using the Spelling Checker to Review Your Work

There are two ways you can proofread and review your work. One way is to use PowerPoint's spelling checker to make sure that there are no embarrassing typographical errors in either your presentation visuals or your handouts. Your credibility is immediately diminished when an audience member points out an error in a slide or an overhead — and there is a breed of human created specifically for this purpose! The second way of reviewing your work is to use the Slide Show and Slide Sorter views to make sure that your arguments are presented in the proper order.

Checking your spelling

To check your spelling, choose the Tools⇨Spelling command or use the F7 keyboard shortcut. PowerPoint immediately begins spell checking your document. If PowerPoint discovers a misspelled word or a word it doesn't recognize, it stops at the word, displays the slide, and displays the Spelling dialog box, too.

Suppose, for example, that you accidentally typed the word *ise* instead of *is* in a slide. PowerPoint stops at the word *ise* in the slide and displays the Spelling dialog box (see Figure 8-15). Notice that PowerPoint offers you two alternatives, *ice* and *is*. You have the following options at this point:

- You can accept the highlighted suggestion — *ice,* for example — by clicking on the Change button.

- If you want to accept a suggestion that is not selected — *is*, for example — click on it and then click on the Change button. Or double-click on the selection, which immediately accepts it.

- If you feel you may have misspelled the word elsewhere in your presentation, click on the Change All button. Every instance of the misspelled word is automatically changed — for example, all instances of *ise* will be replaced with *is*. Clicking on this button can speed up your spell checking by eliminating the need to stop at every instance of the misspelled word.

- Click on the Add button if the word that PowerPoint locates is actually the correct spelling of a word that is unique to your industry and that you will encounter over and over again. You can add the word to the default CUSTOM.DIC or to another dictionary, if you have created a personal or client-specific dictionary.

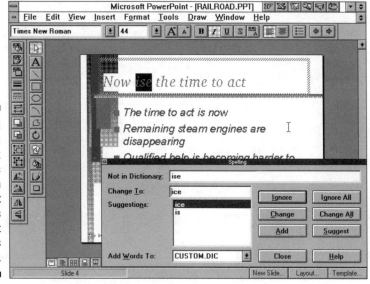

Figure 8-15: The Spelling dialog box appears when PowerPoint encounters a word not found in its dictionary.

Suppose that you make another mistake by typing *bigbucks* rather than *big bucks*. The spelling checker stops at *bigbucks*. In the Change To text box, click an insertion point between the *g* and the *b* and press the spacebar. PowerPoint prompts you with the statement The word "big bucks" is not in the dictionary. Change anyway? Click on OK. After PowerPoint is finished spell checking your slides, it prompts you and asks permission to close. Click on OK or press Enter.

Creating a summary for your presentation

By now, you've put a lot of work into your presentation. It would be a shame to lose it because of a momentary power outage. Accordingly, select File➪Save, enter a name for your slide presentation, and press the Enter key. The Summary Info dialog box appears, where you can save more information about your presentation, making it easy to identify and retrieve it at a later date. You can cross-reference the presentation by adding a subject, author, keywords and other comments (see Figure 8-16).

The Summary Info dialog box also allows you to double-check the path leading to the location where you saved the file, and it allows you to cross-reference the template that the presentation is based on. When you are satisfied with the information in the Summary Info dialog box, click on OK or press Enter.

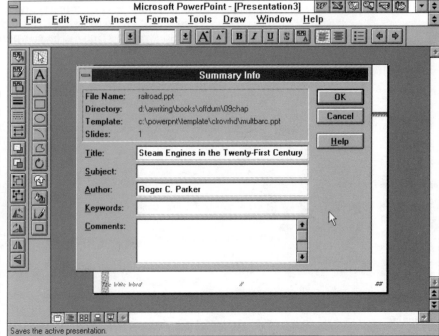

Figure 8-16:
The Summary Info dialog box allows you to save your presentation with more information than is allowed in the standard eight-letter filename.

Using Different Views to Check Your Presentation

There are three ways you can review your presentation to make sure that the arguments are presented in a logical sequence:

Outline View. To review your presentation in Outline view, select View⇨Outline or click on the Outline view button on the horizontal scroll bar at the lower-left side of your screen. As I described earlier in this chapter, Outline view shows unformatted titles and body text.

Slide Show. PowerPoint's Slide Show view allows you to preview your presentation from the audience's point of view. Your presentation visuals fill your computer screen one by one. You can control the movement by clicking the left mouse button or using certain cursor keys. (You can also instruct PowerPoint to automatically display your visuals, but that's a story for a later date....)

Slide Sorter. You can also view formatted presentation visuals at reduced size. In the Slide Sorter view, you can pick up a slide and move it to another location.

Using the Slide Show to review your work

To view your presentation as a Slide Show, select View⇨Slide Show or click on the Slide Show button — the one that looks like a projection screen — on the horizontal scroll bar at the lower-left side of the screen. The Slide Show dialog box opens, where you can choose to preview all or just part of your presentation (see Figure 8-17). At this point, accept the Manual Advance default and click on the Show button. To control the movement of the visuals, you can do the following:

- ✔ To advance forward through your presentation, press the left mouse button, the spacebar, the Page Down key, the down-arrow key, or the right-arrow key.

- ✔ To return to the preceding slide, press the right mouse button, the Page Up key, the up-arrow key, or the left-arrow key.

- ✔ To end the slide show, press the Escape key.

Reorganizing your work in Slide Sorter view

Choose Slide Sorter from the View menu on the menu bar. PowerPoint's Slide Sorter view shows you thumbnails, or reduced-size images, of each of your presentation visuals (see Figure 8-18). You can get a good sense of the flow of your presentation by viewing the thumbnails, and you can easily reorganize your presentation by dragging slides to a new location.

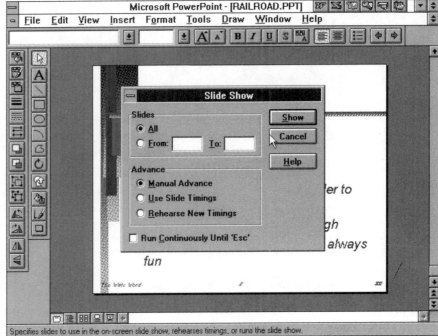

Figure 8-17:
The Slide Show dialog box allows you to determine whether you want to preview all or some of your presentation visuals.

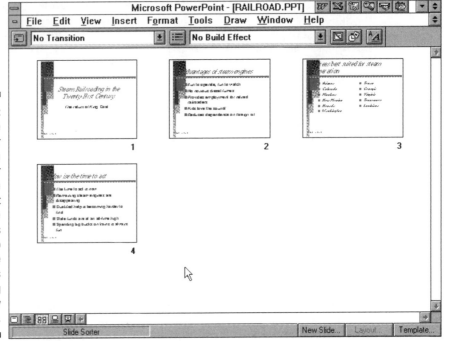

Figure 8-18:
The Slide Sorter shows you each of your presentation visuals at reduced size and permits you to reorganize your slides by dragging them to new locations.

To change the order of your slides, simply click on the slide you want to move. You'll know the slide is selected when a black border appears around it. Then drag the slide to the desired location. Notice that the original slide is now outlined in gray and a vertical dotted line and downward-pointing arrow indicate where the slide will be placed when you release the left mouse button (see Figure 8-19). After you release the mouse button, the slide is relocated and renumbered.

Choosing the right view of your work

You can increase or decrease the number of slides visible in PowerPoint's Slide Sorter by using the Zoom command. You'll find this command handy when preparing long presentations. To adjust the number of slides in the Slide Sorter, you can do either of the following actions:

✔ To display more slides in the Slide Sorter view, select View⇨Zoom and click on the radio button associated with a smaller number than the number currently displayed. Or click on the downward-pointing Percentage arrow until the number of slides you want is displayed. Then click on OK or press Enter.

✔ To display fewer slides at greater magnification in the Slide Sorter view, select View⇨Zoom and click on the radio button associated with a larger number than the number currently displayed. Or click on the upward-pointing Percentage arrow until the number of slides you want is displayed. Then click on OK or press Enter.

Figure 8-19: A vertical dotted line and downward-pointing arrow indicate the location where the slide will be relocated after you release the mouse button.

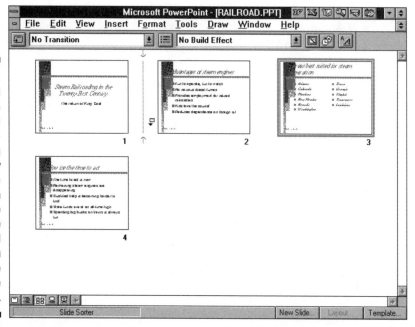

Using the View⇨Zoom command to view a portion of a slide at high magnification increases the size of the slide and permits you to work with greater precision. As you increase the magnification, you display a smaller and smaller part of the slide, but you can place art and text with greater accuracy. You can use the scroll bars to display other areas of the magnified slide. As you decrease magnification, you see more and more of the slide.

Returning to Slide view

After you experiment with other views, there are three ways you can return to Slide view:

- Select View⇨Slides.
- Click on the Slide View button at the lower left side of the horizontal scroll bar.
- Double-clicking on a particular slide in Slide Sorter view takes you directly to the Slide view of that visual.

Reformatting Your Presentation

There are two ways you can reformat an existing presentation: You can choose a new template, or you can modify the master template that you're currently working with. You may encounter several reasons for having to reformat your presentation. For example,

- At the last minute, you may decide to use a different presentation format. Instead of using color overheads, you may decide to create 35mm slides.
- You may want to try out a different color or typeface combination.
- A boss or client may ask you to add the firm's logo to each visual.
- You may want to change repeating information, such as eliminating the date or slide number at the bottom of each slide or replacing the client's name.

Templates can be changed in Outline, Slide, or Slide Sorter views. It makes most sense to change the template in Slide view, however, so that you can immediately see the results of your changes.

To apply a different template, click on the Template button at the lower-right side of your screen. This action takes you to the Presentation Template dialog box. The default directory displayed is the one where your template originally appeared. For example, if you are using a Color Overhead template, the template you have chosen is contained in the CLROVRHD subdirectory. If you are using a Black and White Overhead transparency template, it is located in the BWOVRHD subdirectory. If you are creating 35mm slides or an on-screen presentation, the template you are using is located in the SLDSHOW subdirectory. In the dialog box, you can take the following actions:

✔ To choose a different template, scroll through the list of templates under File <u>N</u>ame by clicking on the up and down arrows on the scroll box, dragging the elevator box, or using the up- and down-arrow keys.

✔ To preview a template, select it by clicking on it. Notice that you can preview your choice in the preview window of the dialog box.

✔ To apply the template, click on the <u>A</u>pply button or press Enter.

When you apply a different template, as shown in Figure 8-20, you lose the custom formatting that you added with Pick a Look Wizard. This information can include repeated text, such as the name of your organization, the slide number, and the date. If you want to include these items, you have to remember to add them to the new Slide Master (or Handouts, Outline, or Notes Master).

If you want to change the presentation format, click on the Template button. When the Presentation Template dialog box appears, click on the Template subdirectory. This step displays the three subdirectories containing the templates for the three categories of templates available: templates for black-and-white overhead transparencies, templates for color overhead transparencies, and templates for slide shows (covering both 35mm slides and on-screen computer-based presentations). Clicking on the desired subdirectory reveals the files they contain.

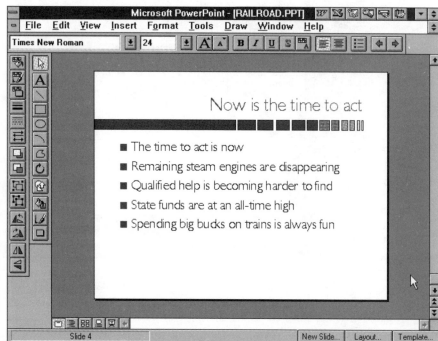

Figure 8-20:
It takes just seconds to reformat your presentation by applying a different template.

WARNING!

Be sure to save your work before applying a different template. *You cannot undo your work by selecting Edit⇨Undo.* After a new slide template has been applied and you want to go back to the original, you must remember its original template name and reapply it to the presentation as if it were a different template.

Editing the Slide Master

Each layout alternative is based on an underlying design, or template, called a Slide Master. The Slide Master contains the background text and graphics that appear as well as the position of the Title Area and AutoLayout Object Area. Changes made to the Slide Master will appear on every slide, regardless of the AutoLayout you choose.

To edit your current template, select View⇨Master followed by Slide Master (or the Master for whichever part of your presentation you want to change), as shown in Figure 8-21. In addition to modifying the Slide Master, you can modify the Notes Master and the Handouts Master.

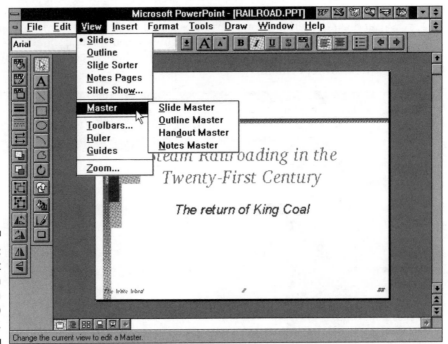

Figure 8-21:
The first step in editing a Master is to select it.

Selecting the Slide Master reveals the *architecture*, or underlying framework, on which your template is constructed. You can do the following things at this point:

✔ Choose a different typeface, type size, type style, or color for the title.

✔ Select a different typeface, type size, type style, color, or line spacing for each level of bulleted text charts.

✔ Change the size of the title area or object area so that they don't overlap other text or graphic elements.

✔ Add a logo that will automatically appear on each slide.

✔ Edit, replace, or delete the firm's name or delete the date or slide number.

To choose a different typeface for the slide titles, for example, all you do is select the Click to edit Master title style object and then choose the Format⇨Font command. When the Font menu appears, as shown in Figure 8-22, you can select a different typeface, type size, type style, and color for the title as well as apply special effects, such as underlining, shadowing, and embossing. Simply click on OK to apply the font changes. Font changes can also be done by using the various buttons on the Formatting toolbar.

Figure 8-22:
From the alternatives displayed in the Font dialog box, you can select a new typeface, type style, type size, and color for your slide titles as well as apply outline effects, such as shadow or emboss.

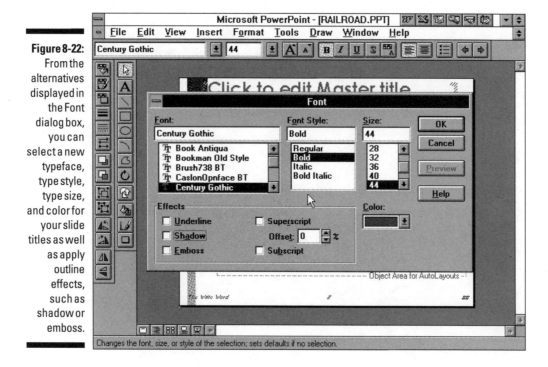

Clicking on the diagonally striped box that surrounds the title permits you to move or resize the title area. For example, by dragging one of the handles on the left toward the right, you can move the title area to the right so that the first letters of the title don't appear against the vertical graduated pattern.

Any changes you make on the Slide Master are repeated on all slides, effectively overriding the decisions that PowerPoint's designers incorporated in the design of the templates. Because PowerPoint's designers spent a lot of time fine-tuning typeface, type size, type style, and choices, you have to be certain that your choices are appropriate. Use the File➪Save As command to save your original presentation so that you can return to it if you don't like the way your reformatted presentation turns out.

To return to the Slide view after editing the Slide Master, select View➪Slides or click on the Slide view button in the horizontal scroll bar.

Congratulations. You've come a long way in a short time. Save your work and take a break. Visuals coming up next; news at 11:00.

Chapter 9

Adding Visuals to Your Slides and Overheads

• •

In This Chapter

▶ Navigating through your presentation

▶ Importing, moving, resizing, cropping, and recoloring clip art

▶ Ungrouping and regrouping clip art

▶ Enhancing clip art with background fills, borders, and shadows

▶ Adding organization charts and tables to your presentation

▶ Turning numbers into graphs

▶ Using PowerPoint's built-in drawing tools

▶ Aligning, grouping, layering, rotating, and duplicating illustrations

▶ Adding text to AutoShapes

▶ Placing text directly on PowerPoint slides

• •

*A*lthough the majority of your presentation will probably consist of words, your audience is likely to find it very boring to watch slide after slide of words alone. In this chapter, I'll show how you can enhance your presentations with visuals. These visuals can take many forms: clip art provided with PowerPoint; illustrations, including your firm's logo, created with other software programs; organization charts, graphs, and tables; and illustrations you create yourself by using PowerPoint's drawing tools.

The skilled and judicious use of illustrations and charts can greatly increase the impact of your presentation by adding character and visual interest while enhancing the communicating power of your charts and graphs. Tables, for example, permit you to easily compare information presented in row and column format; organization charts communicate hierarchies; and graphs permit you to display numeric relationships and trends far better than words alone.

The key to success is to use visuals with restraint. Always ask yourself, "What function does this visual perform? How does it support the conclusion I want my audience to accept?" Your skill as a presenter increases when you employ restraint and restrict your use of visuals to those that contribute to the arguments you are presenting.

Oh, Are You an Artist, Too?

Even if you can't draw a straight line, you can add clip art to your presentations. PowerPoint includes hundreds of high-quality predrawn illustrations, which you can easily add to your presentation. There are steps involved in enhancing your presentation with clip art:

- ✔ Locate the slide where you want to add the clip art.
- ✔ Choose the desired clip art.
- ✔ Manipulate the clip art by resizing, moving, and recoloring it (if necessary).

PowerPoint's clip art library contains a wide variety of useful images. Most have strong symbolic meaning, which can greatly enhance your presentation. Airplanes, for example, nonverbally suggest travel; microscopes, scientific study; and telephones or fax machines, communication. Some illustrations provide a background or framework for words or presentation titles. Other PowerPoint clip art, such as maps of the United States or international maps, is accurate and representational and can both enhance the communicating power of your presentation as well as save you time and money. (Ever try drawing Hawaii's boundaries?)

Navigating through your presentation

Assuming that you're well-rested, restart PowerPoint (either by clicking on the PowerPoint icon in the Windows Program Manager or by clicking on the PowerPoint icon in the Microsoft Office Manager toolbar). When PowerPoint's opening screen appears, click on Open an Existing Presentation. (If PowerPoint is already running, of course, select File⇨Open or use the Ctrl+O keyboard shortcut.)

Select a presentation file and click on the OK button or press Enter. Remember that you can reduce the number of steps involved in opening a file to a single step by double-clicking on the name of the desired file. Notice that the last four files you have saved are listed at the bottom of the File menu, which allows you to select them by simply clicking on the desired filename.

Select Tools⇨Options if you do not want to display the names of the last four saved files at the bottom of the File menu or if you want to display more than four filenames. If you want to eliminate the filenames, click in the check box next to the Recently Used File List option, which removes the default check mark. If you want to change the number of filenames displayed, enter a new number or use the up and down arrows next to the Entries option.

PowerPoint always opens saved presentations to the first, or title, slide; however, there are several ways you can move from slide to slide throughout your presentation:

✔ You can move *forward* slide by slide through your presentation by pressing the Page Down key or the 3 key on the numeric keypad. (*Note:* Pressing the 3, or Pg Dn key, doesn't advance slides if you have pressed the Num Lock key; instead, the number *3* is inserted in a title or text block.)

✔ You can move *backward* slide by slide through your presentation by pressing the Page Up key or the 9 key on the numeric keypad (as long as you haven't pressed the Num Lock key).

✔ If your *entire slide* is visible on-screen, which depends on the Zoom magnification you have chosen, you can move forward or backward through your presentation by clicking on the up and down arrows at the top and bottom of the vertical scroll bar. You can also advance to the next slide by clicking the vertical scroll bar below the elevator box or return to the preceding slide by clicking the space above the elevator box.

✔ If you are working at a high degree of magnification, *with only a portion of the current slide visible on-screen*, the up and down arrows reveal a different part of the slide until they reach the bottom or top of the slide. Then part of the next, or preceding, slide is revealed. (This is the least satisfying way of navigating through your presentation.)

✔ You can move forward through your presentation, one slide at a time, by clicking on the *Next Slide button* — the button containing the two downward-pointing arrows at the bottom of the vertical scroll bar. (If you position the insertion point over this button, the words Next Slide appear on-screen.)

✔ You can move backward through your presentation, one slide at a time, by clicking on the *Previous Slide button* — the button containing the two upward-pointing arrows at the bottom of the vertical scroll bar. (If you position the insertion point over this button, the words Previous Slide appear on-screen.)

✔ You can go directly to the *last slide* in your presentation by using the Ctrl+End keyboard shortcut. You can return to the first slide in your presentation by using the Ctrl+Home keyboard shortcut.

- The fastest way to move from slide to slide, however, is to drag the elevator box in the vertical scroll bar, which makes it easy to quickly and accurately move through even the longest presentation. Click and drag the elevator box in the direction you want to move. A Slide Number box appears next to the elevator box, indicating the slide location where you'll be if you release the mouse button at this point (see Figure 9-1).

Selecting and importing clip art

Drag the elevator box until Slide 3 appears and release the mouse button. After Slide 3 appears, click on the New Slide button. When the New Slide dialog box appears, select the button at the lower left side, the one containing a bulleted list plus an illustration of a man with a big nose. A black border appears around the image, and the words `Text & Clip Art` appear in the AutoLayout description box. Click on OK or press Enter. The new slide is added *after* the current slide, and you are taken directly to it.

Remember that you can work faster and reduce arm and mouse movement by simply double-clicking on the desired AutoLayout thumbnail.

When the slide image appears, double-click in the Double-click to add ClipArt box. This action takes you to the Microsoft ClipArt Gallery (formerly located on lower Fifth Avenue in New York City), as shown in Figure 9-2.

The first step is to choose the appropriate category of Microsoft ClipArt. Scroll through the list of available categories by clicking on the downward-pointing arrow or dragging the elevator box until the category that you want appears and then click on that category. The name of the category appears in the status bar along the bottom of the screen. Because the examples in this chapter deal with trains, I clicked on the Transportation category; `Category: Transportation and Red Sport Car` appeared in the status bar along the bottom of the screen.

When you reach the clip art category that you want, use the lower vertical scroll bar to navigate through the clip art. Each time you click on the downward-pointing arrow in the lower scroll bar, you reveal a different row of illustrations. In the Transportation category, the clip art ranges from automobiles, trucks, earth-moving equipment, airplanes, and finally — a value judgment on Microsoft's part? — a few railroad images.

Click on the illustration you want and then click on OK or press Enter (or double-click on the image). You are returned to the PowerPoint slide you just left. (I double-clicked on the steam locomotive illustration.)

Notice the other buttons in the Microsoft ClipArt Gallery dialog box. Click on Options. After the Options dialog box appears, click on Add to add your own illustrations to the ClipArt Gallery organized in custom categories. You can

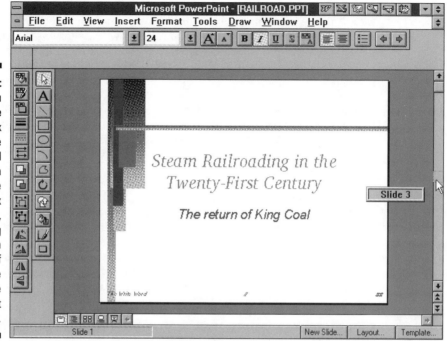

Figure 9-1:
When you drag the elevator box in the vertical scroll bar, a small Slide Number box appears, indicating the location of the slide if you release the mouse button at this point.

Figure 9-2:
The Microsoft ClipArt Gallery dialog box makes it easy to select the appropriate category of illustration.

include frequently used logos, scanned images of your staff, or artwork created with drawing programs, such as Adobe Illustrator, Aldus Freehand, or Corel Draw. The capability to create and name your own categories of illustrations, which you can preview and access through the Microsoft ClipArt Gallery, saves you a great deal of time in locating and retrieving files created with other programs.

Remember, however, that although you can categorize and preview illustrations imported through the ClipArt Gallery dialog box, these illustrations are *copied* rather than embedded or linked. A copied illustration means that its relationship with the originating program is severed, and you cannot easily change or edit it.

In Part V, I'll demonstrate how embedding and linking permits you to place an illustration in a PowerPoint slide and — at a later date — edit the drawing by double-clicking on it. Now you can easily update drawings, if necessary.

After you return to Slide view, the clip art image appears in the Double-click to add ClipArt area, and it is surrounded by eight resizing boxes, or *handles*. Figure 9-3 shows how the steam engine appears in the new slide.

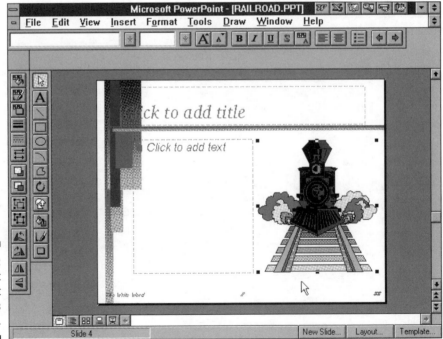

Figure 9-3:
Microsoft
ClipArt, as it
first appears
on a slide.

Manipulating artwork

You can modify imported illustrations in the following six ways:

- Move
- Resize
- Crop
- Recolor
- Add borders and backgrounds
- Ungroup and delete portions of the drawing

Moving an illustration

To move an imported illustration when the handles are visible, simply click anywhere *inside* the illustration and drag the illustration in the desired direction. After you release the left mouse button, the illustration remains where you left it. Try it now. (*I'm waiting!*)

Avoiding distortion when resizing an illustration

There are two ways you can resize clip art. You can distort it, or you can proportionally resize it to maintain its original height-to-width ratio. To distort an illustration, click on one of the middle handles — perhaps the middle handle on the left-hand side. Notice how the handle turns into a line with a pair of right- and left-pointing arrows. Drag *into* the illustration and notice what happens. The illustration remains as tall as it originally was, but the illustration becomes all squished together. Select the middle handle on the left side and, this time, drag *away from* the illustration. You can now stretch the illustration sideways, just as in a mirror in an amusement park fun house. If you select the middle handle along the top border, a line with a pair of up- and down-pointing arrows appears. Drag it down or *into* the illustration. The illustration now looks like it was run over by a steam engine. To return it to its original size, select Edit⇨Undo (or use the Ctrl+Z keyboard shortcut).

To proportionally resize the illustration — retaining its original height-to-width ratio — click on one of the corner handles. The handle turns into a diagonal line pointing into and away from the illustration (see Figure 9-4). Drag *into* the illustration and notice how the illustration becomes proportionately smaller but retains the original height-to-width ratio. A dotted border indicates how large the illustration will appear when you release the mouse button. After you release the mouse button, the image is proportionately resized. Select Edit⇨Undo to return the image to its original size.

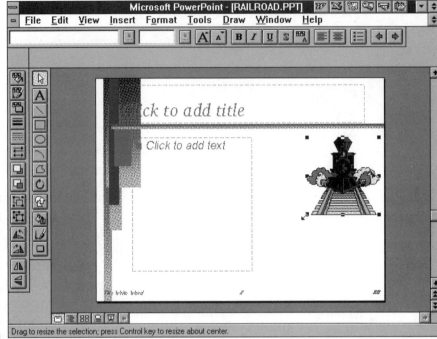

Figure 9-4:
Use the
corner
handles to
proportion-
ately resize
an
illustration.

You can also proportionately resize an illustration by selecting Draw⊅Scale. When the Scale dialog box appears, enter a desired percentage of increase or reduction, or use the up or down arrows to select a desired percentage.

Get that detail out of here!

Cropping an image involves cutting out information along the top, bottom, or sides of the illustration to focus attention on the remaining part of the illustration. In my steam engine example, I eliminated the tracks in front of the engine. To crop the illustration — assuming the image is still selected, as indicated by the eight handles surrounding it — select Tools⊅Crop Picture. A pair of overlapping "carpenter's squares," similar to a picture frame, appear on-screen.

- ✔ If you want to crop from the top, bottom, or sides of the illustration, place the cropping tool over one of the middle handles and drag into the illustration.

- ✔ If you want to crop from both the sides and the top or bottom of the illustration, place the cropping tool over one of the corner handles and drag into the illustration.

To achieve the cropped railroad tracks, I placed the cropping tool over the middle handle along the bottom of the illustration and dragged upward until I reached the point of the cowcatcher — the pointy object at the front of the engine. (No, *cowcatcher* is *not* a Microsoft term relating to file size created by its competitors in Utah.) After I released the mouse button, the engine remained the same size, but the tracks disappeared, as you can see in Figure 9-5. Select Edit⇨Undo to return the image to its original size.

Color coordinating your clip art and presentation color scheme

Take a good look at the illustration on-screen. Is something not quite right with the image? Maybe it's the colors! Perhaps the prominent colors in the rest of your slides are blue, red, and gray, but the imported image appears in purples and blacks. Not to worry. PowerPoint makes it easy to replace the original clip art colors with colors compatible with your presentation's color scheme. Select Tools⇨Recolor Picture, which takes you to the Recolor Picture dialog box (see Figure 9-6), where each of the colors used in the illustration is displayed.

Figure 9-5:
Cropping an image permits you to focus your audience's attention on the most important part of an illustration. (Notice that the cropping tool is displayed here, although it normally disappears when you release the mouse button.)

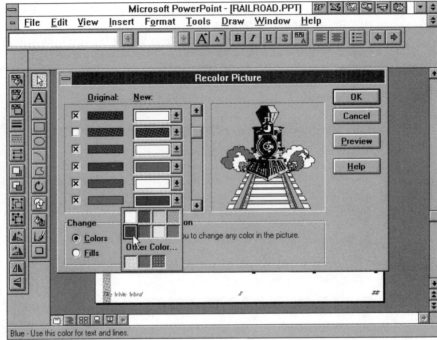

Figure 9-6:
PowerPoint's
Recolor
Picture
dialog box
permits
you to
harmonize
the colors
used in your
illustration
with your
presentation's
color
scheme.

Click on the Colors radio button in the Change box if you want to replace solid colors. Click on the Fills radio button if you want to change pattern fill colors.

To change the color of the clip art, first click on the appropriate color box in the Original color section. Then click on the corresponding pop-up menu in the New section, which displays the colors appropriate to your presentation's color scheme. Click on the desired color to select it.

If you are not happy with the selection provided, or you want a lighter or darker version of it, click on the Other Color option. The Other Color dialog box opens and offers you 88 additional colors to choose from, in addition to black and white. If you make a selection in this dialog box, it is added to the palette that appears each time you select a color from the New selection.

If you *still* don't see what you like, click on the More Colors option. The More Colors dialog box opens, as shown in Figure 9-7, where you can choose the exact colors and shades you want by clicking on the choices. Or you can drag the diagonal pointer next to the vertical column and choose a desired shade (a much easier method). The Color and Solid boxes permit you to preview your choices compared to each other.

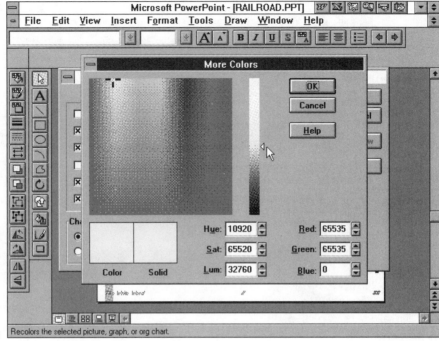

Figure 9-7:
The More
Colors
dialog box
allows you
to define the
exact color,
shade, or
brightness
level that
you desire
for each
part of the
illustration.

Click on the OK button twice to return to the Recolor Picture dialog box. Click on the Preview button to make sure that you are happy with your newly recolored picture. After you are satisfied with the changes you have made recoloring the illustration, click on the OK button or press Enter. When you return to Slide view, the clip art image is recolored to match the rest of your slides.

Adding borders, backgrounds, shadows, and bumps in the night

At this point, your clip art image may still look a bit naked, or uninspired, on your slide. But you can enhance the image by adding a border, a background fill, a shadow, or a combination of the three.

To add a border or a background fill, select the illustration (reveal the handles) and choose Format⇨Colors and Lines. The Colors and Lines dialog box opens, as shown in Figure 9-8, where you can specify a solid, patterned, or shaded background fill as well as define the color and width of the border around the illustration.

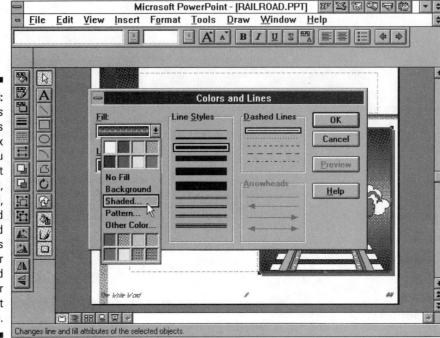

Figure 9-8:
The Colors and Lines dialog box permits you to select a solid, patterned, or shaded background fill as well as a border width and color for your clip art image.

If you select the Shaded option in the Fill area, PowerPoint takes you to the Shaded Fill dialog box (see Figure 9-9), where you can define the direction and range of the transition from light to dark. After you have made your choices in this dialog box, click on OK or press Enter to return to the Colors and Lines dialog box. Click on OK again after you have chosen the desired borders and background fills for your illustration.

To add a shadow box around the illustration, select Format⇨Shadow. The Shadow dialog box allows you to determine the desired color, the size, and the direction and distance of the shadow — the placement of the shadow above, below, to the left, or to the right of the illustration. (Logically enough, the default is down and to the right.) Click on OK or press Enter when you are satisfied with your choices. After you return to your slide, your clip art is as enhanced as you want, as you can see in Figure 9-10.

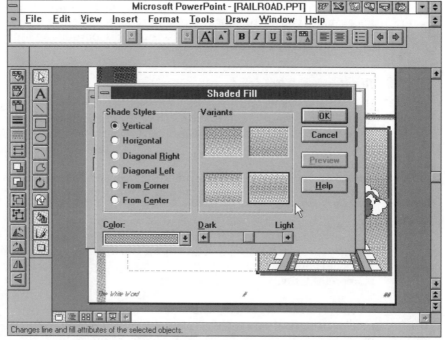

Figure 9-9:
The Shaded Fill dialog box allows you to define the desired shade styles as well as the range from dark to light.

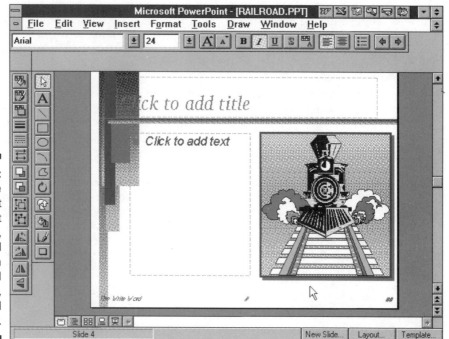

Figure 9-10:
The PowerPoint ClipArt illustration, enhanced with a shaded background, border, and shadow.

You can employ many of these modifying techniques to other types of visuals. For example, you can recolor charts and graphs to match your presentation's color scheme, and you can apply background fills, borders, and shadows to organization charts, graphs, and tables.

Breaking up is hard to do

Ungrouping permits you to customize a piece of PowerPoint clip art by breaking it into its component parts and deleting unwanted elements. Ungrouping permits you to alter the appearance of clip art and achieve totally different effects.

PowerPoint does not allow you to ungroup an illustration *and* add a border, background, or shadow at the same time. You can choose one technique or the other, but not both.

Click on the Next Slide button. Once again, accept the Text plus Clip Art AutoLayout default and import the clip art you want to ungroup. Select Tools⇨Recolor and replace the default colors with colors more appropriate to your presentation's color scheme.

You must recolor a PowerPoint illustration *before* you ungroup it. You cannot recolor an illustration after it has been ungrouped. A prompt appears reminding you that you are making an irreversible decision.

Then select Draw⇨Ungroup. Notice how the eight original handles are replaced by numerous handles. Each group of handles surrounds one of the component parts of the drawing that, together, make up the illustration. In many cases, several levels of Ungroup are possible to reduce the component parts of the drawing down to its basic shapes.

Begin ungrouping the image by selecting a part of it that you don't want to appear in the final slide. Choose Edit⇨Clear (or Delete). Then select the next part of the image that you don't want and delete it. Continue to select and delete the parts of the image that you don't want to appear in the final slide. After you are finished, the image appears by itself.

In my steam engine example, I started by selecting the ties — representing the horizontal pieces of wood the rails rest on — and deleting them, followed by selecting and deleting the rails and the steam billowing to the left and right of the locomotive. *(Note:* To help you see the individual parts of the illustration that I deleted, I dragged the parts to the left in Figure 9-11 rather than deleting them so that you could see how the parts worked together to create the steam engine drawing.)

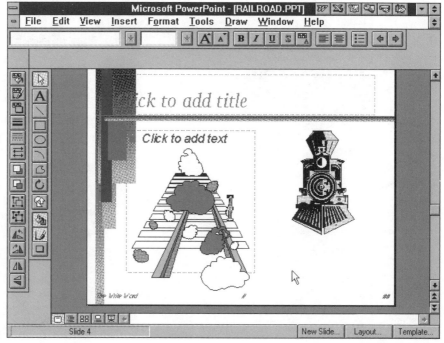

Figure 9-11:
Ungrouping
permits
you to
completely
change the
appearance
of a piece of
clip art by
deleting
unwanted
parts.

If you leave the clip art at this point, it is very unstable because it consists of numerous individual drawings. As a result, it cannot be resized, and you can easily delete an essential part by accident. What you need to do now is regroup the drawing.

To regroup the image, place the insertion point above and to the left of the drawing and drag to the lower right, below the drawing. A dotted border, or *marquis box,* appears. Make sure that the border of this box completely surrounds the drawing. After you release the mouse button, dozens of handles appear on the illustration. With the handles revealed, select Draw⇨Group. Once again, the drawing is surrounded by only eight handles (see Figure 9-12). You can now resize and move the image as a single drawing.

After you have modified the clip art to your satisfaction, click in the Click to add title box to add a title to the slide and click in the Click to add text box to create a bulleted list. Save your work.

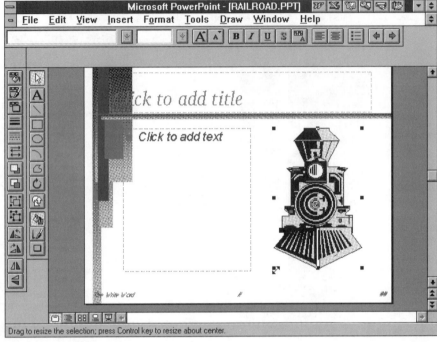

Figure 9-12:
Grouping allows you to resize and move the modified clip art image as a single illustration.

Addressing the Perennial Question: Who's in Charge Here?

Organization charts are one of the most useful types of visuals you can add to your presentations. Organization charts permit you to display hierarchy and responsibility within an organization. Organization charts contain boxes that contain employee names and positions. By locating various individuals' names and positions, you can see to whom they report and whom they supervise.

To add an organization chart, press the New Slide button. After the New Slide dialog box appears, choose the second AutoLayout thumbnail down on the right side. After you select it, the words Org Chart appear in the description box. Click on OK or press Enter.

A new slide appears. Double-click in the Double click to add org chart box. This action loads the Microsoft Organization Chart module, which permits you to create an organization chart and place it in the PowerPoint slide (see Figure 9-13).

You will understand how to create an organization chart much better if you understand the Organization Chart menu.

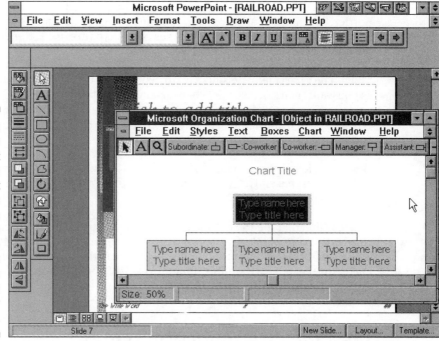

Figure 9-13:
The
Microsoft
Organization
Chart
module
provides the
tools you
need to
add an
organization
chart to
your
presentation.

File. The two most important commands located in the File menu are Exit and Return to (*PowerPoint filename*) and Update (*PowerPoint filename*). You can also save a copy of your organization chart apart from the copy that is saved with the PowerPoint file.

Edit. The Edit menu contains the Select, Select Levels, and Options commands. Select makes it easy to format your organization chart by allowing you to modify every box in the organization chart or just certain categories of boxes, such as Managers, Groups, Branches, or such graphic elements as connecting lines. Select Levels allows you to apply formatting on the basis of how high or low the boxes are in the organizational structure. Options permits you to establish defaults for future organization charts.

Styles. The Styles menu opens to reveal alternative ways of grouping boxes of equal importance vertically, horizontally, or in a cluster.

Text. After you have selected a single box by clicking on it, the Font option permits you to choose a desired typeface, type size, and type style. The Color option permits you to choose from colors appropriate for your presentation's color scheme. You can also choose the Left, Right, or Center justification options. The Text commands are used after you choose the Edit⇨Select or Edit⇨Select Levels commands.

Boxes. The Boxes menu contains the commands needed to format the Box Border, Box Shadow, and Box Color options as well as the Line Thickness, Line Style, and Line Color options. The Boxes commands are used after you choose the Edit⇨Select or Edit⇨Select Levels options.

Chart. The Chart menu permits you to display as much or as little of the chart as you want. You can also add a Background Color here.

Window. The Window menu permits you to work with more than one organization chart at a time and to select between the active charts.

Help. The Help menu explains commands and techniques directly relating to organization charts. The About command displays a prompt informing you of the number of levels and boxes in your chart.

You may find that the easiest and most logical way to create an organization chart is to choose Edit⇨Options and click on the radio button next to Use standard 1-box template for new charts. At least in the beginning, this action makes the meaning of the Subordinate, Co-worker-, -Co-worker, Manager, and Assistant buttons more apparent.

Creating an organization chart

In order to understand how to enter text in boxes and how to use the options offered by the Microsoft Organization Chart toolbar (which is located under the menu), follow these steps to create a 1-box organization chart:

1. **Start by selecting the Chart Title by dragging and typing a new title.**

2. **Click on the single box and press Enter or double-click on the box.**

    The box expands to reveal ⟨Name⟩, ⟨Title⟩, ⟨Comment 1⟩, and ⟨Comment 2⟩. Notice that ⟨Name⟩ is automatically highlighted.

3. **Type in a name and press Enter.**

    Notice that the text selection automatically advances to the ⟨Title⟩ text.

4. **Type in a title for the organization chart.**

    In my example, I replaced ⟨Title⟩ with ORIGINAL POSITION. If you press Enter again, PowerPoint advances you to ⟨Comment 1⟩. If you don't fill in the comments, however, they will automatically be hidden.

5. **To close the box, click elsewhere in the box.**

Adding subordinates, managers, co-workers, assistants, and other unsavory fellow travelers

Now you can enhance the title box (ORIGINAL POSITION) by adding additional boxes. You simply use the toolbar buttons available under the Microsoft Organization Chart menu. Notice that each new box is added in a *different position* relative to the original box. To add more boxes, follow these steps:

1. **Click on the Subordinate button in the Organization Chart toolbar.**

   The Subordinate button becomes lighter than the others, and the mouse pointer turns into the subordinate pointer.

2. **Place the subordinate pointer inside the title box (ORIGINAL POSITION) and click. When a Subordinate box appears, double-click in it.**

   This step reveals the following codes: <Name>, <Position>, <Comment 1>, and <Comment 2>.

3. **Press Enter.**

   This step advances you past the <Name> code and highlights the <Position> code.

4. **Type** Subordinate 1 **and click outside of the box.**

5. **Click on the Subordinate button one more time, position the subordinate pointer inside the title box, and click.**

6. **Double-click to expand the new box, press Enter to skip the name, and type** Subordinate 2.

7. **Repeat Steps 5 and 6 for each subordinate box you want to add to the title position.**

8. **Click on the first Co-worker button, the one with the line pointing to the right of the button. Let's call this the "Co-Worker (left)" button. Again, the mouse button turns into the icon chosen.**

9. **Position the mouse pointer inside the ORIGINAL POSITION box and click.**

   Select the newly-added box and, again, press Enter to pass the <Name> and replace <Position> with Co-worker (left). Click outside the box.

10. **Click on the second Co-worker button, the one with the line pointing to the left of the icon.** Position the Co-worker inside the ORIGINAL POSITION box and click. When the new box appears, press Enter to avoid typing and name and replace <Position> with Co-worker (right). Click outside the box.

11. **Click on the Manager button.** Position the Manager icon inside the ORIGINAL POSITION box and click. When the new box appears, double-click to expand it. Press Enter to skip the name. Replace `<Position>` with Manager. Click outside the box.

12. **Click on the Assistant button.** Position the Assistant icon inside the ORIGINAL POSITION box and click. When the next box appears, double-click to expand it. Press Enter to skip the name and replace `<Position>` with Assistant 1.

13. **Click on the Assistant button again.** Once again, position the Assistant icon inside the ORIGINAL POSITION box and click. Double-click to expand the new box, press Enter to skip the name, and replace `<Position>` with Assistant 2. Repeat once more, and create Assistant 3.

14. **When you have finished, select File⇨Exit and Return to (***PowerPoint filename***).** PowerPoint will prompt you that `This object has been changed. Do you want to Update Object in (`*`PowerPoint filename`*`) before proceeding?` Click on Yes or press Enter to proceed. You can now see the relationship of new boxes to the ORIGINAL POSITION box.

Figure 9-14 shows the following:

✔ The Manager box appears *above* the ORIGINAL box.

✔ The Co-worker boxes always appear *next to* the ORIGINAL POSTION box.

✔ Subordinate and Assistant boxes appear *below* the ORIGINAL POSTION box.

✔ The lines connecting the Assistant boxes to the ORIGINAL POSITION box indicate direct responsibility and little autonomy.

✔ The lines connecting the Subordinate boxes to the ORIGINAL POSTION box indicate parallel authority and individual autonomy.

Deleting and formatting boxes

To edit the organization chart, double-click on it, which returns you to the Microsoft Organization Chart program module. You can then edit in the following ways:

✔ To edit the contents of a box, click on it (to expand it), select the text you want to change, and type in replacement text.

✔ To delete a box, select the box by clicking on it and then choose Edit⇨Clear (or Delete).

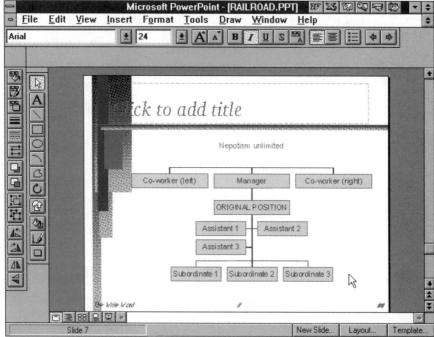

Figure 9-14:
Relation-
ship of
Co-Worker,
Subordinate,
Manager
and
Assistant
boxes to
the
ORIGINAL
POSITION
box.

✔ To reformat all the text in a box, select the box and then choose Text⇨Font, Text⇨Color, or Text⇨Left, Right, or Center. To selectively reformat text, select the box and highlight just the words you want to reformat.

✔ To reformat a box, select it and then choose Boxes⇨Box Border, Boxes⇨Box Shadow, or Boxes⇨Box Color. To reformat the lines around a box, select Boxes⇨Line Thickness, Boxes⇨Line Style, or Boxes⇨Line Color.

✔ To reformat the text or appearance of *all* boxes at a given level, double-click on one of the boxes.

✔ To reformat a line connecting two boxes, click on the line and then choose Boxes⇨Line Thickness, Boxes⇨Line Style, or Boxes⇨Line Color. To reformat more than one line, hold down the Shift key while you select the lines.

✔ To add a background behind the organization chart in order to separate it from the slide background, select Chart⇨Background Color and choose a background from the palette that appears.

After you are finished, choose File⇨Exit and Return to (*PowerPoint filename*) and, when prompted, click on Yes or press Enter.

While creating or editing an organization chart in the Microsoft Organization Chart program module, you can return to PowerPoint by clicking on any part of the slide that is visible behind the chart. These lines indicate that the Microsoft Organization Chart module is running. The lines will disappear when you select File⇨Exit and Return to (*PowerPoint filename*) in the Microsoft Organization Chart module.

Now that you are familiar with the operation of the position buttons in the Microsoft Organization Chart module, you may want to select Edit⇨Options and click on the radio button next to Use standard 4-box template for new charts. This option provides a more familiar framework for your new organization charts.

Adding Tables — and with Any Luck, Chairs — to Your Presentation

Tables permit you to visually display information in an understandable row-and-column format. Tables make it easy for your audience to compare alternatives. Information that would be lost when presented in paragraph format becomes easy to comprehend when reduced to key words and presented in a side-by-side arrangement.

Tables are entered in a three-step process. First, you create the table by using the Microsoft Word Table module. Then you apply Word's AutoFormatting tools to choose the correct typography, grid, and background colors. Finally, you fine-tune the table by using PowerPoint's Format⇨Colors and Lines and Format⇨Shadows commands.

Adding a table and entering text

To add a table to your presentation, click on the New Slide button. After the New Slide dialog box appears, click on the Table AutoLayout thumbnail at the lower-right side. Notice that the word Table appears on-screen. Click on OK or press Enter.

After the new slide appears, double-click in the Double-click to add table area. The Insert Word Table dialog box appears, where you can enter the desired number of columns and rows by clicking on the up or down arrows or typing in the appropriate numbers. Create a table with four columns and five rows. Click on OK or press Enter.

1. Type: (Tab), **Steam** (Tab), **Electric** (Tab), **Diesel** (Tab), followed by Enter.

2. Type: **Acquisition cost** (Tab), **Low** (Tab), **Low** (Tab), **High**, followed by Enter.

3. Type: **Fuel distribution** (Tab), **Low** (Tab), **High** (Tab), **Medium**, followed by Enter.

4. Type: **Labor** (Tab), **Volunteer** (Tab), **Medium** (Tab), **Medium**, followed by Enter.

5. Type: **Insurance** (Tab), **High** (Tab), **Low** (Tab), **Low**, followed by Enter.

When you are finished entering the information in your table, it may look something like the one in Figure 9-15 — hardly what you expected!

Improving table appearance

To choose a more attractive appearance for the table, start by double-clicking on the table to return to the Table Editor. You'll know you're in the right place when a border of diagonal lines appears around the table. Select Table⇨Table AutoFormat, which opens the Table AutoFormat dialog box (see Figure 9-16). Click in the Color check box and scroll through the list of available table formats. Notice that each option is previewed in a large size.

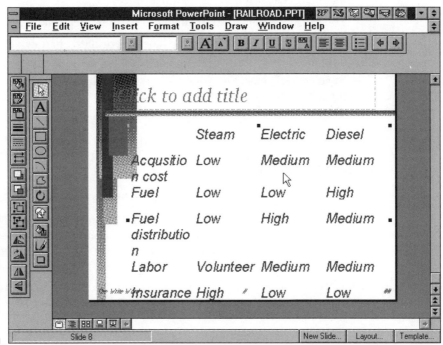

Figure 9-15: A table with unformatted text and no borders or background fills.

Notice the many border, background, and grid options available. Be sure to investigate all options.

You can speed up scrolling through the many Table AutoFormat options by using the up- and down-arrow keys instead of clicking on each individual format name.

When you locate a possible format, double-click on the name of the format, or click on the name of the format and click on OK or press Enter. To illustrate Figure 9-17, I chose the format named Colorful 2.

Be sure you remember to click in the check box marked <u>C</u>olor if you are creating 35mm color slides, color overheads, or visuals designed for computer presentation or projection.

Fine-tuning table appearance

There are numerous ways you can fine-tune the appearance of the table. The first technique is by using PowerPoint's tools. First, select the table by clicking it once and then do any of the following actions:

- ✔ By dragging one of the corner handles, you can proportionately increase or decrease the size of the table. (Avoid dragging one of the middle handles because this action distorts the text.)

- ✔ You can move the table by dragging it to a new location.

- ✔ By selecting F<u>o</u>rmat⇨<u>C</u>olors and <u>L</u>ines or F<u>o</u>rmat⇨S<u>h</u>adow, you can set the table apart from the remainder of the slide background.

- ✔ By selecting <u>T</u>ools⇨<u>R</u>ecolor, you can replace the Table AutoFormat's preselected colors with others more compatible with your presentation's color scheme.

You can also fine-tune the appearance of the table by double-clicking on the table and returning to the Microsoft Word Table Editor, where you can do the following things to the table:

- ✔ You can edit text by double-clicking on the words and typing in new ones.

- ✔ You can selectively reformat individual rows and columns by clicking anywhere in the row or column and selecting either T<u>a</u>ble⇨Select <u>R</u>ow or T<u>a</u>ble⇨Select <u>C</u>olumn followed by F<u>o</u>rmat⇨F<u>o</u>nt or Format⇨<u>B</u>orders and Shading.

- ✔ You can highlight an individual cell by double-clicking on it and choosing F<u>o</u>rmat⇨F<u>o</u>nt or F<u>o</u>rmat⇨<u>B</u>orders and Shading.

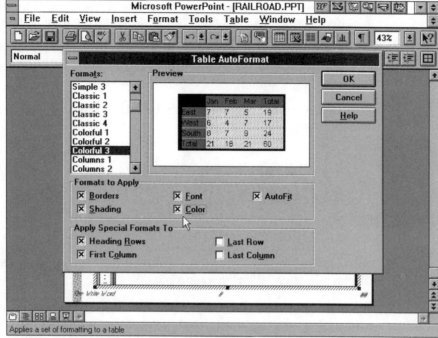

Figure 9-16:
The Table
AutoFormat
dialog box
permits you
to preview
numerous
table
formats
before
making a
choice.

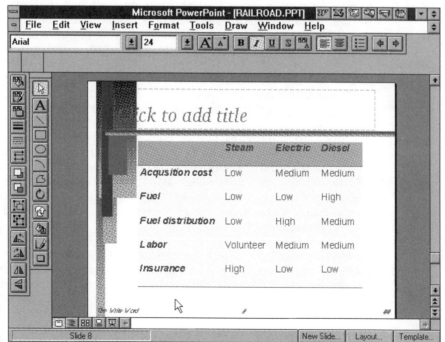

Figure 9-17:
A table
formatted
with the
Colorful 2
format.

> ✔ If content demands, you can increase the size of the table by placing the insertion point at the point in the table where you want more rows and selecting Table➪Insert Rows. Then click on either the Insert Entire Row radio button or the Insert Entire Column radio button. Likewise, you can reduce the size of your table by selecting Table➪Delete Cells followed by Delete Entire Row or Delete Entire Column.

Choose File➪Save or use the Ctrl+S keyboard shortcut after completing your table. It's time to move on!

A Number of Ways to Avoid Boring Numbers

Numbers are boring — there are no two ways about it. One of the best ways you can improve presentations is to replace numbers with graphs that visually display numeric relationships and trends.

There are two ways you can add graphs to PowerPoint. In this section, I'll discuss the easiest and most straightforward way: using the Microsoft Graph feature. Later in this book, you'll investigate the second, more advanced alternative, which involves importing and linking graphs created with Microsoft Excel. There are two primary advantages to importing and linking Excel graphs: the same graph can also be used with other applications, such as in a Word document. And if you choose to link the chart, your PowerPoint presentation is automatically updated if the source data is modified.

Graphs don't have to appear all by themselves on a slide. PowerPoint includes AutoLayouts that combine graphs with bulleted text lists. These AutoLayouts permit you to place the text to the right or the left of the graph.

To add a chart to your presentation, click on the New Slide button. After the New Slide box appears, click on the AutoLayout thumbnail at the upper-right side. When the word Graph appears on-screen, click on OK or press Enter. After the new slide appears, double-click on the Double click to add graph area. This launches the Microsoft Graph module, which includes a datasheet for entering information as well as the menus and tools necessary to create good-looking graphs (see Figure 9-18).

If your computer screen is large enough, drag the Datasheet toolbar toward the bottom of the screen. By being able to see more of the chart, you can see how changes in data entries and toolbar options are reflected in the chart.

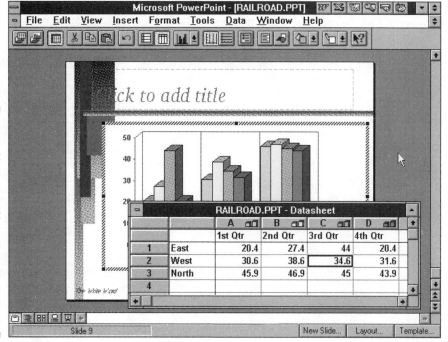

Figure 9-18:
The
Microsoft
Graph
module
includes a
datasheet
for entering
numbers as
well as the
tools you
need to
format the
graph.

Choosing the right type of graph

The first and most important decision you make when working with the
Microsoft Graph module is to choose the right type of graph. To preview the
available options, select Format➪Chart type. The Chart Type dialog box, as
shown in Figure 9-19, permits you to view the various types of charts.

While you are comparing options in the Chart Type dialog box, click the 3-D
radio button. Notice how dramatically the appearance of the charts changes.

After you have become comfortable selecting chart types, use the Chart type
pull-down button in the Microsoft Graph toolbar to choose the desired type of
graph. For the examples in this section, I chose the pie chart.

Entering data

There are two ways you can enter data into a graph. You can enter data directly
into the datasheet, or you can import data from a previously created spreadsheet.

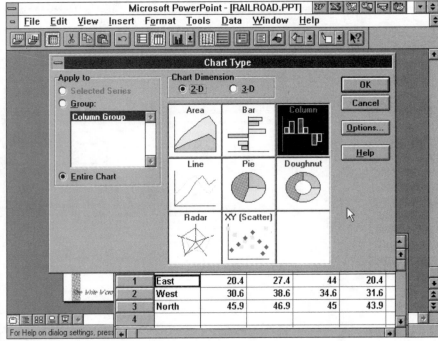

Figure 9-19:
The Chart
Type dialog
box permits
you to
compare the
various
types of
graphs
available.

To enter data in a datasheet, start by replacing the default data in the
datasheet. Highlight the first entry in the first two columns and type the
following:

1. **Acquisition** (Tab), **450,000**

2. **Fuel** (Tab), **750,000**

3. **Labor** (Tab), **110,000**

4. **Trackage** (Tab), **1,250,000**

5. **Insurance** (Tab), **950,000**

Use the up- and down-arrow keys and the left- and right-arrow keys to navigate
through the datasheet when you are entering data.

Importing data from previously created spreadsheets

To import data from a previously created spreadsheet, select Edit⇨Import Data or click on the Import Data tool at the extreme left of the Microsoft Graph toolbar. After the Import Data dialog box appears (see the accompanying figure), identify the appropriate subdirectory file that contains the data you want. Double-click the filename.

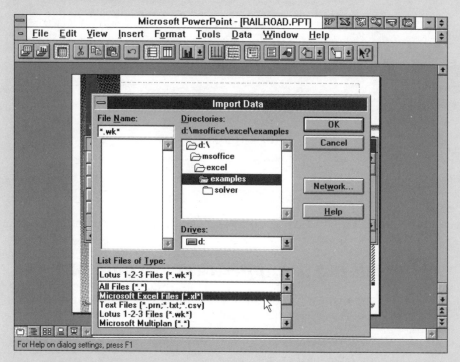

After locating the appropriate spreadsheet, indicate whether you want to import the entire spreadsheet or just a range (which you enter at the lower-left side of the Import Data dialog box).

When you are finished entering data in the graph, click on the graph behind the datasheet to close the datasheet. Then select Data⇨Series in Columns. When you are finished, your chart should resemble the one in Figure 9-20, if you chose a pie chart. When you are satisfied with its appearance, click on the slide to close Microsoft Graph and return to PowerPoint.

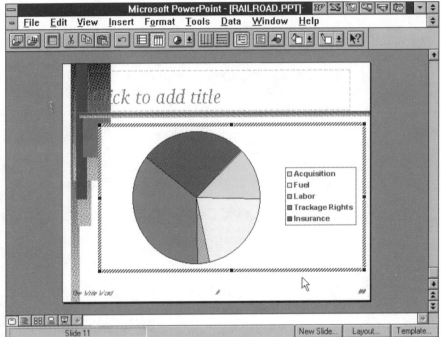

Figure 9-20:
An
unformatted
pie chart
based on
data entered
earlier in
this section.

Fine-tuning the appearance of your graph

Here are some of the ways you can enhance the appearance of the pie chart. Start by double-clicking on the chart to return to the Microsoft Graph.

- ✔ Select Insert⇨Data Labels. After the Data Labels dialog box appears, click on Show Label and Percent.

- ✔ Click on the Legend, the boxed color key that identifies each chart element. Select Edit⇨Clear or press the Delete key.

Click on the PowerPoint slide and return to it. Click on the graph to select it.

1. **Select Format⇨Colors and Lines.** When the Colors and Lines dialog box appears, select a Fill color to provide a background to help separate the graph from the slide background. Select a Line to outline the graph area.

2. **Select Format⇨Shadow and select a color that will extend below and to the right of the box.**

3. **Select Tools⇨Crop Picture and eliminate the space where the Legend previously appeared.**

4. **Select one of the corner handles and enlarge the pie chart as much as possible.**

When you are finished, your chart should resemble the one in Figure 9-21.

In a similar manner, you can fine-tune the appearance of every type of chart. Different options are available depending on the type of graph you are using, including different options for two-dimensional and three-dimensional charts. If you are working with bar graphs, for example, you can include major and minor grid lines as well as add titles to the x- (horizontal) and y- (vertical) axes. You can also display the exact numeric figure for each bar in the graph and vary the depth of three-dimensional graphs.

Working with PowerPoint's Drawing Tools

All drawings, even those that seem very complicated, are ultimately based on a series of carefully assembled, but very basic, smaller drawings. This section provides you with a working knowledge of PowerPoint's drawing tools so that you, too, can think about creating your own drawings!

Click on the New Slide button and select the Title Only AutoLayout located on the bottom row. Take a few moments to explore the Drawing and the Drawing+ toolbars located along the left-hand edge of the PowerPoint screen. Note how a description of each tool's function appears as you position the mouse pointer over each tool.

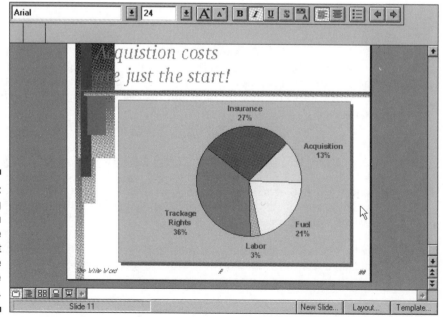

Figure 9-21:
Fine-tuning permits you to unify the pie chart and the slide background.

Creating lines and shapes

Feel free to experiment with the drawing tools as you read through this section. Drawings are created by a combination of lines and shapes.

1. **Start by selecting the Rectangle tool (it resembles a square).** While you hold down the mouse button, drag to create a horizontal rectangle. Notice the eight handles surrounding the rectangle.

2. **Select the Fill Color tool at the upper left.** This permits you to choose a different color for the rectangle or choose an empty, patterned, or shaded background.

3. **Select the Line Style tool—the fourth tool from the top with the horizontal lines—and choose a heavier line thickness.**

4. **Select the Rectangle tool**. This time, hold down the Shift key as you drag. Notice that this creates a square instead of a rectangle. Select the Fill Color tool again and choose a different Fill Color.

5. **Select the Ellipse tool (that resembles an egg).** Hold down the Shift key and drag to create a circle. With the circle selected, select the Fill Color tool and choose a contrasting color. Select the Line Style tool and choose a heavier line width. Select the Line Color tool, the second from the top, and choose a light color. Select the Shadow color tool, the third from the top, and choose a contrasting color.

When you're finished, your screen should look like the one in Figure 9-22. These drawings provide the basis you need for further exploration of PowerPoint's drawing tools.

Other drawing tools you should investigate include the Ellipse drawing tool, which resembles a half circle. The Ellipse drawing tool permits you to draw partial circumferences of uniform radius. The Freeform tool, a hybrid circle and rectangle, turns the mouse pointer into a pencil point and permits you to draw irregular lines and objects.

Aligning, layering, and rotating objects

To align any objects that you draw, start by holding down the Shift key and selecting the objects one by one. Then choose Draw⇨Align followed by one of the following options:

Lefts. Left alignment maintains the original vertical placement of each object but aligns the objects along the left-most edge of the objects.

Centers. Center alignment maintains the original vertical placement of each object but aligns the objects along an imaginary axis through the center of each object.

Rights. Right alignment maintains the original vertical placement of each object but aligns the objects along the right-most edge of the objects.

Tops. Top alignment maintains the horizontal position of the objects but aligns them along the topmost part of the highest object.

Middles. Middle alignment maintains the horizontal position of the objects but aligns the objects along an imaginary axis through the center of each object.

Bottoms. Bottom alignment maintains the horizontal position of the objects but aligns them along the bottommost part of the lowest object.

If you draw several objects with different shapes and you select the Middles option, your drawing should resemble the one in Figure 9-23. Notice that the square is hidden behind the circle because their position depends on the order they were added to the slide. Because the circle was added last, it appears on top.

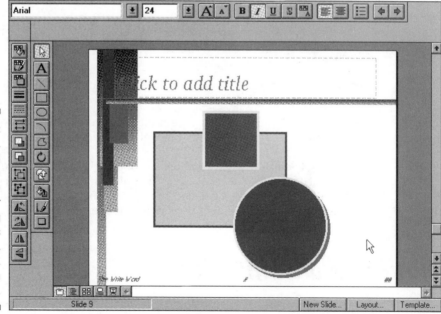

Figure 9-22: A rectangle, square, and circle provide the basis for exploring PowerPoint's layering, alignment, and rotation tools.

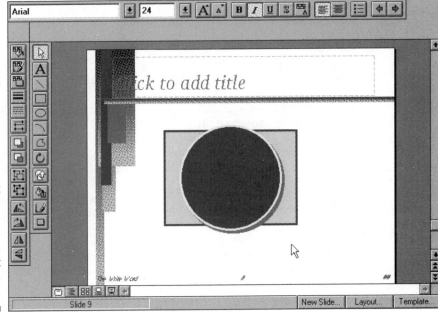

Figure 9-23:
When the three drawings are middle aligned, the first object placed on the slide appears on the bottom; the latest appears on top.

There are two ways you can reveal the square hidden behind the circle. First deselect the drawings by clicking elsewhere on the slide; then do either of the following:

- ✔ Select the circle and choose Draw⇨Send to Back. Now the circle appears behind *both* the square and the rectangle.

- ✔ Select Edit⇨Undo (restoring the circle in the front). Select Draw⇨Send Backward. The circle now appears between the square and the rectangle.

Choose Edit⇨Select All when you "lose" an object — that is, when you can't locate a text or graphic element because it is hidden behind another one. While you hold down the Shift key, deselect the other objects one by one until only the handles of the hidden object are visible. Then select Draw⇨Bring to Front.

Turning Words into Art

A text object consists of words added to PowerPoint tools with the Text tool (the tool with the large *A* on it). Text placed directly on the slide does not appear in the Outline view, but it can be used for annotations or to draw attention to other text objects. You can also use this kind of text for large quotations or "Questions, anyone?" or "Break time!" announcements.

To place text directly on the slide, follow these steps:

1. **Press Ctrl+End to go to the last slide.**

2. **Click on the Next Slide button and choose the very last AutoLayout option, described as Blank.**

3. **Select the Text tool (the tool with the large A).**

   Drag from upper left to lower right, defining the area where you want the text to appear.

4. **Type** Steam will appear in different parts of the country at different times.

First, format the text itself as well as the object it's placed in. Here are some of your options (while the text block is selected, as indicated by the eight handles around it):

- ✔ Click on the Increase Point Size button in the Formatting toolbar—the one with the large A. Type size will increase each time you click the button.

- ✔ Click on the Center Alignment button in the Formatting toolbar—the one with the lines of different length (third from the right).

- ✔ Click on the Text Shadow button, the one with the S, to add impact to the text.

Next, format the object, or container, where the text is located:

1. **Select the Fill Color tool and choose Shaded Background.**

   Choose one of the Color Scheme colors that appear or select Other Color. A light gray works best. When the Shaded Fill dialog box appears, select From Corner and move the Dark/Light slider bar to the center so that the dark area will not be so dark.

2. **Select the Line Color tool and choose a color for the border of the text.**

3. **Select the Line Type tool and choose a thicker line to make the border heavier.**

4. **Select the Shadow Color tool and add a contrasting shadow to the text box.**

5. **Click on the text object and reposition it by dragging it to another location on the slide.**

When you are finished, admire your work and save your presentation. You now have a strong closing slide (see Figure 9-24).

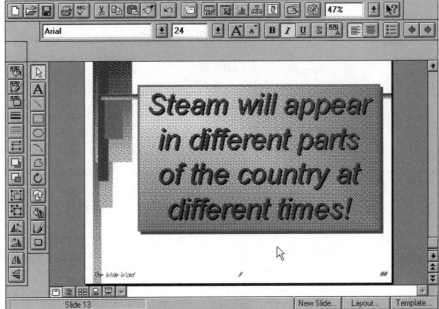

Figure 9-24:
Conclude
your
presentation
with a large,
heavily
formatted
quotation!

Part IV
Working with and Exchanging Information

The 5th Wave   By Rich Tennant

"It's a Windows application that more fully reflects an actual office environment. It multi-tasks with other users, integrates shared data and then uses that information to network vicious rumors through an inter-office link-up."

In this part...

1 f you've ever been scared by the term *database,* it's time to put away the tissues and quit hiding like a little kid.

Sounds tough, huh? The only reason I can say that it *isn't* tough is because of Access, the database program included with Microsoft Office Pro. Access is famous for its ease of use, power, and flexibility for all kinds of info-storage — from recipes to isotope charts.

And that's just the beginning. The advanced data-sharing and communication features of Access and the rest of Microsoft Office put you right in the loop — whether you're in Dodger Stadium in Los Angeles or George's Gas-N-Grub in Zanesville, Indiana.

Chapter 10

Organizing Your Time and Your Assets

• •

In This Chapter

▶ Database 101

▶ Storing names, addresses, and phone numbers

▶ Time is money

▶ Tracking your office assets

▶ Searching a database

▶ Sorting a database

• •

Despite the sophistication of personal computers, many people still insist on storing important names, addresses, and phone numbers in Rolodex files, on index cards, or on sheets of paper stuffed into folders. Although effective, paper solutions are terrible at storing and analyzing information. Just look at a typical Rolodex file, and ask yourself how long it would take to find all the names and phone numbers of people who live in Missouri.

As the database portion of Microsoft Office, Microsoft Access allows you not only to store and retrieve information, but also to sort, manipulate, and analyze it to spot trends or patterns in your data. The more you know about your information, the better you can act to can wipe your less knowledgeable, computer-illiterate competitors off the face of the earth.

Database 101

Microsoft Access is nothing more than a fancy filing cabinet that allows you to dump information in and yank it back out again. Before you can dump information into Access, however, you have to design your database structure. A database consists of the following three elements:

✔ The database file

✔ One or more database tables

✔ One or more fields

Creating a database file

The *database file* is a file that physically exists on your hard disk (or floppy disk) and that has the funny file extension MDB, which stands for <u>M</u>icrosoft <u>DataB</u>ase. Think of a database as being a filing cabinet devoted to holding one type of data, such as information related to taxes or business.

To create a database file, follow the following steps:

1. **From the <u>F</u>ile menu, choose the <u>N</u>ew Database command (or press Ctrl+N).**

   The New Database dialog box appears (see Figure 10-1).

2. **Type the name that you want to give your database.**

   Don't type a file extension because Access automatically adds the MDB extension.

Figure 10-1:
The New
Database
dialog box.

3. Click OK.

Access creates a new database file and displays it in a database window (see Figure 10-2).

Figure 10-2:
A newly
created
Access
database
file.

Creating a database table

After creating a database file, you have to create one or more *database tables*. Database tables are like the separate drawers of a filing cabinet. If your entire filing cabinet contains tax information, for example, one drawer may contain information on tax deductions, and another drawer may contain information on taxable income. Every database file needs at least one database table.

To create a database table, follow these steps:

1. From the File menu, choose Open Database (or press Ctrl+O) unless the the file that you want is already open.

The Open Database dialog box appears (see Figure 10-3).

2. Select the database file that you want to use and click OK.

The database window appears.

3. Click the Table tab and then click the New button.

The New Table dialog box appears (see Figure 10-4).

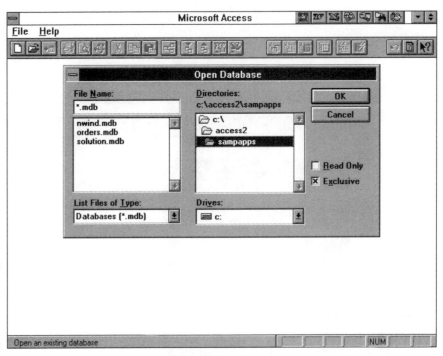

Figure 10-3:
The Open Database dialog box.

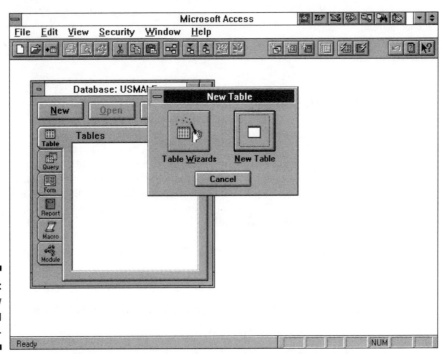

Figure 10-4:
The New Table dialog box.

When you create a table, Access gives you the choice of using its Table Wizard or creating a table from scratch. If you want to create a database table quickly, use the Table Wizard. If you want to create a custom database table (and you know what you're doing), ignore the Table Wizard and create a table from scratch.

Creating database fields

Within each database table, you have to define the information that you want to save, such as names, addresses, and phone numbers. Each bit of information gets stored in a *field*. Think of a typical form that asks you to fill in your name and address. The blank line where you write your name is one field, and the blank line where you write your address is another field.

To create database fields with the Table Wizard, follow these steps:

1. **With the New Table dialog box on-screen, click the Table Wizards button or type** W.

   The Table Wizard dialog box appears (see Figure 10-5).

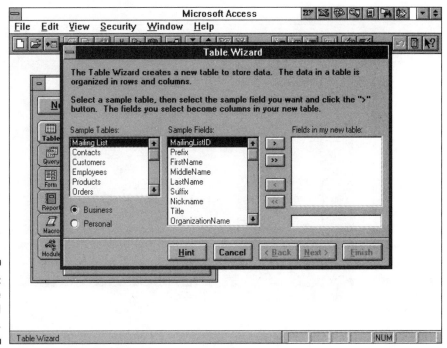

Figure 10-5:
The Table Wizard dialog box.

2. **In the Sample Tables list, click the type of table that you want to create.**

3. **In the Sample Fields list, click each field that you want to include in your table, and then click the > button.**

4. **Repeat Step 3 until you finish inserting all the fields you want for your new table.**

5. **Click the Next button.**

   A new Table Wizard dialog box appears (see Figure 10-6).

6. **Type the name that you want to give your table and click the Next button.**

   Still another Table Wizard dialog box appears.

7. **Click the Finish button.**

   Access displays your completed table in a row-and-column format that looks suspiciously like a spreadsheet (called the *datasheet view*).

The columns in the datasheet view represent your separate fields. The rows in the datasheet view represent records. Each record contains all the information for a single person.

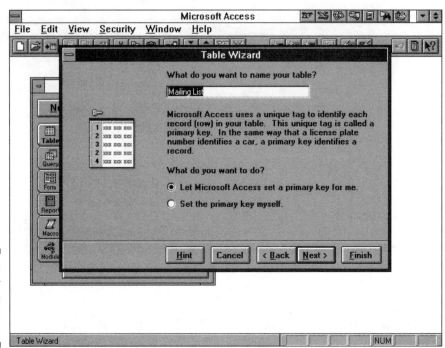

Figure 10-6:
Another
Table
Wizard
dialog box.

After you create a database file, define one or more database tables, and define one or more fields within each database table, you're (finally) ready to store some real information in your database. The various parts of a Microsoft Access database are shown in Figure 10-7.

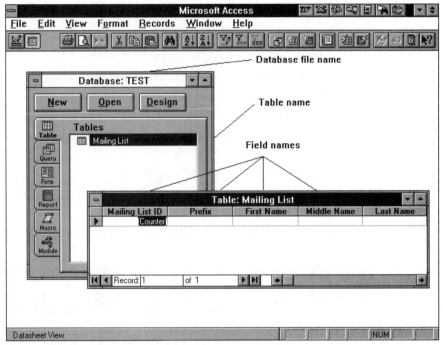

Figure 10-7:
The parts of
a typical
Microsoft
Access
database.

Modifying your data

The longer you store data, the more likely you are to need to modify the information as people move, change phone numbers, or disappear altogether. Modifying data can mean

- Adding new records
- Editing existing records
- Deleting fields from existing records
- Deleting entire records

When you need to add a new name, address, and phone number, you have to add a record. If someone moves or gets a new phone number, you have to edit that person's existing record. If your changes are extensive, sometimes it's easier just to wipe out the old data and type new data. In these situations, you may find it easier to delete a field from an existing record.

For those people whom you no longer need to see, you can delete an entire record, effectively wiping their names out of your Access database. Use this procedure sparingly, of course, because it's just as easy to wipe out important names and addresses as it is to delete useless ones.

To add a record to a database, follow these steps and see Figure 10-8:

1. **From the File menu, choose Open Database (or press Ctrl+O).**

   The Open Database dialog box appears.

2. **Highlight the database file that you want to open and click the OK button.**

   Access displays the database window.

3. **In the database window, highlight the table to which you want to add a record and click the Open button.**

   The datasheet view of your table appears.

4. **Move the cursor to the last record marked by the New record symbol (*) in the very left of your table window.**

5. **Type the data for each field and press Tab in between each entry.**

Figure 10-8:
How to add a new record to a database.

To edit data in a database, follow these steps and also refer to Figure 10-9:

1. **From the File menu, choose Open Database (or press Ctrl+O).**

   The Open Database dialog box appears.

2. **Highlight the database file that you want to open and click the OK button.**

   Access displays the database window.

3. **In the database window, highlight the table that contains the data you want to edit and click the Open button.**

   The datasheet view of your table appears.

4. **Click the field that you want to edit.**

5. **Make your corrections.**

   Press the left-and right-arrow keys to move the cursor in the field. Press Backspace to delete characters to the left of the cursor and Delete to delete characters to the right of the cursor.

6. **Press Tab when you finish.**

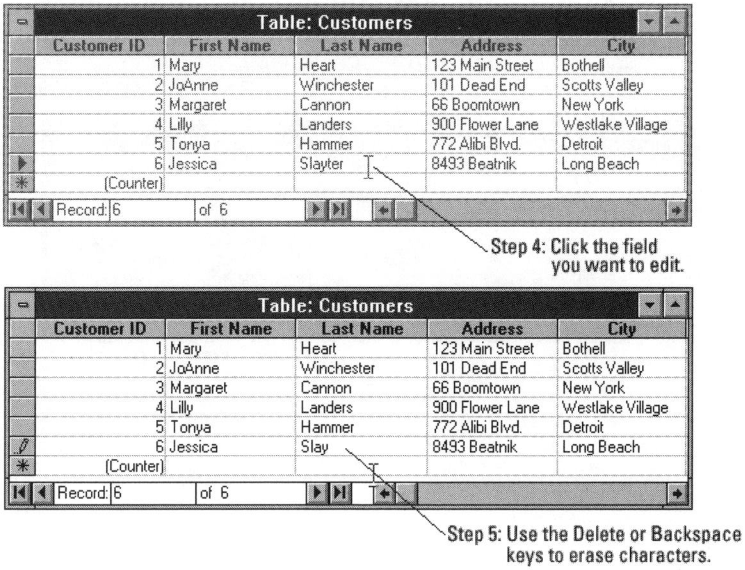

Step 4: Click the field you want to edit.

Figure 10-9:
How to edit
a record in a
database.

Step 5: Use the Delete or Backspace keys to erase characters.

To delete data from a database field, do the following:

1. **From the File menu, choose Open Database (or press Ctrl+O).**

   The Open Database dialog box appears.

2. **Highlight the database file that you want to open and click the OK button.**

   Access displays the database window.

3. **In the database window, highlight the table and click the Open button.**

   The datasheet view of your table appears.

4. **Use the arrow keys to highlight the data that you want to delete.**

5. **Press Delete.**

   Access deletes the highlighted data, as shown in Figure 10-10.

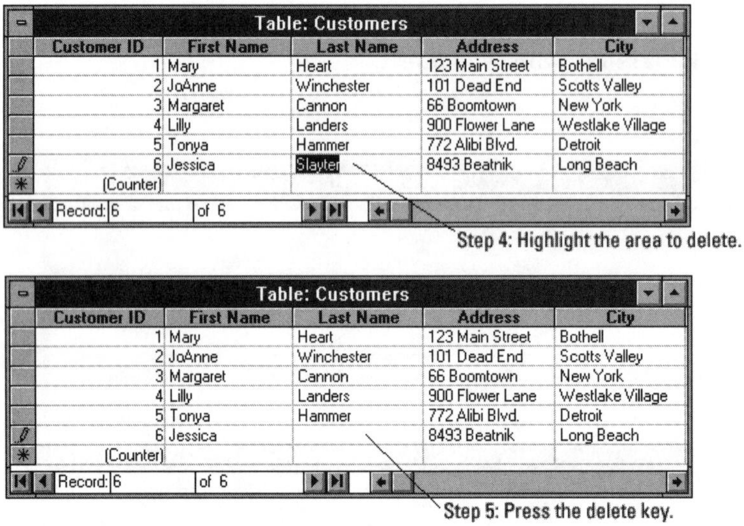

Table: Customers				
Customer ID	**First Name**	**Last Name**	**Address**	**City**
1	Mary	Heart	123 Main Street	Bothell
2	JoAnne	Winchester	101 Dead End	Scotts Valley
3	Margaret	Cannon	66 Boomtown	New York
4	Lilly	Landers	900 Flower Lane	Westlake Village
5	Tonya	Hammer	772 Alibi Blvd.	Detroit
6	Jessica	Slayter	8493 Beatnik	Long Beach
	(Counter)			

Record: 6   of 6

Step 4: Highlight the area to delete.

Figure 10-10:
How to delete data stored in a field.

Table: Customers				
Customer ID	**First Name**	**Last Name**	**Address**	**City**
1	Mary	Heart	123 Main Street	Bothell
2	JoAnne	Winchester	101 Dead End	Scotts Valley
3	Margaret	Cannon	66 Boomtown	New York
4	Lilly	Landers	900 Flower Lane	Westlake Village
5	Tonya	Hammer	772 Alibi Blvd.	Detroit
6	Jessica		8493 Beatnik	Long Beach
	(Counter)			

Record: 6   of 6

Step 5: Press the delete key.

To delete an entire record from a database, follow these steps:

1. **From the File menu, choose Open Database (or press Ctrl+O).**

   The Open Database dialog box appears.

2. **Highlight the database file that you want to open and click the OK button.**

   Access displays the database window.

3. **In the database window, highlight the table that contains the record you want to delete and click the Open button.**

   The datasheet view of your table appears.

4. **Place the mouse pointer to the left of the record row that you want to delete.**

   The mouse pointer turns into an arrow pointing to the right (see Figure 10-11).

5. **Click one time.**

   Access highlights the entire record row.

6. **Press Delete.**

   Access deletes the entire record.

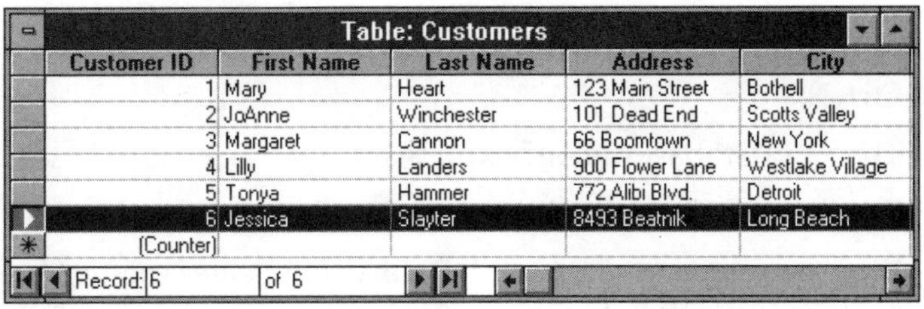

Figure 10-11:
How to
delete an
entire
record.

Customer ID	First Name	Last Name	Address	City
1	Mary	Heart	123 Main Street	Bothell
2	JoAnne	Winchester	101 Dead End	Scotts Valley
3	Margaret	Cannon	66 Boomtown	New York
4	Lilly	Landers	900 Flower Lane	Westlake Village
5	Tonya	Hammer	772 Alibi Blvd.	Detroit
6	Jessica	Slayter	8493 Beatnik	Long Beach
(Counter)				

Table: Customers

Record: 6   of 6

Storing Names, Addresses, and Phone Numbers

Because the most common types of information that most people need on a regular basis are names, addresses, and phone numbers, let Access bring you into the modern age: store this information on your computer. After you've stored names, addresses, and phone numbers in a database, you'll never again be at a loss for someone's phone number or address. (Unless, of course, you lose your database.)

Creating a phone and address database

To create a phone and address database, you need to create a new MDB database file, define a table in your database, and then set up fields within that table to actually store the information. By the time you finish creating a database, guess what? It's empty.

When you create a database, you essentially create a cookie-cutter device for storing information. After you finish creating your database, it's time to start dumping in data.

To create a phone and address database, follow these steps:

1. **From the File menu, choose the New Database command (or press Ctrl+N).**

   The New Database dialog box appears.

2. **Type a name that contains up to eight characters and press Enter.**

   You can use a name such as MyData, your business name (Acme), or something creative. For the sake of having an honest-to-goodness example, however, pretend that you're running a business called U.S. Male, which provides male escorts for women. So type **USMALE** and press Enter. The database window appears.

3. **Click the Table tab and then click the New button.**

   The New Table dialog box appears.

4. **Click the Table Wizards button or type W.**

   The Table Wizards dialog box appears.

5. **In the Sample Tables category, highlight Customers.**

6. **In the Sample Fields category, highlight the following fields, clicking the > button after each one:**

> CustomerID
>
> FirstName
>
> LastName
>
> Address
>
> City
>
> State
>
> PostalCode
>
> Country
>
> PhoneNumber
>
> FaxNumber
>
> Note

7. **Click the Next button.**

   Another Table Wizard dialog box appears, asking you what you want to name your database table. By default, Access assumes that you want to call it Customers.

8. **Click the Next button.**

   Still another Table Wizard dialog box appears, asking, What do you want to do? By default, Access selects the Enter data directly into the table option.

9. **Click the Finish button.**

   Access cheerfully displays the datasheet view of your table, organized in rows and columns much like a spreadsheet (see Figure 10-12).

10. **From the File menu, choose Close.**

    Access displays your Customers table in the database window (see Figure 10-13).

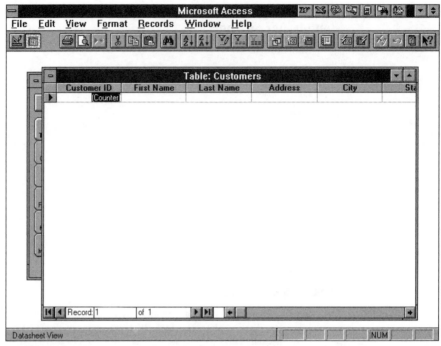

Figure 10-12:
The datasheet view of the Customers table.

Figure 10-13:
The Customers table, highlighted in the USMALE database window.

Entering data in your phone and address database

When you finish creating a database file, tables, and fields (or when the person you hired to do it finishes), you're ready to start entering information.

For consistency, always enter your data the same way. For example, some people like spelling out state names (*Michigan*), others abbreviate it in their own way (*Mich.*), and still others use the official two-letter abbreviation (*MI*). Whichever method you choose, use it throughout your database. Otherwise, your database won't be able to find all your data because that data will have been stored with different words (*Michigan, Mich.*, and *MI*).

To enter data in your phone and address database (see Figure 10-14), follow these steps:

1. **In the USMALE database window, highlight the Customers table, and then click the O̲pen button (or press Ctrl+O).**

   The datasheet view of your Customers table appears.

2. **Press Tab to move the cursor to the FirstName field.**

3. **Type a first name (such as** Mary**) and press Tab to move to the LastName field.**

4. **Type a last name (such as** Heart**) and press Tab to move to the Address field.**

5. **Type an address (such as** 123 Main Street**) and press Tab to move to the City field.**

6. **Type a city (such as** Bothell**) and press Tab to move to the State field.**

7. **Type a state (such as** WA**) and press Tab to move to the PostalCode field.**

8. **Type a postal code (such as** 98041-3022**) and press Tab to move to the Country field.**

   Notice that Access automatically inserts the dash into the postal code.

9. **Type a country (such as** USA**) and press Tab to move to the PhoneNumber field.**

10. **Type a phone number (such as** (206) 123-4567**) and press Tab to move to the FaxNumber field.**

    Notice that Access automatically formats the phone number with parentheses and dashes.

11. **Type a fax number (such as** (206) 123-0987**) and press Tab to move to the Note field.**

Notice that Access automatically formats the fax number with parentheses and dashes.

12. **Type a memo (such as** Has a $3,000 credit limit**) and press Tab.**

13. **Repeat Steps 2 through 12 for each person whose information you want to store in your database.**

14. **When you finish adding information, open the File menu and choose Close.**

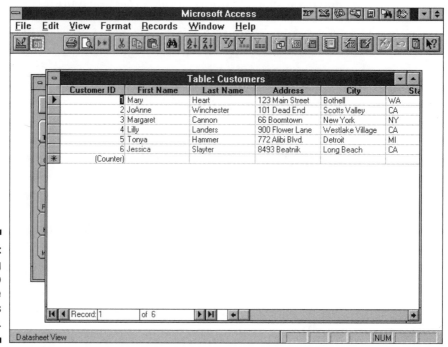

Figure 10-14: Entering data into your phone and address database.

Time Is Money

Rather than being paid a flat fee (and spending most of the time complaining that they aren't paid enough anyway), many professionals, such as consultants and attorneys, are paid by the hour. For these people, time really is money, because the more time they spend on a project, the more money they can collect later (they hope).

Because tracking your time is crucial when it comes to delivering a bill, you need precise accuracy (partially so that you can justify the outrageous expenses). To help you track your time, this section shows you how to create a simple time-tracking database.

Creating a time-tracking database

Although you can create a time-tracking database and store it in a separate MDB database file, you're more likely to track your time with a particular client. Rather than type a client's address and phone number over and over in a separate MDB database file, it's easier to create separate tables stored in the same MDB file.

One table can contain customer information, such as names, addresses, and phone numbers; and the second table can contain the actual time-tracking information. Then you can use the amazing powers of Microsoft Access to create a *relationship* between the tables (see Figure 10-15).

Relationships between separate tables give you more flexibility than dumping every bit of information into a single database table. For example, you might store names, addresses, phone numbers, time billed, and project names in one database table. But what happens if you have a second or third project that you need to bill to the same client?

You could keep adding separate fields for each project, but a better solution is to keep time-tracking information separate and create a relationship between the customer data and the time-tracking data, as shown in Figure 10-15. That way, you theoretically can bill multiple projects to a single client (useful for government contractors that bill $593.86 hammers, $45.00 paper clips, and $3,902.00 toilet seats to the military).

To create a time-tracking database, follow these steps:

1. **From the File menu, choose the Open Database command (or press Ctrl+O).**

   The Open Database dialog box appears.

2. **Highlight the USMALE.MDB database file and click OK.**

   The USMALE database window appears.

3. **Click the Table tab and then click the New button.**

   The New Table dialog box appears.

4. **Click Table Wizard or type** W.

   The Table Wizards dialog box appears.

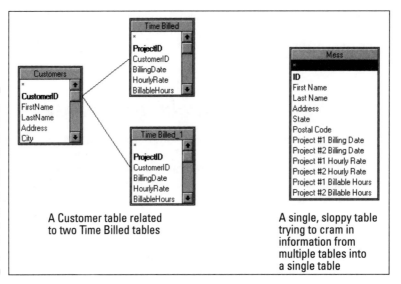

Figure 10-15:
Dumping all
your data
into one
table,
compared
with
establishing
relationships
between
tables.

A Customer table related
to two Time Billed tables

A single, sloppy table
trying to cram in
information from
multiple tables into
a single table

5. **In the Sample Tables category, select Time Billed.**

6. **In the Sample Fields category, select the following fields, clicking the >
button after each one:**

> ProjectID
>
> CustomerID
>
> BillingDate
>
> HourlyRate
>
> BillableHours
>
> Note

7. **Click the Next button.**

Another Table Wizard dialog box appears, asking for the name you want to
give the database table. Access assumes that you want to call the table
Time Billed.

8. **Click the Next button.**

Still another Table Wizard dialog box appears, asking whether this table is
related to any other table in your database. Access assumes that you want
to relate this table to the Customers table.

9. **Click the Next button.**

   Yet another Table Wizard dialog box appears, asking whether you want to start entering data in your new table.

10. **Click the Finish button.**

    The datasheet view of the Time Billed table appears (see Figure 10-16).

11. **From the File menu, choose Close.**

    Access displays your Time Billed table in the database window (see Figure 10-17).

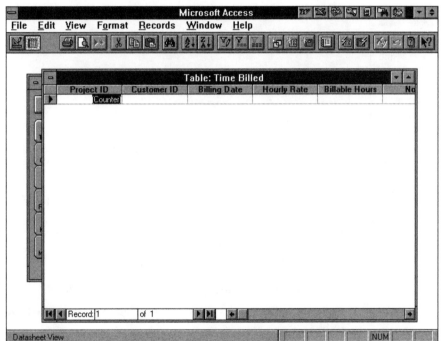

Figure 10-16:
The datasheet view of the Time Billed table.

Entering data in your time-tracking database

Unlike the familiar structure of names, addresses, and phone numbers, the time-tracking database stores hourly billing rates, hours, and customer ID numbers. Because both the Customer table and the Time Billed table store the customer ID number, you can use this relationship to link multiple Time Billed records to a single client.

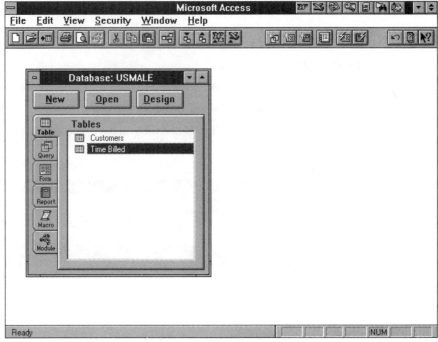

Figure 10-17:
The Time
Billed table,
highlighted
in the
USMALE
database
window.

To enter data in your time-tracking database, follow these steps:

1. **In the USMALE database window, highlight the Time Billed table and click the Open button (or press Ctrl+O).**

   The datasheet view of your Time Billed table appears.

2. **Press Tab to move the cursor to the CustomerID field.**

3. **Type a number (such as 1) and press Tab to move to the BillingDate field.**

4. **Type a billing date (such as 10/18/95) and press Tab to move to the HourlyRate field.**

5. **Type an hourly rate (such as 50.25) and press Tab to move to the BillableHours field.**

   Notice that Access automatically formats this number so that it appears as $50.25.

6. **Type the number of billable hours (such as 8) and press Tab to move to the Note field.**

7. **Type a note (such as** Deadline is New Year's Eve**) and press Tab.**

8. **Repeat Steps 2 through 7 for each record that you want to store in your database.**

9. **When you finish adding information, open the File menu and choose Close.**

The finished product should look like Figure 10-18.

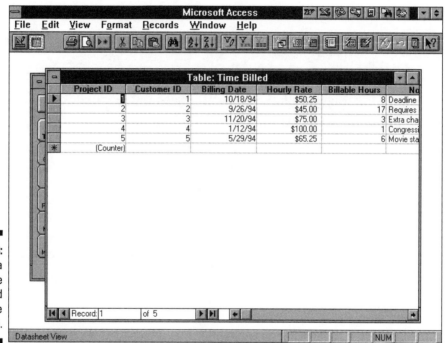

Figure 10-18:
Sample data
stored in the
Time Billed
database
table.

Tracking Your Office Assets

Quick — recite the model names and serial numbers of all the valuable equipment that you own! Sound easy? If so, skip this section. But if you're like the rest of us who need to keep track of valuables for insurance and tax purposes, you may need a fixed-asset database.

A fixed-asset database allows to you track what you own and how much it's worth. Armed with this information, you can provide your insurance company with proof that thieves really did break into your office and steal a 747 jumbo jet, convince the government that your Super Nintendo unit actually is an office computer, and persuade the boss that your new Ferrari really is a company car.

Creating a fixed-asset database

To create a fixed database, you could create a new MDB database file, define a table in your database, and then set up fields within that table to store the information. But because your fixed assets are related to your business, a better idea is to store this information as a separate table in your existing business MDB database file.

To create a fixed-asset database, follow these steps:

1. **From the _F_ile menu, choose the _O_pen Database command (or press Ctrl+O).**

    The Open Database dialog box appears.

2. **Highlight the USMALE.MDB database file and click OK.**

    The USMALE database window appears.

3. **Click the Table tab and then click the _N_ew button.**

    The New Table dialog box appears.

4. **Click Table _W_izards or type** W.

    The Table Wizard dialog box appears.

5. **In the Sample Tables category, select Fixed Assets.**

6. **In the Sample Fields category, select the following fields, clicking the > button after each one:**

    FixedAssetID

    AssetName

    Make

    Model

    ModelNumber

    SerialNumber

    BeginningValue

    CurrentValue

    Description

7. **Click the _N_ext button.**

    Another Table Wizard dialog box appears, asking for the name that you want to give the database table. Access assumes that you want to call the table Fixed Assets.

8. Click the Next button.

Still another Table Wizard dialog box appears, asking whether this table is related to any other table in your database. Because the Fixed Assets table does not use any fields contained in the other tables, Access assumes that this table is unrelated to any other table.

9. Click the Next button.

Yet another Table Wizard dialog box appears, asking whether you want to start entering data in your new table.

10. Click the Finish button.

The datasheet view of the Time Billed table appears (see Figure 10-19).

11. From the File menu, choose Close.

Access displays your Fixed Assets table in the database window (see Figure 10-20).

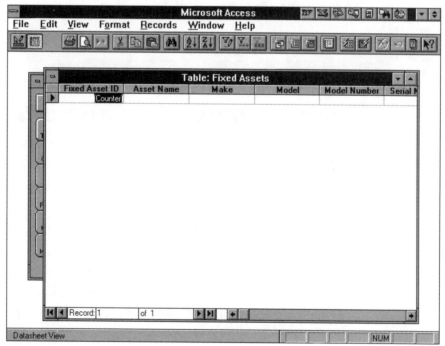

Figure 10-19:
The datasheet view of the Fixed Assets table.

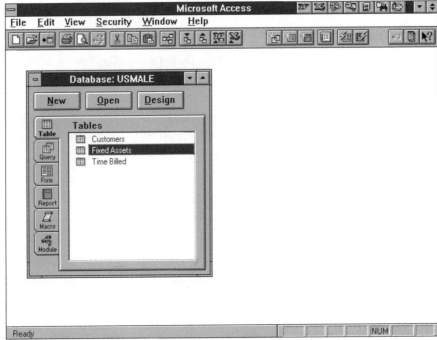

Figure 10-20:
The Fixed
Assets table,
highlighted
in the
USMALE
database
window.

Entering data in your fixed-asset database

Your fixed-asset database can store information about your business equipment. (Of course, your fixed-asset database will be worthless if someone steals your computer.)

To enter data in a fixed-asset database, follow these steps:

1. **In the USMALE database window, highlight the Fixed Assets table and click the Open button (or press Ctrl+O).**

   The datasheet view of your Fixed Assets table appears.

2. **Press Tab to move the cursor to the AssetName field.**

3. **Type the name of your asset (such as** 486 computer**) and press Tab to move to the Make field.**

4. **Type the make of your asset (such as** Big Brother Computers**) and press Tab to move to the Model field.**

5. **Type the model of your asset (such as** Model T**) and press Tab to move to the ModelNumber field.**

6. **Type the model number (such as** 1234**) and press Tab to move to the SerialNumber field.**

7. **Type the serial number (such as** 0093651**) and press Tab to move to the BeginningValue field.**

8. **Type a beginning value (such as** 3500**) and press Tab to move to the CurrentValue field.**

   Notice that Access automatically formats this number so that it appears as $3,500.00.

9. **Type the current value of the asset (such as** 2000**) and press Tab to move to the Description field.**

   Notice that Access automatically formats this number so that it appears as $2,000.00.

10. **Type a description (such as** The big ugly one that doesn't work**) and press Tab.**

11. **Repeat Steps 2 through 10 for each record that you want to store in your database.**

12. **When you finish adding information, open the File menu and choose Close.**

   The Fixed Assets database table shold look like Figure 10-21.

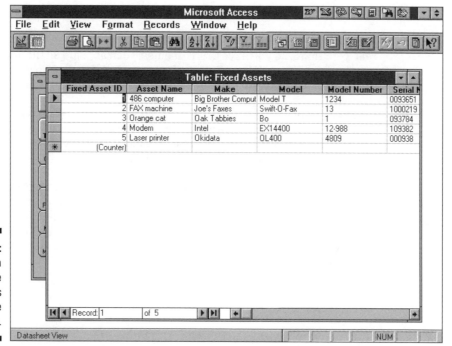

Figure 10-21: Sample data stored in the Fixed Assets database table.

Searching a Database

After you create a database and stuff information into it, guess what? It's useless unless you can retrieve information from it again. After all, you could store the names and addresses of all your elementary-school teachers since the second grade, but unless you'll need that information in the future for some reason, there's no reason to store it, let alone to retrieve it. If you want to store stuff that you never intend to retrieve again, use your attic, basement, or garage instead.

Typical paper databases — such as filing cabinets, Rolodex files, and paper folders — are designed for storing and retrieving information alphabetically. By contrast, Access can find and retrieve information any way you want: by area code or ZIP code, alphabetically by last name or first name, by state, or by date.

Searching a database is great for retrieving specific information, such as a specific person's phone number, all the people who live in Minnesota, or all the people who live in a certain area code. Access provides two ways to search a database:

- ✔ Finding a specific record
- ✔ Finding one or more records by using a filter

Finding one specific record

To find a specific record, you have to know part of what you want. Access can't read your mind, so you have to give it clues, such as "Find all the addresses of people who live in Alaska," "Find the first names of people whose last name is Black," or "Find the phone number of James Earl Jones."

When you want to find a specific record, you have to know at least one bit of data about that record. If you want to find a specific phone number, for example, you have to know the first or last name of the person you want to call. (Otherwise, what's the sense of looking up a phone number?)

The more specific the data that you already know, the faster Access can find the record you want. Asking Access to find the phone number of someone who lives in California is going to be a lot slower than asking Access to find the phone number of someone whose last name is Bangladore. Lots of people live in California, but how many people have such an odd last name as Bangladore?

When you want to tell Access to find something for you, you have to use a dialog box. This dialog box allows you to specify several options:

✔ The Find What option tells Access exactly what you want it to find. This could be part of a word, a single word, or an entire phrase.

✔ The Where option tells Access where to look for the data you specified in the Find What option. Following are your three choices:

Any Part of Field (a search for *Ann* would find both *MaryAnne* and *AnnMarie*)

Match Whole Field (a search for *Ann* would find only records containing *Ann*)

Start of Field (a search for *Ann* would find *AnnMarie* and *Ann* but not *MaryAnne*)

✔ The Search In option tells Access which fields to search for the data specified in the Find What option. Your choices are Current Field (where the cursor appears) and All Fields.

✔ The Direction option tells Access which way to start looking for the data specified in the Find What option. Your choices are Up and Down. Up tells Access to search all records, starting from the record that currently contains the cursor and going up to the first record in the table. Down tells Access to search all records, starting from the record that currently contains the cursor and going down to the last record in the table.

✔ The Match Case option is for finicky people who only want exactly what's typed in the Find What option. Choosing this option means that if you search for *AnN*, Access will find records containing *AnN* but not records containing *Ann, ann*, or *aNN*.

✔ The Search Fields as Formatted option is for searching for data that appears in a different format from the one in which it was stored. For example, Access can display a date as 10/14/95 but store it as 14-Oct-95. Choosing this option tells Access to search for data only as it appears on-screen.

To find a specific record in the Customers database table, follow these steps:

1. **From the File menu, choose the Open Database command (or press Ctrl+O).**

   The Open Database dialog box appears.

2. **Highlight the USMALE.MDB database file and click OK.**

   The database window appears.

Figure 10-22:
The Find in
Field dialog
box.

3. Click the Customers table, and then click the Open button.

The Customers table appears in datasheet view.

4. Click the field containing the data that you already know.

For example, if you want to find a person's phone number but know only that person's last name, click the LastName field.

5. From the Edit menu, choose Find (or press Ctrl+F).

The Find in Field dialog box appears, as shown in Figure 10-22.

6. Type a last name that you want to find (such as Heart**) and click the Find First button.**

Access highlights the first record that contains *Heart* as the last name.

7. Click the Close button to close the Find in a Field dialog box.

Finding one or more records by using a filter

To find one or more records, you have to create a filter. A filter tells Access something like "Show me all the people who live in Oregon and have the last name of Smith." Using this filter, Access rummages through your entire database and shows you the names, addresses, and phone numbers of all the Smiths who live in Oregon.

When you want to use a filter, you have to use the Filter dialog box, which is shown in Figure 10-23. This dialog box allows you to specify several options:

- The Field option tells Access which fields you want to search. You can choose one or more fields.

- The Sort option tells Access to sort records in alphabetical order (*ascending*), to sort records in reverse alphabetical order (*descending*), or to not bother sorting at all (*not sorted*).

- The Criteria option tells Access what to look for. You can specify two or more criteria, such as "Find all the addresses of people who live in Oregon *or* California" or "Find all the addresses of people who live in Oregon *and* California."

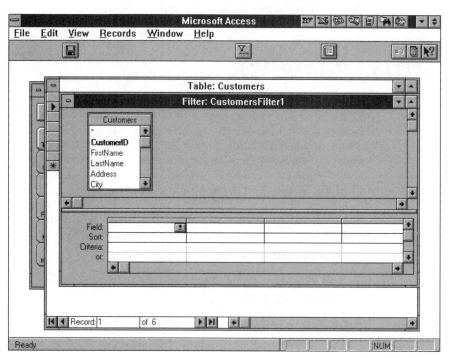

Figure 10-23:
The Filter
dialog box.

To find one or more records in the Customers database table by using a filter, follow these steps:

1. **From the File menu, choose the Open Database command (or press Ctrl+O).**

   The Open Database dialog box appears.

2. **Highlight the USMALE.MDB database file and click OK.**

   The database window appears.

3. **Click the Customers tab and then click the Open button.**

   The Customers table appears in datasheet view.

4. **From the Records menu, choose Edit Filter/Sort.**

   The Filter dialog box appears.

5. **Click the Field list-box arrow and choose State.**

6. **Click the Criteria box and type NM.**

7. **From the Records menu, choose Apply Filter/Sort.**

   Access displays only those records containing *NM* in the State field.

8. **From the File menu, choose Close.**

Sorting a database

To sort a database, you have to tell Access which field you want to sort and how you want to sort it (in ascending or descending order). For example, you can sort your database alphabetically by last name, by ZIP code, or by city. Unlike searching, which shows only part of your database, sorting simply shows your entire database from a different point of view.

To sort the Customers database table, follow these steps:

1. **From the File menu, choose the Open Database command (or press Ctrl+O).**

   The Open Database dialog box appears.

2. **Highlight the USMALE.MDB database file and click OK.**

   The database window appears.

3. **Click the Customers table and then click the Open button.**

   The Customers table appears in datasheet view.

4. Click the LastName field.

5. From the Records menu, choose Quicksort and then choose Ascending.

Access obediently sorts your records alphabetically by last name (see Figure 10-24).

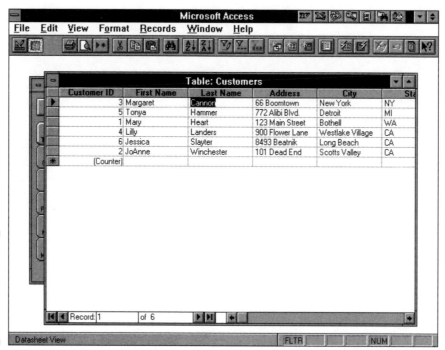

Figure 10-24:
The Customers table, sorted alphabetically by last name.

Chapter 11

Making the Most of Stored Information

In This Chapter

▶ Asking questions with queries

▶ Making reports so that your data looks good

▶ Making mailing labels

▶ Forms: seeing your data from another perspective

*A*fter you store information in a database, the real fun comes in using that information somehow. After all, it's useless to store all the names and addresses of your customers if you don't use this information to help you make more money (which is what business is all about).

To help you use your stored information effectively, Access provides different ways to view, print, and examine your data. Unlike the static-looking information stored in Rolodex files, address books, and paper forms, data stored in Access can be molded, shaped, and manipulated like Silly Putty.

Asking Questions with Queries

Query is just a fancy term for a question that you can ask Access. After you store information in a database, queries help you get that information out again. A query can be as simple as finding the names and phone numbers of all the people in your database who live in Arkansas, or it can be as sophisticated as making Access retrieve all salespeople who made more than $50,000 in sales and who live in California, Nevada, or Arizona.

What's the difference between queries and the Find command?

Both queries and the Find command tell Access to retrieve and display certain data from your database. The main difference between the two is that the Find command can search only for specific data in one field, whereas queries can search for data in one or more fields.

A second crucial difference is that you can save queries as part of your database file so that you can use them over and over without defining what you want to look for each time. With the Find command, you have to define what you want to look for each time.

Use the Find command when you need to search through one field and you only need to make this search one time. Use queries when you need to search through two or more fields and you need to make this search periodically.

Because queries can be so flexible and powerful, they constitute a whole subject that you can study all by itself. (In fact, the Microsoft Access manual devotes four chapters to explaining queries, and many computer programmers spend entire semesters studying database queries, so don't feel bad if you don't master the topic of queries in 21 days.)

Do you need to use queries? No, but they can make life a whole lot easier for you if you do. As an alternative, you can examine your entire database and try to make some sense of it, but it's much easier to have Access dig through your database and find what you want.

For example, a query could list all the names and addresses of customers who haven't paid their bills in the past 60 days. Trying to find this information on your own would be time-consuming and tedious. By comparison, having a query find it for you is fast and accurate. The whole secret to using queries is knowing what you want and telling Access how to find it. (Not always an easy task. If you've ever told a child to bring you something cold to drink and he came back with a bottle of liquid fertilizer, you already know the problem of giving accurate commands.)

Creating a query

When you create a query, you must specify what type of data you want Access to find. How you specify what to find is called *search criteria*. To give you an idea of how complicated queries can get, here are some of the most common types of search criteria:

✔ *Exact matches* tell Access to find all records containing certain information, such as all people with the last name of Jones who live in Idaho and work as lumberjacks.

✔ *Partial matches* tell Access to find all records containing certain information, such as all people whose last names begin with *B* and whose job titles contain the word *computer.*

✔ *Less than* tells Access to find all records containing information that is less than a specific value, such as finding all people who make less than $30,000 a year, have been married for less than three years, and fly on a commercial airline fewer than four times a year.

✔ *Greater than* tells Access to find all records containing information that is greater than a specific value, such as finding all people who own more than three yachts, earn more than $50,000 a month, and haven't paid any taxes in more than five years.

✔ *Between* tells Access to find all records that fall between two specific values, such as finding all people born between 1960 and 1970 who earn more than $30,000 a year but less than $90,000 and who have more than two but fewer than five children.

Queries can get fairly complicated. You could ask Access to find the names of all people who earn less than $75,000 a year, live in Seattle or Detroit, have owned their homes for more than six years, work in computer jobs, own a personal computer, and subscribe to more than three but fewer than six magazines a year.

Just remember that the quality of your answers depends heavily on the quality of your queries (questions). If you create a poorly designed query, Access probably won't find all the data that you really need and may overlook important information that could save your business or your job.

To create a query for your Customers and Time Billed tables, follow these steps:

1. **From the File menu, choose the Open Database command (or press Ctrl+O).**

   The Open Database dialog box appears.

2. **Highlight the USMALE.MDB database file (created in Chapter 10), and click OK.**

   The database window appears.

3. **Click the Query tab and then click the New button.**

   The New Query dialog box appears (see Figure 11-1).

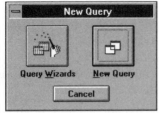

Figure 11-1:
The New
Query dialog
box.

4. Click the New Query button.

The Add Table dialog box appears (see Figure 11-2).

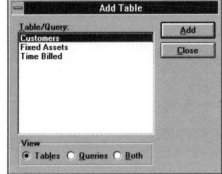

Figure 11-2:
The Add
Table dialog
box.

5. Choose Customers and click the Add button.

6. Choose Time Billed, click the Add button, and then click the Close button.

The Select Query window appears.

7. Double-click FirstName in the Customers table.

Access displays FirstName in the first field at the bottom of the query window (see Figure 11-3).

8. Double-click LastName in the Customers table.

Access displays LastName in the second field at the bottom of the query window.

9. Double-click PhoneNumber in the Customers table.

Access displays PhoneNumber in the third field at the bottom of the query window.

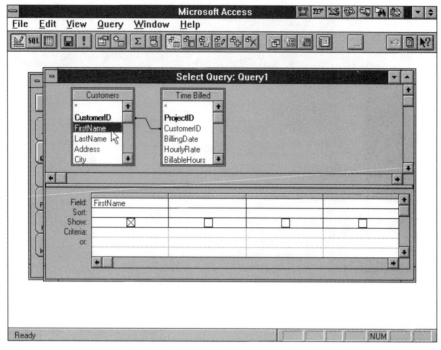

Figure 11-3:
FirstName
displayed in
the first field
at the
bottom of
the query
window.

10. **Double-click BillingDate in the Time Billed table.**

    Access displays `BillingDate` in the fourth field at the bottom of the query window.

11. **Click the Criteria row below the BillingDate column.**

12. **Click the Build button.**

    This is the ellipses button in the toolbar. The Expression Builder window appears (see Figure 11-4).

13. **Type** Between 1-Oct-94 and 31-Dec-94 **and click the OK button.**

    Access displays your search criteria at the bottom of the query window.

14. **From the Query menu, choose Run.**

    Access displays the result of your query (see Figure 11-5).

15. **From the File menu, choose Save Query (or press Ctrl+S).**

    The Save As dialog box appears.

16. **Type** Fourth quarter billings **and press Enter.**

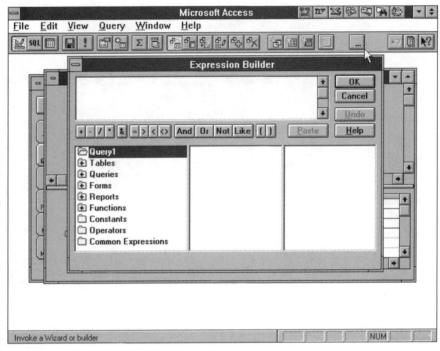

Figure 11-4:
The
Expression
Builder
window and
the Build
button in the
toolbar.

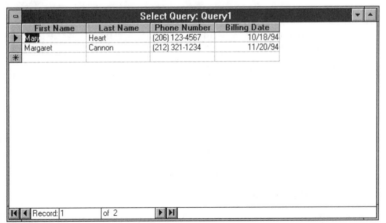

Figure 11-5:
The result of
a successful
query.

17. **From the File menu, choose Close.**

Access displays your query name in the database window (see Figure 11-6).

Figure 11-6:
The query
name in the
database
window.

Using a query

After you create and save a query, you can use that query as many times as you want, no matter how much you add, delete, or modify the records in your database. Because some queries can be fairly complicated ("Find all the people in North Dakota who owe more than $10,000 on their credit cards, own their own farms, and have declared bankruptcy in the past 30 days"), saving and reusing queries helps save you time—which is the whole purpose of computers.

To use an existing query in the USMALE database, follow these steps:

1. **If USMALE.MDB is not already open, choose the Open Database command from the File menu (or press Ctrl+O).**

   The Open Database dialog box appears.

2. **Highlight the USMALE.MDB database file and click OK.**

   The database window appears.

3. **Click the Query tab, highlight** Fourth quarter billings **and then click the Open button.**

   Access immediately displays the result of your query.

4. **From the File menu, choose Close.**

Deleting a query

Eventually, a query no longer may serve its purpose as you add, delete, and modify the data in your database. To keep your database window from overflowing with queries, delete the ones that you don't need any more.

Deleting a query does *not* delete any data. When you delete a query, you're deleting only the criteria that you use to search your database.

To delete a query, follow these steps:

1. **From the File menu, choose the Open Database command (or press Ctrl+O).**

   The Open Database dialog box appears.

2. **Highlight the MDB database file that you want to use and click OK.**

   The database window appears.

3. **In the database window, click the Query tab.**

4. **Click the query that you want to delete.**

5. **From the Edit menu, choose Delete (or press Delete).**

   Access displays a dialog box, asking whether you really want to delete the query.

6. **Click OK.**

   Your query disappears from the database window.

If you suddenly realize that you deleted a query by mistake, don't cringe in horror—immediately choose Undo from the Edit menu (or press Ctrl+Z). Access undoes your last command and restores your query to its preceding pristine condition. Whenever you do something by mistake, the Undo command can correct it. Just make sure that you choose the Undo command immediately after screwing up; otherwise, Access may not be able to recover from your mistake.

Making Reports So That Your Data Looks Good

If you store valuable information in your databases, chances are that you'll need to show somebody what you have. Rather than drag someone to your computer and display the data on your pretty new color monitor, print out your data in a report instead.

Besides being more convenient than making someone look at your computer, reports can selectively display data, calculate new results, and make everything look pretty enough so that other people think you put out more effort than you really did.

To make a report from your Fixed Assets table, follow these steps:

1. **From the File menu, choose the Open Database command (or press Ctrl+O).**

   The New Database dialog box appears.

2. **Highlight the USMALE.MDB database file and click OK.**

   The database window appears.

3. **Click the Report tab in the database window and then click the New button.**

   The New Report dialog box appears.

4. **Click the arrow next to the Select a Table/Query list box and select Fixed Assets.**

5. **Click the Report Wizards button.**

   A Report Wizards dialog box appears, asking Which Wizard do you want? (see Figure 11-7).

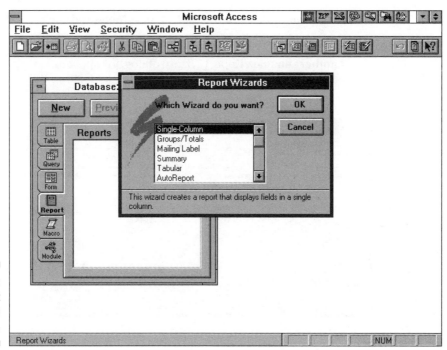

Figure 11-7:
The Report
Wizards
dialog box.

6. Choose Summary and click OK.

A Summary Report Wizard dialog box appears, asking `Which fields do` `you want to group by, if any?` (see Figure 11-8).

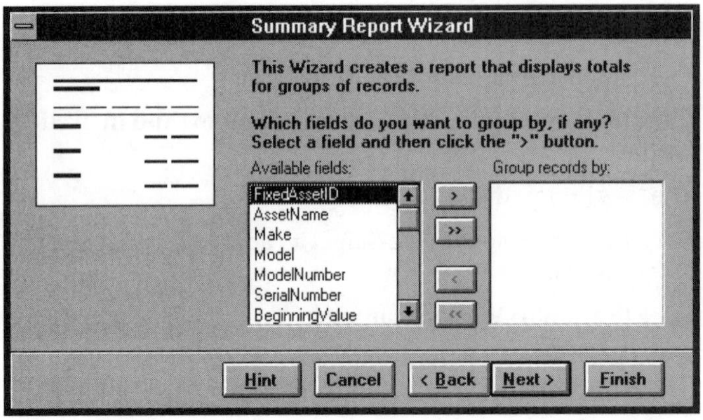

Figure 11-8:
The
Summary
Report
Wizard
dialog box.

7. In the Available Fields list, select AssetName and click the > button.

8. Click the Next button.

Another Summary Report Wizard dialog box appears, asking `How do you` `want to group data in each field?` (see Figure 11-9).

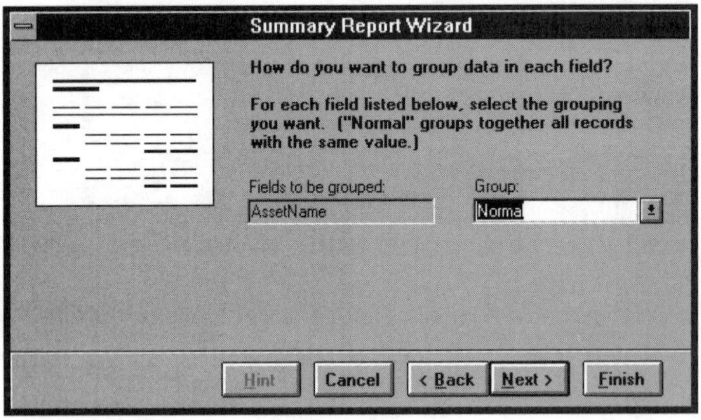

Figure 11-9:
Another
Summary
Report
Wizard
dialog box.

9. Click the Next button.

Still another Summary Report Wizard dialog box appears, asking `Which` `fields do you want on your report?` (see Figure 11-10).

Figure 11-10:
Yet another
Summary
Report
Wizard
dialog box.

10. **In the Available Fields list, select CurrentValue, and click the > button.**

11. **Click the Next button.**

    Another Summary Report Wizard dialog box appears, asking `What style do you want for your report?` (see Figure 11-11).

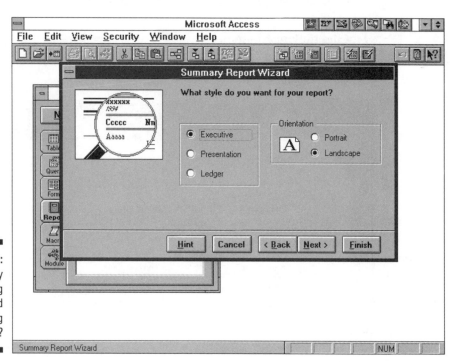

Figure 11-11:
How many
more dialog
boxes could
this thing
have?

12. Click the <u>N</u>ext button.

Another Summary Report Wizard dialog box appears, asking `What title do you want for your report?` (see Figure 11-12).

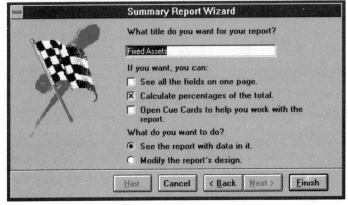

Figure 11-12:
Checkered
flag — at
last!

13. Click the Calculate percentages of the total option to remove the check mark.

14. Click the <u>F</u>inish button.

Access displays your report on-screen (see Figure 11-13).

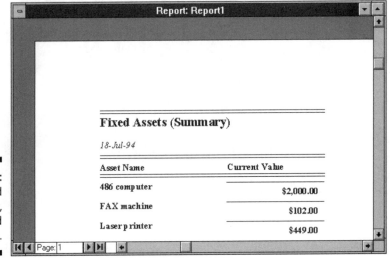

Figure 11-13:
The finished
report,
displayed
on-screen.

15. **From the File menu, choose Print (or press Ctrl+P).**

   The Print dialog box appears.

16. **Click OK.**

   Access prints your report (as long as your printer doesn't jam).

17. **From the File menu, choose Save (or press Ctrl+S).**

   The Save As dialog box appears.

18. **Type the name under which you want to save the report (such as Fixed-asset report) and press Enter.**

19. **From the File menu, choose Close.**

   Access displays your fixed-asset report in the database window.

Making Mailing Labels

Mailing labels are those little stickers that you can paste on envelopes so that you don't have to write complete addresses yourself. If you send mass mailings to the same people periodically, you can save time by letting Access print mailing labels for you.

By storing names and addresses in an Access database, you can print mailing labels any time you want — or you can sell your database to a mailing-list company so that everyone in your database starts receiving junk mail from organizations that nobody had heard of before.

To make mailing labels from the Customers table, follow these steps:

1. **From the File menu, choose the Open Database command (or press Ctrl+O) unless USMALE.MDB is already open.**

   The New Database dialog box appears.

2. **Highlight the USMALE.MDB database file and click OK.**

   The database window appears.

3. **Click the Report tab and then click the New button.**

   The New Report dialog box appears.

4. **Click the arrow next to the Select a Table/Query list box and select Customers.**

5. **Click the Report Wizards button.**

   A Report Wizards dialog box appears (see Figure 11-14).

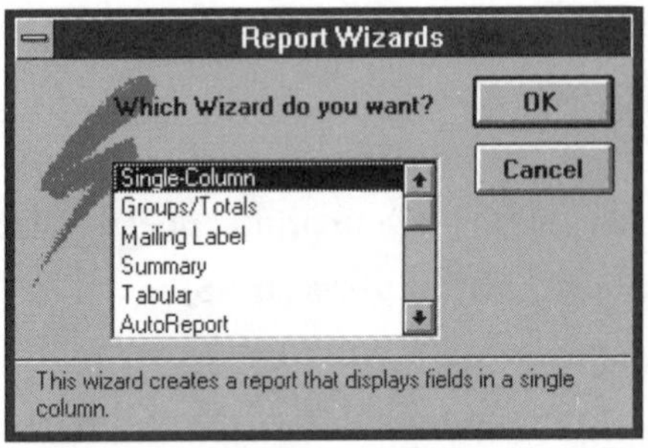

Figure 11-14:
The Report
Wizards
dialog box.

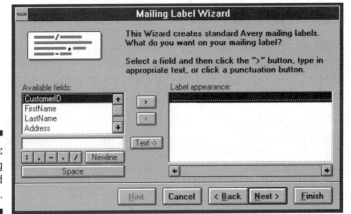

6. **Choose Mailing Label and click OK.**

   A Mailing Label Wizard dialog box appears (see Figure 11-15).

Figure 11-15:
The Mailing
Label Wizard
dialog box.

7. **In the Available Fields list, select FirstName and click the > button.**

8. **Click the Space button (the button in the dialog box — not the spacebar on your keyboard).**

9. **In the Available Fields list, select LastName and click the > button.**

10. **Click the Newline button.**

11. **In the Available Fields list, select Address and click the > button.**

12. **Click the Newline button.**

13. **In the Available Fields list, select City and click the > button.**

14. **Click the comma (,) button.**

15. **Click the Space button.**

16. **In the Available Fields list, select State and click the > button.**

17. **Click the Space button.**

18. **In the Available Fields list, select PostalCode and click the > button.**

19. **Click the Next button.**

    Another Mailing Label Wizard dialog box appears, asking `Which fields do you want to sort by?`

20. **In the Available Fields list, select PostalCode and click the > button.**

21. **Click the Next button.**

    Still another Mailing Label Wizard dialog box appears, asking `What label size do you want?`

22. **Choose the Avery-label number of the mailing labels that you're using and click the Next button.**

    Another Mailing Label Wizard dialog box appears, asking `What font and color do you want?`

23. **Choose the font, size, font weight, and color that you want to use and then click the Next button.**

    Yet another Mailing Label Wizard dialog box appears (see Figure 11-16).

Figure 11-16:
The final
Mailing
Label Wizard
dialog box.

24. **Click the Finish button.**

    Access shows you what your mailing labels will look like (as long as your printer doesn't screw up), as shown in Figure 11-17.

Figure 11-17:
A print
preview of
your mailing
labels.

25. **Turn on your printer and shove in your mailing labels.**

26. **From the File menu, choose Print (or press Ctrl+P).**

    The Print dialog box appears.

27. **Click OK.**

    If your printer works, your mailing labels appear printed neatly on each label.

28. **From the File menu, choose Close.**

    A dialog box appears, asking whether you want to save your report.

29. **Click Yes.**

    The Save As dialog box appears.

30. **Type the name under which you want to save your mailing-label report (such as Mailing labels) and click OK.**

    Access displays the name of your mailing-label report in the database window (see Figure 11-18).

Figure 11-18:
Access lists
your mailing-
label report
in the
Reports
window.

Forms: Seeing Your Data from Another Perspective

Normally, when you look at your data, Access displays that data in rows and columns as though it were an ugly spreadsheet. This view, called datasheet view, is great for looking at multiple records at the same time. Datasheet view, however, bears no resemblance to ordinary paper databases such as Rolodex cards and address books, which means that Access can seem to be more confusing and intimidating than necessary.

But don't fret! Access can display data in either datasheet view (the ugly spreadsheet appearance) or form view (which resembles a paper form — hence the name). Unlike datasheet view, form view can show only one record at a time (see Figure 11-19).

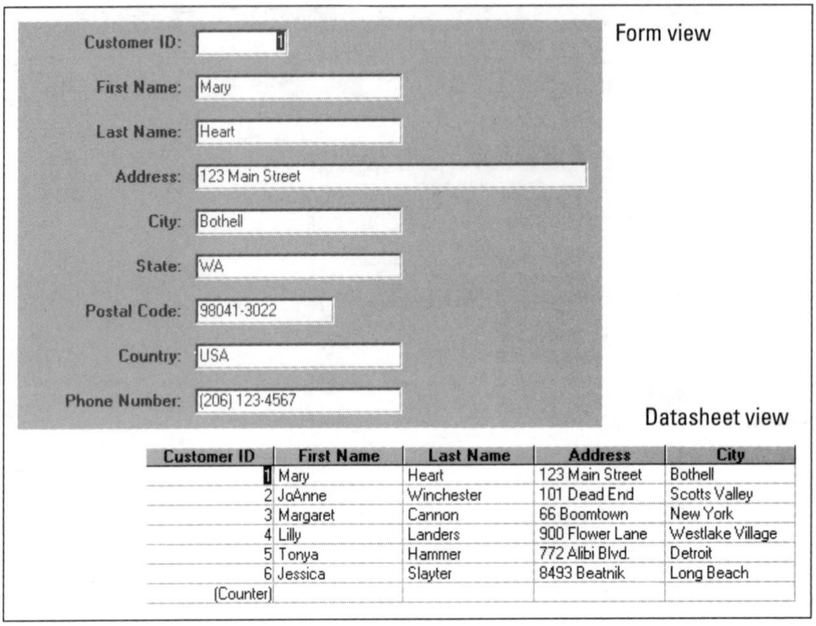

Figure 11-19:
The
differences
between
datasheet
view and
form view.

Creating a form

Access gives you two ways to create a form: use the Form Wizard or create a form from scratch. Unless you need to create a custom form, let the Form Wizard create forms for you automatically.

To create a Customers form with the Form Wizard, follow these steps:

1. **From the File menu, choose the Open Database command (or press Ctrl+O), unless USMALE.MDB is already open.**

   The Open Database dialog box appears.

2. **Highlight the USMALE.MDB database file and click OK.**

   The database window appears.

3. **Click the Form tab and then click the New button.**

   The New Form dialog box appears (see Figure 11-20).

4. **Click the arrow next to the Select a Table/Query list box and select Customers.**

Figure 11-20:
The New
Form dialog
box with the
Select a
Table/Query
list box.

5. **Click the Form Wizards button.**

   Another Form Wizards dialog box appears, asking `Which Wizard do you want?`.

6. **Choose AutoForm and click OK.**

   After a few moments (depending on how slow your computer may be), Access displays your form, as shown in Figure 11-21.

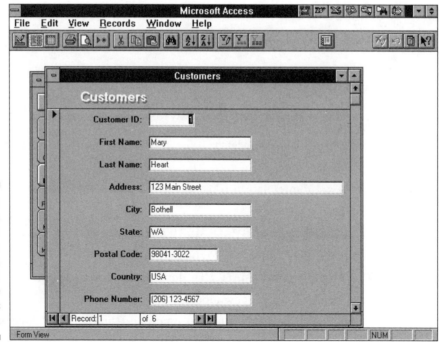

Figure 11-21:
The form
created
by the
AutoForm
Wizard
from the
Customers
table.

7. **From the File menu, choose Save Form (or press Ctrl+S).**

The Save As dialog box appears.

8. **Type** Customers, **and click OK.**

9. **From the File menu, choose Close.**

Access displays your Customers form in the database window (see Figure 11-22).

Figure 11-22:
The Customers form in the USMALE database window.

Using a form

A form is more than just a pretty way to display your data. You also can use a form to enter new data or edit existing data. Because a form shows only one record at a time, a form lets you see whether you filled in all the fields for each record.

To view and enter data in a Customers form, follow these steps:

1. **From the File menu, choose the Open Database command (or press Ctrl+O), unless USMALE.MDB is already open.**

The Open Database dialog box appears.

2. **Highlight the USMALE.MDB database file and click OK.**

The database window appears.

3. **Click the Form tab, click Customers and then click the Open button.**

Access displays the Customers form.

4. **Click the Last Record button.**

   Access displays the last record.

5. **Click the Next Record button.**

   Access displays a blank record.

6. **Type your data and then press Tab to move the cursor to the next field.**

7. **Repeat Step 6 until you finish entering data.**

8. **From the File menu, choose Close.**

Modifying a form

Although Access can create forms for you automatically through the wonder of the Form Wizard, you may want to customize your form's appearance anyway, just to show Access that you still possess free will.

Forms consist of one or more fields and field labels (see Figure 11-23). A field contains the information stored in your database, and the field label simply identifies your data.

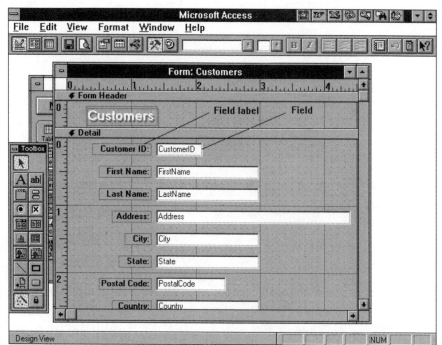

Figure 11-23:
Identifying fields and field labels in a form.

Modifying a form allows you to

- ✔ Change the position, size, and text appearance of your fields and field labels.
- ✔ Add labels of your own.

Moving fields and field labels in a form

Although Access's Form Wizard can create forms automatically, you may like to modify your form to suit your own taste. For that reason, Access allows you to move fields and field labels around a form until the entire form looks exactly the way you want it to.

To move fields and field labels in a form, follow these steps:

1. **In the database window, click the Form tab.**

   Access displays a list of your forms.

2. **Click the form that you want to modify and then click the Design button.**

   Access displays your form.

3. **Click the field or field label that you want to move.**

   On the upper-left side of the field or field label, Access displays a little gray handle. This is the *move handle* (see Figure 11-24).

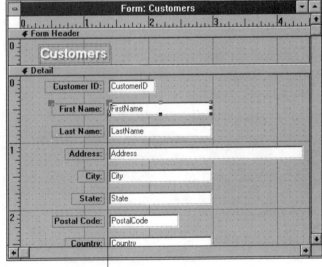

Figure 11-24:
The move handle on the upper-left side of a selected field.

The move handle

4. Place the mouse pointer on the move handle.

The mouse pointer changes to a little black pointing hand (see Figure 11-25).

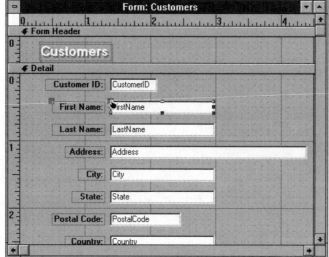

Figure 11-25:
The little
black
pointing
hand.

5. Hold down the mouse button and drag the mouse.

The field or field label moves with the mouse.

6. Place the field or field label where you want it and release the mouse button.

Resizing fields and field labels

When Access creates a form for you, it tries to create fields and field labels that are large enough to show all your data. However, sometimes a field is too small (or too large). Rather than suffer such imperfection, you can resize your fields and field labels.

To resize fields and field labels, follow these steps:

1. In the database window, click the Form tab.

Access displays a list of your forms.

2. Click the form that you want to modify and then click the Design button.

Access displays your form.

3. **Click the field or field label that you want to resize.**

   Access displays little gray handles around the field or field label. Tiny black boxes also appear around the edges of the field or field label. These tiny black boxes are called the *size handles*.

4. **Place the mouse pointer on one of the size handles.**

   The mouse pointer changes to a double arrow (see Figure 11-26).

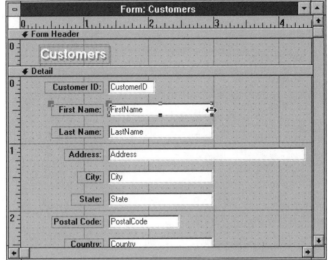

Figure 11-26:
The double arrow enables you to size the field or field label.

5. **Hold the mouse button down and drag the mouse.**

   The field or field label changes size.

6. **Release the mouse button when the field or field label is the size you want.**

Changing the text appearance of fields and field labels

Because Access lacks an active imagination, it tends to create dull fields and field labels that appear in black and white, in 8-point size in the MS Sans Serif font, with left alignment.

To spice up your fields and field labels to highlight important information — or just to give yourself something important to do while you're at work — you can change background and foreground colors, fonts, size, and alignment (left, center, or right).

Be careful that you don't alter the appearance of your fields and field labels too drastically. It's possible to display information in shocking pink, 48-point size, and some bizarre font never before seen by humans. But such wildly creative fields and field labels may detract from the purpose of your form, which is to display data so that you can see and understand it.

To change the text appearance of fields and field labels, follow these steps:

1. **In the database window, click the Form tab.**

   Access displays a list of your forms.

2. **Click the form that you want to modify and then click the Design button.**

   Access displays your form.

3. **Click the field or field label whose text appearance you want to change.**

   Access displays little gray handles around the field or field label.

4. **Click the appropriate toolbar buttons to change the text appearance of the selected field or field label (see Figure 11-27).**

Figure 11-27:
The toolbar with the color palette, font, size, bold, italic, and alignment buttons.

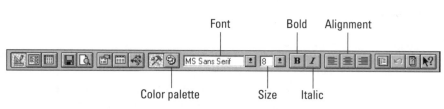

Adding labels of your own

Each field in a form has a corresponding field label. Sometimes, however, you may want to add labels of your own, which can contain company names, short instructions, or explanations.

To satisfy this creative urge, Access allows you to create your own labels and plop them anywhere in a form. Such labels are purely decorative, so make sure that you really need them before messing up your form any more than you must.

To add your own labels to a form, follow these steps:

1. **In the database window, click the Form tab.**

   Access displays a list of your forms.

2. **Click the form that you want to modify and then click the Design button.**

   Access displays your form.

3. **Click the Label tool (the button with the letter A) in the toolbox (see Figure 11-28).**

Label tool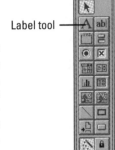

Figure 11-28:
The Toolbox,
featuring the
world-
famous
Label tool.

4. **Place the mouse pointer in the form where you want the upper-left corner of your label to appear.**

5. **Hold down the mouse button and move the mouse pointer to the location where you want the lower-right corner of your label to appear.**

   Access displays your label as a box made from dots.

6. **Release the mouse button.**

   Access draws your label in the form.

7. **Type the text that you want to appear in the label and press Enter when you finish.**

   At this point, you can go back and modify the color, font, size, attributes, or alignment of your label.

Deleting a form

In case you decide that you don't need to use a form to view, enter, or edit data, you can always delete it. Deleting a form does *not* delete any data. When you delete a form, you're deleting only the pretty form that displays the data; you're not deleting the data itself.

To delete the Customers form, follow these steps:

1. **In the database window, click the Form tab.**

   Access displays a list of your forms.

2. **Click the form that you want to delete.**

3. **From the Edit menu, choose Delete (or press Delete).**

   Access displays a dialog box, asking whether you really want to delete the form.

4. **Click OK.**

   Your form disappears from the database window.

If you suddenly realize that you deleted a form by mistake, don't cringe in horror: immediately choose Undo from the Edit menu (or press Ctrl+Z). Access undoes your last command and restores your form to its preceding pristine condition. Whenever you do something by mistake, the Undo command can correct it. Just make sure that you choose the Undo command immediately after screwing up; otherwise, Access may not be able to recover from your mistake.

The 5th Wave By Rich Tennant

"NO, THEY'RE NOT REALLY A GANG, JUST A PARTICULARLY AGGRESSIVE LAN."

Chapter 12

Chatting at the Electronic Watercooler with Microsoft Mail

*W*hen you buy a copy of Microsoft Office, Microsoft generously gives you a slip of paper known as a license. This license gives you permission to use (and, of course, buy) the full-blown version of Microsoft Mail and install it on your network. If you're not using Microsoft Office on a network or have no desire to talk to anyone else even if you are connected to a network, then don't bother reading this chapter.

But if your computer is connected to a network and your boss thinks that electronic mail is the way to improve morale and communication among people who don't like each other in the first place, then you may be lucky (or unlucky) enough to have to use Microsoft Mail.

What Is Microsoft Mail?

Microsoft Mail is a program that you can use only on a network. (You can use it on a single isolated computer, but it's about as useful as talking on a telephone that isn't connected to a phone line.) If you have a network and need Microsoft Mail, be prepared to dish out several hundred dollars more to buy the program.

Essentially, Microsoft Mail lets people communicate through the network by sending files or simple messages back and forth to anyone else on the network. Files can consist of Word documents, Excel worksheets, Access databases, or PowerPoint presentations. Messages are simple text that you type at your keyboard.

The Secret of Passwords

Anyone can send messages through Microsoft Mail. Each time a message is sent, Microsoft Mail takes care of tracking the return address so that you know who sends the messages.

If you really want some fun, you can send a message to your boss from someone else's computer and really tell him what you think of his lousy managerial skills. Because you used another computer, your boss would think that the other person sent the message, and you'd never get the blame!

But to prevent such unauthorized use of electronic mail, Microsoft Mail requires that you type the proper password. Without the right password, you can't get into other people's Microsoft Mail program and send messages in their names.

Choose a password that has special meaning to you but to no one else, such as the name of your favorite teddy bear you had as a kid or the real name you would love to call your boss if you wouldn't get fired over it. The more distinctive your password is, the less likely someone will be able to guess it.

Also, keep your password safely stored away where someone won't be able to find it. Don't tape your password to your computer monitor, the inside top drawer of your desk, or on the side of your computer. If you must write down your password, store it some place where nobody would think of finding it — such as on the wall of the third stall in the men's room.

Using your password to log on to Microsoft Mail

You must use your password to log on to Microsoft Mail. Think of your password as a key. If you lose your password, you can't use Microsoft Mail (which isn't always such a bad thing).

To start Microsoft Mail with your password, follow these steps:

1. Double-click on the Microsoft Mail icon from within Windows.

The Mail Sign In dialog box appears, as shown in Figure 12-1.

Figure 12-1:
The Mail
Sign In
dialog box.

2. Type your password and click OK.

The Microsoft Mail screen appears (see Figure 12-2).

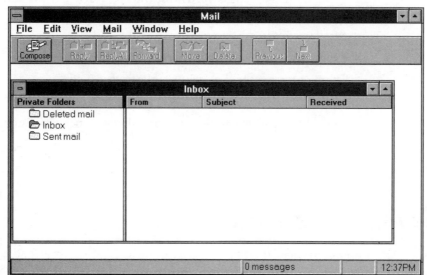

Figure 12-2:
The
Microsoft
Mail screen.

Rather than type your password each time, click on the Remember password option in the Mail Sign In dialog box. Now, the next time you load Microsoft Mail, it doesn't bug you for your password. Of course, this convenience for you also means that anyone else can just log on to Microsoft Mail and send nasty messages to your boss, so think about this option before deciding to use it.

Changing your password

It's a good idea to change your password periodically, just to make sure that somebody isn't plotting to send dirty messages to someone else using your electronic mail address.

To change your password, follow these steps:

1. From the Mail menu, choose Change password.

The Change Password dialog box appears, as shown in Figure 12-3.

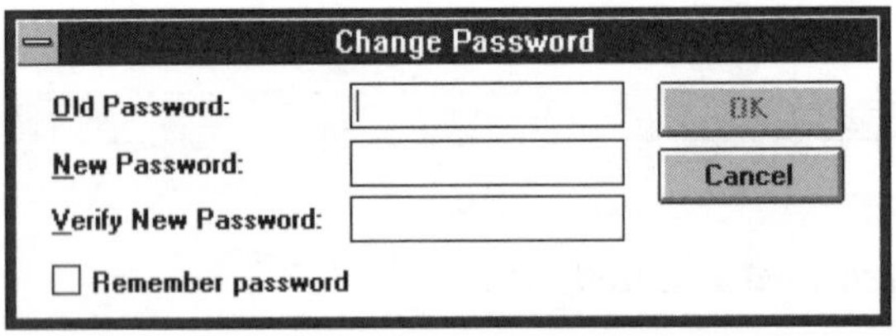

Figure 12-3:
The Change
Password
dialog box.

Change Password
Old Password: [   ]   OK
New Password: [   ]   Cancel
Verify New Password: [   ]
☐ Remember password

2. Type your current password in the Old Password text box and press Tab.

Notice that Microsoft Mail masks your password with asterisks. The cursor moves to the New Password field.

3. Type your new password and press Tab.

The cursor moves to the Verify New Password field.

4. Click OK.

A dialog box appears, letting you know that you successfully changed your password.

5. Click OK.

Sending Messages

Any time you need to pass a memo to someone, don't use a valuable slip of pink memo paper or a yellow Post-it note and leave it on that person's desk. Instead, send an electronic message through Microsoft Mail. Unlike the national postal system, where disgruntled postal workers can stash mail in their garages out of anger, Microsoft Mail guarantees that your mail will reach its destination.

To create and send a message, follow these steps:

1. **From the Mail menu (see Figure 12-4), choose Compose Note, press Ctrl+N, or click on the Compose button.**

   The Send Note window appears, as shown in Figure 12-5.

2. **Type the name of the person you want to send your message to or click the Address button and select a person's name. Then press Tab.**

3. **Type the name of a second person you want to send your message to. (You can leave this blank if you want.) Then press Tab.**

4. **Type a brief description of your message topic in the Subject field and press Tab.**

5. **Type your message.**

6. **When you're done, click on the Send button.**

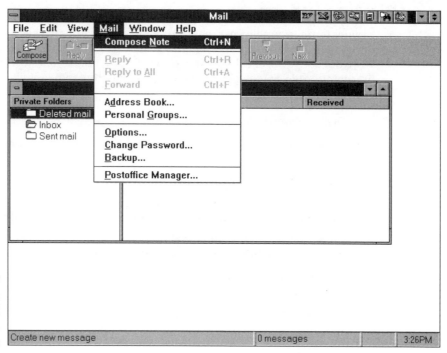

Figure 12-4:
The Mail
menu.

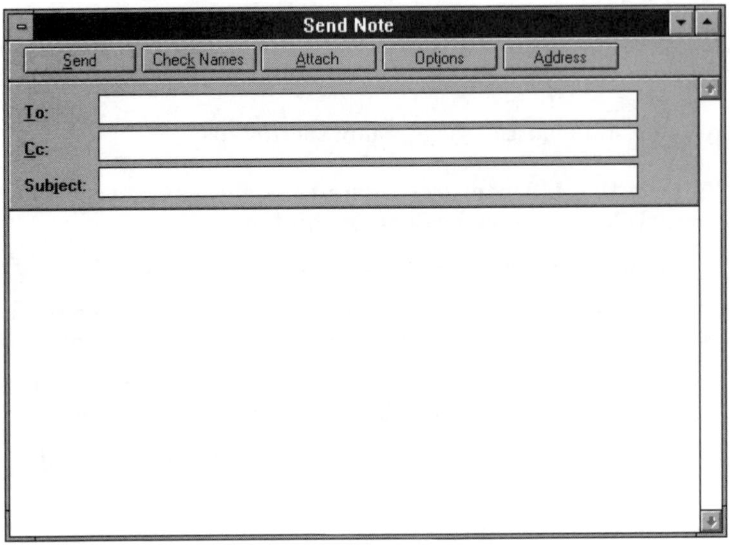

Figure 12-5:
The Send
Note
window.

Sending Files

Besides letting you send messages to people you'd rather not see in person but have to get along with anyway, Microsoft Mail also lets you send a complete Word document, an Excel worksheet, an Access database, or a PowerPoint presentation file. Sending files is convenient for letting someone else review your work.

To send a file, follow these steps:

1. **From the Mail menu, choose Compose Note, press Ctrl+N, or click on the Compose button.**

   The Send Note window appears.

2. **Type the name of the person you want to send your message to or click the Address button and select a person's name. Then press Tab.**

3. **Type the name of a second person you want to send your message to. (You can leave this blank if you want.) Then press Tab.**

4. **Type a brief description of your message topic in the Subject field and press Tab.**

5. **Type your message.**

6. **Click the Attach button.**

   An Attach dialog box appears (see Figure 12-6).

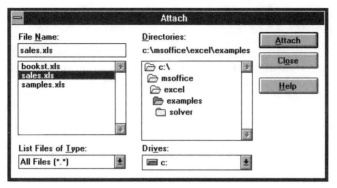

Figure 12-6:
The Attach
dialog box.

7. **Choose the drive, directory, and name of the file you want to send and click the Attach button.**

8. **Click the Close button.**

Your attached file appears as an icon on-screen, as shown in Figure 12-7.

9. **Click the Send button.**

Figure 12-7:
An attached
file appears
as an icon.

Reading Your Mail

No matter how much you may detest junk mail at home, you're sure to get bombarded with junk mail at work through the wonders of Microsoft Mail. Any time you receive mail, Microsoft Mail thoughtfully beeps to let you know that mail has arrived.

To read your mail, follow these steps:

1. **Double-click on the Microsoft Mail icon from within Windows.**

   The Mail Sign In dialog box appears.

2. **Type your password and click OK.**

   The Microsoft Mail screen appears.

3. **Under Private Folders, double-click on Inbox.**

   Microsoft Mail shows you all the mail you've received (see Figure 12-8). Ordinary messages appear as a folded envelope. Messages with files attached appear as a folded envelope with a paper clip icon next to it.

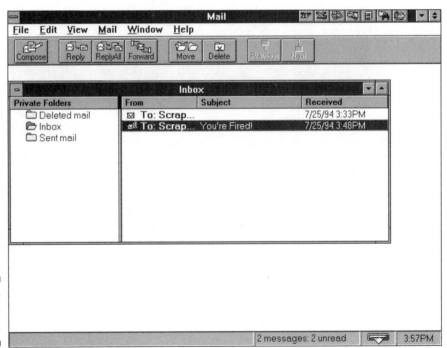

Figure 12-8:
Mail in the
Inbox.

4. Double-click on the mail you want to read.

The Read Note window appears, as shown in Figure 12-9. If a message contains an attached file, you can double-click on the file to view it, but only if you have the program that created it. For example, if a message contains an attached Excel file, you can only view this file if you have Excel on your computer.

5. Choose one of the following:

- Click the Delete button to get rid of any unwanted mail.

- Click the Reply button to write a reply to one message.

- Click the Reply All button to write a single reply to all of your messages, such as "The company picnic is on Friday! Bring lots of junk food."

- Click the Forward button to send a copy of your message to someone else.

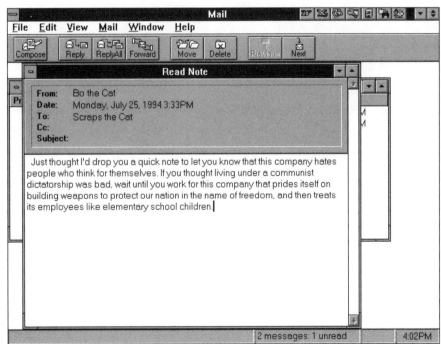

Figure 12-9:
The Read
Note
window.

Part V
Putting It All Together

By Rich Tennant

"OH SURE, IT'LL FLOAT ALRIGHT, BUT INTEGRATION'S GONNA BE A KILLER."

In this part...

Microsoft Office is more than just a collection of applications. In fact, this suite is one of the few concoctions that live up to the old cliché that the whole is more than the sum of its parts. Some might even say that an Office in the hand is worth two in the bush. (I even heard someone say that a stitch in time saved her nine megabytes of hard disk space.)

With Microsoft Office, you can link data from one application to another. In other words, you can link your Access baseball card database to your Excel asset workbook — every time another Hall of Famer buys the farm, you can watch your net worth skyrocket!

Chapter 13

Working Efficiently in the Windows Environment

· ·

In This Chapter

▶ Switching between programs (the old-fashioned way)

▶ Putting MOM (the Microsoft Office Manager) to work

▶ Customizing the Microsoft Office Manager

· ·

*I*n the old days, computers could run only one program at a time, and even then, those programs looked as stark and unappealing as the New York Stock Exchange listing in *The Wall Street Journal*. With the introduction of Microsoft Windows, programs began looking pretty and colorful, as well as offering pull-down menus, overlapping windows, and mouse support — which would have been a revolutionary idea if Macintosh users hadn't already been using a similar interface for the past ten years.

Although Microsoft Windows makes computer programs easier to use, its main benefit is allowing users to run two or more programs simultaneously. Instead of continually loading and exiting your word processing, spreadsheet, and database programs, you can use Windows to load all three programs and switch among them at the touch of a button.

By making all your programs available to you in an instant, Windows allows you to spend less time loading programs and more time actually getting some work done (or at least creating the illusion that you're getting some work done).

Switching between Programs (the Old-Fashioned Way)

Microsoft Windows provides four ways to switch between two or more programs that you have loaded:

- ✔ Press Alt+Tab.
- ✔ Press Ctrl+Esc to use the Task List.
- ✔ Click the window of the program you want to use (if the window is visible).
- ✔ Press Alt+Esc.

You can use any or all of these different methods to switch between programs, although most people usually stick to one or two ways and forget the others.

Pressing Alt+Tab

This is probably both the quickest and easiest way to switch between applications. First, however, you have to make sure that the option is turned on. From the Windows Program Manager, double-click the Control Panel icon (usually found in the Main program group). Once inside the Control Panel, double-click the Desktop icon. In the Applications box, make sure that the Fast "Alt+Tab" Switching box is checked, then click OK (if it is already checked, you can still click OK). To get out of the Control Panel, press Alt+F4. Now you're ready to do some fast switching.

Hold down the Alt key and press (then release) Tab, keeping the Alt key held down the whole time. You will see a box in the center of your screen with the name of another application. If you release the Alt key now, you will switch to that application. But wait—there's more.

Keep Alt held down (I know, your thumb is getting tired) and press Tab again. Now there's another application name in the center of your screen (possibly the same application you were using in the first place). Pressing Tab additional times brings the names of all running applications to the center of your screen. When you find the one you want, just release the Alt key, and you jump right to that application.

Using the Task List

No matter what program you're using, when you press Ctrl+Esc, the Task List pops up on-screen, listing all the programs you have already loaded. To switch to another program, just highlight the program you want and click the Switch To button.

The Task List is a most convenient way to see which programs you've already loaded (so that you don't try loading them again). But for switching between programs rapidly, it's fairly slow, because the moment you press Ctrl+Esc, Windows wastes time displaying the Task List.

Clicking another window

Rather than display the Task List, you can minimize the currently displayed program, which will expose the windows of any other programs you've loaded. Then you can click the window of the program that you want to use next.

This method is faster but can be clumsy because you have to keep minimizing and clicking different program windows. If one program window overlaps another, you may not even know that the other program is there.

Pressing Alt+Esc

An even faster method of switching between programs is pressing Alt+Esc. Each time you press Alt+Esc, Windows displays another currently loaded program. Just keep pressing Alt+Esc until you find the program that you want.

If you have only two or three programs loaded, pressing Alt+Esc can be fast. But if you have five or more programs loaded, you may have to press Alt+Esc several times to get to the program that you want.

Putting MOM (the Microsoft Office Manager) to Work

Microsoft Office isn't just a collection of separate programs that Microsoft threw together as a slick marketing tactic (although it may look that way). Instead, Microsoft Office is a collection of separate programs that Microsoft linked through a program dubbed the Microsoft Office Manager, or MOM.

I'll tell you right now, I'm not making this up. Borland International, the maker of another suite of applications called Borland Office, chose to call its application-linking program the Desktop Application Director, or DAD. Isn't that just about the biggest coincidence you've ever seen?

Although Microsoft Office can do glamorous things, such as linking information between programs and preparing address labels for invitations to your Halloween party, it's a good idea to learn what else the program can do before you use it. By making the most of the Microsoft Office Manager, you'll be able to use Microsoft Office to its maximum potential (just as soon as you figure out how to use your computer).

So what makes MOM so special? Besides never complaining if you forget Mother's Day, MOM makes it easy to load and switch between programs.

Normally, you have to load a program this way:

1. **Point to the icon representing the program that you want to load.**

2. **Double-click the mouse button to load the program (see Figure 13-1).**

Figure 13-1:
The old-fashioned way to access Microsoft Office programs is to double-click their icons in the Microsoft Office Group in the Windows Program Manager.

This two-step process is fairly clumsy, especially if your finger slips and you double-click too slowly. Because this is the world of computers and technological sophistication, you'd think that there has to be a better way — and there is.

The answer is the Microsoft Office Manager, which can display a customizable toolbar containing buttons that represent the programs in Microsoft Office (see Figure 13-2). Rather than double-click the program icon to load Microsoft Word, Excel, PowerPoint, or Access, just click the program's button in the Microsoft Office Manager or pull down the Microsoft Office Manager menu and click the program that you want to use.

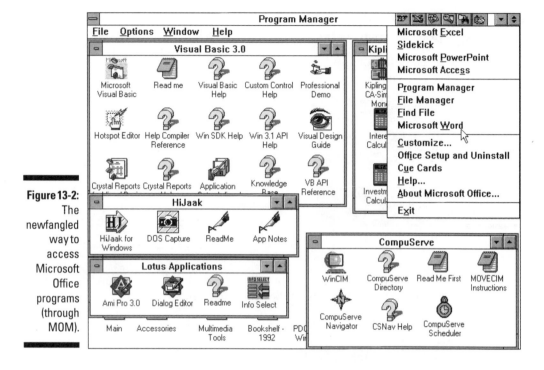

Figure 13-2:
The
newfangled
way to
access
Microsoft
Office
programs
(through
MOM).

Customizing the Microsoft Office Manager Toolbar

Because this is your computer, you can adapt MOM to your way of working by customizing the Microsoft Office Manager toolbar in several ways:

- Changing the size of MOM's buttons
- Changing the position of MOM
- Changing the number and type of buttons in MOM
- Changing the appearance of MOM's menus

Changing the size of MOM's buttons

Like the 1957 movie *The Three Faces of Eve*, which told the story of a woman with three personalities, the Microsoft Office Manager also has three faces (see Figure 13-3):

↙ Small Buttons

↙ Regular Buttons

↙ Large Buttons

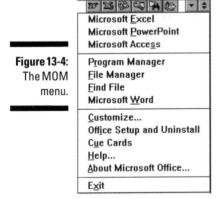

Small buttons

Regular buttons

Large buttons

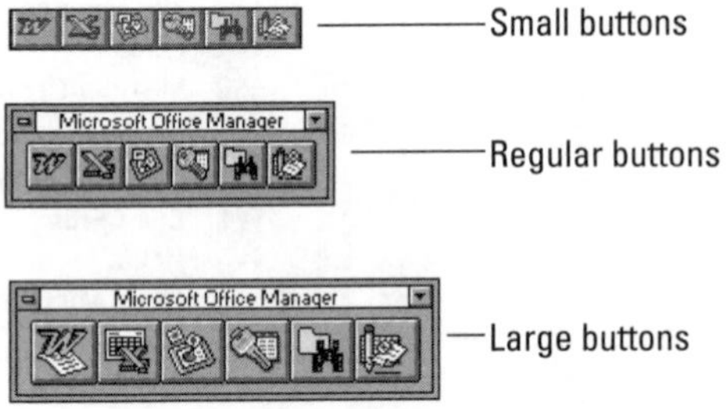

Figure 13-3:
The three
faces of
MOM.

By default, Microsoft Office displays MOM with small buttons to keep the buttons out of the way and unobtrusive. But if you like bigger buttons that don't require you to squint, you can change MOM's appearance.

To change MOM's appearance, follow these steps:

1. Click the Microsoft Office button in the MOM toolbar.

The MOM menu appears, as shown in Figure 13-4. (In case the toolbar is hidden, display it by using the clumsy method of double-clicking the Microsoft Office icon in the Microsoft Office program group.)

Figure 13-4:
The MOM
menu.

Microsoft **E**xcel
Microsoft **P**owerPoint
Microsoft Acce**s**s

Program Manager
File Manager
F**i**nd File
Microsoft **W**ord

Customize...
Offi**c**e Setup and Uninstall
C**u**e Cards
Help...
About Microsoft Office...

E**x**it

2. Choose Customize or type C.

The Customize dialog box appears (see Figure 13-5).

3. Click the View tab.

The View tab of the Customize dialog box appears (see Figure 13-6).

4. **Click Small Buttons, Regular Buttons, or Large Buttons.**

5. **Click the OK button.**

The MOM toolbar magically changes its appearance.

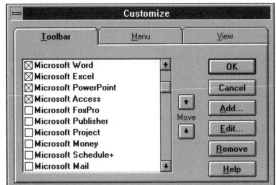

Figure 13-5:
The
Customize
dialog box.

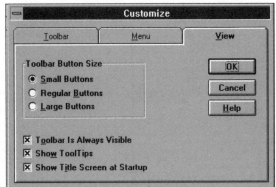

Figure 13-6:
The View
tab of the
Customize
dialog box.

Changing the position of MOM

Unless you specify otherwise, MOM's toolbar appears in the upper-right corner of your screen, tucked neatly out of the way. If you want to move the toolbar to another location, however, you can.

You can move MOM's toolbar only if you have changed the button size to Regular Buttons or Large Buttons.

To move MOM's location, follow these steps:

1. **Place the mouse pointer on the title bar of the MOM toolbar.**

2. **Hold down the mouse button and drag the mouse.**

   The gray outline of the MOM toolbar moves along with the mouse (see Figure 13-7).

3. **Release the mouse button when the toolbar is where you want it.**

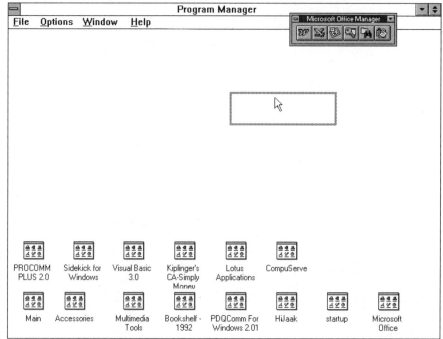

Figure 13-7:
Moving the
MOM
toolbar.

Changing MOM's buttons

By default, the MOM toolbar displays only buttons for Microsoft Word, Excel, PowerPoint, Access, and Microsoft Office. You can change the position of these buttons as well as add or delete buttons that represent other programs.

Deleting and adding buttons

For kicks, you can delete all the buttons that represent Microsoft programs and put in buttons that represent those programs' biggest competitors, such as WordPerfect, Lotus 1-2-3, Harvard Graphics, and Paradox. Because the MOM toolbar retains its Microsoft Office Manager title, you can make it look as though Microsoft is endorsing its competitors' products.

To add or delete buttons representing Microsoft applications from MOM's toolbar, follow these steps:

1. Click the Microsoft Office button in the MOM toolbar.

The MOM menu appears.

(If the toolbar is hidden, first display it by double-clicking the Microsoft Office icon in the Microsoft Office program group.)

2. Choose Customize or type C.

The Customize dialog box appears.

3. Click the Toolbar tab.

The Toolbar tab of the Customize dialog box appears (see Figure 13-8).

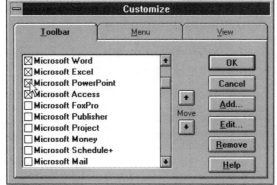

Figure 13-8:
The Toolbar
tab of the
Customize
dialog box.

4. Click the appropriate check boxes.

If you want to add a program that is not already on the MOM toolbar, click the check box of the program you want to add.

To delete a program, click the check box of the program you want to remove from the toolbar. An empty check box means that the button won't appear in the toolbar. (If you're removing a non-Microsoft program from the toolbar, you can click the Remove button to remove the program name from the button list.)

5. Click the OK button.

MOM obediently adds or removes any buttons that you specified.

To add buttons representing non-Microsoft programs to MOM's toolbar, follow these steps:

1. Click the Microsoft Office button in the MOM toolbar.

The MOM menu appears.

(If the toolbar is hidden, first display it by double-clicking the Microsoft Office icon in the Microsoft Office program group.)

2. **Choose Customize or type** C.

   The Customize dialog box appears.

3. **Click the Toolbar tab.**

   The Toolbar tab of the Customize dialog box appears.

4. **Click the Add button.**

   The Add Program to Toolbar dialog box appears (see Figure 13-9).

Figure 13-9:
The Add
Program to
Toolbar
dialog box.

5. **Click the Browse button.**

   The Browse dialog box appears (see Figure 13-10).

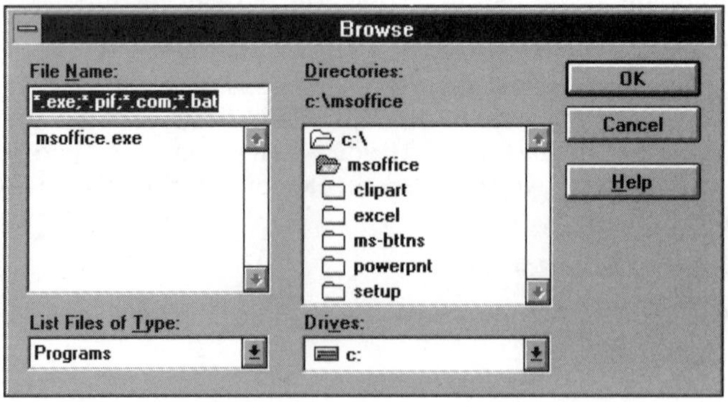

Figure 13-10:
The Browse
dialog box.

6. Double-click the directories in the Directories list box.

In the list box under File Name, highlight the program file that you want to add to the toolbar and then click the OK button. The Toolbar tab of the Customize dialog box shows your new program in the program list (see Figure 13-11).

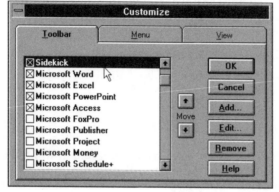

Figure 13-11:
A new program added to the program list.

7. Click the OK button.

The MOM toolbar displays the program button (see Figure 13-12).

Figure 13-12:
The MOM toolbar with a new program button.

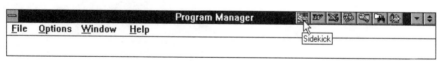

Moving buttons in MOM's toolbar

Besides adding or deleting buttons from the toolbar, you can rearrange the positions of the buttons. By rearranging buttons, you can truly make your toolbar personal.

To rearrange MOM's toolbar buttons, follow these steps:

1. Click the Microsoft Office button in the MOM toolbar.

The MOM menu appears. (If the toolbar is hidden, first display it by double-clicking the Microsoft Office icon in the Microsoft Office program group.)

2. **Choose Customize or type** C.

   The Customize dialog box appears.

3. **Click the Toolbar tab.**

   The Toolbar tab of the Customize dialog box appears.

4. **Highlight the name of any program that appears with a check in its check box and click the up or down Move arrows to the right of the scroll box (see Figure 13-13).**

5. **Click the OK button when you finish moving programs around.**

   The MOM toolbar shows your newly arranged buttons.

Changing MOM's menus

As an alternative to choosing programs from the toolbar, MOM gives you the option of choosing programs from a menu. Because MOM is a Microsoft program, the menu naturally displays only Microsoft programs (see Figure 13-14). You can, however, add, delete, or rearrange program names in the menu to customize the menu exactly the way you want it.

The Move buttons

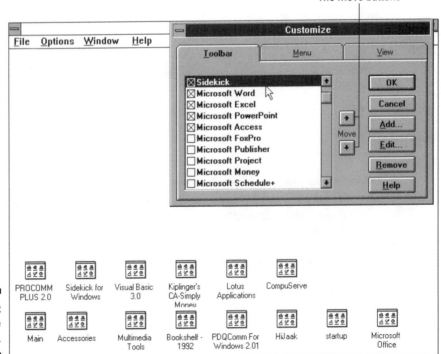

Figure 13-13:
The Move
arrows.

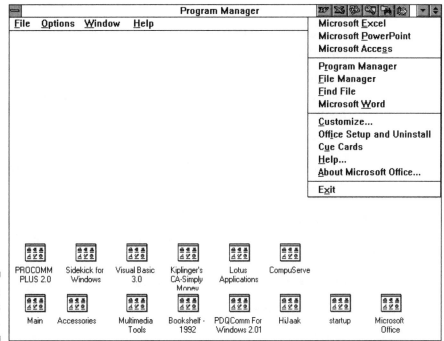

Figure 13-14: MOM's menu.

The programs that appear as buttons in the toolbar can be completely different from the programs that appear in MOM's menus. Changing the programs that appear in the toolbar has no effect on programs that appear in the menu, and vice versa.

Deleting and adding programs

Menus are great for people who like to see all their choices before making a decision. With that in mind, MOM allows you to add or delete menu programs, based on what you find most convenient. After all, if you rarely need to create presentation graphics with PowerPoint, there's no sense in having PowerPoint clutter MOM's menu.

To delete programs from MOM's menu, follow these steps:

1. Click the Microsoft Office button in the MOM toolbar.

The MOM menu appears.

(If the toolbar is hidden, first display it by double-clicking the Microsoft Office icon in the Microsoft Office program group.)

2. Choose Customize or type C.

The Customize dialog box appears.

3. Click the Menu tab.

The Menu tab of the Customize dialog box appears (see Figure 13-15).

4. Click the check box next to the program that you want to remove from the menu.

An empty check box means that the menu won't appear in the toolbar. (If you're removing a non-Microsoft program from the menu, you can click the Remove button to remove the program name from the menu list.)

5. Click the OK button.

MOM removes the programs that you specified.

To add programs representing Microsoft programs to MOM's menu, follow these steps:

1. Click the Microsoft Office button in the MOM toolbar.

The MOM menu appears.

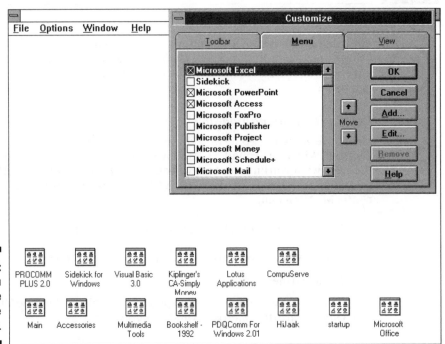

Figure 13-15:
The Menu tab of the Customize dialog box.

(If the toolbar is hidden, first display it by double-clicking the Microsoft Office icon in the Microsoft Office program group.)

2. **Choose C̲ustomize or type** C.

The Customize dialog box appears.

3. **Click the M̲enu tab.**

The M̲enu tab of the Customize dialog box appears.

4. **Click the check box next to the Microsoft program that you want to add to the menu.**

5. **Click the OK button.**

To add programs representing non-Microsoft programs to MOM's menu, follow these steps:

1. **Click the Microsoft Office button in the MOM toolbar.**

The MOM menu appears.

(If the toolbar is hidden, first display it by double-clicking the Microsoft Office icon in the Microsoft Office program group.)

2. **Choose C̲ustomize or type** C.

The Customize dialog box appears.

3. **Click the M̲enu tab.**

The M̲enu tab of the Customize dialog box appears.

4. **Click the A̲dd button.**

The Add Program to Menu dialog box appears (see Figure 13-16).

5. **Click the B̲rowse button.**

The Browse dialog box appears.

6. **Double-click in the D̲irectories list box until you find the directory with the file you want.**

In the list box under File N̲ame, highlight the program file that you want to add to the menu and then click OK.

The Add Program to Menu dialog box shows your new program added to the program list (see Figure 13-17).

7. **Click the OK button.**

The MOM menu displays the program name (see Figure 13-18).

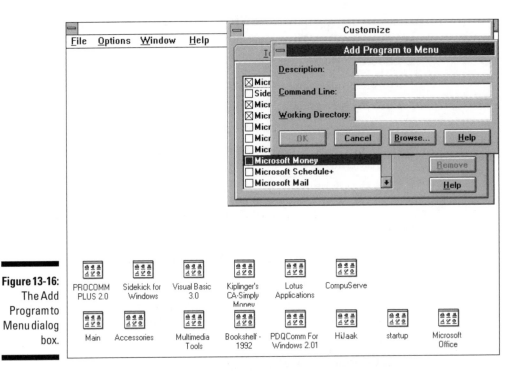

Figure 13-16:
The Add
Program to
Menu dialog
box.

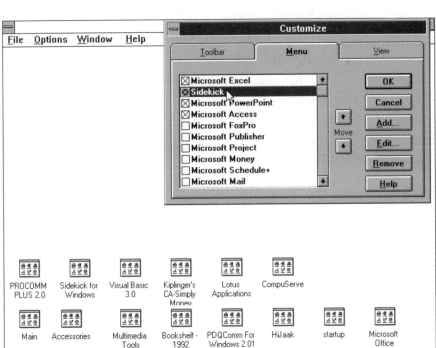

Figure 13-17:
A new
program
added to the
program list.

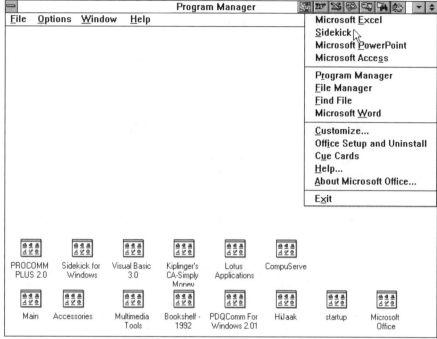

Figure 13-18:
The MOM
menu with a
new
program
name.

Moving programs in MOM's menu

Besides adding or deleting programs from the menu, you can rearrange the position of each program. That way, you can put your most frequently used programs at the top (or bottom) of the menu and bury your least used programs somewhere in the middle.

To rearrange MOM's menu programs, follow these steps:

1. **Click the Microsoft Office button in the MOM toolbar.**

   The MOM menu appears.

   (If the toolbar is hidden, first display it by double-clicking the Microsoft Office icon in the Microsoft Office program group.)

2. **Choose Customize or type** C.

   The Customize dialog box appears.

3. **Click the Menu tab.**

   The Menu tab of the Customize dialog box appears.

4. **Highlight the name of any program that appears with a check in its check box and click the up or down Move arrow (just to the right of the scroll bar).**

5. **Click the OK button when you finish moving programs around.**

   The MOM menu shows your newly arranged program names.

Hiding and displaying MOM

Although MOM tries to stay tucked neatly out of the way, it still can be disconcerting to see the MOM toolbar floating around your screen. To hide the toolbar, you have two options:

✔ Minimize the MOM toolbar by changing the button size to regular or large and then clicking the MOM window's Minimize button (the button on the right side of MOM's title bar).

✔ Temporarily hide the MOM toolbar by overlapping it with the current program window.

If you hide the MOM toolbar, you can bring it back into view by using the Task List (pressing Ctrl+Esc) or pressing Alt+Esc.

To minimize the MOM toolbar, follow these steps:

1. **Click the Microsoft Office button in the MOM toolbar.**

   The MOM menu appears.

   (If the toolbar is hidden, first display it by double-clicking the Microsoft Office icon in the Microsoft Office program group.)

2. **Choose Customize or type C.**

   The Customize dialog box appears.

3. **Click the View tab.**

   The View tab of the Customize dialog box appears.

4. **Choose Regular Buttons or Large Buttons and click the OK button.**

   The MOM toolbar appears as a tiny window with a close box on the left side of the toolbar and a Minimize button on the right side of the toolbar (see Figure 13-19).

5. **Click the Minimize button.**

   The MOM toolbar disappears from view.

Figure 13-19:
The MOM toolbar with the close box and Minimize button.

Close box

Minimize button

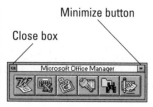

To hide the MOM toolbar behind the current program window, follow these steps:

1. **Click the Microsoft Office button in the MOM toolbar.**

   The MOM menu appears.

   (If the toolbar is hidden, first display it by double-clicking the Microsoft Office icon in the Microsoft Office program group.)

2. **Choose Customize or type C.**

   The Customize dialog box appears.

3. **Click the View tab.**

   The View tab of the Customize dialog box appears.

4. **Click the check box next to the Toolbar is Always Visible option so that a check mark does not appear.**

5. **Click the OK button.**

   The MOM toolbar appears as a tiny window with a close box and a Minimize button.

6. **Click anywhere in the window of a currently loaded program.**

   The MOM toolbar disappears from view. Use the Alt+Tab keyboard shortcut (described in the beginning of this chapter) to show the toolbar again.

Displaying MOM's ToolTips

In the old days, programs required you to memorize and type cryptic commands if you wanted the computer to do anything. Then some genius came up with the idea of pull-down menus. As if to speed the spread of illiteracy, other geniuses came up with the idea of displaying icons below the pull-down menus. Each icon represented a specific command, and by clicking the appropriate icon, you could bypass menu commands altogether.

Unfortunately, most icons are less than intuitive. Microsoft Word, for example, has an icon that looks like a finger pointing at a grid. If you guessed that this icon represents the Insert Autotext command, congratulations!

If playing guessing games with icons that are supposed to make programs easier to use isn't your idea of fun, MOM can come to the rescue. With MOM on the lookout, any time you place the mouse pointer on an icon in any Microsoft program, a little yellow description of the icon appears. This little box, called a *ToolTip*, explains the function of each icon so that you don't have to guess anymore (see Figure 13-20).

Figure 13-20:
A MOM
ToolTip.

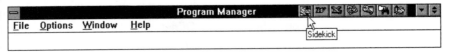

To turn MOM's ToolTips off or on, follow these steps:

1. **Click the Microsoft Office button in the MOM toolbar.**

   The MOM menu appears.

   (If the toolbar is hidden, first display it by double-clicking the Microsoft Office icon in the Microsoft Office program group.)

2. **Choose Customize or type C.**

   The Customize dialog box appears.

3. **Click the View tab.**

   The View tab of the Customize dialog box appears.

4. **Click the Show ToolTips check box, if appropriate.**

   An X in the check box means that MOM will show ToolTips. No X, no ToolTips.

5. **Click the OK button.**

   As you move the mouse pointer slowly over icons or the MOM toolbar, notice whether ToolTips appear.

Chapter 14

Exchanging Information between Word and Other Programs

- -

In This Chapter

▶ Exchanging data between programs

▶ Exchanging words with Word

▶ Exchanging spreadsheets with Excel

▶ Exchanging data with Access

▶ Exchanging pretty pictures with PowerPoint

- -

*T*he most popular kind of program is word processing. Despite the efficiency of telephones, television, and other devices that begin with *tele*, writing remains one of the most common ways that people communicate with one another (besides using obscene hand gestures).

No matter how pretty you make your graphs with PowerPoint or how often you calculate complex results with Excel, you'll always need to write words that explain what this information means. For that reason, Microsoft Office provides plenty of ways to exchange data between Word, Excel, Access, and PowerPoint. By combining words with spreadsheets, data, and graphs, you can create sophisticated reports that will look pleasing, even if you have nothing important to say.

Exchanging Data Between Programs

Microsoft Windows makes it easy to exchange data between different programs. Just copy the data you want from one program and paste it into another. Depending on what you want to do, Windows provides four ways to share data between programs:

✔ Copy it.

✔ Move it.

✔ Link it.

✔ Embed it.

The Windows Clipboard

Whenever you copy or move data, Windows stores this information temporarily in an area of memory affectionately known as the Clipboard. The Clipboard can hold globs of data, but only one glob at a time. The moment you copy or move another glob of data, the Clipboard immediately erases the data that it's currently holding and replaces it with the new data.

After you copy or move data to the Clipboard, you can paste it into a Word, Excel, PowerPoint, or Access window as many times as you want. But the moment you copy or move new data to the Clipboard, the Clipboard forgets all the old data that was stored on it.

Copying data

Copying data is useful when you want certain data to appear in more than one program, such as names and addresses in both an Access database and a Word form letter.

To copy data, follow these steps:

1. **Highlight the data that you want to copy.**

   Either hold down the mouse button and drag the mouse over the data that you want to copy, or hold down the Shift key and press the arrow keys to highlight the data.

2. **Press Ctrl+C or click the Copy button (see Figure 14-1).**

   Although you can't see it, Windows temporarily stores your highlighted data in the Clipboard.

3. **Position the insertion point where you want to paste the data that you highlighted in step 1.**

4. **Press Ctrl+V or click the Paste button (see Figure 14-2).**

Figure 14-1:
The Copy button in the Standard toolbar.

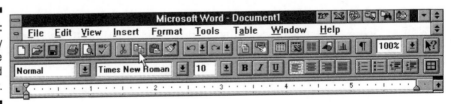

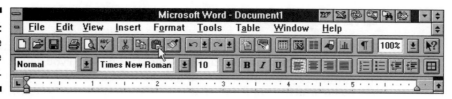

Figure 14-2:
The Paste
button in the
toolbar.

Moving data

Moving data is useful when certain data appears in one file but you want it to appear in another file instead — for example, when you're moving text from one Word document to another or moving a spreadsheet from Excel to Word.

To move data, follow these steps:

1. **Highlight the data that you want to move.**

   Either hold down the mouse button and drag the mouse over the data that you want to move, or hold down the Shift key and press the arrow keys to highlight the data.

2. **Press Ctrl+X, or click the Cut button (see Figure 14-3).**

   Although you can't see it, Windows temporarily stores your highlighted data on the Clipboard.

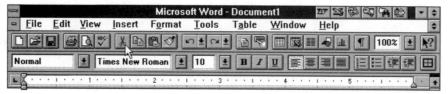

Figure 14-3:
The Cut
button in the
toolbar.

3. **Position the insertion point where you want to paste the data that you highlighted in step 1.**

4. **Press Ctrl+V or click the Paste button.**

When you cut data from a program, that data exists only on the Clipboard, so paste it to a new document or location right away. If you cut or copy additional data before pasting the first chunk of data, the Clipboard will erase the first data cut to it and replace it with the new data copied or cut to it. This means that you'll lose the first chunk of data that you cut to the Clipboard.

Whenever you use the Cut command, always follow it immediately with the Paste command unless you want to lose your data.

Linking data

Linking data allows you to create a graph in PowerPoint and to have that graph appear in a Word document. Linking is most useful when you need to share data with several people. If you have a graph that five other people need to use, you could print five copies and pass them around the office. Naturally, this procedure would be time-consuming and inconvenient.

But if you link your graph to those five people's Word documents, you can just change the graph in PowerPoint; the link would update the graphs in their Word documents automatically.

To link data, follow these steps:

1. **Open the program containing the data that you want to link.**

   If you want to link a PowerPoint graph to a Word document, for example, open PowerPoint.

2. **Highlight the data that you want to link.**

   Either hold down the mouse button and drag the mouse over the data that you want to link, or hold down the Shift key and press the arrow keys to highlight the data.

3. **From the Edit menu, choose Copy (or press Ctrl+C).**

4. **Open the program to which you want to link your data.**

   If you're linking a PowerPoint graph to a Word document, for example, open Word.

5. **Position the insertion point where you want the linked data to appear.**

6. **From the Edit menu, choose Paste Special.**

   The Paste Special dialog box appears (see Figure 14-4).

7. **Choose Paste Link and click OK.**

To link data to Access, you must switch to design view in Access.

Besides linking data between different programs, you can link data between different files created by the same program. For example, you can create a link between two or more Word documents.

Editing links

Linked data can be changed only by the original program. If you create a graph in PowerPoint and link it to a Word document, for example, the only way to modify that graph is from within PowerPoint.

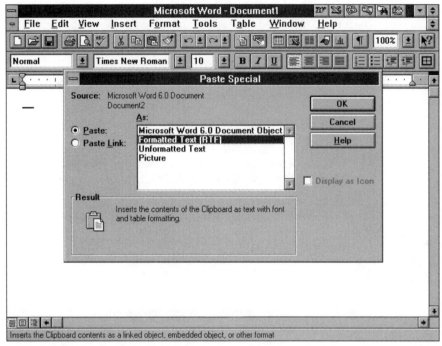

Figure 14-4:
The Paste
Special
dialog box.

You can edit linked data with the original program in two ways:

- ✔ Open the program that created the linked data.
- ✔ Open the program that contains the linked data and double-click that data to open the program that created it.

If you know that the data is linked to other programs, it's easier and faster to open that program first. If you have a PowerPoint graph linked to a Word document, just open PowerPoint and make your changes in the linked graph.

If you're not sure which data is linked to another program, you have no choice but to open the program that contains the linked data. If you have a PowerPoint graph linked to a Word document, but you have no clue where to find the PowerPoint graph on your hard disk, open Word and double-click the graph. Microsoft Office goes through the nuisance and trouble of finding the linked graph that you want to edit.

Breaking links

You can break a link at any time. When you break a link, the linked data remains but cannot be updated or re-connected again, so be careful about breaking links.

You can break a link only from within the program that contains the linked data. If you have a PowerPoint graph linked to a Word document, you have to break the link from within Word.

To break a link, follow these steps:

1. **From the Edit menu, choose Links.**

   The Links dialog box appears (see Figure 14-5).

2. **Click the Break Link button.**

   A dialog box appears, asking whether you're sure that you want to break the link. When you do break the link, there's no way to unbreak it.

3. **Click the Yes button.**

To break a link within Microsoft Excel, highlight the linked data and press Delete. The three-step process described in this section won't work with Excel because Microsoft hasn't gotten integration to work smoothly in all programs in Microsoft Office.

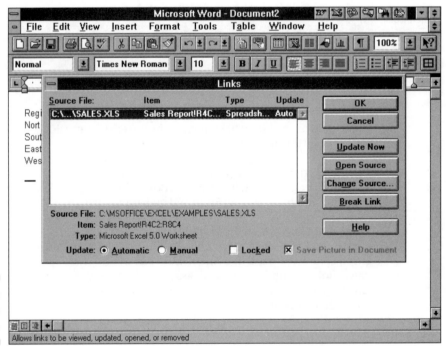

Figure 14-5:
The Links
dialog box.

Linking vs. embedding

Should you link or embed data? Linking shares data between two or more separate files, whereas embedding crams data into a single file. As a result, embedded files tend to get fat and large, while linked files stay lean.

On the other hand, sharing linked data files is a pain in the neck. Not only do you have to give each person a copy of all your linked data files, but each person also must have a copy of each program that created the linked data. If you linked an Excel spreadsheet to a Word document, for example, you would have to give someone else your Excel spreadsheet file and your Word document file, in addition to making sure that the other person has a copy of Excel and Word on his or her computer.

Sharing embedded data files is easy: just give one file to the other person, and you're done. Even if your embedded file contains Excel data and the other person doesn't have Excel on his computer, embedded files still can display the Excel spreadsheet data.

If you want to share files with other people who don't have the same programs that you have, embed your data. If you want to keep your files small and separate, link data.

Embedding data

When you embed data, you physically store data from one program in another program, such as embedding an Excel spreadsheet in a Word document. The main difference between linking and embedding is that embedding creates a single document that contains all the data.

This means that you can embed Excel, Access, and PowerPoint data in a Word document and then view, edit, or print that document on another computer — even if that computer does *not* have a copy of Excel, Access, or PowerPoint. When you embed data, the data resides in a single file. When you link data, the data resides in two separate files.

To embed data, follow these steps:

1. **Open the program containing the data that you want to embed.**

   If you want to embed a PowerPoint graph in a Word document, for example, open PowerPoint.

2. **Highlight the data that you want to embed.**

   Either hold down the mouse button and drag the mouse over the data that you want to embed, or hold down the Shift key and press the arrow keys to highlight the data.

3. **From the Edit menu, choose Copy (or press Ctrl+C).**

4. **Open the program in which you want to embed the data.**

   If you're embedding a PowerPoint graph in a Word document, for example, open Word.

5. **Position the insertion point where you want to embed the data.**

6. **From the _E_dit menu, choose Paste _S_pecial.**

   The Paste Special dialog box appears.

7. **Choose the _P_aste option.**

8. **Choose the option that ends with the word _Object_.**

   For example, you might choose Microsoft Word 6.0 Document Object or Microsoft Excel 5.0 Worksheet Object.

9. **Click the OK button.**

Editing embedded data

To edit embedded data, just double-click the embedded data. After you double-click embedded data, two changes immediately occur:

✔ The menu and toolbar change to match the program that created the embedded data. If you double-clicked an Excel spreadsheet that is embedded in a Word document, Excel's menus and toolbar temporarily replace Word's menus and toolbars (see Figure 14-6).

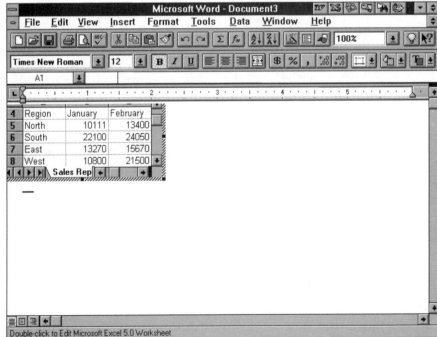

Figure 14-6:
Menus and
toolbars
change
when you
edit
embedded
data.

✔ The embedded data immediately changes its appearance to the way it would look in the program that created it (see Figure 14-7). An embedded Excel spreadsheet, for example, would display row numbers, column labels, and worksheet tabs.

Notice that during editing, embedded data appears
as it would in the program that created it.

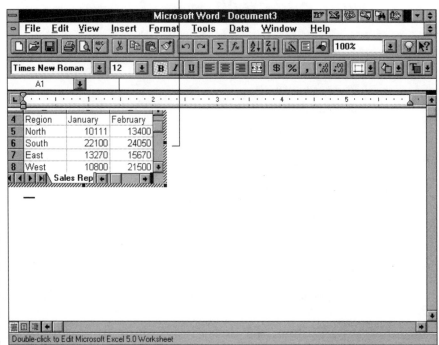

Figure 14-7:
Embedded
data
changes its
appearance
during
editing.

When you're through editing embedded data, click anywhere outside the embedded data.

Deleting embedded data

To delete embedded data, highlight it with the mouse or arrow keys, and then press Delete. Simple, isn't it?

When you delete linked data, that data still exists in a separate file. When you delete embedded data, that data may or may not exist in another file. Before deleting embedded data, make sure that you won't need it again.

Exchanging Words with Word

If you're creating a fancy report, you can write your text in Word and spruce it up with numbers from Excel, data from Access, and pretty pictures from PowerPoint.

Word and Excel

Word can display Excel worksheet data in four ways:

- ✔ As text
- ✔ As a picture
- ✔ As a table
- ✔ As a spreadsheet

Importing Excel data as text

When you paste Excel data into Word as text, you have to manually align the numbers in neat rows and columns. The main reason for copying Excel data as text is to display that data in a format other than rows and columns.

To import Excel data as text into Word, follow these steps:

1. **Open Excel.**

2. **Open the worksheet containing the data that you want to import into Word.**

3. **Highlight the data that you want to import.**

   Either hold down the mouse button and drag the mouse over the data that you want to import, or hold down the Shift key and press the arrow keys to highlight the data.

4. **From the Edit menu, choose Copy (or press Ctrl+C).**

5. **Switch to Word.**

6. **Position the insertion point where you want the Excel data to appear.**

7. **From the Edit menu, choose Paste Special.**

   The Paste Special dialog box appears.

8. **Choose the Paste option.**

9. **In the As: list box, choose Unformatted Text (see Figure 14-8).**

10. **Click the OK button.**

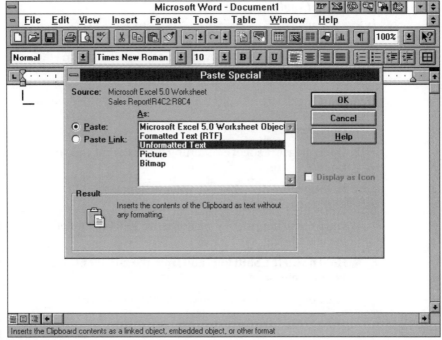

Figure 14-8:
The
Unformatted
Text option
in the As:
list box.

Importing Excel data as a table

A table allows Word to display Excel numbers in neat rows and columns that you can edit, but Word can't use Excel formulas or functions to calculate any results. Tables are useful when you need to display numbers in rows and columns but don't need to use Excel's formulas or functions.

To import Excel data as a table into Word, follow these steps:

1. **Open Excel.**

2. **Open the worksheet containing the data that you want to import into Word.**

3. **Highlight the data that you want to import.**

   Either hold down the mouse button and drag the mouse over the data that you want to import, or hold down the Shift key and press the arrow keys to highlight the data.

4. **From the Edit menu, choose Copy (or press Ctrl+C).**

5. **Switch to Word.**

6. **Position the insertion point where you want the Excel data to appear.**

7. **From the Edit menu, choose Paste (or press Ctrl+V).**

Importing Excel data as a picture

A picture allows you to display Excel numbers in neat rows and columns but won't let you edit the numbers in any way. Pictures are most useful when you want to display numbers that you don't want someone to edit by mistake (or on purpose).

To import Excel data As a picture into Word, follow these steps:

1. **Open Excel.**

2. **Open the worksheet containing the data that you want to import into Word.**

3. **Highlight the data that you want to import.**

   Either hold down the mouse button and drag the mouse over the data that you want to import, or hold down the Shift key and press the arrow keys to highlight the data.

4. **Hold down the Shift key, and from the Edit menu, choose the Copy Picture command.**

   The Copy Picture dialog box appears (see Figure 14-9).

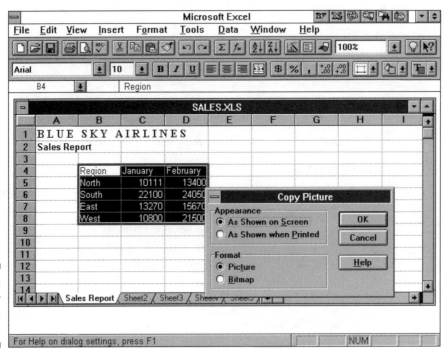

Figure 14-9:
The Copy
Picture
dialog box.

5. **Click the OK button.**

6. **Switch to Word.**

7. **Position the insertion point where you want the Excel data to appear.**

8. **From the Edit menu, choose Paste (or press Ctrl+V).**

Importing Excel data as a spreadsheet

A spreadsheet allows Word to display Excel numbers in neat rows and columns, with the additional benefit of being capable of using Excel formulas or functions to calculate results. The only two ways to display a spreadsheet in Word are to link or embed data from Excel to your Word document.

To import Excel data into Word, follow these steps:

1. **Open Excel.**

2. **Open the worksheet containing the data that you want to import into Word.**

3. **Highlight the data that you want to import.**

   Either hold down the mouse button and drag the mouse over the data that you want to import, or hold down the Shift key and press the arrow keys to highlight the data.

4. **From the Edit menu, choose Copy (or press Ctrl+C).**

5. **Switch to Word.**

6. **Position the insertion point where you want the Excel data to appear.**

7. **From the Edit menu, choose Paste Special.**

   The Paste Special dialog box appears.

8. **Choose Paste Link.**

9. **In the As: list box, choose Microsoft Excel 5.0 Worksheet Object.**

10. **Click the OK button.**

To embed Excel data in Word, follow these steps:

1. **Open Excel.**

2. **Open the worksheet containing the data that you want to embed in Word.**

3. **Highlight the data that you want to embed.**

   Either hold down the mouse button and drag the mouse over the data that you want to embed, or hold down the Shift key and press the arrow keys to highlight the data.

4. **From the Edit menu, choose Copy (or press Ctrl+C).**

5. **Switch to Word.**

6. **Place the insertion point where you want the Excel data to appear.**

7. **From the Edit menu, choose Paste Special.**

   The Paste Special dialog box appears.

8. **Choose Paste.**

9. **In the As: list box, choose Microsoft Excel 5.0 Worksheet Object.**

10. **Click the OK button.**

Creating spreadsheets within Word

Sometimes you need to create from scratch a spreadsheet that you want to use in a Word document. You could open Excel, create your spreadsheet, and then copy and paste it into Word. That method is clumsy, though, and we all know that computers make life easier than that (except when you try reading the manuals).

As a shortcut, you can create an Excel spreadsheet directly within Word, complete with all of Excel's formulas and functions. When you save your Word document, the Excel spreadsheet is saved (embedded) within your Word document file.

To create Excel data in Word, follow these steps:

1. **Open Word.**

2. **Open a document.**

3. **Place the insertion point where you want to create an Excel spreadsheet.**

4. **Click the Insert Microsoft Excel Worksheet button in the toolbar.**

   A grid appears (see Figure 14-10).

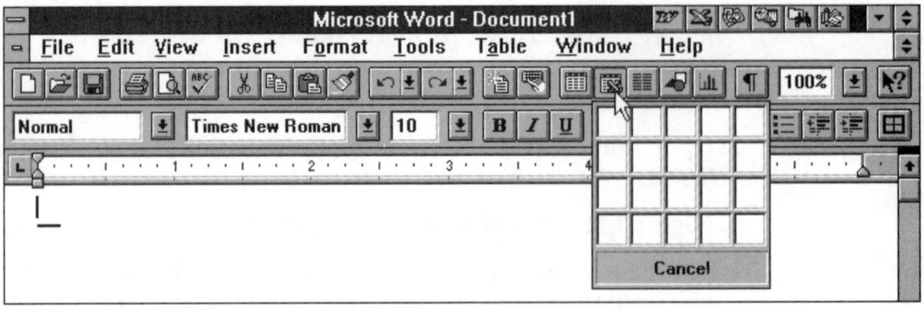

Figure 14-10: The Insert Microsoft Excel Worksheet button and its grid.

5. **Click the box that corresponds to the size of the spreadsheet that you want to create.**

If you click the box in the bottom-right corner of the grid, for example, you'll create a spreadsheet that consists of four rows and five columns.

6. **Type any numbers, functions, or formulas that you want to use in the spreadsheet.**

When the insertion point appears inside a spreadsheet embedded in Word, Excel's menus and toolbar temporarily replace Word's menus and toolbar.

To resize your spreadsheet, drag the spreadsheet's resize handles. This action creates a bigger or smaller spreadsheet.

Word and Access

Normally, Access data (which is covered in Chapter 15) is most useful for creating form letters, mailing labels, and other annoying instruments of junk mail. You also can insert Access data as a table into a Word document, however.

To import Access data as a table into Word, follow these steps:

1. **Open Word.**

2. **Open a document.**

3. **Place the insertion point where you want to put the Access data.**

4. **From the Insert menu, choose Database.**

The Database dialog box appears (see Figure 14-11).

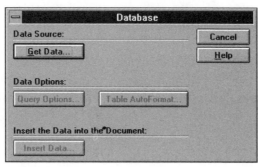

Figure 14-11:
The
Database
dialog box.

5. **Click the Get Data button.**

The Open Data Source dialog box appears (see Figure 14-12).

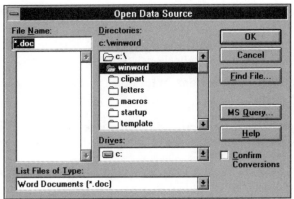

Figure 14-12:
The Open
Data Source
dialog box.

6. **Click the arrow in the List Files of Types list box, and choose MS Access Databases (*.mdb).**

7. **Choose the directory and MDB file that you want to import into your Word document and click the OK button.**

   The Microsoft Access dialog box appears (see Figure 14-13).

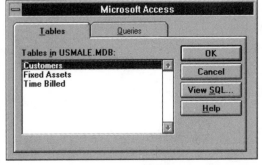

Figure 14-13:
The
Microsoft
Access
dialog box.

8. **Click the Tables or Queries tab.**

9. **Choose the table or query that you want to insert into your Word document and then click the OK button.**

   The Database dialog box appears (see Figure 14-14).

10. **Click the Table AutoFormat button.**

    The Table AutoFormat dialog box appears (see Figure 14-15).

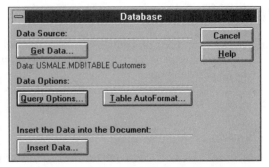

Figure 14-14:
The
Database
dialog box.

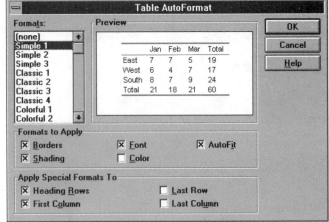

Figure 14-15:
The Table
AutoFormat
dialog box.

11. **Choose the table format that you want to use and click the OK button.**

    The Database dialog box appears again.

12. **Click the Insert Data button.**

    The Insert Data dialog box appears (see Figure 14-16).

13. **Choose to insert All the records, or type the range of records that you want to insert.**

    For example, you might type **1** in the From: box and **12** in the To: box for records 1 through 12.

14. **Click the OK button.**

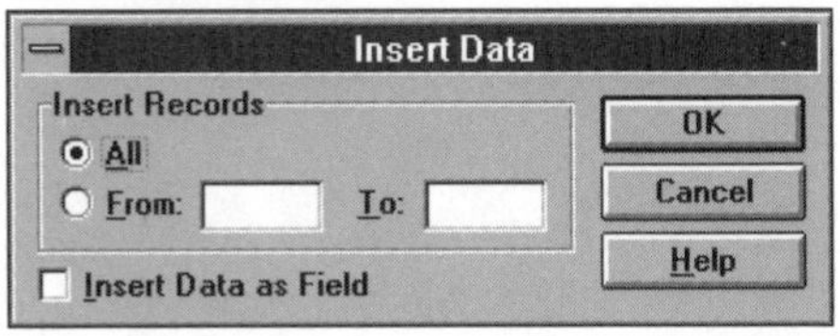

Figure 14-16:
The Insert
Data dialog
box.

Word and PowerPoint

PowerPoint is a great program to use to create slides, overheads, and outlines. Because Word is useful mostly for writing, and its weak drawing program can't match PowerPoint's artistry, you can take advantage of both programs' capabilities. Just create a fancy, colorful PowerPoint presentation, and paste either the text or graphic objects into Word.

Pasting text from PowerPoint into Word

Text most commonly appears in PowerPoint as an outline, a slide title, or a text box. Any time you move the mouse over text, PowerPoint helpfully turns the mouse pointer into an I-beam pointer (see Figure 14-17).

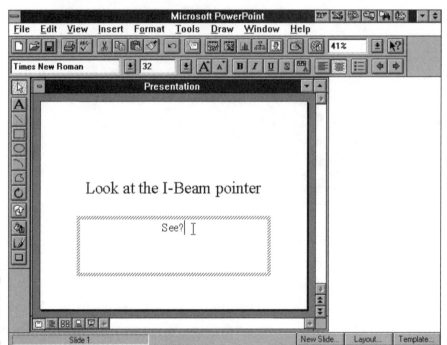

Figure 14-17:
The I-beam
pointer.

What appears to be text in a PowerPoint presentation may actually be a graphic object, such as fancy titles or headlines. If you move the mouse pointer over text and the pointer doesn't change into an I-beam pointer, chances are that the text is really a graphic object.

To import PowerPoint text into Word, follow these steps:

1. **Open PowerPoint.**

2. **Open a PowerPoint presentation file.**

3. **Select the data that you want to import.**

   Either hold down the mouse button and drag the mouse over the data that you want to import, or hold down the Shift key and press the arrow keys to highlight the data.

4. **From the Edit menu, choose Copy (or press Ctrl+C).**

5. **Switch to Word.**

6. **Position the insertion point where you want to import the PowerPoint text.**

7. **From the Edit menu, choose Paste (or press Ctrl+V).**

Pasting graphics from PowerPoint into Word

PowerPoint graphics appear in a Word document as an object that you can resize, move, or even edit from within Word. That way, you can make sure that your text flows nicely around the graphic object, and you can use Word as a crude desktop publisher for creating simple newsletters, flyers, and other things that people will throw away the moment they're finished looking at them.

To import PowerPoint Ggaphics into Word, follow these steps:

1. **Open PowerPoint.**

2. **Open a PowerPoint presentation file.**

3. **Click the graphic object that you want to import.**

   PowerPoint displays resize handles around any graphic object that you click.

4. **From the Edit menu, choose Copy (or press Ctrl+C).**

5. **Switch to Word.**

6. **Place the insertion point where you want to import the PowerPoint graphic.**

7. **From the Edit menu, choose Paste (or press Ctrl+V).**

Exchanging Numbers with Excel

Although Excel mainly is used to calculate numeric results, you can copy and paste data from Word, PowerPoint, or Access into an Excel worksheet. Rather than type text in a worksheet cell, for example, you might find it easier to copy text from Word.

Excel and Word

When you copy text from Word into Excel, you have three options:

- ✓ Paste the text into a worksheet cell.
- ✓ Paste the text into a worksheet text box.
- ✓ Paste a Word table into multiple worksheet cells.

Copying text to a worksheet cell

When you copy text from Word to an Excel worksheet, you can paste the text in a single worksheet cell. Unfortunately, if you paste a long phrase or paragraph in a worksheet cell, all the text tries to cram into that cell. The result is that the text overflows into the neighboring cells and the worksheet looks like a mess (see Figure 14-18).

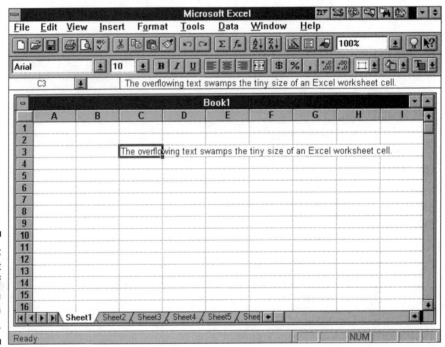

Figure 14-18:
What happens if you copy a paragraph to a single cell.

To import Word text into an Excel worksheet cell, follow these steps:

1. **Open Word.**

2. **Open a document.**

3. **Select the data that you want to import.**

   Either hold down the mouse button and drag the mouse over the data that you want to import, or hold down the Shift key and press the arrow keys to highlight the data.

4. **From the Edit menu, choose Copy (or press Ctrl+C).**

5. **Switch to Excel.**

6. **Place the insertion point in the cell into which you want to import the Word text.**

7. **From the Edit menu, choose Paste (or press Ctrl+V).**

Copying text to a worksheet text box

As an alternative to copying text from Word and pasting it into an Excel worksheet cell, you can paste the text into an Excel worksheet text box (see Figure 14-19). For long phrases or paragraphs, text boxes are more convenient because you can see all your text at the same time.

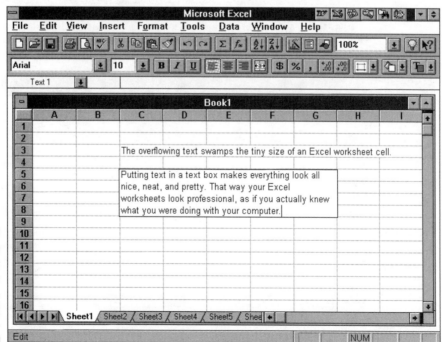

Figure 14-19: How a text box handles a paragraph, compared with a cell.

To import Word text into an Excel text box, follow these steps:

1. **Open Word.**

2. **Open a document.**

3. **Highlight the data that you want to import.**

   Either hold down the mouse button and drag the mouse over the data that you want to import, or hold down the Shift key and press the arrow keys to highlight the data.

4. **From the Edit menu, choose Copy (or press Ctrl+C).**

5. **Switch to Excel.**

6. **Click the Text Box icon in the toolbar (see Figure 14-20).**

7. **Place the insertion point in the worksheet where you want the upper-left corner of the text box to appear.**

8. **Drag the mouse to where you want the lower-right corner of the text box to appear and let go of the mouse button.**

   Excel draws a box in the worksheet, with the insertion point inside the box.

9. **From the Edit menu, choose Paste (or press Ctrl+V).**

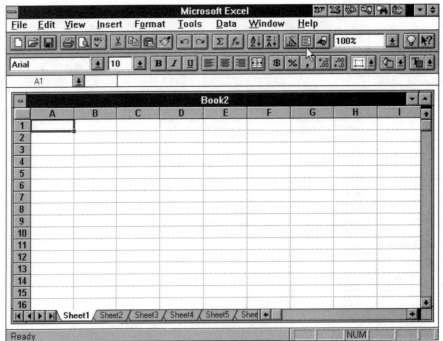

Figure 14-20:
The Excel
Text Box
icon in the
toolbar.

Copying a table from Word to Excel

When you copy a table stored in a Word document and paste it into an Excel worksheet, Excel thoughtfully places each cell of your Word table in corresponding cells in the worksheet.

To import a Word table into Excel, follow these steps:

1. **Open Word.**
2. **Open a document.**
3. **Highlight the table that you want to import.**

   Either hold down the mouse button and drag the mouse over the data that you want to import, or hold down the Shift key and press the arrow keys to highlight the data.

4. **From the Edit menu, choose Copy (or press Ctrl+C).**
5. **Switch to Excel.**
6. **Click the cell where you want the upper-left corner of the table to appear.**
7. **From the Edit menu, choose Paste (or press Ctrl+V).**

Linking Word text to an Excel worksheet

Linking text to Excel ensures that any changes made in the Word document automatically get updated in Excel without any effort on your part, and we all know that people want to do as little as possible when they can get away with it (and still get paid).

To link text to Excel, follow these steps:

1. **Open Word.**
2. **Open a document.**
3. **Highlight the text that you want to link.**

   Either hold down the mouse button and drag the mouse over the data that you want to link, or hold down the Shift key and press the arrow keys to highlight the data.

4. **From the Edit menu, choose Copy (or press Ctrl+C).**
5. **Switch to Excel.**
6. **Click the cell where you want the linked text to appear.**
7. **From the Edit menu, choose Paste Special.**

   The Paste Special dialog box appears.

8. Choose Paste Link.

9. In the As: list box, choose Microsoft Word 6.0 Document Object.

10. Click the OK button.

Excel and Access

Access gives you two ways to copy data from an Access database to Excel:

- ✔ Copy and paste data from individual fields.
- ✔ Convert entire Access datasheets, forms, or reports into an Excel XLS format and open the file into Excel.

Copying data from Access fields to Excel

Although Access can show data in form or datasheet view, it won't allow you to highlight multiple records and fields. Instead, you have to highlight fields one at a time. If you need to copy data from only a few fields stored in Access, use this method. Otherwise, it's faster to convert the entire Access datasheet, form, or report to an Excel XLS file.

To copy fields to Excel, follow these steps:

1. Open Access.

2. Open a database file.

3. Choose the table, form, query, or report that you want to use.

4. Highlight the text stored in a field.

   Either hold down the mouse button and drag the mouse over the data that you want to copy, or hold down the Shift key and press the arrow keys to highlight the data.

5. From the Edit menu, choose Copy (or press Ctrl+C).

6. Switch to Excel.

7. Click the cell where you want the text to appear.

8. From the Edit menu, choose Paste (or press Ctrl+V).

Converting data to an Excel XLS file

Any time you need to copy massive amounts of Access database information to Excel, the easy way is to have Access convert your entire database to an Excel XLS file.

To convert an Access database to an Excel XLS file, follow these steps:

1. **Open Access.**

2. **Open a database file.**

3. **Choose the table, form, query, or report that you want to convert to an Excel XLS file.**

4. **From the File menu, choose Output To.**

   The Output To dialog box appears (see Figure 14-21).

5. **Choose Microsoft Excel (*.xls) and click the OK button.**

   Another Output To dialog box appears.

6. **Choose the drive, directory, and file where you want to store your Access data and click the OK button.**

7. **Switch to Excel.**

8. **From the File menu, choose Open (or press Ctrl+O).**

   The Open dialog box appears.

9. **Highlight the file that you chose in Step 6 and click the OK button.**

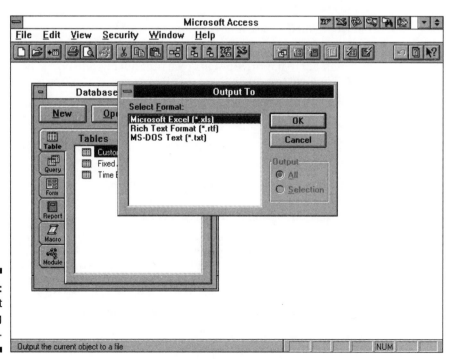

Figure 14-21:
The Output
To dialog
box.

Excel and PowerPoint

PowerPoint can make prettier pictures than Excel, so it's only natural that you might want to copy a graphic object from PowerPoint and dump it into Excel. Besides allowing you to copy graphics from PowerPoint to Excel, Microsoft Office allows you to copy text from a PowerPoint presentation to Excel so that you don't have to type the same words over and over.

Pasting text from PowerPoint into Excel

Text most commonly appears in PowerPoint as an outline, a slide title, or a text box. Any time you move the mouse pointer over text, PowerPoint helpfully turns the mouse pointer into an I-beam pointer.

What appears to be text in a PowerPoint presentation may actually be a graphic object, such as fancy titles or headlines. If you move the mouse pointer over text but the pointer doesn't change into an I-beam pointer, chances are that the text is really a graphic object.

To import PowerPoint text into Excel, follow these steps:

1. **Open PowerPoint.**

2. **Open a presentation file.**

3. **Highlight the data that you want to import.**

   Either hold down the mouse button and drag the mouse over the data that you want to import, or hold down the Shift key and press the arrow keys to highlight the data.

4. **From the Edit menu, choose Copy (or press Ctrl+C).**

5. **Switch to Excel.**

6. **Position the insertion point in the cell or text box where you want to import the PowerPoint text.**

7. **From the Edit menu, choose Paste (or press Ctrl+V).**

Pasting graphics from PowerPoint into Excel

PowerPoint graphics appear in an Excel worksheet as objects that you can resize or move from within Excel. By adding colorful graphics from PowerPoint, you can disguise the fact that the numbers in your Excel worksheet show that your company is going bankrupt and can't afford to pay its employees any longer.

To import PowerPoint graphics in Excel, follow these steps:

1. **Open PowerPoint.**

2. **Open a presentation file.**

3. **Click the graphic object that you want to import.**

   PowerPoint displays resize handles around any graphic object that you click.

4. **From the Edit menu, choose Copy (or press Ctrl+C).**

5. **Switch to Excel.**

6. **Position the insertion point in the cell where you want the upper-left corner of the PowerPoint graphic to appear.**

7. **From the Edit menu, choose Paste (or press Ctrl+V).**

Exchanging Data with Access

Because Access stores data in fields, any information that you copy from another program must fit into an Access database field. This means that you can copy text but not graphic objects.

Access and Excel

Access gives you two ways to copy data from Excel and paste it into Access:

- ✔ Copy data from Excel and paste it into an Access database field.
- ✔ Convert an Excel XLS file to an Access database table.

Copying data from Excel to an Access database field

If you need to copy only a few items from Excel, it's quicker and more convenient just to copy the data items individually and paste them into Access.

To import Excel data into Access, follow these steps:

1. **Open Excel.**

2. **Open a worksheet file.**

3. **Highlight the data that you want to import.**

   Either hold down the mouse button and drag the mouse over the data that you want to import, or hold down the Shift key and press the arrow keys to highlight the data.

4. **From the Edit menu, choose Copy (or press Ctrl+C).**

5. **Switch to Access.**

6. **Open a database table and click where you want to paste the Excel data.**

7. **From the Edit menu, choose Paste (or press Ctrl+V).**

Converting an Excel worksheet to an Access database table

If you need to copy lots of data from Excel into Access, it's easier to convert the whole thing to an Access database table and then open the file into Access for further analysis, manipulation, or whatever else you want to do with the information.

Make sure that each row of your Excel worksheet contains data and that the data in each column is of the same data type (such as numbers, text, or currency).

To convert an Excel file to an Access file, follow these steps:

1. **Open Excel.**

2. **Make any changes you want in the Excel worksheet file that you want to convert.**

3. **Save your file.**

4. **From the File menu, choose Close.**

5. **Switch to Access.**

6. **From the File menu, choose Open Database (or press Ctrl+O).**

7. **Choose the MDB database file in which you want to store the Excel data.**

   The database window appears.

8. **From the File menu, choose Import.**

   The Import dialog box appears (see Figure 14-22).

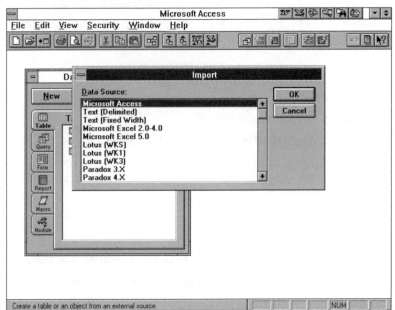

Figure 14-22:
The Import
dialog box.

9. **In the Data Source list box, choose Microsoft Excel 5.0.**

10. **Click the OK button.**

    The Select File dialog box appears.

11. **Choose the drive, directory, and file that you want to import.**

12. **Click the Import button.**

    The Import Spreadsheet Options dialog box appears (see Figure 14-23).

13. **Choose the options you want.**

14. **Click the OK button.**

Access and Word

Access gives you two ways to copy data from Word and paste it into Access:

  ✔ Copy data from Word and paste it into an Access database field.

  ✔ Convert a Word document file to an Access database table.

Copying data from Word to an Access database field

If you need to copy only a few items from Word, it's quicker and more convenient just to copy the data items individually and paste them into Access.

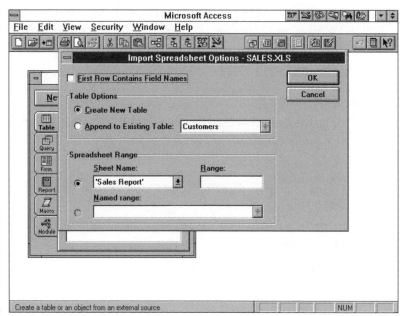

Figure 14-23:
The Import
Spreadsheet
Options
dialog box.

To import Word data into Access, follow these steps:

1. **Open Word.**
2. **Open a document.**
3. **Highlight the data that you want to import.**

   Either hold down the mouse button and drag the mouse over the data that you want to import, or hold down the Shift key and press the arrow keys to highlight the data.
4. **From the Edit menu, choose Copy (or press Ctrl+C).**
5. **Switch to Access.**
6. **Open a database table.**
7. **Click where you want to paste the Word data.**
8. **From the Edit menu, choose Paste (or press Ctrl+V).**

Convert a Word document file to an Access database table

You can convert a Word document file to an Access database table only if you have organized the Word document as a delimited text file. A *delimited text file* simply means that the data for each field is separated by a character, such as a comma or a tab. Following is an example of a delimited text file:

"Bob", "Smith", "123 Main Street", "AnyTown", "State", "Zip"

Delimited text files often are created by the mail-merge feature of word processing programs, such as Ami Pro. Rather than type all this information again, you can import it into Access.

To import a delimited text file into Access, follow these steps:

1. **Open Word.**
2. **Open the delimited text file that you want to import into Access.**
3. **From the File menu, choose Save As.**

   The Save As dialog box appears.
4. **Choose the drive, directory, and file where you want to save the delimited text file.**
5. **In the Save File As Type list, choose Text Only With Line Breaks.**
6. **Click the OK button.**
7. **Switch to Access.**

8. From the File menu, choose Open Database (or press Ctrl+O).

9. Choose the MDB database file in which you want to store the delimited text file.

   The database window appears.

10. From the File menu, choose Import.

    The Import dialog box appears.

11. In the Data Source list box, choose Text (Delimited).

12. Click the OK button.

    The Select File dialog box appears.

13. Choose the drive, directory, and file that you want to import.

14. Click the Import button.

    The Import Text Options dialog box appears (see Figure 14-24).

15. Choose the options you want.

16. Click the OK button.

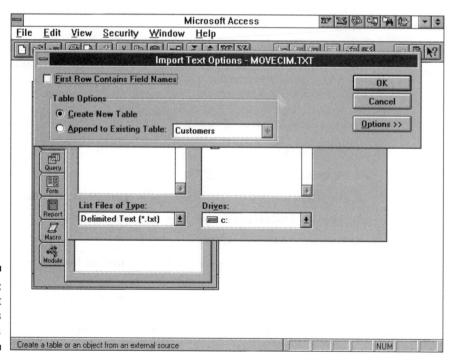

Figure 14-24:
The Import Text Options dialog box.

Exchanging Pretty Pictures with PowerPoint

PowerPoint can help you make presentations (otherwise known as dog-and-pony shows) to persuade others that your ideas are worthwhile — or at least that your opponent's ideas are worth ignoring. To that end, PowerPoint allows you to import text and graphics from Excel and Word.

From Excel, you can import a worksheet or a graph. From Word, you can import an outline, a graphic object, or just plain ol' text.

PowerPoint and Excel

You can display Excel data in a PowerPoint presentation in three ways:

- ✔ Copy and paste the data.
- ✔ Link the data.
- ✔ Embed the data.

Copying and pasting Excel data into PowerPoint

If you have labels or numbers in an Excel worksheet that you want to copy into PowerPoint because you don't feel like typing them again, just copy and paste them from Excel into PowerPoint.

To import Excel text or graphics into PowerPoint, follow these steps:

1. **Open Excel.**
2. **Open an Excel worksheet file.**
3. **Highlight the text or click the graphic object that you want to import.**
4. **From the <u>E</u>dit menu, choose <u>C</u>opy (or press Ctrl+C).**
5. **Switch to PowerPoint.**
6. **For text, click where you want to paste the Excel data. For graphics, skip to Step 7.**
7. **From the <u>E</u>dit menu, choose <u>P</u>aste (or press Ctrl+V).**

After you paste a graphic object into PowerPoint, you can resize or move the graphic to make it pretty.

Linking Excel data to PowerPoint

Because a PowerPoint presentation should display the latest information possible, it won't do you any good to copy Excel data to PowerPoint only to have the data change later. To make sure that your PowerPoint data remains current, you can link Excel text or graphics to PowerPoint.

To link Excel text or graphics to PowerPoint, follow these steps:

1. **Open Excel.**
2. **Open a worksheet file.**
3. **Highlight the text or click the graphic object that you want to link.**
4. **From the Edit menu, choose Copy (or press Ctrl+C).**
5. **Switch to PowerPoint.**
6. **From the Edit menu, choose Paste Special.**

    The Paste Special dialog box appears.

7. **Choose Paste Link.**
8. **Choose Microsoft Excel 5.0 Worksheet Object (if you're linking text) or Microsoft Excel 5.0 Graphic Object (if you're linking graphics).**
9. **Click the OK button.**

Embedding an Excel worksheet in PowerPoint

You can embed an Excel worksheet in a PowerPoint presentation in two ways:

✔ Embed an existing Excel worksheet in PowerPoint.

✔ Embed a new Excel worksheet in PowerPoint.

If you need to display an existing Excel worksheet or graph in a PowerPoint presentation, it's often easier to link the data from Excel to PowerPoint. Linking, however, stores data in two or more separate files. If you want to store all the data in a single file, it's easier to embed the data instead.

To embed an existing Excel worksheet in PowerPoint, follow these steps:

1. **Open PowerPoint.**
2. **Place the insertion point where you want the Excel worksheet to appear.**
3. **From the Insert menu, choose Object.**

    The Insert Object dialog box appears (see Figure 14-25).

4. **Choose the Create from File tab.**

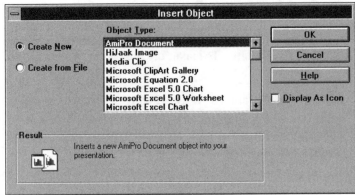

Figure 14-25:
The Insert
Object
dialog box.

5. **Click the Browse button.**

   The Browse dialog box appears.

6. **Choose the drive, directory, and filename of the Excel worksheet that you want to embed in PowerPoint.**

7. **Click the OK button.**

   The embedded object appears within PowerPoint.

8. **Use the mouse to resize or move the object.**

9. **To edit the object, double-click it.**

If you embed an existing Excel worksheet in PowerPoint and later change the data from within PowerPoint, any changes that you make will *not* be reflected in the existing Excel file. Likewise, if you change the data in the existing Excel worksheet, your changes will *not* be reflected in the embedded data in PowerPoint.

Embedding data also is useful for creating a new worksheet or graph. It's too cumbersome to open Excel, open a blank worksheet, and type new numbers just so that you can link the data to your PowerPoint presentation. Instead, simply embed a blank Excel worksheet in PowerPoint and modify the data from within PowerPoint.

To embed a new Excel worksheet in PowerPoint, follow these steps:

1. **Open PowerPoint.**

2. **Place the insertion point where you want the Excel worksheet to appear.**

3. **From the Insert menu, choose Object.**

   The Insert Object dialog box appears.

4. **Choose the Create New tab.**

5. **In the Object Type list box, choose Microsoft Excel 5.0 Worksheet.**

6. **Click the OK button.**

   PowerPoint displays a blank Excel worksheet.

7. **Click the embedded worksheet to type in numbers.**

PowerPoint and Word

You can display Word text or graphics in a PowerPoint presentation in two ways:

✔ Copy and paste the data.

✔ Link the data.

Copying text and graphics to PowerPoint

You can copy both text and graphics from Word to PowerPoint, although you must copy text and graphics separately.

To import text or graphics into PowerPoint, follow these steps:

1. **Open Word.**

2. **Open a document.**

3. **Highlight the text or click the graphic object that you want to import.**

4. **From the Edit menu, choose Copy (or press Ctrl+C).**

5. **Switch to PowerPoint.**

6. **For text, click where you want to paste the text or graphic object. For graphics, skip to Step 7.**

7. **From the Edit menu, choose Paste (or press Ctrl+V).**

Linking text to PowerPoint

Sometimes you may base your PowerPoint presentations on text in a Word document that changes periodically. For example, you may write a quarterly report and want to display the results in PowerPoint. Rather than copy and paste this information each time the text changes in Word, you can link the text from Word to PowerPoint so that any changes made in Word automatically appear in PowerPoint.

To link text to PowerPoint, follow these steps:

1. **Open Word.**

2. **Open a document.**

3. **Highlight the text that you want to link.**

   Either hold down the mouse button and drag the mouse over the data that you want to link, or hold down the Shift key and use the arrow keys to highlight the data.

4. **From the Edit menu, choose Copy (or press Ctrl+C).**

5. **Switch to PowerPoint.**

6. **From the Edit menu, choose Paste Special.**

   The Paste Special dialog box appears.

7. **Choose Paste Link.**

8. **Click the OK button.**

If you resize the text box that contains the linked text, the text may appear to be smashed together.

Converting Word documents to PowerPoint outlines

You may have a brilliantly written report that you'd like to convert to a PowerPoint presentation. Rather than rewrite the whole thing in PowerPoint, you can convert your Word document to an outline and then have PowerPoint suck the whole thing in to create a complete presentation.

To convert an entire Word document to PowerPoint, follow these steps:

1. **Open Word.**

2. **Open a document.**

3. **From the View menu, choose Outline.**

4. **Arrange your Word document in an outline with different headings.**

5. **From the File menu, choose Save (or press Ctrl+S).**

6. **Switch to PowerPoint.**

7. **From the File menu, choose Open (or press Ctrl+O).**

   The Open dialog box appears.

8. **In the List Files Of Type list box, choose Outlines.**

9. **Choose the drive, directory, and file name of the Word document that you want to import into PowerPoint.**

10. **Click the OK button.**

Chapter 15

Using Form Letters and Address Labels to Get the Word Out Fast

- -

In This Chapter

▶ Getting Access and Word to cooperate

▶ Making mailing labels

▶ Making form letters and other "personalized" mail

▶ Making selective form letters

▶ Sorting data to merge in form letters

- -

*A*lthough Microsoft Word is perfectly capable of creating form letters and mailing labels all by itself, why store names and addresses in Microsoft Word if you have a copy of Microsoft Access handy? Microsoft Access can not only help you create form letters, but also help you choose those names and addresses that you want.

If you need to print form letters for all customers who live in California and make more than $50,000 a year, Microsoft Access can help you find this information. If you had those names and addresses stored in Word, Microsoft Word would have no clue how to help you choose certain names and addresses.

Combining Access and Word gives you the most flexibility in printing form letters. That way, you can create "personalized" letters that may actually read as though they were written by someone with more time than you have.

Getting Access and Word to Cooperate

Creating a form letter or mailing label requires two separate files:

- A data source
- A document

The data source contains names and addresses; the document determines the appearance and position of the names and addresses on a mailing label or within a form letter. Obviously, an Access file is the data source, and a Word file is the document.

First, you must create a data source, which means storing names and addresses (or whatever else you want) in an Access database. When you have a data source, you can use Word to create the document that will display this data.

Making Mailing Labels

Mailing labels are nothing more exciting than names and addresses on stickers that you paste on envelopes.

To create mailing labels in Word, do the following:

1. **Open Word.**
2. **From the File menu, choose New (or press Ctrl+N).**

   A New dialog box appears.
3. **Click the OK button.**
4. **From the Tools menu, choose Mail Merge.**

   The Mail Merge Helper dialog box appears (see Figure 15-1).
5. **Click the Create button.**

   A list box appears (see Figure 15-2).
6. **Choose Mailing Labels.**

   A Microsoft Word dialog box appears.
7. **Click the Active Window button.**
8. **Click the Get Data button.**

   A list box appears (see Figure 15-3).

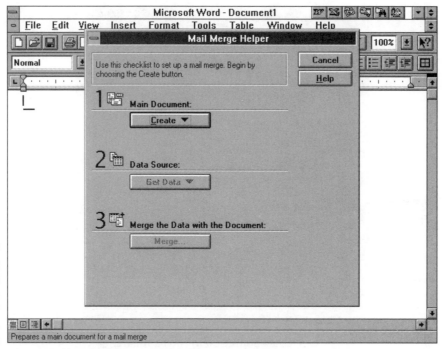

Figure 15-1:
The Mail
Merge
Helper
dialog box.

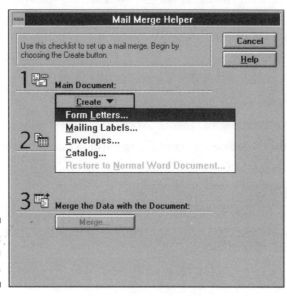

Figure 15-2:
The Create
list box.

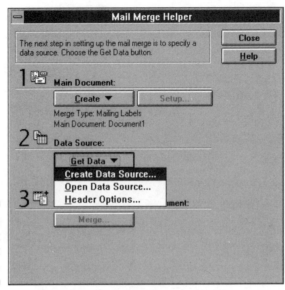

Figure 15-3:
The Get
Data list
box.

9. **Choose Open Data Source.**

   The Open Data Source dialog box appears.

10. **In the List Files of Type list, choose MS Access Databases (*.mdb).**

11. **Choose the drive, directory, and filename of the Access database containing the data that you want to use.**

12. **Click the OK button.**

   The Microsoft Access dialog box appears (see Figure 15-4).

13. **Click either the Tables or Queries tab.**

   The Tables or the Queries tab of the Microsoft Access dialog box appears.

14. **Highlight the table or query containing the data that you want to use.**

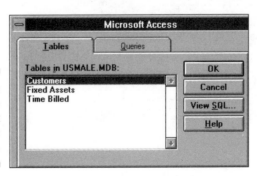

Figure 15-4:
The
Microsoft
Access
dialog box.

15. **Click the OK button.**

A Microsoft Word dialog box appears.

16. **Click the Set Up Main Document button.**

The Label Options dialog box appears (see Figure 15-5).

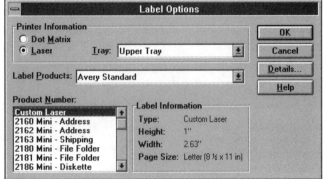

Figure 15-5:
The Label
Options
dialog box.

17. **Choose Dot Matrix or Laser.**

18. **In the Product Number list, choose your mailing-label type.**

19. **Click the OK button.**

The Create Labels dialog box appears (see Figure 15-6).

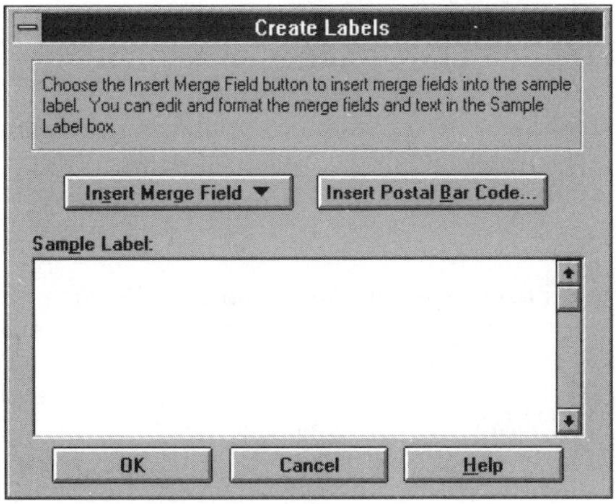

Figure 15-6:
The Create
Labels
dialog box.

20. **Click the Insert Merge Field button.**

    A list box appears, showing all the fields of your chosen database table.

21. **Choose the fields that you want to display.**

    Make sure that you insert spaces, commas, and new lines (by pressing the Enter key) to display your addresses the way you want.

22. **Click the OK button.**

    The Mail Merge Helper dialog box appears.

23. **Click the Merge button.**

    The Merge dialog box appears (see Figure 15-7).

24. **Click the Merge button again.**

Figure 15-7:
The Merge
dialog box.

Creating Form Letters and Other "Personalized" Mail

Everyone has received a form letter, such as the Publishers Clearing House sweepstakes letter notifying you that *you* may have just won $10 million. Besides containing different names and addresses, form letters can contain other data that needs to vary from letter to letter.

If you're writing a letter to salespeople, for example, urging them on to greater glory and profits, you may want each letter to contain the salesperson's monthly sales results as well as his or her name and address. If you're writing letters to potential life insurance customers, you may want to mention their children's names and the horrible consequences that those children might suffer if the prospects don't send you money every month in the guise of a premium.

Any time that you need to write custom letters that contain different but predictable data, you can save time by writing a form letter.

To write a form letter in Word follow these steps:

1. **Open Word.**

2. **From the File menu, choose New (or press Ctrl+N):**

   The New dialog box appears.

3. **Click the OK button.**

4. **From the Tools menu, choose Mail Merge.**

   The Mail Merge Helper dialog box appears.

5. **Click the Create button.**

   A list box appears.

6. **Choose Form Letters.**

   A Microsoft Word dialog box appears.

7. **Click the Active Window button.**

8. **Click the Get Data button.**

   A list box appears.

9. **Choose Open Data Source.**

   The Open Data Source dialog box appears.

10. **In the List Files of Type list, choose MS Access Databases (*.mdb).**

11. **Choose the drive, directory, and filename of the Access database containing the data that you want to use.**

12. **Click the OK button.**

    A Microsoft Access dialog box appears.

13. **Click either the Tables or the Queries tab.**

    The Tables or the Queries tab of the Microsoft Access dialog box appears.

14. **Highlight the table or query containing the data that you want to use.**

15. **Click the OK button.**

    A Microsoft Word dialog box appears.

16. **Click the Edit Main Document button.**

    The Database toolbar appears (see Figure 15-8).

Figure 15-8:
The
Database
toolbar.

17. **Type your form letter.**

When you want data from your Access database to appear in a certain spot, click the Insert Merge Field button. A list box appears, displaying all the available fields.

18. **Choose the field containing the data that you want to appear in your form letter.**

Microsoft Word displays data fields with special brackets. Suppose that you inserted a field named LastName. Figure 15-9 shows how that field appears in Word.

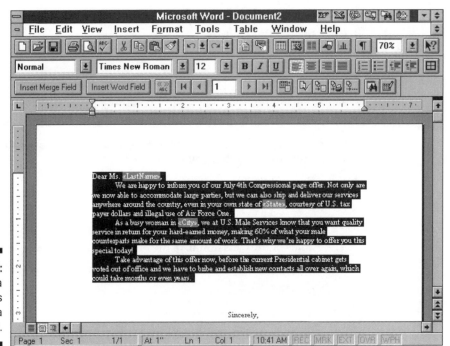

Figure 15-9:
How data
fields
appear in a
form letter.

19. **When you finish writing your form letter and inserting data fields, click the View Merged Data button (see Figure 15-10).**

    Word shows you how your form letter will look with actual data displayed.

Figure 15-10: The View Merged Data, First Record, Previous Record, Next Record, and Last Record buttons in the Database toolbar.

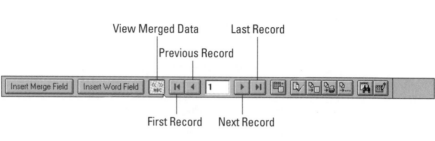

20. **Click the First Record, Previous Record, Next Record, or Last Record buttons to view different record data displayed in your form letter.**

21. **Click the View Merged Data button again to display the data fields.**

22. **Click the Merge to Printer button (see Figure 15-11).**

    The Print dialog box appears.

Figure 15-11: The Merge to Printer button.

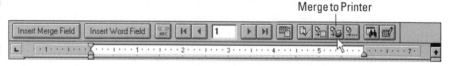

23. **Click the OK button.**

24. **From the File menu, choose Save (or press Ctrl+S).**

    A Save dialog box appears.

25. **Type the filename under which you want to save your form letter.**

26. **Click the OK button.**

Creating Selective Form Letters

You may have a long list of names and addresses stored in a database but want to send form letters to only some of those names, such as all those people who live in California or who have the last name Jones. In these situations, you need to tell Access and Word to merge only that data that meets your criteria.

Word provides the following eight filtering criteria to help you choose only records that contain the data you want to use:

- *Equal to* chooses only records that contain certain information. For example, you could tell Word to merge only data in which the State field is Equal to MO. Only if a record contains MO in its State field will Word merge it with your form letter.

- *Not Equal to* chooses only records that do not contain certain information. If you want to send form letters to everyone except people who live in MO, you could tell Word to merge all records in which the State field is Not Equal to MO.

- *Less Than* chooses only records that contain information less than a certain value. For example, you could send form letters to all addresses in which the PostalCode field is Less Than 50000. When you use the Less Than criteria with text, Word examines text alphabetically. The word *Smith*, for example, is considered to be Less Than *Jones*. Word ignores whether text appears in uppercase or lowercase.

- *Greater Than* chooses only records that contain information greater than a certain value. You could send form letters to all addresses in which the PostalCode field is Greater Than 50000. When you use the Greater Than criteria with text, Word examines text alphabetically. The word *Jones*, for example, is considered to be Greater Than *Smith*. Word ignores whether text appears in uppercase or lowercase.

- *Less Than or Equal* chooses only records that contain information less than or equal to a certain value. You could send form letters to all addresses in which the PostalCode field is Less Than or Equal to 50000. When you use the Less Than or Equal to criteria with text, Word examines text alphabetically. The word *Smith* is considered to be Less Than *Jones*. Word ignores whether text appears in uppercase or lowercase.

- *Greater Than or Equal* chooses only records that contain information greater than or equal to a certain value. You could send form letters to all addresses in which the PostalCode field is Greater Than or Equal to 50000. When you use the Greater Than or Equal to criteria with text, Word examines text alphabetically. The word *Jones* is considered to be Greater Than *Smith*. Word ignores whether text appears in uppercase or lowercase.

✔ *Is Blank* chooses only records that contain certain blank fields. For example, you could tell Word to merge only those records in which the PhoneNumber field Is Blank. In this case, you might be writing form letters to people, asking for their phone numbers.

✔ *Is Not Blank* chooses only records that do not contain certain blank fields. For example, you could tell Word to merge only those records in which the Male field Is Not Blank. In this case, you might be writing form letters only to the males in your database, such as for sending out invitations to a bachelor party.

In addition to these filtering criteria, Word allows you to combine multiple filtering criteria by using the magical words AND or OR.

You may want only those records in which the State field is Equal to CA or the State field is Equal to NV. Or you may want only those records in which the State field is Equal to MI and the LastName field is Less Than or Equal to Smith. By combining multiple filtering criteria with AND and OR, you can create sophisticated criteria that find only the records that you really want.

To select certain data to merge with a form letter, do the following:

1. **Open Word.**

2. **From the File menu, choose Open (or press Ctrl+O).**

   The Open dialog box appears.

3. **Choose the file containing the form letter that you want to use.**

4. **Click the Mail Merge Helper button (see Figure 15-12).**

   The Mail Merge Helper dialog box appears.

Mail Merge Helper button

Figure 15-12:
The Mail
Merge
Helper
button.

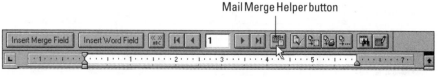

5. **Click the Query Options button.**

   The Query Options dialog box appears (see Figure 15-13).

6. **Click the Field list box and choose the field name that you want to use in your filtering criteria (such as State, PostalCode, or LastName).**

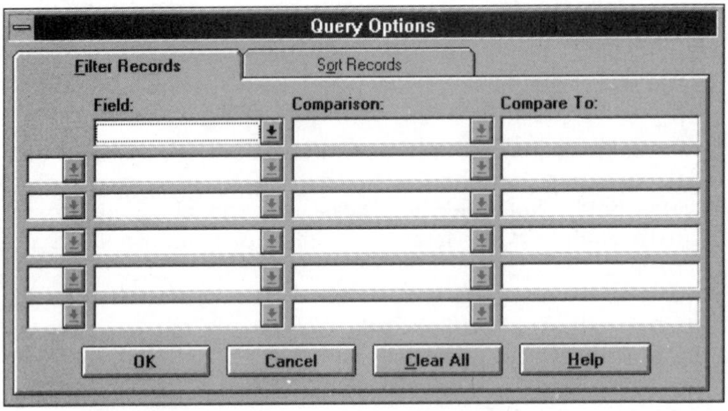

Figure 15-13:
The Query
Options
dialog box.

7. Click the Comparison list box and choose filtering criteria (Equal to, Not Equal to, and so on).

8. In the Compare To box, type a value for your filtering criteria.

Word automatically displays AND next to the blank criteria fields below (see Figure 15-14).

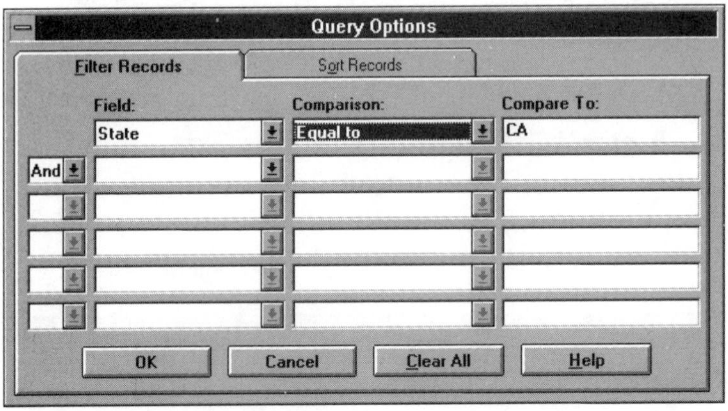

Figure 15-14:
A completed
query in the
Query
Options
dialog box.

9. Click the AND box and change the entry to OR or AND.

10. Repeat Steps 6 through 8 until you finish defining your filtering criteria.

11. Click the OK button.

The Mail Merge Helper dialog box appears.

12. Click the Close button.

13. **Click the View Merged Data button again to display the data fields.**

14. **Click the Merge to Printer button.**

    The Print dialog box appears.

15. **Click the OK button.**

16. **From the File menu, choose Save (or press Ctrl+S).**

    The Save dialog box appears.

17. **Type the filename under which you want to save your form letter.**

18. **Click the OK button.**

Sorting Data to Merge in Form Letters

In case you want to print your form letters alphabetically by last name, you can. To make sure that your data appears in the order that you want, Word allows you to specify up to three fields on which to sort your form letters.

To sort data to merge with a form letter, follow these steps:

1. **Open Word.**

2. **From the File menu, choose Open (or press Ctrl+O).**

    The Open dialog box appears.

3. **Choose the file containing the form letter that you want to use.**

4. **Click the Mail Merge Helper button.**

    The Mail Merge Helper dialog box appears.

5. **Click the Query Options button.**

    The Query Options dialog box appears.

6. **Click the Sort Records tab.**

    The Sort Records tab of the Query Options dialog box appears (see Figure 15-15).

7. **Click the Sort By list box and choose the field you want to sort by.**

8. **Click the Ascending or Descending option.**

9. **Click the two Then By list boxes if you want to specify additional fields to sort by.**

10. **Click the OK button.**

    The Mail Merge Helper dialog box appears.

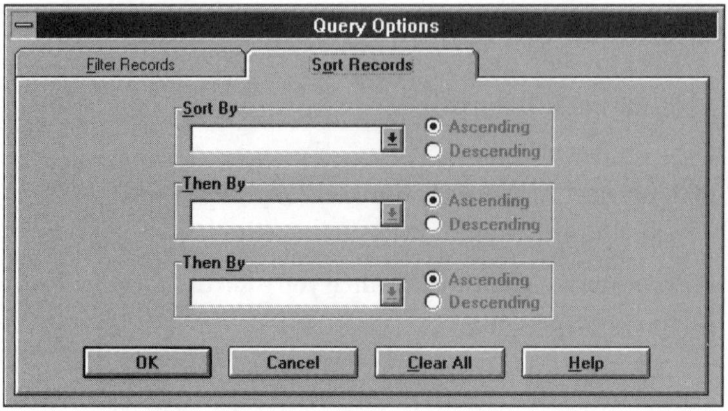

Figure 15-15:
The Sort
Records tab
of the Query
Options
dialog box.

11. **Click the Close button.**

12. **Click the View Merged Data button again to display the data fields.**

13. **Click the Merge to Printer button.**

    The Print dialog box appears.

14. **Click the OK button.**

15. **From the File menu, choose Save (or press Ctrl+S).**

    The Save dialog box appears.

16. **Type the filename under which you want to save your form letter.**

17. **Click the OK button.**

Part VI

The Part of Tens—
101 Design and
Efficiency Tips

The 5th Wave   By Rich Tennant

YEAH, BUT YOU SHOULD SEE HOW NICELY IT CENTERED EVERYTHING.

In this part...

Okay, you've worked hard. You've earned it. You can process words, build a 3-D pie chart, and knock the sales force off its feet. You even made it through the *database* chapters! But isn't there anything else?

There sure is. This section is crawling with tips and techniques designed to get your project done fast and right — the first time. No more documents that print sideways, no more missing data, and no more static cling! (I just can't get rid of that sales force…)

Chapter 16

Ten Ways to Create Better-Looking Word Documents

• •

A few relatively simple, commonsense design concepts can make a big difference in the appearance of the documents that you create with Word 6.

Add space above and below header and footer text or borders

When you work with headers, pressing the Enter key one or more times before you insert the publication or chapter title adds white space between the top of the page and the header text. You can control the amount of white space by increasing or decreasing the type size of the "phantom paragraph" added by the Enter key. Likewise, pressing the Enter key one or more times after you insert the publication title or page numbers adds white space between the header and the text that follows. (Word 6's default setting doesn't add enough white space between the header and the paragraphs of text that follow.)

Likewise, pressing the Enter key before you type footer text adds white space between the footer and the last line of text above the footer. Pressing the Enter key after you enter the page number or footer text adds white space between the footer and the bottom of the page.

Use uppercase type with discretion

Words set in uppercase type are harder to read than words set in lowercase type because words set in uppercase type lack the distinct shapes that words set in lowercase type have. Lowercase letters vary in their height as well as their depth (distance below the baseline). These variations, found in letters such as *y, p, g,* and *q,* provide important clues that readers use to recognize words quickly.

In short, words set in uppercase type are longer and lack the distinctive shapes needed for instant recognition.

Avoid underlining

Underlining does not make words easier to read; it makes them *harder* to read. Underlining obscures *descenders* — the portions of letters that extend below the baseline on which the type rests. Use alternatives such as boldface, italics, or small caps for titles or to add selective emphasis.

The only reason you should ever underline text is to identify the text so that you can later use Word's Find and Replace feature to change the typeface, perhaps substituting Old Style Figures for Lining Figures or True Small Caps for small caps.

Place border rules above subheads

Border rules permit you to create visual barriers between text and subheads. Border rules above a subhead clearly indicate that the subhead belongs to the text that follows. When you place the rule below the subhead — or, worse yet, underline a subhead — you're creating a barrier between the subhead and the text that it is supposed to introduce.

Avoid using narrow columns of justified text

Narrow columns of justified text typically are characterized by excessive hyphenation and irregular, visually distracting word spacing. To achieve justification, lines that contain a few long words will have exaggerated word spacing, and lines that contain numerous short words will have compressed word spacing. Restrict the use of justified text to lines that are long enough to permit justification without noticeably affecting word spacing.

Always use Word's paragraph-spacing commands

Word's Spacing Before and Spacing After options (accessed by choosing Format⇨Paragraph and then choosing the Indents and Spacing tab in the Paragraph dialog box) can improve the appearance of body-copy text as well as headlines and subheads. Spacing Before and Spacing After measurements should be built into the styles that you create for the various elements of page architecture. These measurements permit you to fine-tune the appearance of your documents with precision.

✔ Spacing Before enables you to add white space above headlines and subheads. Spacing Before isolates the headline or subhead from the preceding text and focuses the reader's eyes on the headline or subhead.

✔ Spacing After improves the appearance of body-copy text by allowing you to precisely control the amount of white space between paragraphs. You can emphasize paragraph spacing without creating the distracting horizontal gaps that appear if you press the Enter key twice between paragraphs.

Avoid isolated or split headlines and subheads

When you create styles for headlines and subheads, choose Format⇨Paragraph and then choose the Text Flow tab in the Paragraph dialog box. Select the following options: Widow/Orphan Control, Keep Lines Together, and Keep with Next.

✔ Widow/Orphan Control keeps Word from printing the last line of a headline or subhead at the top of a page or column or isolating the first line of a headline or subhead at the bottom of a page or column.

✔ Keep Lines Together keeps multiple-line headlines and subheads from being split across two columns or two pages.

✔ Keep With Next ensures that the subhead appears immediately before the paragraph that it introduces. If you don't choose this option, the subhead could appear at the bottom of a column or page, separated from the paragraph that it introduces.

Avoid using two spaces after periods

Show the world that you're a word processing professional by pressing the spacebar only one time after periods. Periods followed by two spaces create excessive sentence spacing. Worse, in narrow columns of justified text, this excessive spacing can create annoying ribbons snaking vertically through your text. Break yourself of the habit, or use Word's Edit⇨Replace command to search through your document and replace every period followed by two spaces with a period followed by one space.

Reduce character spacing in headlines

You can improve the appearance of headlines set in a large type size by reducing letter spacing. To experiment with various spacing alternatives, follow these steps:

1. **In Page Layout view, select the headline text.**

2. **Choose Format⇨Font to display the Font dialog box.**

3. **Choose the Character Spacing tab.**

4. **Drop down the Spacing list and choose Condensed.**

5. **Click the up or down arrow next to the By box to choose a spacing alternative.**

   You can observe the effect of varying character-spacing settings in the Preview box.

6. **When you finish, click OK to close the dialog box.**

To reduce letter spacing between selected pairs of letters, such as an upper-case *W* next to a lowercase *a* (instead of reducing letter spacing by the same amount throughout the headline), place the insertion point between the letters, choose Format⇨Font, and manipulate the Spacing setting in the Character Spacing tab.

Use the Shrink to Fit command to eliminate awkward document endings

Have you ever noticed how often the last line of a fax appears on a page by itself, or the signature appears by itself at the top of the last page of a letter? Isn't this frustrating? To eliminate these ugly frustrations, choose File⇨Print Preview, and click the Shrink to Fit button in the Print Preview toolbar. Word 6 goes through your entire document, reduces the type size in half-point inter-vals, and repaginates until the offending text block is brought back to the bottom of the preceding page.

Chapter 17
Ten Ways to Work Faster with Word

● ●

*G*etting into the habit of working as efficiently as possible right from the start can save you tremendous amounts of time in the future (perhaps enough time to allow you to go home early or to get a second job at Wal-Mart so that you can purchase health insurance). Although the following tips may appear to be elementary, they can greatly enhance your productivity.

Select words for editing or formatting by double-clicking them

Rather than drag the mouse to select a word for cutting, copying, or formatting, double-click the word. (You may have to experiment a bit to get the hang of it, but in the long run, learning this procedure is time well spent.)

Notice that there is a subtle difference between double-clicking — clicking twice in rapid succession — and clicking twice. You'll know that you have selected the word when it appears in a color that contrasts to the rest of the text.

Another advantage of double-clicking a word to select it is the fact that Word 6 automatically selects the space that follows the word (a space that you normally want to delete or move anyway) but does *not* select the punctuation, which you usually don't want to select (a human-engineering feature not found in WordPerfect). Normally, you don't want to carry or delete punctuation when you move or delete individual words.

Use Ctrl+click to select sentences

Instead of selecting a sentence by holding down the left mouse button as you drag through the sentence, hold down the Ctrl key while clicking anywhere inside the sentence. Instantly, the entire sentence is selected for editing or formatting.

Select a paragraph by triple-clicking inside the paragraph or double-clicking in the left margin

Avoid the wasted effort of dragging with the mouse when you want to select an entire paragraph for deletion, copying, or formatting. Triple-clicking inside a paragraph selects the entire paragraph, and double-clicking in the margin to the left of the paragraph also selects the entire paragraph.

Use shortcut menus for editing or formatting

To cut, copy, or format a sentence or paragraph, select it and then click the right mouse button. This action displays a shortcut menu that contains the Cut, Copy, and Paste editing commands as well as the commands that access various formatting dialog boxes.

Apply styles by clicking inside paragraphs rather than selecting the entire paragraph

This tip is a biggie. When you apply a paragraph style, avoid the time-wasting (and wrist-wasting) temptation to select the entire paragraph by dragging the mouse. Instead, simply click anywhere inside the paragraph and apply the desired style. Word automatically applies the style to the entire paragraph.

Use keyboard shortcuts to apply styles

You can work faster and reduce the chance of muscle strain or injury by using keyboard shortcuts instead of the mouse to open menus and apply styles. To assign a keyboard shortcut to an existing style, follow these steps:

1. Choose Format⇨Style to display the Style dialog box.

2. Click Modify to display the Modify Style dialog box.

3. Click Shortcut Key to display the Customize dialog box.

4. Choose the <u>K</u>eyboard tab and type the desired keyboard shortcut in the Press <u>N</u>ew Shortcut Key box.

5. Click OK to return to the Modify Style dialog box.

6. Click the Close button to return to the Style dialog box.

7. Click <u>A</u>pply and then click Close.

You now can apply the style quickly, without removing your hands from the keyboard.

Use the Format Painter to copy formatting attributes

Although the Format Painter is not a substitute for styles, it can be handy for occasions when you want to copy the attributes of a text or graphic object. To use the Format Painter, display the Formatting toolbar and then follow these steps:

1. **Select a formatted text or graphic element.**

2. **Click the Format Painter button in the Standard toolbar.**

You'll know when the formatting has been copied because a small paint-brush appears to the left of the insertion point.

3. **"Paint" another text or graphic element by dragging the insertion point over it.**

The amount of formatting that is copied depends on whether styles or just individual character and formatting attributes have been chosen or on how much of the text is selected with the insertion point.

Use AutoCorrect for speed and accuracy

You can work faster, as well as more accurately, if you use Word's <u>T</u>ools⇨<u>A</u>utoCorrect feature to insert frequently used terms and proper names. Why take a chance on misspelling "Bumstead, Bundy, Dagwood, and Seinfeld, Architects and Auctioneers, Gesellschaft" when Word can spell it correctly every time you type **bdb**?

Use keyboard shortcuts to access frequently used symbols and special characters

Efficiency is as important as the ability to know when to use em and en dashes, nonbreaking spaces, and optional hyphens. To review the keyboard shortcuts for frequently used symbols, as well as the commands used to insert nonbreaking spaces (so that names and dates won't be split over two lines) and optional hyphens (which permit you to determine where words will be hyphenated if they need to be hyphenated), choose Format⇨Symbol and choose the Special Characters tab in the Symbol dialog box. You can scroll through the list of characters to view the default keyboard shortcuts (and change them, if you so desire).

Chapter 18

Ten Ways to Customize Word for Efficiency and Safety

. . . .

*T*he following tips will help you work faster and safeguard your work as you create it.

Edit in Normal view by using the Draft Font and Wrapped to Window options

By suppressing formatting and working with a single typeface and type size in Normal view, you can work faster by concentrating on the content, rather than the appearance, of your document. Normal view hides headers, footers, multicolumn formatting, and graphics.

To customize Normal view, follow these steps:

1. **Choose View⇨Normal.**

2. **Choose Tools⇨Options, followed by the View tab.**

3. **Click Draft font (or click the Draft Font box) to replace the actual typeface, type size, and type style used in your document with Word's draft font, which is a large, easy-to-read, sans-serif font.**

   (You can switch back at any time to view the actual typeface, type size, and type style by choosing View⇨Page Layout.)

4. **Click Wrap to Window (or click the Wrap to Window box).**

   On-screen line breaks now will be determined by the text on your screen, rather than the actual line breaks of the text in your document when printed. This option eliminates a lot of unnecessary scrolling if you are using a small type size. The same number of words will appear in each line on-screen, regardless of how many words actually appear when you print your document. (To check actual line breaks, choose View⇨Page Layout or File⇨Print Preview.)

Have Word save your work automatically at frequent intervals

There's nothing more frustrating than losing work because of a momentary power outage because you were reaching for the flyswatter to hit the cat that knocked your hot chocolate onto your keyboard. To reduce the possibility of this problem, choose Tools⇨Options to display the Options dialog box and then choose the Save tab. Click Automatic Save, and enter a desired interval in the box (or click the up or down arrow) to specify an Automatic Save interval.

Always make two copies of each file

You can instruct Word to always save two copies of each file. The backup copy is indicated by the .BAK extension. To instruct Word to save a backup copy, choose Tools⇨Options, choose the Save tab in the Options dialog box, and click Always Create Backup Copy.

Double-click to choose spell-check alternatives

When you check the spelling in your document, you can replace three steps with one. Instead of scrolling through the list of suggested alternative spellings — highlighting the desired alternative and clicking OK — simply double-click the alternative that you want to use. Word immediately inserts your choice and moves on to the next questionable word.

Instruct Word's spelling checker to disregard words set in uppercase type and words that contain numbers

Word's spelling checker checks for irregular capitalization as well as words that contain numbers. If your documents contain words that are deliberately set in uppercase type or formulas that contain numbers, you can customize Word's spelling checker to disregard those items.

To customize the way that Word spell checks your document, follow these steps:

1. **Choose Tools⇨Options to display the Options dialog box.**
2. **Choose the Spelling tab.**
3. **Click Words in UPPERCASE if you want Word to disregard words set in capital letters.**
4. **Click Words with Numbers if you want Word to disregard formulas and other items in which words and numbers are mixed.**
5. **Click OK.**

Use the Don't Hyphenate option in headline and subhead styles

When you create styles for headlines, subheads, pulled quotes, and (possibly) captions, choose Format⇨Paragraph, choose the Text Flow tab in the Paragraph dialog box, and then click Don't Hyphenate. This option prevents text formatted with the style from being hyphenated, even if the rest of the document is hyphenated.

Add formatted tables to the AutoCorrect library

Formatting tables can take a lot of time. Rather than reinvent the wheel each time you need another table, after you create and format a table with the headings, borders, and fills that you're likely to need again and again, simply copy the table to the AutoCorrect library.

To copy a formatted table, follow these steps:

1. **To select the entire table, choose Table⇨Select Table (or press Alt+5).**
2. **Choose Tools⇨AutoCorrect to display the AutoCorrect dialog box.**

   Notice that a portion of the table appears in the With: Formatted Text box.

3. **In the Replace box, enter the text that you want to use to insert the table (perhaps 1tab).**
4. **Click OK.**

Whenever you type the "magic letters," the formatted table will appear in your document!

Add formatted and locked frames to the AutoText library

You can save frames created for pulled quotes, illustrations, and other items in the AutoText library. To reuse a formatted frame, follow these steps:

1. **Choose Format⇨Frame to display the Frame dialog box.**

2. **Apply the desired text-wrap, size, and position options.**

3. **Choose Edit⇨Copy (or press Ctrl+C).**

4. **Choose Edit⇨AutoText to display the AutoText dialog box.**

   A portion of the frame appears in the Preview window.

5. **Enter a name for the frame.**

6. **Click Add.**

7. **Close the document.**

8. **To insert the frame into another document, choose Edit⇨AutoText to display the AutoText dialog box.**

9. **Select the name of the frame and then click Insert (or double-click the name).**

   The frame appears in your document.

Use the right mouse button to add and remove toolbars

To add or remove toolbars, rather than choosing View⇨Toolbar, simply click the right mouse button on any portion of any open toolbar. A list of all the toolbars appears. If the desired toolbar is already visible, and if a check mark appears next to its name in the list, you can remove it from the screen by clicking its name to remove the check mark. If the desired toolbar is not visible, you can display it by clicking its name in the list.

Always display paragraph marks

Paragraph marks are very important to Word. If you delete a paragraph mark, you lose all of the paragraph's formatting; the paragraph will join the following paragraph and adopt its formatting.

To reduce the possibility of inadvertently deleting a paragraph mark, follow these steps:

1. **Choose Tools⇨Options to display the Options dialog box.**
2. **Choose the View tab.**
3. **Click Paragraph Marks in the lower-right corner of the View tab.**
4. **Click OK.**

   Paragraph marks now will be visible in both Normal and Page Layout views, reducing the possibility of accidental deletion.

Chapter 19

Excel's Ten Most Important Commands

• •

Mastery of Excel is elusive at best. So many commands . . . so little time! If only someone would give you a Top 10 list to focus on. Where's Dave when you really need him? Well, Dave wasn't available, but learn these ten commands, and you'll be in command of Excel in no time.

AutoSum

Using this command is the quickest way to add a group of numbers. Click an empty cell just below or to the right of the numbers that you want to sum and then double-click the AutoSum button in the Standard toolbar.

Spelling

Nothing says "don't take this spreadsheet seriously" as loudly as spelling errors. Click the Spelling button in the Standard toolbar to have Excel proofread your worksheets.

Don't get cocky, though — you still must proofread your work. Excel doesn't know the difference between *they're* and *their* or between *to* and *too*. (See, its not two smart.)

Format Painter

Can't remember all the formats that you applied to that slick-looking title? Wish that you could wave a magic wand and copy all the formatting to another cell or range? No problem. Click the cell that contains the cool formatting, and then click the Format Painter button in the Standard toolbar. Finally, click the cell or drag across the range to which you want to apply the formatting.

Undo

Of course *I* never make any mistakes. (Sure.) But in case you do, get to know the Undo command, which can undo almost any foolish thing that you may do. Undo can reverse data entries, formatting, sorting, you name it. Just click the Undo button in the Standard toolbar (or press Ctrl+Z).

Print Preview

Don't you hate sending a document to the printer, waiting for it to come out, and then discovering that you didn't have it set up correctly to print the way you wanted? Get used to checking how your documents will print before sending them to the printer. Click the Print Preview button in the Standard toolbar for a quick peek.

TipWizard

The TipWizard is your own personal coach, always looking over your shoulder, gently suggesting better — or at least other — ways to perform the task that you just performed. When the TipWizard has a suggestion for you, the light bulb on the TipWizard toolbar button lights up (turns yellow). Just click the TipWizard button to see the suggestion, which appears in the TipWizard toolbar just below the Formatting toolbar.

ChartWizard

Let the ChartWizard be your guide to turning numbers into persuasive charts. Select the data to be included in the chart, click the ChartWizard button in the Standard toolbar, drag the mouse across the cells in which you want the chart to appear, and enter the information that the ChartWizard dialog boxes request.

Zoom

Want to see more of your worksheet? Perhaps you used some fine print in your worksheet to discourage other people from reading the bad news, and now you're having trouble reading it. Use the Zoom command to zoom out to see the big picture or to zoom in to enlarge the data.

Click the Zoom button in the Standard toolbar to display a drop-down list of zoom percentages. Click a large number (say, 200) to zoom in or a small number (say, 50) to zoom out. You also can type your own percentage to get just the amount of zoom that you want.

Splitting Panes

If you have data spread far and wide, you may want to view separate portions of the worksheet without scrolling back and forth. Use the vertical split box to scroll the columns on either side of the split independently. Use the horizontal split box to scroll rows above and below the split independently.

Create a vertical split by positioning the mouse pointer on the vertical split box (the black bar just to the right of the horizontal scroll bar) and dragging to the left, into the worksheet, until the vertical bar is positioned where you want it. Create a horizontal split by positioning the mouse pointer on the horizontal split box (the black bar just above the vertical scroll bar) and dragging down until the horizontal bar is positioned as desired. You can get rid of a split bar by double-clicking it.

Save, Save, Save!

I saved the most important Excel command for last. Until you use the Save command, all the work that you've done since the last time you saved is at risk. Save every 10 to 20 minutes or so. That way, if something goes wrong, you won't lose too much work.

Click the Save button in the Standard toolbar to save your workbook. The first time you save, you'll have to assign a filename. After you name the file, just click the Save button every time you want to save, and continue working.

Chapter 20

Ten Important Excel Shortcuts

• •

*I*f saving time is what computing is all about, that's what this chapter is all about ten times over. Here are my ten favorite tips for cutting daunting Excel tasks down to size.

Opening files

When you want to open a workbook that you used recently, you don't have to search for it. If that file was one of the four files you used most recently, you'll find it listed at the bottom of the File menu. Click File and then click the name of the file that you want to open at the bottom of the menu.

Getting from here to there

Use the name box just to the left of the formula bar or the Edit⇨Go To command to zip around in the worksheet. Just click the name box, type the address or range name of the cell to which you want to go, and press Enter. You also can press F5 (the Go To key), type a cell address or range name, and press Enter.

Macros

Macros can be the greatest time-savers of all. They allow you to record a series of actions and then have Excel automatically play back those actions whenever you want. You can use a macro to record your company's name and address, for example, so that you don't have to retype it for every worksheet.

To record a macro, choose Tools⇨Record Macro⇨Record New Macro. Enter a name for the macro in the Record New Macro dialog box.

To make it really easy to play your macro later, click the Options button and assign the macro to the Tools menu or a shortcut key. Click OK, perform any Excel tasks that you want to include in your macro, and then click the Stop Macro button that appears in the worksheet when you start recording.

Play the macro by pressing its shortcut key; by choosing it from the Tools menu; or by choosing Macro from the Tools menu, typing the name of the macro in the Macro dialog box, and clicking OK.

Goal Seek

Excel can adjust the values in your worksheet to give you the answer that you want. Click the cell in which you want the new result to appear and then choose Tools⇨Goal Seek. In the To value box, enter the desired value. In the By changing cell box, enter the address of the cell to be changed. Finally, click OK.

AutoFormat

Excel can format the tables in your worksheet for you. Select the table that you want to format and then choose AutoFormat from the Format menu. Click one of the table formats and then click the OK button.

AutoFill

There's no need to type a series of dates or numbers when Excel's AutoFill feature can create the series for you. After entering the first date or number, position the mouse pointer on the fill handle in the lower-right corner of the cell pointer, hold down the Ctrl key, and drag right or down to increment the series. Drag left or up to decrement the series.

Shortcut menus

Don't guess how you can manipulate an object on the Excel screen; use the object's shortcut menu to get to all the options for that object. Right-click the object to display its shortcut menu and then click one of the shortcut menu commands.

Keyboard shortcuts

As handy as the mouse is, it's often more efficient to press a couple of keys on the keyboard to carry out a task. For example, you can apply the **bold** attribute to a cell by clicking the Bold button in the Formatting toolbar, or you can keep your hands on the keyboard and press Ctrl+B. The shortcut for *italic* is Ctrl+I; the shortcut for <u>underlining</u> is Ctrl+U; and the shortcut for the Currency format is Ctrl+Shift+$.

You can see a complete list of keyboard shortcuts in Excel's Help system. Click Help➪Contents➪Reference Information➪Keyboard Guide and then any of the categories of keyboard shortcuts that you want to see.

AutoFit column widths

Don't strain your brain trying to figure out how wide to make your columns. After entering data that's too wide for a column, double-click the right border of its column heading. Excel increases the column width to just a bit wider than the longest entry. If all the data is narrower than the current column width, double-clicking decreases the column width.

Getting the help you need

Click the Help button in the Standard toolbar to display Help's Search dialog box. Enter the name of the Excel feature on which you need help. When the feature that you're looking for is highlighted, click OK. Then click the Help topic in the bottom portion of the dialog box that most closely meets your needs. A Help screen appears, answering your question.

The 5th Wave   By Rich Tennant

"I SAID I WANTED A NEW MONITOR FOR MY BIRTHDAY! MONITOR! MONITOR!"

Chapter 21

Ten Ways to Improve Your Access to Information

· ·

Microsoft Access is one of the most popular databases around because it's so easy to use — and powerful as well. Yet despite its user-friendliness and flexibility, it can't do everything for you. With a little bit of foresight and planning, creating and using an Access database can be simple. With a little bit of carelessness, however, creating and using an Access database can be an exercise in frustration.

To make sure that you don't have to read any more of the Access manuals than you really want to, here are some tips to keep in mind when you use Microsoft Access to create a database.

Design your database correctly

Before touching your computer or a copy of Microsoft Access, design your database on paper. Jot down the type of information that you want to store in your database; how you want that information to appear on your computer screen; and different ways in which you may want to manipulate the data to display it, analyze it, or hide it so that you can embezzle millions without anyone's noticing until you've left the country.

By designing your database on paper first, you can avoid wasting time designing your database in Microsoft Access and then realizing that you screwed up so badly that you have to start all over again. Here are some key questions to ask yourself when you create a database:

> ✔ *What's important to me?* If you want to keep track of people so that you can mail them flyers, bills, or ransom notes, you'll want each person's name and address, but not necessarily his or her phone number, fax number, shoe size, Social Security number, or birthday.

✔ *How long will I need this information?* The longer you need to save information, the more useful a database can be. Storing the names, addresses, and phone numbers of your customers is smart. Storing the names, addresses, and phone numbers of people whom you meet in an elevator is not smart.

✔ *What do I want to do with my information?* Microsoft Access is a great database for storing information, but stored information is worthless if you don't use it somehow. If you just want to find a person's name and phone number, your database will look a lot different than if you want to find the top salesperson in your company and how many products that person sold during the past three months in all states whose names end with the letter *A*.

✔ *Will I be the only one using the database?* If you're creating a database just for yourself, you can afford to be quirky, eccentric, and downright bizarre in designing your database. If other people need to add, delete, edit, or view information trapped in your database, however, you'll want your database to be easy to use. The harder a database is to use, the less likely anyone will use it at all — and the more likely that your company will replace you with someone who can do your job more effectively.

✔ *What about the future?* Although your business may sell only to customers in the United States, ask yourself what may happen if you suddenly have to store phone numbers and addresses for people in England, South Africa, or Taiwan. If you haven't planned your fields correctly, you may have to go through the time-consuming effort (not to mention the nuisance) of modifying your database.

By thinking ahead, you can ensure that the database you design today can still be used tomorrow. Besides, the real purpose of using Access is to store and retrieve information, not to design databases.

Store data in as many fields as possible

Make a list of all the information that you want to store in your database, such as names, addresses, phone numbers, company names, postal codes, and country names. Whenever possible, store information in separate fields.

Rather than create one long field to store a person's complete name, for example, use two separate fields. One field can store the first name, and the second field can store the second name. When you store people's names in FirstName and LastName fields, Access can sort your information by a person's first name or last name. (Whee! Aren't databases fun?)

Besides using separate fields for a person's first and last name, use separate fields for addresses. One field could contain the street address; another could contain the city, state (or province), postal code, and country name.

In general, the more separate fields in which you store your information, the more ways Access can sort and search through your information. Just make sure that you don't get carried away and create separate fields for street numbers, street names, and apartment numbers; you'll probably never want to find all the people in Connecticut who live in apartment number 3B.

Use tables to organize your data

A database can contain any type of information, from names and phone numbers to details on how your family members like their steaks cooked. Although you can dump all your information into a single Access database, you can use tables to categorize the information further.

Rather than haphazardly dump names and phone numbers into a database, for example, use tables to store certain names and phone numbers in the categories Customers and Suppliers.

Separating related information in tables helps keep your data organized and also gives you the chance to add information that may not appear elsewhere. A list of names and phone numbers stored in a Suppliers table, for example, may include fax numbers, e-mail addresses, and pager numbers; a similar list of names and phone numbers stored in the Customers table may contain only phone numbers.

If the data stored in separate tables is unrelated (if your suppliers never are your customers, for example), it's easier to store this information in separate database files. But if your suppliers sometimes are your customers, and vice versa, store the information in separate tables in the same database file. That way, you don't have to type the same information twice.

Make data entry mindless

A database is only as useful as the accuracy of the information that it contains. To prevent anyone from entering wildly incorrect information — or even no information at all — make data entry as simple as possible by using default values, list boxes, and combo boxes.

Default values allow you to specify that a field will contain certain information unless the user makes a conscious effort to enter new information. Suppose that you want a field to list the date on which a record was last updated. Rather than force (and expect) someone who earns minimum wage to do this all the time, make Access use the current date as a default value instead. That way, someone can enter data, and Access can enter the date automatically.

Besides default values, use list boxes and combo boxes. A list box lists all possible items that could be stored in a field. If your business buys supplies only from three suppliers, for example, a list box could list the names of these suppliers. Instead of wasting time by typing the supplier's name (and risking typos in the process), use a list box to provide acceptable values.

Combo boxes work like list boxes, except that they give you the choice of typing information yourself or choosing information from a list of acceptable items. A list box containing the names of all the suppliers that your company normally uses may be fine, but what if you suddenly start buying from a new supplier? In that case, a combo box would give you the ability to type a new name that isn't contained in the combo box list.

Use default values or combo boxes whenever you want to give the user a list of possible choices or the ability to store new information in a field. Use list boxes when you want to restrict the information that a user can store in a field.

Use input masks

If the information in a field conforms to a specific, unchanging format, use input masks. An input mask simply provides blanks that show the exact number of characters that the user needs to type.

For example, phone numbers in the United States usually follow a specific format: a three-digit area code and a seven-digit number, such as (XXX) XXX-XXXX. When you use an input mask, there's no chance that a user may type **555-123-4567** one time and **(555) 123-4567** another time. Because input masks allow the user to focus on typing the data without concern about its actual appearance, all data appears uniform and consistent.

The problem with input masks, of course, is that they can be too restrictive. An input mask of (XXX) XXX-XXXX doesn't leave room for phone-number extensions or country codes for overseas phone numbers. Input masks can make data entry easier, but make sure that they don't prevent you from entering the data that you really need.

Have Access check your data

To prevent someone from storing incorrect data in your database fields, use validation rules so that Access can determine whether any typed data is acceptable. You may have a database that lists yearly salaries, for example. Through an honest typing mistake, someone could type a yearly salary of $1 — or $15,000,000. Because few companies willingly pay such low or high salaries (which explains why embezzling is so popular), these numbers obviously are incorrect. Unfortunately, finding all incorrect data entries can be like looking for the proverbial needle in the haystack.

To catch data-entry errors as they occur, use validation rules to tell Access, "OK, when someone enters a salary, check to make sure that it's $10,000 or higher, or $250,000 or lower." Thereafter, if someone tries to enter $1 or $15,000,000 as a yearly salary, Access checks the validation rules, refuses to accept this information, and tells the user to stop goofing around and type a valid answer before he gets fired.

Ask questions intelligently

In school, your teachers may have encouraged you to ask questions, saying that's the only way you could learn. The moment that you started asking questions, though, they told you to shut up and listen so that they can get on with their lesson plans.

Fortunately, asking questions of an Access database isn't as intimidating. After you store information in a database, you can use queries to yank out that information.

A query allows you to ask your Access database to retrieve certain information for you — for example, "Find all the engineers in our company who speak a foreign language, have oil-drilling experience, and get on my nerves on a consistent basis." When you know this information, you'll know which engineers you can send to Saudi Arabia because they're qualified and because you want to place them as far away from you as possible. In this case, Access isn't just storing information anymore; it's giving you choices and power!

Think of queries as showing you different points of view about your data. The more sophisticated the way in which you define your query, the more information Access will reveal to you. Facts such as the names of California residents who also own yachts may seem to be dull and unimportant, but if you publish a yachting magazine, this information can be crucial to your financial survival.

Remember that information stored in databases is useless by itself. It's when you look at that information from different angles (using different queries) that you can make sense of it for your own needs.

Back up, back up, back up!

Want to make life completely unbearable? Erase a database file containing valuable information that you've collected over the past five years, and then see how well you get along without this information. If this scenario sounds completely unreasonable, it's no more shortsighted than never making a backup copy of your database files and praying that a disaster won't strike.

Unless you want to destroy the advantages of a computer in the first place, always make backup copies of your database files. Many people make backups once a month, once a week, or (for the truly paranoid or security-minded) once a day. Consider how often you update your database and then ask yourself how much information you're willing to lose at any given time. This answer will determine how often you should make backups of your database files.

Ideally, you should make copies of your database files on floppy disks or tape cartridges, and then store these backup copies in a separate place far away from your computer — preferably in another building, neighborhood, or city. That way, if a tornado or earthquake wipes out your office, you'll still have a copy of your database files. (You just won't have a computer or an office in which you can use them.)

Compact your databases periodically

The longer you have a database, the more likely it is that you'll add, edit, and delete information periodically. Each time you modify a database, you physically change its structure. Deleting or editing information causes tiny gaps to appear in the database file. When you add information to the database file, Access shoves the new information into the gaps left by previous deleting or editing. Because the new information isn't always the same size as the gaps created by the deleted or edited information, more gaps can appear in the database file.

Such gaps cause file fragmentation. Each time you load and search through a fragmented database file, Microsoft Access needs more time to find all the pieces and paste them back together again — which means that Access will run sluggishly, no matter how fast your computer is.

To solve this problem, compact your databases periodically. Compacting simply removes any gaps in the files and streamlines the database to facilitate fast access to your information. To compact a database, open the File menu and choose the Compact Database command.

Don't depend on your database (at first)

After you create a database in Microsoft Access, congratulate yourself, eat some ice cream as a reward, and then avoid storing any valuable information in your new database for the first few days or so.

Huh? Why would you want to spend all that time designing a Microsoft Access database if you're not going to use it right away?

You don't use the database right away for the same reason that airlines don't put passengers on newly designed planes that haven't flown off the ground yet. No matter how well you think that you designed something, there's a good chance that you forgot, overlooked, or ignored something that could become a big problem if you don't catch it right away.

In the world of databases, it's perfectly possible to design a database, stuff it full of valuable information, and then realize that your database doesn't really organize your information the way you want. If the changes are minor, you can modify your database. But if the changes are major, it may actually be easier to wipe out your existing database and start again from scratch.

When you create a database, test it with some information that you don't mind losing if something goes wrong. After stuffing your database with a little bit of information, you'll have a better idea of what needs to be fixed or modified. At this point, you can overhaul your database and then reload it with the rest of your information.

Alternatively, you can ignore this tip, stuff your database with information, find something wrong, erase the entire database file, create a new one, and then reload the same information all over again until you get it right. If you have that much time on your hands, maybe you need to get another hobby.

Chapter 22

Ten Things to Check Before You Print

● ●

*B*ad things happen to good people when they print prematurely. Although the Windows Print Manager contains a handy Cancel button, this button often doesn't work; the document may already have passed through the Windows Print Spooler to the printer. Canceling a printer by clicking the Off-Line or Reset button (or, worse, turning the printer on and off) is an invitation to frustration and stress. Canceling a print job after it has reached the printer wastes time and frequently results in wasted materials; the printer takes on a mind of its own and insists on printing some pages or prints partial pages.

Here are some of the things that you should check before you choose File⇨Print.

Did you run the spelling checker one last time and review page breaks in Print Preview?

Always run your spelling checker one more time. Deadline madness often causes spelling errors in last-minute edits. These errors always seem to occur in extremely noticeable locations, such as slide titles, headlines, and captions. The only way to avoid embarrassing errors is to run your spelling checker one last time.

File⇨Print Preview helps you make sure that page breaks occur at normal places in Word and Excel. Check to see that subheads aren't isolated at the bottom of pages and that spreadsheet subtotals aren't isolated at the top of pages. Print Preview also helps you make sure that charts appear next to the data on which they're based.

Did you select the correct printer?

The age of the single-printer computer is over. Computers running Office 4 applications often are connected to several printing devices. Frequently, configurations include a black-and-white laser printer and a color inkjet printer. In addition, you may have a fax/modem connected to your computer. And if you're a PowerPoint user, you probably installed the Autographix driver (for preparing 35mm slides and high-quality color transparencies). Before printing, make sure that you selected the right printer.

Did you load the proper materials?

There's nothing quite like the feeling of despair that you get when you notice that you're printing letters or proposals on overhead-transparency film, or that you're printing your presentation on draft paper. Likewise, if your luck is anything like mine, just when you're down to your last four or five sheets of letterhead, you accidentally start printing drafts of your next project on letterhead instead of cheap paper.

Did you select the proper orientation?

Presentation visuals and spreadsheets usually are printed in landscape orientation — that is, the long edge of the paper extends along the top of the page instead of the bottom. Make sure that you switch to portrait orientation when you switch back to printing correspondence.

Did you select the proper Paper Source?

Many laser printers (including the Hewlett-Packard LaserJet IIID) include two separate paper bins. These bins permit you to print the first page of your document on letterhead that contains full address and telephone/fax information and the remaining pages on second sheets that contain only your firm's logo. Alternatively, you can load the first bin with letterhead and the second bin with everyday paper for drafts. Before printing, make sure that you're targeting the correct paper bin.

Did you choose the proper page range?

In most programs, if you click the Print button in the toolbar, or if you click the OK button in the Print dialog box too soon, the program prints the entire document, even though you may have wanted to print only the current page (or, in PowerPoint, the current slide). Likewise, with PowerPoint, make sure that you do not have Slides selected if you really want to print Notes or Handouts. When printing from Excel, you can print a highlighted Selection, a Selected Sheet (or Sheets), or an Entire Workbook.

Do you want output collated?

When you need multiple copies of a document, you can save a lot of post-printing time by instructing Word, PowerPoint, and other programs to collate the output automatically. Although printing may take longer, you won't have to hand-separate the copies. Also, the Windows Print Manager will spool the copies for you, freeing your computer for other duties while you're printing.

Did you select the desired print quality?

You often can save time (and toner) by choosing Draft mode. Depending on the type of printer that's connected to your computer, Draft mode may speed the printing process by printing only text and omitting graphics.

When you print from PowerPoint, click the check boxes next to Black & White or Pure Black and White to optimize the quality of color images printed on black-and-white inkjet and laser printers.

When you print from Excel to a Hewlett-Packard LaserJet 4 series printer, you can save toner and speed the printing process by selecting reduced resolution when printing drafts.

Does your document contain the latest version of linked data?

To make sure that your document has the most current information before you print, select File⇨Print⇨Options. In the Print tab of the Options dialog box, make sure that Update Links is checked. This ensures that your printed document contains the latest version of data that you linked from other application programs.

Did you choose the proper graphics quality?

Excel documents that contain complex graphics may require more memory than your printer has. If your document is too complex, charts and graphics may be split across two separate pages. To modify Excel's printer defaults, click the Options button in the Print dialog box and change the Graphics Quality setting to Low or Medium. You also can choose Page Protection On if you experience difficulties.

Chapter 23

Ten Things to Remember When Sharing Information between Programs

• •

Although Microsoft Office lets you share data effortlessly between Word, Excel, Access, and PowerPoint, there are still some pitfalls to watch out for. While the dream of copying text or graphics from one program and pasting it into another works most of the time, here are some points to remember so that sharing data between programs doesn't cause you any more problems than you deserve.

Watch your fonts

As any desktop publishing fanatic can tell you, it's not what you write but how it looks. You could write the most memorable essay ever read, but if it's scrawled on the back of a wrinkled envelope covered with bacon grease, not many people are going to take the effort to read it, much less even look at it.

That's why the wonderful world of Windows offers an incredible variety of fonts, type styles, and point sizes so that you can make your text look immense, soft, forbidding, fragile, dainty, or bold. When you copy and paste text between programs, however, Microsoft Office copies only the text — not any of the fonts, type styles, or point sizes that make the text look pretty.

When linked text appears in a file, the appearance of the text depends on the formatting of the destination program. For example, if you link text from Word to Excel, the formatting of the text depends on Excel.

When embedded text appears in file, the appearance of the text depends on the formatting of the source program. For example, if you embed text from Word to Excel, the formatting of the text depends on Word.

Copy Excel data as a picture to save file space

If you need to insert an Excel cell range into a Word document and you don't need to update this data in the future, copy and paste it as a picture. Not only will this prevent anyone from accidentally messing up the Excel data from within Word, but the file will be smaller than if you had copied the data as text.

To copy an Excel cell range as a picture, follow these steps:

1. **Highlight the cell range in Excel that you want to paste into Word.**
2. **Press Shift and from the Edit menu, choose Copy Picture.**

   A Copy Picture dialog box appears.
3. **Click the OK button.**
4. **Switch to Word and move the cursor where you want to paste the cell range.**
5. **From the Edit menu, choose Paste or press Ctrl+V.**

Know when to link data

Linking lets you copy data from one file (called the source document) and paste it in another file (called the destination document). Use linking whenever you need to do any of the following:

- ✔ Control the accuracy of certain data.
- ✔ Update data in one or more files on a regular basis.
- ✔ Keep files as small as possible.

If you need to display data from one file to another file only once, copy and paste the data instead. If you need to pass around copies of your file to others, then embed your data.

Know when to embed data

Embedding lets you store data from one type of a program (such as Excel) and paste it in a file created by another type of a program (such as Word). Use embedding whenever you need to do any of the following:

- ✔ Give files to other people.
- ✔ Allow anyone to edit data stored in a file.
- ✔ Store data in a single file for convenience.

If you need to display data from one file to another file only once, copy and paste the data instead. If you need to control the accuracy of your data and don't trust anyone else, then link your data.

Know where your linked files are at all times

Whenever you link data from one file (the source file) to another (the destination file), Microsoft Office automatically keeps track of the drive, directory, and filename of the source file. If you move the source file to another drive or directory, guess what? You've just broken your link. This means that any changes you make in the source file won't update any linked destination files because Microsoft Office no longer knows where to find your source file.

To prevent this disaster from occurring, it's a good idea to keep all source files in a single directory so you'll always know where to find them. If you move a source file and want to reestablish your links to your destination files, here's what you have to do:

1. **Open the destination file.**
2. **From the Edit menu, choose Links.**

   A Links dialog box appears.
3. **Click the Change Source button.**

   A Change Links dialog box appears.
4. **Type the drive, directory, and filename of the source file and then click the OK button.**

Switch to manual linking

Every time you change data in a source file, Microsoft Office cheerfully updates the data in any linked destination files. Unfortunately, if you're making extensive changes to the data in your source file, Microsoft Office repeatedly rushes off to update your linked destination files.

This means that every few moments, you'll get to see that silly hourglass icon on your screen as Microsoft Office updates all your linked files. If you have only a few linked files, this time delay may be acceptable. But if you have ten or more linked files that require updating, this time delay can be unreasonable.

Such automatic linking ensures that all linked files receive the most current data, but it also means that you wait during this updating. To save your sanity, turn automatic linking off and switch to manual linking.

With manual linking, you can make as many changes as you want to the data in your source file. Microsoft Office will update the data in your linked destination files only when you're ready.

To turn on manual linking, follow these steps:

1. **Load the destination file.**
2. **From the Edit menu, choose Links.**

   A Links dialog box appears.
3. **Choose the link that you want to change to manual linking.**
4. **Choose the Manual option button.**
5. **When you want to update the destination file, click the Update Now button.**

Name your cell ranges in Excel before linking

When you take Excel data that is stored in a range of cells and link it to another program (such as Word), be careful. Microsoft Office simply links the cell range to the other file, such as all the data from row 1 and column 1 (A1) to row 6 and column 9 (F9). Any data you change within this cell range automatically appears in any linked files as well.

But if you add a row or column within this cell range, certain data may be shoved outside the linked cell range, as shown in Figure 23-1. Now any changes you make to data shoved outside the linked cell range won't be reflected in any linked files.

To prevent this problem from ever occurring (yes, it is preventable), name your ranges before linking them to another file. After you've named a cell range, Microsoft Office uses the cell range name and not the physical dimensions of the cell range. Now you can insert as many columns or rows as you want, and Microsoft Office will always correctly link the entire named cell range.

To name a cell range in Excel, follow these steps:

1. **Highlight the cell range that you want to link.**
2. **From the Insert menu, choose Name.**

   A submenu appears.
3. **Choose Define.**

   A Define Name dialog box appears (see Figure 23-2).
4. **Type the name you want to give your cell range (four-letter names work just as well) and click the OK button.**

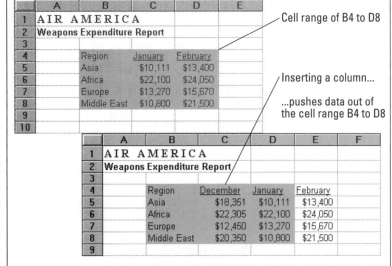

Cell range of B4 to D8

Inserting a column...

...pushes data out of the cell range B4 to D8

Figure 23-1:
Inserting a new row or column can move data outside a linked cell range.

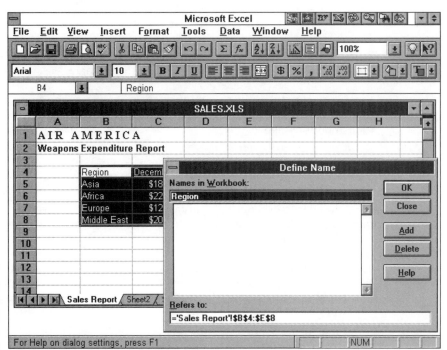

Figure 23-2:
The Define Name dialog box.

Use toolbar buttons to embed objects

From within all Microsoft Office programs, you can embed an object from the Insert menu by choosing Object. But if you're using Word or PowerPoint, there's an easier way.

From within PowerPoint, you can embed a Word table or Excel worksheet by clicking the Insert Microsoft Word Table or the Insert Microsoft Excel Worksheet button on the toolbar (see Figure 23-3).

Figure 23-3:
Insert Microsoft Word Table and Insert Microsoft Excel Worksheet buttons.

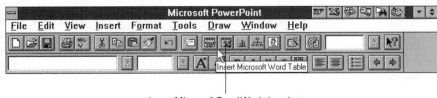

Insert Microsoft Excel Worksheet button.

From within Word, you can embed a blank Excel worksheet by clicking on the Insert Microsoft Excel Worksheet button on the toolbar.

You can still use the clumsy, multiple-step process of embedding objects from the Insert menu in either program, but for speed and convenience, use the toolbar buttons instead.

Use toolbar buttons to convert files

From the File menu in Access, you can choose Export to convert a database table into an Excel worksheet. But there's an even faster way to convert a database table into an Excel worksheet.

To convert an Access database table into an Excel worksheet, follow these steps:

1. **Highlight the database table that you want to convert into an Excel worksheet.**

2. **Click on the Analyze It with MS Excel button, shown in Figure 23-4.**

   Within seconds, Excel loads and displays your database table as an Excel worksheet.

Figure 23-4:
The Analyze It with MS Excel button on the Access toolbar.

Use a Wizard to share data between Access and Word

Access and Word work together just fine for creating mailing labels or form letters. To make the whole process of mail merge completely effortless, have the Mail Merge Wizard guide you step-by-step so nothing gets fouled up beyond repair.

To use the Mail Merge Wizard from within Access, follow these steps:

1. **Highlight the database table that you want to use.**

2. **Click the Merge It button on the toolbar (see Figure 23-5).**

   The Mail Merge Wizard dialog box appears.

3. **Follow the instructions of the Mail Merge Wizard.**

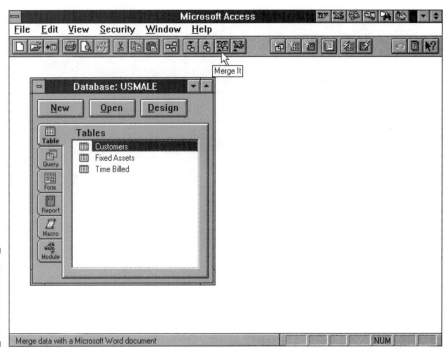

Figure 23-5:
The Merge
It button on
the Access
toolbar.

Installing Microsoft Office

Microsoft Office isn't a single program; it's a collection of Microsoft's five most popular programs, which have WordPerfect, Lotus 1-2-3, Paradox, cc:Mail, and Harvard Graphics on the run. If you want the ultimate in software firepower from one company, Microsoft Office is the package for you.

Installing Microsoft Office can be a real pain in the neck. Luckily, you have to go through the process only once (twice, if your hard disk fails or if you need to install Microsoft Office on a second computer). If you're *really* lucky, someone at work will already have installed Microsoft Office on your computer so that you won't have to. But if you must, here's what you can expect when you install Microsoft Office.

The Two Faces of Microsoft Office

Microsoft Office comes in two versions: Standard and Professional. Both versions come with the following programs:

- Microsoft Word (for word processing)
- Microsoft Excel (for number-crunching)
- Microsoft PowerPoint (for creating graphic presentations)
- Microsoft Mail (for sending electronic mail through a network)

Unlike the other three programs, Microsoft Mail is not a complete program. To use Microsoft Mail, you need a network and the server edition of Microsoft Mail (which Microsoft sells separately, meaning that it's going to cost you more money to get it to work).

In addition to these four programs, the Professional edition of Microsoft Office includes Microsoft Access (for storing and retrieving data).

If you're brand-new to computers, buying the complete Microsoft Office package can be a quick (but not necessarily inexpensive) way to get every program you need to get started using your computer.

However, if you already own another popular word processing, spreadsheet, database, or graphics program (such as Lotus 1-2-3, Quattro Pro, WordPerfect, WordStar, or Harvard Graphics, among others), you can purchase the special upgrade (translate that to mean the "defection") version of Microsoft Office for hundreds of dollars less.

Unlike the nonupgrade version of Microsoft Office, the upgrade version of Microsoft Office won't install on your computer unless it detects the existence of a popular competing program on your hard disk. Because you often can buy older versions of popular programs (such as WordPerfect or WordStar) at swap meets and garage sales, the combined cost of an old program plus the upgrade version of Microsoft Office can be hundreds of dollars less than the complete nonupgrade version of Microsoft Office.

In other words, you can save a bundle of money if you buy the upgrade version of Microsoft Office instead.

Floppy Disks Galore

Microsoft Offices comes on more than 25 high-density floppy disks, and because you have to insert each floppy disk one at a time, you should be prepared for a long installation process. To prevent any more aggravation than absolutely necessary, make sure that you have the following items, which Microsoft Office needs to run, before you start installing the program. If you lack any of these items, you can't use Microsoft Office, so don't even bother wasting your time installing it.

To run Microsoft Office, you need the following:

- ✓ MS-DOS version 3.1 or later. (If you have an earlier version, you need to get out of the Ice Age and get MS-DOS 6 or later, because these versions are more finely tuned to work with Windows.)

- ✓ Microsoft Windows 3.1 or later. (This category includes all the Windows variants, such as Windows for Workgroups 3.1 or later and Windows NT version 3.1 or later.)

- ✓ A computer with at least an 80386 microprocessor. (Realistically, though, you need at least an 80486 just to run Windows. Who does Microsoft think it's kidding?)

✔ At least 4MB of RAM. (To do anything useful, however, you really need 8MB of RAM.)

✔ A hard disk with at least 21MB of space available. (100MB is more realistic, especially if you're installing the Professional edition of Microsoft Office.)

If your computer meets all of these ungodly requirements, you're ready to install Microsoft Office on your hard disk.

If you misplace even one of the many floppy disks that come with Microsoft Office, you may not be able to install the parts of Microsoft Office that you want. So don't lose those floppies!

The Four Installation Options

Microsoft Office provides four options for installing the programs on your hard disk:

✔ *Typical.* This option installs the most common features and programs that Microsoft has determined the general public wants to use.

✔ *Complete/Custom.* This option allows you to choose which programs and features you install. If you don't want Microsoft Mail or PowerPoint, for example, use this option to keep these programs off your hard disk.

✔ *Laptop.* This option is provided in case you've lost your mind and decided to cram Microsoft Office onto the minuscule hard disks that most laptop computers come with. Laptop allows you to install the absolute bare minimum number of files you need to actually run Microsoft Office.

✔ *Workstation.* This option allows you to install Microsoft Office on a network so that you don't have to waste hard disk space on your own computer.

To install Microsoft Office, follow these steps:

1. **Find Disk 1 (good luck) among the many floppy disks that come with Microsoft Office.**

2. **Insert Disk 1 into your floppy disk drive.**

3. **Run Microsoft Windows.**

4. **From the File menu, choose Run.**

   The Run dialog box appears.

5. **Click the Browse button.**

   The Browse dialog box appears.

6. Choose the drive that contains Disk 1, highlight the SETUP.EXE file, and click the OK button.

See Figure A-1 for a glimpse of the opening installation screen.

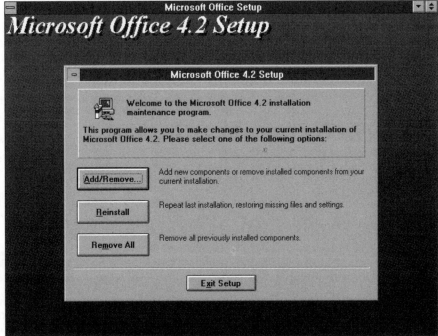

Figure A-1:
The setup
options
of the
Microsoft
Office
installation
program.

7. Grab a book, watch TV, or stare out your window.

The installation program painstakingly copies files off each floppy disk and demands that you insert Disk 2, Disk 3, Disk 4, and so on at periodic intervals, none of which will occur at any convenient time.

Good luck. Depending on which options and programs you've chosen to install, you could be in for a long wait.

Any time that you want to add or remove Microsoft Office features or programs, just run the SETUP.EXE program again.

Glossary

● ●

*O*ften, the best way to master a software program is to become familiar with its important commands, features, and terms. This glossary provides a sample of the most important terms you'll encounter when working with the programs in Microsoft Office 4.

By looking over the following terms, newcomers will gain a quick overview of the commands and features in one or more of the programs that comprise Microsoft Office 4. Users who have already read this book will find the glossary to be a helpful way of reviewing what they've just learned.

Annotations. A PowerPoint feature that allows you to draw your audience's attention to key words and chart elements by adding on-screen circles and lines during electronic presentations.

Auditing. An Excel feature that helps you locate errors in your spreadsheet by displaying relationships between cells. The Trace Precedents button in the Auditing toolbar draws arrows to all cells that directly supply values to a given cell; the Trace Dependents button draws arrows to all cells that depend on values in the cell.

(Also an IRS feature that often causes grief for successful computer-book authors.)

AutoCorrect. A new Word 6 feature that corrects common spelling errors automatically as you make them. You can enter your own frequently misspelled words in the AutoCorrect list. More important, you can use AutoCorrect to spell out long names (such as *Feinstein, Feinstein, Feinstein, and Feinstein Professional Association, Limited*) when you type the abbreviation associated with the name (such as 4F).

AutoDialer. An Access feature that allows you to dial a telephone number listed in the phone-number field of a form or table,

saving time and eliminating misdials (assuming that you have a modem connected to your computer, of course).

AutoFill. An Excel feature that fills in the days of the week or the months of the year automatically as you create column headers. AutoFill also can fill cells with amounts that increase by a predetermined increment (for example, 2, 4, 6, 8, and so on).

AutoFormat. A new feature in Word 6, Excel 5, and PowerPoint 4 that speeds document formatting by making coherent and consistent decisions about elements such as typeface, type size, type style, alignment, border, shading, and color. You can AutoFormat entire documents or presentations, or only parts such as charts and tables.

Automatic Save. A Word and Excel feature that saves your file automatically at predetermined intervals, thus preventing bloodshed when pets and family members accidentally unplug your computer before you save your work.

(Similar to feelings of guilt caused by not backing up your hard disk, as in "I auto back up my hard disk this week.")

AutoShape. A PowerPoint feature that allows you to add custom or existing shapes to a presentation and then add text to the shapes. The text remains with the shapes even if you move or resize them.

AutoSum. An Excel feature that guesses the range of cells whose contents you want to sum. You also can identify a range you want to add up by dragging, followed by pressing Enter.

AutoText. A Word feature that allows you to name and then easily retrieve text phrases in your documents. AutoText is not limited to text; you also can retrieve fully formatted graphic objects such as frames and tables.

Bookmark. A Word feature that allows you to identify and go directly to a desired document location, even if you don't know the page number.

Borders. Horizontal and/or vertical lines that can be placed above, below, or around pages, or used to add selective emphasis to individual paragraphs or cells in a table or spreadsheet.

Browse. An Access command used to review records in database tables.

Cell. The building block of tables and spreadsheets. Information is inserted into cells, which are the intersections of rows and columns.

Character-level formatting. An often-unnoticed, but important, addition to Word 6 that enables you to create separate styles for characters and paragraphs. Character-formatting attributes include typeface, type size, type style, letter spacing, and color. Character-level styles permit you to create paragraphs that contains sentences formatted with two or more different styles, such

as a introductory sentence formatted differently from the remaining sentences. (Also see *Paragraph-level formatting*.)

ChartWizard. A timesaving Excel feature that guides you through the steps necessary to create a new chart or modify an existing chart. The ChartWizard presents alternatives and formats the chart on the basis of your responses.

Clear. Edit menu function, also accessed by pressing the Delete key, that allows you to remove text or graphics without placing them in the Windows Clipboard. This means that you cannot move the information to another location. (Also see *Clipboard*, *Cut*, *Copy*, and *Paste*.)

Clipboard. A Windows feature that allows you to place a single text or graphic element in your computer's temporary memory, allowing it to be moved to another location in the same (or different) document or copied (leaving the original intact). (Also see *Cut, Copy, Clear, Paste*, and *Spike*.)

Color scheme. A unique combination of foreground (i.e., text and accent) and background colors used throughout a presentation. Often referred to as a palette, the colors used in 35mm slides, overhead transparencies, and computer-based presentations should remain consistent throughout your presentation.

Compose. A Microsoft Mail command used to prepare a message by identifying the recipient, the subject, and the recipients of courtesy copies, followed by the text of the message in the Message box.

Constrain keys. Holding down the Shift key when resizing objects (charts, illustrations, scanned images, and so on) in various Office programs proportionately increases or reduces both the object's height and width. When using Word or PowerPoint's drawing tools, holding down the Shift key when drawing new objects creates circles and squares instead of ovals or rectangles. In addition, holding down the Ctrl key while resizing an object resizes it from its center; the top, bottom, and sides are increased or reduced in size, while the object's center remains in the same location.

Copy. Edit menu function that allows you to duplicate an object in the same or different document, leaving the original in the same location. (Also see *Clear*, *Clipboard*, *Cut*, and *Paste*.)

Crop Picture. A Word and PowerPoint feature that allows you to cut out parts of an imported graphic from the top, bottom, or sides. Cropping focuses attention on the important parts of the illustration or scanned image (often located far from the edges).

Cue Cards. On-screen advice, available in many Office programs, that provides step-by-step guidance on accomplishing common tasks.

Cut. Common Edit menu function involving removing text or graphics from one location, placing it in the Windows Clipboard, and inserting, or pasting, it in another location in the same, or different, document. (Also see *Clear*, *Clipboard*, *Copy*, and *Paste*.)

DataSeries. When you are creating Excel and PowerPoint charts, the DataSeries command permits you to determine whether the series being displayed is selected from rows or columns of a datasheet.

Delete. Similar to Clear. When you delete text or graphics, you cannot move the deleted information to another location because that information does not displace information in the Windows Clipboard.

Demote. Changing the level of a topic in a Word or PowerPoint outline. When you demote a topic, it becomes subordinate to the preceding topic, and its formatting (typeface, type size, type style, color, and accompanying graphics, such as bullets and borders) is likely to change.

Design view. Access command used to create or modify a form which allows you to enter and view portions of a database record without viewing the entire record (for example, seeing all of the information, or fields, it contains).

Destination document. When exchanging information between documents, the destination document (often a Word document) contains a copy of the data or object created by using a different program, such as an Excel chart. (Also see *Source document.*)

Detail Data. An Excel Pivot Table feature, similar to Word's Outline view, that allows you to selectively hide or reveal rows and columns that contribute to subtotals and totals.

Drag-and-drop editing. A shortcut procedure, based on dragging, that eliminates the need to cut and paste. Similar to drag-and-drop copying (hold down the Ctrl key while dragging), which does not disturb the original.

Drill Down. A PowerPoint feature that allows you to return to the source document temporarily and examine the way in which a linked or embedded object (such as an Excel chart or Word table) was created.

Drop Cap. A Word design feature that allows you to introduce a new paragraph with a large capital letter.

Embedding. Embedded objects are created by an application (such as Excel) and inserted into documents created in different applications (such as Word or PowerPoint).

Field. Fields are the building blocks of an Access database. Fields are organized in horizontal rows. Each field contains a specific category of information, such as street address, date of purchase, and quantity.

Filter. An Access feature that permits you to restrict records displayed to those that meet predetermined criteria.

Format Painter. A handy Word, Excel, and PowerPoint feature that allows you to share text and graphic formatting attributes between objects without creating styles. The attributes that are shared depend on the type of text or object that is being copied, as well as on whether the original object was saved as a style.

Formatting. Commands and activities that involve the appearance, as opposed to the content, of a text or graphic object. Text formatting attributes include typeface, type size, and type style. Paragraph formatting attributes involve line spacing within the paragraph, space before and after paragraphs, and border and shading options.

Form view. A simplified view of an Access database that allows the user to concentrate on a single task (such as entering names and addresses) by displaying only the fields in which data is to be entered. Form view often includes prompts that contain instructions.

Forwarding a message. A Microsoft Mail feature that allows you to add comments to a message that was sent to you, allowing you to share your comments with others who received the original message or are next in line to receive it.

Frame. A frame is a Word object used as a container for a table, imported text file, headline, scanned image, or chart. Frames permit objects to extend over column boundaries. You can anchor frames to specific paragraphs (if you want the frame to float as preceding text is added or deleted), or you can anchor the frame to a specific page location (where it will remain whether or not preceding text is added or deleted).

Freeze Pane. An Excel feature that allows row and column headings to remain on-screen while you scroll through a large spreadsheet.

Full Screen. A Word and PowerPoint feature that allows you to fill your screen temporarily with a portion of a document or a complete presentation visual without menus or toolbars. This feature gives you a fresh, magnified look at your work.

Goal Seek. An Excel command that permits you to specify a desired, minimum, or maximum value for a cell and then works backward to achieve that value by modifying the values in cells.

Group/Ungroup. The Group command located in Word's Drawing toolbar and PowerPoint's Draw menu allows you to create a single object from individual text and graphic objects, allowing you to move and resize those objects as a single object. The Ungroup command (often used with imported clip art) permits you to return the object or drawing to its components so that you can eliminate unwanted elements or selectively recolor parts of the drawing.

Hidden Slide. A PowerPoint feature, active during electronic (computer-based) presentations, that allows you to create slides that will be displayed only if necessary. You can use this feature to provide supporting information and arguments that you may not need to include in your presentation.

Hyphenation. A word processing feature applied to words that are too long to fit on a single line. Hyphenation breaks the word at a logical point and places the remainder of the word at the beginning of the next line. Although text type nearly always should be hyphenated, never hyphenate headlines, and try to avoid hyphenating captions.

Keyboard shortcuts. A timesaving feature that allows you to access frequently used commands (and apply Word styles) without clicking a toolbar button or opening a menu and navigating through dialog boxes. Keyboard shortcuts typically consist of a single letter (usually one associated with the most easily remembered word or the word that best describes the command) pressed in combination with the Shift, Ctrl, or Alt key. When applying keyboard shortcuts, Word displays a list of currently used keyboard shortcuts so that you don't accidentally erase an existing keyboard shortcut.

Legend. An Excel or PowerPoint chart feature that provides a visual, color-coded link between chart slices or bars and the data series that the chart elements represent.

Link. A method used to exchange dynamic, or changing, data between programs rather

than simply pasting static copies of the original information or object. When information in the source document is modified (for example, information in an Excel spreadsheet), links inform the destination document (often a chart in a Word proposal or PowerPoint slide) that the data has been changed. If both programs are open, the object in the destination document is updated. If the destination document is closed, Word asks you whether you want to update the information or object when you open the file.

Macro. A file containing the commands used to perform a frequently repeated function — for example, a Word macro used to eliminate unwanted spaces after periods, an Excel macro used to search for maximum and minimum values that fall in a certain range, and an Access macro used to print individual records or reports.

Merge. You can print form letters, envelopes, and labels by merging a Word document with the names and addresses contained in an Access database. You can specify the database files that will be included, and you can preview your document and letter on-screen before printing (or automatically print the document).

Microsoft Office Manager toolbar. Customizable Office 4 feature containing buttons that represent the programs included in Office as well as other popular Microsoft programs. The Microsoft Office Manager toolbar makes it easy to launch or switch between programs and also to access Windows features like the Program Manager, File Manager, and Print Manager.

Normal view. A Word 6 view, normally used while entering and editing text, that shows text formatting without headers and footers. Normal view suppresses multicolumn layouts; it also indicates the size and location of imported graphics but doesn't show the graphics.

Page Layout view. A Word feature that displays formatted text and multicolumn documents as well as headers and footers. (Also see *Normal view.*)

Paragraph-level formatting. Paragraph styles that contain line spacing, text alignment, and border and background shading information. (Also see *Character-level formatting.*)

Paragraph marks. A Word feature that displays the hard returns that indicate paragraph breaks. Paragraph formatting is contained in the paragraph mark, and if you inadvertently delete the paragraph mark, the paragraph is reformatted with the typeface, type size, alignment, and line spacing of the following paragraph.

Password. A Word feature that limits other users' access to sensitive documents. You can lock other people out completely or allow them to read, but not modify, the original document. A password consists of up to 15 letters, numbers, and spaces that must be entered in exactly the right order, with the appropriate uppercase and lower-case letters, to open the original document. (Also see *Read Only* and *Write Protected.*)

Paste Special. A command used in sharing information between documents. Paste Special allows you to specify whether you want to paste a picture (static image) of an object that will not change if the original document changes or whether you want to use a link, which means that the object in the destination document will change if the data in the source document is modified.

PivotTable. An Excel feature that permits you to create a worksheet table that summarizes and analyzes data in existing worksheets, providing a different view of the information contained in the original spreadsheet. You can temporarily eliminate unwanted details, consolidate information, or sort rows and columns. You can update a pivot table at any time. The PivotTable Wizard guides you through the creation of a PivotTable.

Print Preview. A Word, Excel, and Access feature that permits you to view the way a document will look when printed. Word permits you to display up to six pages at a time, which helps you review the flow of your document.

QBE. Stands for Query By Example, an Access feature that allows you to establish query criteria by dragging fields from the top to bottom of the Query dialog box. (It is also a new home-shopping network, featuring Joan Rivers, that displays information available through the Internet.)

Query. An Excel command used to locate and display or print desired information. Also an Access command used to locate or summarize information. *Select queries* display query results without changing the original data. *Action queries* change, update, or move the original data. *Crosstab queries* compute total values for individual rows and columns.

Question-mark pointer. A feature of many Office programs that allows you to access context-sensitive help by clicking the Help button in the Standard toolbar (or by pressing Shift+F1). When the question-mark pointer appears, click the command or feature on which you want information. In addition, in Word, clicking on a text or graphic object with the question-mark pointer displays character and paragraph formatting of text objects (or the attributes of graphic elements).

Read Only, Write Protected. A password feature that allows other users to open and read a Word document but not to modify or save their changes. This feature is useful when you are sharing instructions or procedures on a network. (Also see *Password*.)

Recolor Picture. A PowerPoint feature that allows you to harmonize the colors of an imported clip art illustration with your presentation's existing color scheme, eliminating the "tuba in a string quartet" appearance of inappropriate colors. Recolor Picture permits you to maintain visual consistency throughout your presentation.

Record. As a verb, a macro feature that saves keystrokes in a separate file; to repeat the keystrokes, you run the macro. As a noun, *record* refers to information in an Access database contained in rows. Records include fields that, together, describe an individual firm (such as name and address) or an individual transaction (such as shipping information, date and quantity ordered, and total price).

Record set. A combination of previously selected records that can be treated as a single object.

Rehearse New Timings. A PowerPoint Slide Show feature that keeps track of the time spent rehearsing each slide and displays the time spent on each slide in Slide Sorter view.

Reply. A Microsoft Mail command that permits you to respond to a message. You can direct your comments to the sender or to everyone who received a courtesy copy of the message. You can include the original message in your reply.

Report. An Access feature that prints a summary of information contained in a database table. Reports can be as detailed or as concise as desired.

Return receipt. A Microsoft Mail option that informs you when a message has been read by the recipient. Microsoft Mail permits you to save copies of all receipts acknowledging that messages have been received.

Routing slip. A Microsoft Mail feature that allows you to include a message with a Word, Excel, or PowerPoint file sent to other users on your computer network.

Saved Search. Excel feature that allows you to save a complicated search containing multiple variables so that you can modify or repeat the search later without re-entering search criteria. The Saved Searches dialog box displays a list of Saved Searches.

Send Mail. A command in Office programs that allows you to include a copy of the current document, spreadsheet, presentation, or Access database report to other users on your computer network, along with an explanatory message.

Sheets. Multilayer Excel spreadsheets that have a common format and layout and are devoted to a single time period or product line. Sheets are contained in workbooks, and the totals can be consolidated.

Shortcut menus. An Office feature displayed by right-clicking a text or graphic object. A shortcut menu displays the commands most often used with the object (Cut, Copy, Paste, Font, Paragraph, and so on). The menu displayed differs, depending on the object selected.

Slide Master. The underlying structure that determines the appearance of a PowerPoint presentation. Slide Master elements include the position of the title and other objects (such as text charts or illustrations), repeating elements (such as the slide number and presentation date), as well as the presentation's color scheme.

Slide Show. A PowerPoint feature that allows you to review your presentation on-screen by hiding menus and toolbars. During a slide show, you can advance from one slide to another by clicking the mouse or pressing keyboard keys, or you can set up self-running presentations that advance from slide to slide automatically.

Solver. An Excel feature that permits you to enter a goal amount (or a minimum or maximum value) in a target cell and then work backward to achieve that goal by changing values in adjustable cells. You also can enter constraints that must be satisfied — for example, you cannot enter labor costs of zero to increase profits.

Sorting. Rearranging information (such as items in a list or information in rows or columns) in ascending or descending order.

Source document. Refers to the program and file containing information that is linked to, or embedded in, a document created in another program. Often, an Excel spreadsheet is the source document for a chart that appears in a Word document or PowerPoint slide.

Spike. An AutoText feature that allows you to cut, copy, or paste multiple text and graphic objects from several locations to one location. (It is also hardware used by railroads to keep rails from getting out of alignment.)

Style Gallery. A Word feature that permits you to preview templates (formatted document layouts) that can be applied to an existing document or serve as the basis of a new document.

Table. As used in Word and PowerPoint, refers to graphic objects containing information displayed in row-and-column format. In Excel, refers to the entire spreadsheet. In Access, refers to the structure of a database, typically containing individual records in rows and fields and categories of information in columns.

Tabs. A dialog box feature in many Office programs that permits a single dialog box to contain several layers. You can switch among the layers by clicking the tabs to reveal a different set of formatting options. The Font dialog box, for example, contains Font and Character Spacing tabs; the Paragraph dialog box contains the Indents, Spacing, and Text Flow tabs. Word's Options dialog box contains 12 tabs.

Templates. Read-only documents that contain styles and repeating elements (such as logos, borders, and header/footer information). Templates save time by permitting you to share formatting between documents.

Tick marks. Small horizontal and vertical marks added to the horizontal and/or vertical axis of Excel and PowerPoint charts to indicate values between the gridlines (major divisions).

TipWizard. Context-specific Excel Help information that shows you how to perform common tasks as quickly and easily as possible.

Toolbar. A feature in Office 4 programs that allows you to access frequently needed commands by clicking the buttons that represent those commands. Toolbars can be customized; you can move them around the screen and add or delete buttons.

ToolTips. Short, descriptive words and phrases that appear when you place the mouse pointer on a toolbar button. ToolTips help you identify the function that each button performs.

Undo/Redo. You can use Undo to reverse most editing and formatting changes — that is, you can restore deleted text and restore typeface, type size, and color to their original settings. Redo permits you to restore your changes, in case you're not convinced that they were as bad as you thought.

Update. A command used when information in a source document is linked to an object in a destination document. Update shares changes in the source document with objects in the destination document.

View buttons. Buttons located at the left end of Word's and PowerPoint's horizontal scroll bars that permit you to change your view of your document or presentation. Word's view buttons permit you to switch among Normal, Page Layout, and Outline view. PowerPoint's view buttons permit you to switch among Slide, Outline, Slide Sorter, Slide Show, and Notes view. (When you hold down the Shift key in PowerPoint, you can go to the Slide Master, Outline Master, and Notes Master views, which allow you to establish formats to be repeated throughout your presentation.)

Viewer. The PowerPoint Viewer is a stand-alone program that you can freely distribute to other users, allowing them to view PowerPoint presentations on their computers even if they have not installed PowerPoint. This feature permits you to distribute copies of your presentation to people who were not able to attend it.

Wizards. Word, Excel, PowerPoint, and Access include numerous wizards that interactively help you learn faster and work more efficiently. Word's wizards provide suggestions for document content. Excel's wizards help you format charts. PowerPoint's wizards help you determine the content and formatting of your presentation. Access wizards help you set up a database that will satisfy your information-management goals.

WordArt. Word utility that allows you to modify TrueType fonts, change letter spacing, rotate and stretch clip art, add callouts to Word documents, and create logos by manipulating letters and graphics that can be saved and resized as a single object.

Word Count. A feature that allows you to count the words in a Word file (or part of a file).

WordDraw. Powerful Word feature that allows you to import and modify clip art, add callouts to Word documents, and create logos by manipulating letters and adding graphic accents (such as shaded backgrounds), which can be saved and resized as a single object.

Workbook. Excel feature that allows a single file to contain several individual spreadsheets that can be consolidated. Individual spreadsheets can represent the various months of the year (consolidated into a single yearly spreadsheet) or separate departments (consolidated into company-wide totals).

Zoom. A Word, Excel, and PowerPoint feature that allows you to see as much, or as little, of your document as possible. Working at large magnification increases the accuracy with which you place text and objects. Working at small magnification provides a better view of the overall appearance of your document or presentation visual.

Index

● *T* ●

• *Z* •

Title	Author	ISBN	Price

INTERNET / COMMUNICATIONS / NETWORKING

Title	Author	ISBN	Price
CompuServe For Dummies™	by Wallace Wang	1-56884-181-7	$19.95 USA/$26.95 Canada
Modems For Dummies™, 2nd Edition	by Tina Rathbone	1-56884-223-6	$19.99 USA/$26.99 Canada
Modems For Dummies™	by Tina Rathbone	1-56884-001-2	$19.95 USA/$26.95 Canada
MORE Internet For Dummies™	by John R. Levine & Margaret Levine Young	1-56884-164-7	$19.95 USA/$26.95 Canada
NetWare For Dummies™	by Ed Tittel & Deni Connor	1-56884-003-9	$19.95 USA/$26.95 Canada
Networking For Dummies™	by Doug Lowe	1-56884-079-9	$19.95 USA/$26.95 Canada
ProComm Plus 2 For Windows For Dummies™	by Wallace Wang	1-56884-219-8	$19.99 USA/$26.99 Canada
The Internet For Dummies™, 2nd Edition	by John R. Levine & Carol Baroudi	1-56884-222-8	$19.99 USA/$26.99 Canada
The Internet For Macs For Dummies™	by Charles Seiter	1-56884-184-1	$19.95 USA/$26.95 Canada

MACINTOSH

Title	Author	ISBN	Price
Macs For Dummies®	by David Pogue	1-56884-173-6	$19.95 USA/$26.95 Canada
Macintosh System 7.5 For Dummies™	by Bob LeVitus	1-56884-197-3	$19.95 USA/$26.95 Canada
MORE Macs For Dummies™	by David Pogue	1-56884-087-X	$19.95 USA/$26.95 Canada
PageMaker 5 For Macs For Dummies™	by Galen Gruman	1-56884-178-7	$19.95 USA/$26.95 Canada
QuarkXPress 3.3 For Dummies™	by Galen Gruman & Barbara Assadi	1-56884-217-1	$19.99 USA/$26.99 Canada
Upgrading and Fixing Macs For Dummies™	by Kearney Rietmann & Frank Higgins	1-56884-189-2	$19.95 USA/$26.95 Canada

MULTIMEDIA

Title	Author	ISBN	Price
Multimedia & CD-ROMs For Dummies™, Interactive Multimedia Value Pack	by Andy Rathbone	1-56884-225-2	$29.95 USA/$39.95 Canada
Multimedia & CD-ROMs For Dummies™	by Andy Rathbone	1-56884-089-6	$19.95 USA/$26.95 Canada

OPERATING SYSTEMS / DOS

Title	Author	ISBN	Price
MORE DOS For Dummies™	by Dan Gookin	1-56884-046-2	$19.95 USA/$26.95 Canada
S.O.S. For DOS™	by Katherine Murray	1-56884-043-8	$12.95 USA/$16.95 Canada
OS/2 For Dummies™	by Andy Rathbone	1-878058-76-2	$19.95 USA/$26.95 Canada

UNIX

Title	Author	ISBN	Price
UNIX For Dummies™	by John R. Levine & Margaret Levine Young	1-878058-58-4	$19.95 USA/$26.95 Canada

WINDOWS

Title	Author	ISBN	Price
S.O.S. For Windows™	by Katherine Murray	1-56884-045-4	$12.95 USA/$16.95 Canada
MORE Windows 3.1 For Dummies™, 3rd Edition	by Andy Rathbone	1-56884-240-6	$19.99 USA/$26.99 Canada

PCs / HARDWARE

Title	Author	ISBN	Price
Illustrated Computer Dictionary For Dummies™	by Dan Gookin, Wally Wang, & Chris Van Buren	1-56884-004-7	$12.95 USA/$16.95 Canada
Upgrading and Fixing PCs For Dummies™	by Andy Rathbone	1-56884-002-0	$19.95 USA/$26.95 Canada

PRESENTATION / AUTOCAD

Title	Author	ISBN	Price
AutoCAD For Dummies™	by Bud Smith	1-56884-191-4	$19.95 USA/$26.95 Canada
PowerPoint 4 For Windows For Dummies™	by Doug Lowe	1-56884-161-2	$16.95 USA/$22.95 Canada

PROGRAMMING

Title	Author	ISBN	Price
Borland C++ For Dummies™	by Michael Hyman	1-56884-162-0	$19.95 USA/$26.95 Canada
"Borland's New Language Product" For Dummies™	by Neil Rubenking	1-56884-200-7	$19.95 USA/$26.95 Canada
C For Dummies™	by Dan Gookin	1-878058-78-9	$19.95 USA/$26.95 Canada
C++ For Dummies™	by Stephen R. Davis	1-56884-163-9	$19.95 USA/$26.95 Canada
Mac Programming For Dummies™	by Dan Parks Sydow	1-56884-173-6	$19.95 USA/$26.95 Canada
QBasic Programming For Dummies™	by Douglas Hergert	1-56884-093-4	$19.95 USA/$26.95 Canada
Visual Basic "X" For Dummies™, 2nd Edition	by Wallace Wang	1-56884-230-9	$19.99 USA/$26.99 Canada
Visual Basic 3 For Dummies™	by Wallace Wang	1-56884-076-4	$19.95 USA/$26.95 Canada

SPREADSHEET

Title	Author	ISBN	Price
1-2-3 For Dummies™	by Greg Harvey	1-878058-60-6	$16.95 USA/$21.95 Canada
1-2-3 For Windows 5 For Dummies™, 2nd Edition	by John Walkenbach	1-56884-216-3	$16.95 USA/$21.95 Canada
1-2-3 For Windows For Dummies™	by John Walkenbach	1-56884-052-7	$16.95 USA/$21.95 Canada
Excel 5 For Macs For Dummies™	by Greg Harvey	1-56884-186-8	$19.95 USA/$26.95 Canada
Excel For Dummies™, 2nd Edition	by Greg Harvey	1-56884-050-0	$16.95 USA/$21.95 Canada
MORE Excel 5 For Windows For Dummies™	by Greg Harvey	1-56884-207-4	$19.95 USA/$26.95 Canada
Quattro Pro 6 For Windows For Dummies™	by John Walkenbach	1-56884-174-4	$19.95 USA/$26.95 Canada
Quattro Pro For DOS For Dummies™	by John Walkenbach	1-56884-023-3	$16.95 USA/$21.95 Canada

UTILITIES / VCRs & CAMCORDERS

Title	Author	ISBN	Price
Norton Utilities 8 For Dummies™	by Beth Slick	1-56884-166-3	$19.95 USA/$26.95 Canada
VCRs & Camcorders For Dummies™	by Andy Rathbone & Gordon McComb	1-56884-229-5	$14.99 USA/$20.99 Canada

WORD PROCESSING

Title	Author	ISBN	Price
Ami Pro For Dummies™	by Jim Meade	1-56884-049-7	$19.95 USA/$26.95 Canada
MORE Word For Windows 6 For Dummies™	by Doug Lowe	1-56884-165-5	$19.95 USA/$26.95 Canada
MORE WordPerfect 6 For Windows For Dummies™	by Margaret Levine Young & David C. Kay	1-56884-206-6	$19.95 USA/$26.95 Canada
MORE WordPerfect 6 For DOS For Dummies™	by Wallace Wang, edited by Dan Gookin	1-56884-047-0	$19.95 USA/$26.95 Canada
S.O.S. For WordPerfect™	by Katherine Murray	1-56884-053-5	$12.95 USA/$16.95 Canada
Word 6 For Macs For Dummies™	by Dan Gookin	1-56884-190-6	$19.95 USA/$26.95 Canada
Word For Windows 6 For Dummies™	by Dan Gookin	1-56884-075-6	$16.95 USA/$21.95 Canada
Word For Windows For Dummies™	by Dan Gookin	1-878058-86-X	$16.95 USA/$21.95 Canada
WordPerfect 6 For Dummies™	by Dan Gookin	1-878058-77-0	$16.95 USA/$21.95 Canada
WordPerfect For Dummies™	by Dan Gookin	1-878058-52-5	$16.95 USA/$21.95 Canada
WordPerfect For Windows For Dummies™	by Margaret Levine Young & David C. Kay	1-56884-032-2	$16.95 USA/$21.95 Canada